Unified Objects:
Object-Oriented Programming Using C++

IEEE Computer Society Press
Mohamed E. Fayad
Editor-in-Chief, Practices for Computer Science and Engineering

SELECTED TITLES

Distributed Objects: Methodologies for Customizing Operating Systems
    Nayeem Islam

Software Engineering Risk Management
    Dale Karolak

Digital Design and Modeling with VHDL and Synthesis
    K.C. Chang

Industrial Strength Software: Effective Management Using Measurement
    Lawrence Putnam and Ware Myers

Unified Objects: Object-Oriented Programming Using C++
    Babak Sadr

Interconnection Networks: An Engineering Approach
    José Duato, Sudhakar Yalamanchili, and Lionel Ni

SPICE: The Theory and Practice of Software Process Improvement and Capability Determination
    Khaled El Emam, Jean-Normand Drouin, and Walcélio Melo

Meeting Deadlines in Real-Time Systems: The Rate Monotonic Analysis
    Daniel Roy and Loic Briand

Executive Briefings

Controlling Software Development
    Lawrence Putnam and Ware Myers

Unified Objects:
Object-Oriented Programming Using C++

Babak Sadr

IEEE
COMPUTER
SOCIETY

Los Alamitos, California

Washington • **Brussels** • **Tokyo**

Library of Congress Cataloging-in-Publication Data

Sadr, Babak.
    Unified objects: object-oriented programming using C++ / Babak Sadr.
        p.   cm.
    Includes bibliographical references.
    ISBN 0-8186-7733-3
        1. Object-oriented programming (Computer science)   2. C++ (Computer program language).
I. Title.
QA76.64.S25   1998
005.13 ' 3—dc21   96-45236
                                                                                      CIP

IEEE Computer Society Press Order Number BP07733
Library of Congress Number 96-45236
ISBN 0-8186-7733-3

Additional copies can be ordered from

IEEE Computer Society Press	IEEE Service Center	IEEE Computer Society
Customer Service Center	445 Hoes Lane	Watanabe Building
10662 Los Vaqueros Circle	P.O. Box 1331	1-4-2 Minami-Aoyama
P.O. Box 3014	Piscataway, NJ 08855-1331	Minato-ku, Tokyo 107-0062
Los Alamitos, CA 90720-1314	Tel: (732) 981-0060	JAPAN
Tel: (714) 821-8380	Fax: (732) 981-9667	Tel: +81-3-3408-3118
Fax: (714) 821-4641	mis.custserv@computer.org	Fax: +81-3-3408-3553
Email: cs.books@computer.org		tokyo.ofc@computer.org

Publisher: Matt Loeb
Manager of Production, CS Press: Deborah Plummer
Advertising/Promotions: Tom Fink
Production Editor: Denise Hurst
Cover Design: Alex Torres

Printed in the United States of America
99 98   2   1

To my parents

For who I am, what I am,
And where I am,
It is all because of you.
So this is for you
                    —Babak (January 1996)

Contents

List of Figures and Tables

Foreword

Without a doubt, object-oriented technology is part of the mainstream of software development. OOP has been used to develop and deploy systems in domains as diverse as patient health care, avionics, aerospace, trading systems, automotive electronics, telecommunications, and computer animation. Furthermore, OOP knows no political boundaries. I've encountered successful, industrial strength projects in every developed country and on every continent.

It is amazing to realize that this technology is really not that new. Indeed, it has already been 10 years since C++ was first introduced, and the basic OOP concepts go back even earlier. That is actually good news: there is considerable experience with technologies such as C++, and this helps new projects start with lower risk and more mature organizations improve over time.

Babak was a part of the OOP community for almost a decade and he understood some of the best practices that distinguish successful projects from unsuccessful ones. In this book you will learn about these practices, especially as they relate to applying sound software engineering concepts to C++.

Grady Booch
Chief Scientist
Rational Software Corporation
August 1996

Prologue

BACKGROUND

In the late 1970s, as computers grew more powerful, the complexity of the software developed for these systems increased. Large-system development was plagued by schedule and cost overruns. When systems were actually delivered they often lacked the required functionality, quality, and reliability [Jones 1995]. The problems have been well documented in government and privately sponsored studies. For example, a review by the US Department of Defense (DoD) of 17 major contracts showed all projects suffered schedule delays [Saiedian 1995]. In "The Mythical Man-Month," author Fred Brooks described the development of the IBM 360 Operating System and the problems associated with large software development projects [Brooks 1995]. While hardware technology blossomed in the 1980s away from mainframe to workstations and personal computers, the lack of progress in solving software development problems was designated the "software crisis." This term was coined with respect to DoD software projects. Early efforts to address the "software crisis" by the DoD in particular included the following:

1. **Software Standards:** The DOD-STD-2167 development standard defined the "waterfall" development life cycle, consisting of requirements analysis, design, code/unit test, component test, and system test. Each life cycle phase had entry and exit criteria and the phases were sequential.

2. **Modern Programming Languages**: The DoD mandated the development and use of the Ada Language for Mission Critical Systems (1985). The use of this modern programming language was intended specifically to address the maintenance problems caused by the proliferation of processors and languages. Ada was developed to standardize software development environments and to address programming methods for real-time embedded systems. Ada introduced the concept of language support for software engineering practices such as data abstraction and encapsulation.

Since the cost overruns, schedule delays, and low quality were certainly not limited to the DoD, similar efforts such as those culminating in the IEEE software standards, were carried out by the commercial sector. In parallel, the commercial side of the business was dominated by migration of software development to Unix and the C-language.

By the late 1980s, it was clear that the structure of the development process imposed by DOD-STD-2167 was not the solution to the software crisis. In addition, object-oriented methods and languages were not compatible with the standards. Even though DOD-STD-2167[1] was revised, the "waterfall" life cycle, which involves a sequential flow of activities was found impossible to sustain. This was due to uncertainty and dynamic changes in the functional requirements of most large systems. Feedback between the waterfall phases of DOD-STD-2167 was cumbersome and time consuming.

To find solutions to the "software crisis," the Advanced Research Development Agency (ARPA) of the US Government funded the Software Engineering Institute (SEI) at Carnegie Mellon University in 1984. The SEI,

---

[1]DOD-STD-2167A has been superseded by DOD-STD-498

under the direction of Watts Humphrey, developed the concept of the software process as described in his book *Managing the Software Process*. The SEI formalized the software process into a *Capability Maturity Model (CMM)* framework (Figure 1). This process identifies procedures and activities such as project planning and tracking, configuration management, requirements management, and training. These activities guide the development of high-quality, reliable software. The CMM defines five levels of software process maturity. Level 1 identifies the software development activities as basically "ad hoc." Level 1 organizations demonstrate no repeatable process for conducting software development or maintenance. Each product depends solely on the skills of the team assembled to develop and/or maintain it. The higher levels are characterized by *Key Process Areas (KPAs)* that are put in place by a development organization. These areas specify activities that will continuously improve the software development process [Paulk 1993].

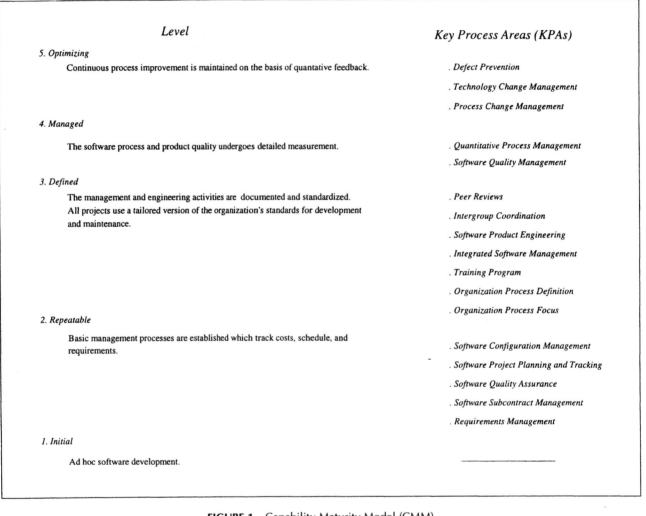

FIGURE 1 Capability Maturity Model (CMM).

On the basis of the SEI's CMM, an organization performs a self-assessment in cooperation with an SEI-licensed vendor. An organization's current development process is evaluated against the CMM KPAs and the assessment provides the organization with the actions that need to be taken to improve its development process. The CMM measures a software development organization's ability to develop software products reliably, on time, and within budget.

Other recent software process models, such as the European ISO-9000 standards are similar to the CMM. ISO-9000 provides guidelines for an organization's software quality management system. Companies are ISO-9000 certified via an evaluation process similar to the SEI Software Process Assessments. Both the CMM and ISO-9000 require documented software development procedures.

PROJECT MANAGEMENT

In recent years object-oriented technology and C++ have become increasingly popular. The rush to adopt this technology and language has created a naive perception that software developed using C++ results in self-maintainable and reliable code. However, writing a program in C++ is only one of the steps in a complete software development process. The steps that go before and after code production are just as important to the ultimate successful execution of the program. Learning the syntax and semantics of a programming language is again only one of the essential elements for producing high-quality, reliable computer applications. A software development organization needs to address the following areas:

1. **Software Processes**: Software process models such as CMM, ISO-9000, or Capers Jones Model should be adopted in order to formalize the development process and to create an environment that results in maintainable and reliable software products.

2. **Software Development Strategy**: The most prominent methods are the *modified waterfall*, *spiral*, and *rapid prototype*:

   a. *Modified Waterfall*: The normal phases are repeated for segments of the project. Components are designed, coded, and tested in parallel. Integration and test is usually accomplished by "builds," each successive build containing more functionality than the preceding build.

   b. *Spiral Model*: The development process is iterative and based on cycles. In each cycle, the objectives, constraints, and alternatives are defined; project risks are identified and analyzed; requirements are specified; software is developed and tested; and finally the next phase is planned. The cycle is repeated until the project is complete [Boehm 1988].

   c. *Rapid Prototype*: System functionality is quickly prototyped (hardware and software) to demonstrate and evaluate system requirements. Using the knowledge gained in building and evaluating the prototype, operational software is then produced.

3. **Design Methodology**: The above software development process defines the development life cycle. In addition, a design methodology is necessary in order to have a consistent method for analyzing software requirements and designing the software. Major methodologies are:

   a. *Structured Analysis*: This methodology concentrates on flow of data through a system. It is a top-down approach, with design being refined in stages. The design is captured via diagrams that illustrate data and control flow through a system. These diagrams are known as *data flow* diagrams. In addition, other textual and visual tools such as design by structure charts and state transition diagrams are also used.

   b. *Object-Oriented Design*: Analysis defines real-world objects, and associated processing requirements. Object-oriented design has gained popularity in recent years because of its potential to provide software reusability. Inherently it provides modularity, low coupling (independence between objects), and high cohesion (functional correlation between data and processing).

4. **Software Standards**: Software standards such as the IEEE documents formalize different areas of the software development life cycle (Figure 2).

In conclusion, there is no single "silver bullet" that will make the "software crisis" disappear. The solution to the software crisis has been gradual and will continue to be based on the improvements made in the software process by all of the above-described efforts and technologies. The solution is a combination of process and technology. Each software developer can contribute individually to the solution by addressing all the steps in the software development life cycle. At the organizational level an organization will improve its ability to meet quality, reliability, schedule, and cost objectives for software development projects by incorporating and establishing a structured software development program. The program should address the above-cited areas of process management, life cycle development, standards, methodologies, and languages and tools.

Patricia Dousette
Babak Sadr

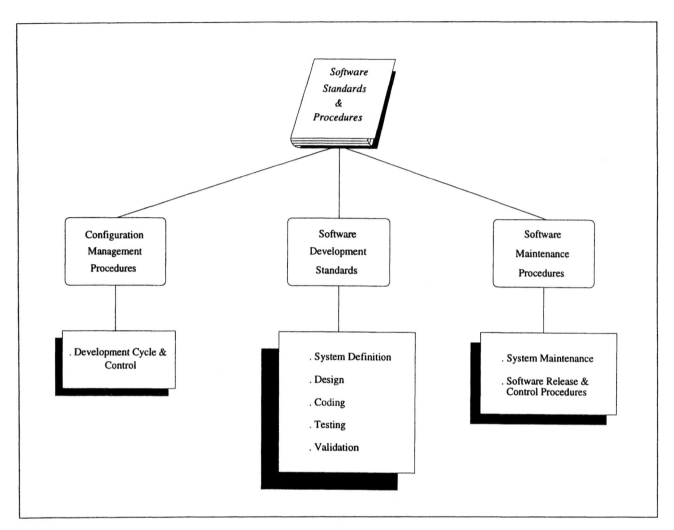

FIGURE 2   Software standards.

Preface

INTRODUCTION

This book has been developed from my course notes at the University of California, Los Angeles (UCLA). My eight years of teaching experience and students feedback have been the basis for the development and approach of this book. The book was written with the following objectives in mind:

1. **Overall Focus**: Since proper design and implementation represent an important part of software development, this book's primary objective is to create a balance between object-oriented programming (OOP) and C++ by bridging the gap between design and implementation. The C++ features are mapped to object-oriented concepts with less focus on language and syntax.
2. **Structure**: Since the book is structured around object-oriented concepts, each chapter addresses a specific area in OOP. For example, the beginning chapters focus on *encapsulation* and *abstraction* and the later chapters on *design hierarchies*.
3. **Object-Oriented (OO) Methodology**: This book provides formal definitions for object-oriented concepts and describes how they relate to features in C++.
4. **Complexity**: The examples are kept simple and concise and the book intentionally avoids complicated examples. I have found that extensive and complex examples only frustrate students and interfere with their comprehension of OO design concepts.

   When appropriate, a single example is consistently developed throughout a chapter. This keeps the reader's attention focused. In addition, it allows an example to evolve and address the more complex issues.
5. **Graphical Presentations**: An emphasis is placed on using graphical presentations to amplify the text. Pictorial representation has always helped my students absorb the course material more easily than just plain text.
6. **Object-Oriented Notation**: An object-oriented notation is a vehicle for conveying the design of a system in a clear and standard manner. The book primarily uses **Booch-93** notation for its examples. Booch-93 notation was selected to teach my students one of the industry's popular notations.

   This book also describes the **Unified Modeling Language (UML)**, which combines the object modeling technique (OMT) and Booch notations. The Unified Modeling Language has been developed by Grady Booch, James Rumbaugh, and Ivar Jacobson at Rational Software Corporation. The presentation of Booch-93 and UML allows the reader to select the notation that is most appropriate for his/her design.

   In addition, other diagrams such as the Wassermann-Pircher-Muller and function hierarchy diagrams are also used to help convey additional information.

AUDIENCE

The text assumes the reader has prior knowledge of the C language. This assumption maintains the focus on OOP and corresponding features of C++. The book has been written for the following audiences:

1. **Students**: This textbook is designed for an upper division university course. It introduces the student to object-oriented design and programming. In addition, the student gains a basic understanding of Booch notation.
2. **Professional Software Developers and Engineers**: This book is intended for use by engineers who want to transition to OOP and C++.

FLOW

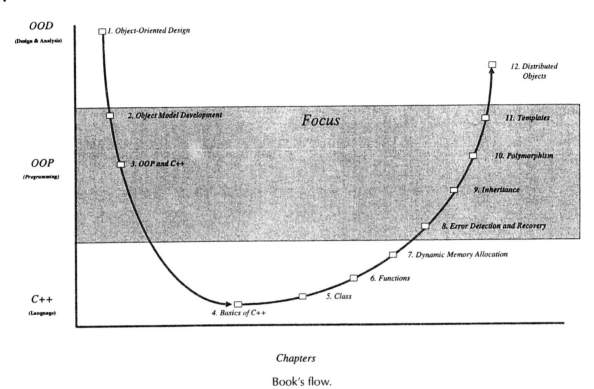

Book's flow.

The text is divided into several major segments which are identified below. Figure 1 depicts the general flow and structure of the book:

1. **Introduction**: the introduction segment begins by providing an overview of object-oriented design (OOD) and object-oriented programming (OOP) (chapters 1 through 3).

    Chapter 1 introduces the framework of object-oriented design and describes the graphical notation used.

    Chapter 2 continues to build on OOP and describes the development of an object model from requirement specification to testing. This chapter discusses the macro- and micro-development processes. It also describes how an object-oriented design captures both *dynamic* and *static* behaviors of the system.

    Chapter 3 correlates the features in C++ to the framework of an object model.
2. **C++**: To build a solid foundation on the language, Chapters 4 through 7 focus on C++. These chapters relate *encapsulation*, *abstraction*, and *modularity* from the *object model* to C++ features.
3. **Object-Oriented Programming**: Chapters 8 through 11 build on the earlier C++ work and discuss important OOP issues such as design hierarchies. These chapters describe exception handling, inheritance, polymorphism, templates, and their use in software design and implementation.
4. **Distributed Objects**: Chapter 12 introduces the reader to advanced topics such as distributed architectures. The chapter describes *concurrency* and *persistence* issues. In addition, a brief overview of the emerging standards such as the Common Object Request Broker Architecture (CORBA) standard is provided.

While this book was in its completion phase, two related significant industry developments were: the Java programming language began to gain enormous popularity, and Booch, Rumbaugh, and Jacobson consolidated the Booch, Object-Modeling Technique (OMT), Object-Oriented Software Engineering (OOSE) notations under the Unified Modeling Language (UML). Therefore, two additional chapters have been included to discuss these areas:

1. **Introduction to Java**: Chapter 13 provides a brief overview.
2. **Unified Modeling Language (UML)**: Chapter 14 concludes this book with an overview of the UML.

STANDARD C++ CLASS LIBRARIES

This book provides high-level coverage on the following ANSI C++ libraries:

1. *Stream I/O* class library: Chapters 3, 5, and 8
2. *string* class: Chapter 5
3. *complex* class: Chapter 5
4. *exception* class library: Chapter 7
5. *Standard Template Library* (STL): Chapter 10

The book describes the use of C++ features in the design of these libraries. For a comprehensive discussion, the reader should refer to a C++ compiler reference manual.

EXAMPLES

Except for the embedded application examples, the examples are available on a companion MS-DOS format disk.

FURTHER READING

This book is geared toward Booch methodology with focus on OOP and C++. The following books will further aid the reader in gaining a better understanding of object-oriented analysis/design and C++:

Booch, G. *Object-Oriented Analysis and Design with Applications.* Redwood City, California: Benjamin/ Cummings, 1994.

Stroustrup, B. *The C++ Programming Language.* New Jersey: Addison- Wesley, 1991.

Ellis, M. and Stroustrup, B. *The Annotated C++ Reference Manual.* New Jersey: Addison-Wesley, 1990.

ERRATA

I have attempted to find every error in this book. I would appreciate it if you, the reader, would notify me of any errors or omissions that you find. I also welcome suggestions for improving and enhancing the book structure and content. An errata sheet will be available with the first edition.

NOTATION

Italic and **bold face** characters are used to amplify the description of C++ examples. The following describes the convention used throughout the book:

1. **name**(): References to function names appear in **bold face**.
2. *comments*: C++ comments in the examples appear in *italic*
3. ***data***: References to data and objects appear in ***italic-bold***.

Italic characters are also used to highlight newly introduced technical terms.
The C++ examples in this book and accompanying disk are based on the following style and layout:

```
/// FILE_NAME.H Header File
#ifndef FILE_NAME_H // multiple file inclusion guard
#define FILE_NAME_H

        #include "Supporting Library Header Filename.h"

        // #define and constant definitions
        #define SYMBOLIC_NAME constant_value
        const  Type name = initialization statement ;

        // typedef definitions
        typedef built-in_type Symbolic_Name ;

        // class definition
        class Name
        {
                private:
                // private interface: data & function declarations

                protected:
                // protected interface: data & function declarations

                public:
                // public interface: function declarations
} ;
// non-member function declarations

// inline member function definition
inline return_type Name:: function_name(parameters, if any)
{
   // function's body
}

#endif

// FILE_NAME.CPP Source File
#include <C++ Library Header Filename.h>

#include "Book's Library Header Filename.h"

// internal (static) function declarations

// initialization statements for static data members, extern, and static objects

// function definitions
return_type Class_Name:: function_name(parameters, if any)
{
   // function's body
}
```

The following identifies the coding convention in this book. An underscore is used to separate words.

1. **Data Type**: Mixed case is used for the class name and *typedef*:

```
typedef int Counter ;

class Linked_List
{
} ;
```

2. **Constants**: Constants, #define, and enum members are defined using upper-case letters:

```
const double PI = acos( -1.0 ) ;

#define BUFFER_SIZE  100

enum Color
{
GREEN, BLUE, RED, YELLOW
} ;
```

3. **Objects**: Objects and variables are defined using lower-case letters:

```
Savings customer ;
```

ACKNOWLEDGMENTS

Writing a book is not an individual achievement. Many individuals contributed to make this book happen, and while finishing this book, I was diagnosed with a rare and advanced type of cancer in May of 1996. During these trying times, I have learned who have been my true friends. These friends have helped me spiritually, emotionally, and physically. I would like to thank especially my beautiful wife, Laura, and my friend, Patricia Dousette. In addition, Grady Booch, a true gentleman, took time away from his busy schedule to assist me in finalizing the last chapter on the Unified Modeling Language. Without their help, I would have been unable to finish this book. As one of my good friends, Alan Cordover, says: "*It does not cost a penny to be human.*" I would like to thank all of my friends for being such great humans; *thank you, my friends.*

I thank my colleagues and students, who devoted their time in proofreading the entire book, especially Patricia Dousette, Mark Turner, Wade Mergenthal, Talin Parseghian, Paul Blumstein, Mike Reese, and Paul Denzer. Their comments have been instrumental in improving the book's quality and clarity.

To lighten up a reasonably dry and technical topic, I asked Mike Reese to use his artistic ability and draw cartoons for this book. On the basis of topics presented in each chapter, Mike and I developed the cartoon themes, and Mike spent his weekends drawing them. I hope the readers will enjoy Mike's sense of humor and his cartoons.

I must thank those members of the IEEE Computer Society who played a strategic role in the publication of this book. Mohammed Fayad, Editor-in-Chief of the Practice Board, recommended this book for publication to the IEEE Computer Society. Matt Loeb, IEEE Assistant Publisher, made this book a reality, and worked closely with me in preparing it for publication. Bill Sanders, Acquisition Editor, came up with the idea for the cover of the book. Cheryl Smith and Lisa O'Conner worked diligently behind the scenes to coordinate the long and laborious process of getting the book reviewed and preparing it for publication. I thank Susan McColl, whose input improved the clarity of my book.

I am also grateful to PARTA Corp. and UCLA for helping make this book possible.

'Cause nothing' lasts forever
Even cold November rain
-Guns N' Roses
Use Your Illusion I

CHAPTER 1

Object-Oriented Design

INTRODUCTION

Distributed computing, virtual reality, multimedia, and other new technologies have increased the complexity of software design. It is common for software development projects in these areas to involve different development platforms and programs consisting of more than 100,000 lines of code. With these types of systems, ad hoc design and development is impractical, if not impossible. The successful delivery of these types of systems relies on a structured and formalized analysis, design, and implementation process.

The object-oriented methodology has gained popularity because the analysis, design, and implementation process revolves around a well-defined framework with focus on minimizing risks and maximizing software *maintainability*, *reliability*, and *reusability*. An object-oriented system undergoes analysis, design, and implementation through an iterative process that is depicted in Figure 1.1. Even though the iterative process is not unique to object-oriented methodology, they work well together:

1. **Object-Oriented Analysis (OOA)**: The software requirements are analyzed and a real-world *object* model is established. The *object* model provides an abstract representation of the actual entities to be modeled by the software application. For example, the object model for a flight control system views the plane's actuators, sensors, engine, and flight control stick as *objects* that interact with each other and keep the plane in flight. In an object-oriented model, the software algorithms such as flight control algorithms become secondary issues.

2. **Object-Oriented Design (OOD)**: The *object* model is further refined. In the design phase, the details of the architecture, and the relationships and interactions between the objects, are specified. The algorithms and processes are mapped to the applicable objects.

3. **Object-Oriented Programming (OOP)**: Using a programming language that supports OOD, the completed design is implemented and tested.

This chapter describes and focuses on Object-Oriented Design (OOD). It presents a formal definition for an object, and identifies the framework for an object model. The chapter also describes how OOD techniques help localize software changes, encourage reusability, and enhance reliability.

Similar to other design methodologies, graphical presentations are important in OOD for capturing and conveying information. Since this book relies on Booch-93 notation for the presentation of the designs, this chapter provides an overview of the Booch notation.

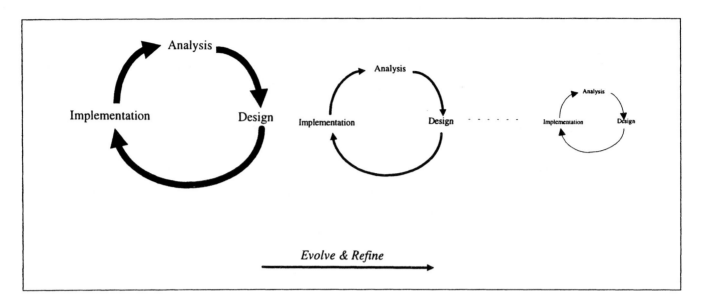

FIGURE 1.1   Iterative design process.

1.1 DEFINITION OF AN OBJECT

In object-oriented designs, software requirements are analyzed and mapped to *objects* instead of processes and functions. Software can be viewed as a collection of *objects* that collaborate with each other to perform the tasks defined by the software requirements. For example, an object-oriented design will translate and map the following system requirement to a *modem* object (Figure 1.2):

> *"The system shall <u>transmit</u> and <u>receive</u> data via an internal **modem** using a minimum transmission rate of 9,600 baud"*

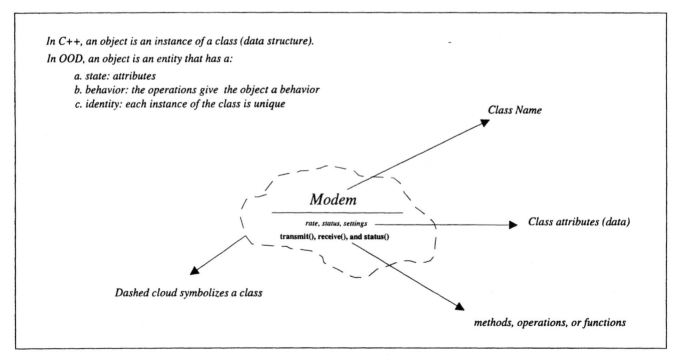

FIGURE 1.2   Modem class.

The **transmit( )** and **receive( )** functions are the *operations (methods)* on the *modem* object. The transmission rate is one of the object's *attributes* and the minimum transmission rate of 9,600 baud identifies the lower threshold for this attribute. Figure 1.2 depicts an abstract view of a *modem* using the Booch-93 notation.

The cloud shape represents an object and highlights the abstraction produced by the design. *Attributes* such as the **transmission rate** and **status** specify the modem's state and characteristics. On the basis of the values and settings, the attributes identify the state of the object. For example, **mode** and **status** specify the object is idle, transmitting, receiving, or in a degraded state. The **transmit( )**, **receive( )**, and **status( )** methods operate on the *attributes* and alter the state of the object. These functions cause the *modem* to transition state, such as going from idle to transmitting.

Other objects use these methods to transmit and receive data via the *modem* object. These *operations* (methods) hide and protect the attribute's name, type, and data architecture from these objects. Since these operations define the external interface of the *modem* object, they also protect the data attributes from being corrupted by other objects. The operations provide a consistent user interface even when their internals change.

An *object* provides an abstract representation of a real entity that is being modeled and mimicks the real entity's behavior. The definition of an *object* has been formalized in OOD as an "*entity that has a state, behavior, and an identity*" [Booch 1994]:

1. **State**: The values of the *attributes* identify the state of the object. Figure 1.3 depicts the possible states of a *modem* object using Booch-93 notation. On the basis of the communication mode and status, the *modem* object may be in idle, setup, transmit, receive, error, or termination states. An event or an operation may cause an object to transition to another state. For example, an incoming phone call will change the state of *modem* from idle to receive. The transition diagram identifies the known states for an object. At any point within its life span, an object must remain in a known and stable state.
2. **Behavior**: *Operations* such as **transmit( )** give the *modem* object a **behavior**. During file transmission, the modem would need to dial the phone number, establish communication with the remote system, transmit data, verify that the transmission has been successful, and then terminate communication. Some of the operations cause changes in the **states** of the object and the object then displays a different behavior.
3. **Identity**: A system may contain several different *modem* objects. Even though each *modem* object has the same attributes and operations, each object has its own unique state. On the basis of the state, each object exhibits its own behavior. For example, one modem may be transmitting a file and the other receiving a fax.

In C++, an *object* does not exist at the source file level. An *object* comes into existence when the software is executed and the memory space for it is reserved and initialized. At the source file level, only the architecture for the object can be defined and is referred to as a *class* definition. A *class* is a type definition (for example, a **struct** definition) and it logically groups data in a set, and functions become the operations on the set (Figure 1.4). The *class* definition identifies the types, names, and layout of the data members. This information defines the size and content of memory space used by an *object*. In addition, it identifies the member functions that are allowed to operate on the data members. An *object* is an instance of a *class*. For example, a *modem* object would be an instance of the *modem* class. Any reference to an *object* is implicitly considered as an instance of a *class*.

1.2 OBJECT MODEL

An object model consists of a collection of objects that interact with each other and represent the design being modeled. For instance, a computer and its peripherals are illustrated as *classes* in Figure 1.5. Through coordinated interaction, these *classes* represent a computer.

Figure 1.5 has loosely coupled the objects and does not depict the relationship and interaction between the objects. In representing a system, an *object model* must not only identify the objects but must also identify states, relationships, and interactions between the objects. The relationships and interactions specify how the objects use each other's services and how they communicate. The object model must reflect and address both static and dynamic information. For instance, a *computer* object may use a *printer* object to print a *document*. The relationship between the *computer* and the *printer* becomes a "*use-a*" relationship. Booch-93 notation provides graphical symbols that represent common relationships such as "*has-a*," "*is-a*," and "*use-a*" between objects in a class diagram:

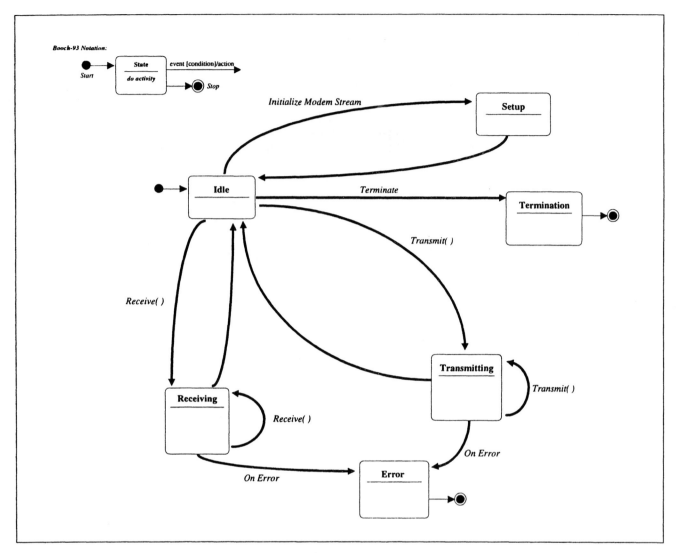

FIGURE 1.3 Modem state transition diagram.

1. **Composition**: When a class uses another class as its data member, the classes form a *"has-a"* relationship. In Figure 1.6, a *computer* contains a *floppy disk*. The *floppy disk* is perceived as a subsystem of the *computer*, and the relationship characterized as the *computer "has-a" floppy disk*.
2. **User**: When a class uses another class in the implementation of its member functions or for the function interfaces, it is *using* the services of the other class. For instance, the computer class may provide a **print()** function. The body of the **print()** function would *"use-a"* *printer* object for printing a document. In Figure 1.6, the *monitor* and *printer* classes are not components of a *computer*, but are used by a *computer* to display and print information, respectively.
3. **Inheritance**: A class may inherit the properties and attributes of another class, which forms a parent-child relationship. The child class becomes a subtype of the parent class. The child class *is-a* more specialized form of its parent class. For example, a *floppy disk* inherits the data members and member functions of the *disk* class, and adds features that are specific to a *floppy disk*. Thus, the *floppy disk "is-a"* subtype of a *disk* class.

Figure 1.6 illustrates a representation of the object model for a personal computer (PC). Figure 1.6 highlights the hierarchical architecture formed by the objects and their relationships, such as the *memory* and *port* classes. For example, a *computer **has*** multiple ports. The *serial* and *parallel* ports *are* different types of ports ("*is-a*" relationship). These relationships are described in greater detail in the subsequent sections.

The framework of an *object model* is partitioned into the following components and the design of an object-oriented system must reflect and encompass them:

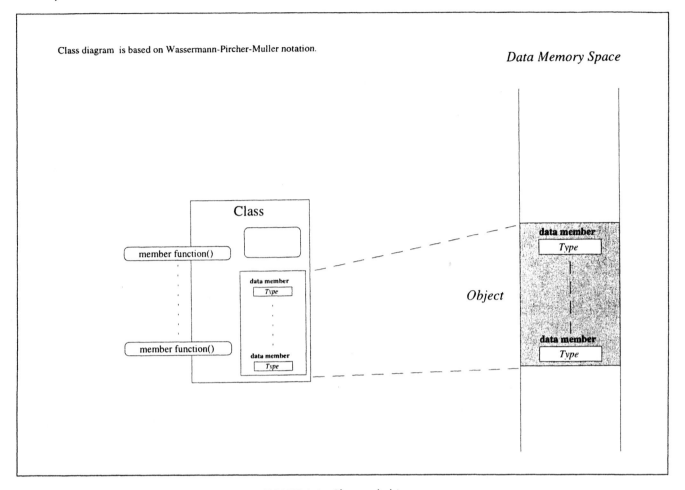

FIGURE 1.4   Class and object.

1. **Modularity:** The internal architectures and designs of the classes must be decoupled from each other. A modular architecture decouples the designs of the classes and results in formation of libraries and independent software modules.

2. **Encapsulation:** The internal architecture and data representation of a class must be kept hidden from other classes. The methods provided by a class specify the design interface for a class, and other objects operate on an instance of the class via these operations.

3. **Abstraction:** The methods must hide the processes and algorithms associated with the functions of a class. For example, the **transmit( )** function of the *modem* abstracts the data transmission process from its clients.

4. **Design Hierarchy:** The classes in the design form hierarchical relationships. As depicted in Figure 1.6, the *floppy* and *hard disk* classes inherit the properties and attributes of the *disk* class. The design of the *disk* classes is hierarchical. This is a crucial criterion in object-oriented designs and will be discussed in greater detail in subsequent sections.

5. **Typing:** Identifies a programming language type conversion and characteristics. For instance, a strong typing means that conversions between different data types in expressions require explicit conversions.

6. **Concurrency:** In *distributed architectures*, objects can be distributed across multiple processors. Since they are no longer controlled by a single process (program), their operations, states, and interactions must be controlled and coordinated in order to avoid resource contention and processing deadlocks.

7. **Persistence:** In *distributed architectures* or database applications, as a process terminates, the state of critical objects associated with the terminated process must be stored in a database or in a file. This provides *persistence*, and objects from other processes can reactivate and interact with each other without loss of information.

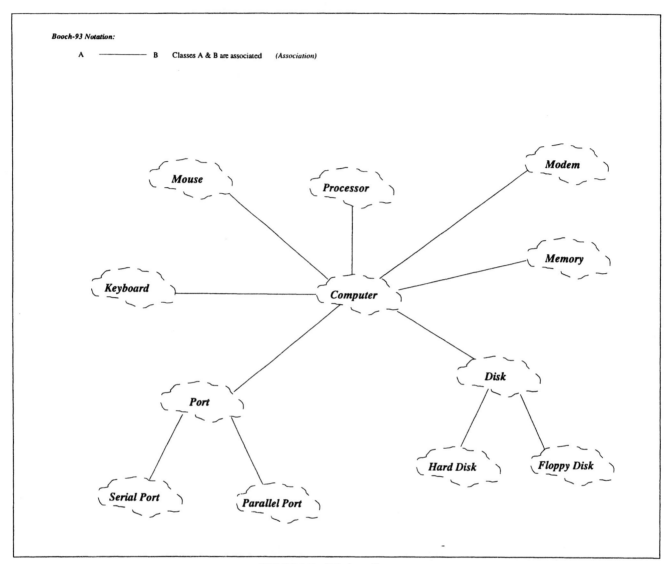

FIGURE 1.5 PC class diagram.

A true object-oriented design supports *modularity, encapsulation, abstraction,* and *design hierarchy* elements [Booch 1994]. If a design lacks any of these four characteristics, it is not considered an *object-oriented* design. For instance, a design that is based on *modularity, encapsulation,* and *abstraction* is considered an *object-based* design rather than an *object-oriented* design because it does not utilize a *design hierarchy*.

Concurrency, persistence, and *typing* are **optional** components of OOD. *Concurrency* and *persistence* usually apply to applications whose objects are distributed across different systems and platforms (*distributed architecture*). *Typing* is controlled by the programming language.

1.2.1 Modularity

During a complete software product life cycle, a product will undergo modifications and enhancements. A modular design makes product maintenance and modification easier since changes can be localized to specific modules. Modular design promotes software reuse across projects and cuts the cost of developing software. Use of common libraries also simplifies integration and evolution of software packages by centralizing functionality. Decoupling the class design improves the maintainability of the software. *Modularity* is achieved by minimizing *coupling* (interdependence between objects), and increasing *cohesion* (functional correlation between data and process).

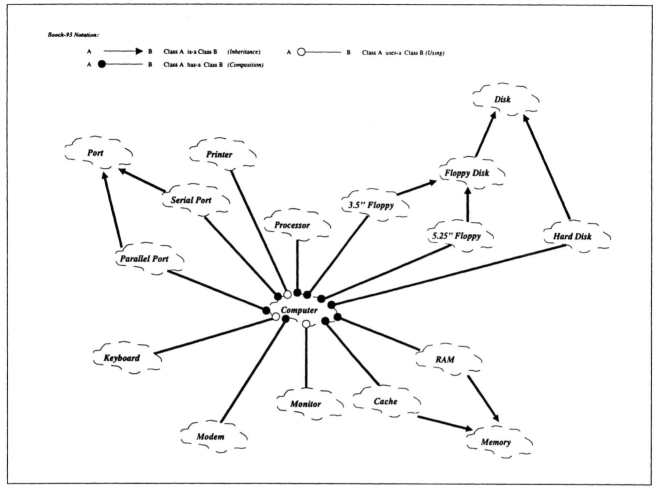

FIGURE 1.6 PC class diagram.

A modular design is created by logically partitioning a system into a group of objects and constraining these objects to interact through well-defined interfaces. In Figure 1.6, a computer system is partitioned into a set of classes by viewing its tangible components and peripherals as classes. The task of storing and retrieving information to/from a floppy disk is mapped to the *floppy disk* class, while the graphical displaying of information is allocated to the *monitor* class. The logical partitioning of classes has created a modular view of the computer.

1.2.2 Encapsulation

In object-oriented design (OOD), the class encapsulates its internal architecture and data representation from other classes. In Figure 1.6, the *floppy disk* class stores and retrieves information to a floppy disk and the *monitor* class displays information on the screen. Each class hides its internal operations and only the methods provided can be used to operate on an object (refer back to Figure 1.2). This approach makes the *computer* class design independent of *monitor* and *floppy disk* designs. For example, changes to *3.5" floppy* are localized to a single point and the *computer* remains unchanged. Furthermore, as long as the interfaces between the computer and these classes remain unchanged, changes to the internal architecture and operations are localized to the modified class.

In addition to maintainability, *encapsulation* enhances the reliability of the design. The likelihood of data corruption and of the object being placed into an *unpredictable* state is minimized. For example, if the *computer* object wrote information directly onto a floppy disk, there is a danger it would accidently corrupt the file allocation table. In such an event, the *floppy disk* object would be placed into an *unpredictable* state and the reliability of the *floppy disk* is adversely affected. By using the **store( )** function provided by the *floppy disk* class (Figure 1.7), the *floppy disk* object would ensure the information is written properly to the disk while keeping the *floppy disk* object in a valid state.

1.2.3 Abstraction

The *operations* provided by a class abstract the internal processes from other classes. For instance, the *computer* class would use the *floppy disk* **store( )** function to store a file to a floppy disk (Figure 1.7). The **store( )** function needs to reserve tracks/sectors on the disk. Then the file content must be partitioned into blocks and the data blocks stored on the medium. As blocks are stored to specific sectors on the disk, the **store( )** function also needs to update the file allocation table to identify the locations of the blocks. The *floppy disk* **store( )** function abstracts the details of the data storage process and hardware interaction from the *computer* object or other users of the *floppy disk*. In addition, the implementation for the storage operation varies among computer systems and operating systems; the abstraction provided by the method localizes and hides these dependencies. *Abstraction* hides the implementation's complexity from other classes.

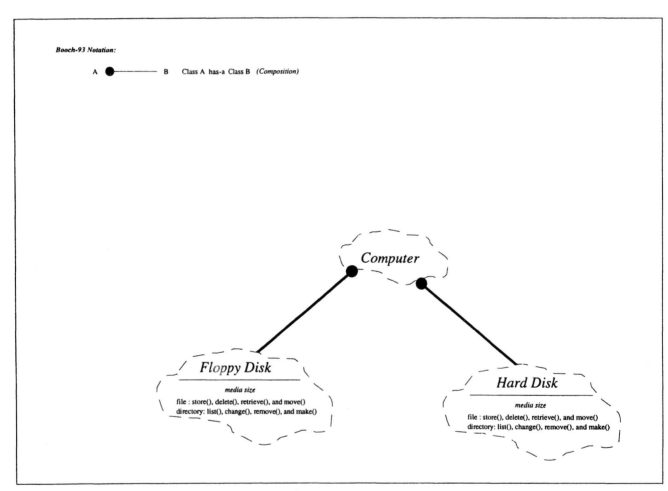

FIGURE 1.7   Disk class diagram.

1.2.4 Design Hierarchy

Design hierarchies are formed by allowing new designs to *inherit* the properties and attributes of the existing designs. Through *inheritance*, a new class inherits the attributes and services of an existing class. In a *design hierarchy*, classes form an "**is-a**" relationship. By inheriting the properties of an existing class, a new class builds on tested and mature classes, while existing designs are reused and development productivity is improved. In

Figure 1.7, both the *hard disk* and *floppy disk* objects provide directory and file services such as the **store( )**, **create( )**, **delete( )**, and **move( )** operations. The implementations for the above operations vary on the basis of system, hardware, and storage medium characteristics. The two objects can be viewed as different types of disks. From the perspective of the *computer*, the disk operations on both *floppy disk* and *hard disk* objects are identical. The design presented in Figure 1.7 does not convey any relationship between the two, which forces the *computer* object to support unique and custom code for using each of them. In addition, the *floppy disk* and *hard disk* objects are duplicating the common attributes and features in the implementation.

The design presented in Figure 1.7 can be modularized and simplified by using a *design hierarchy*. In Figure 1.8, the design for *hard disk* and *floppy disk* classes has been rearchitected. The hierarchy as shown improves the design by providing the following benefits:

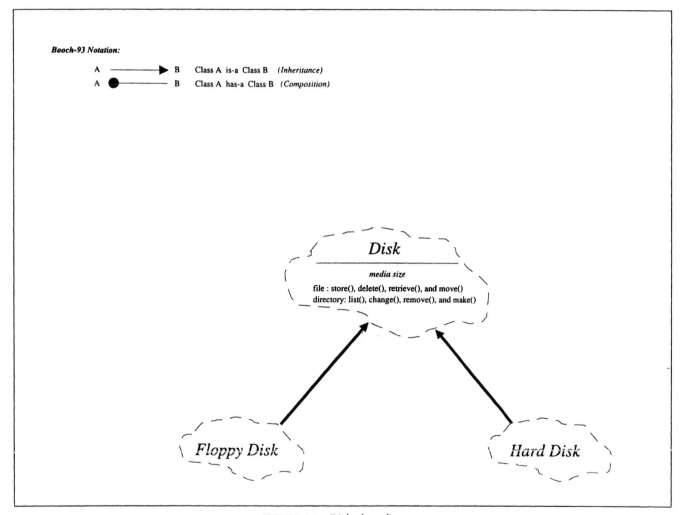

FIGURE 1.8 Disk class diagram

1. **Common Characteristics**: The common attributes and operations between the disk classes are maintained in the common *disk* class, and the *floppy* and *hard disk* classes do not need to provide unique implementations for these common features. Since common properties are inherited through *disk*, changes to the common attributes become localized to *disk*. This localization of changes will reduce redevelopment, test, validation, and integration time. As an added benefit, both the *floppy* and *hard disk* classes are built on a tested *disk* class.

2. **Data Dependencies**: Even though the services such as the **store( )** operation provided by the *floppy* and *hard disk* objects are implemented differently for each distinct object, the client perceives them as the same. By defining a common interface (parameter list) for this function, a greater level of abstraction can be

achieved because the actual **store( )** operation on different media is transparent to the client. This approach allows the client to develop applications that are independent of a specific type of *disk*:

```
disk.store( arguments )
```

The client is not dependent on any specific disk type in the hierarchy. Depending on the type of *disk* object, the applicable **store( )** operation is invoked at run time. This gives the software the ability to operate on different but related data types, and is referred to as *polymorphic* behavior. When a new type of *disk* is later added to the hierarchy, the client's program will require minimal or no modifications. The decoupling of the client's code to specific data types minimizes the data dependencies and limits the scope of redevelopment and retesting.

3. **Customization**: New objects can be added to the design hierarchy simply by creating customized versions of the existing ones. In Figure 1.9, the *floppy disk* object has been customized and two new customized versions are introduced: *3.5"* and *5.25"* floppies. These new objects are built on existing designs that are tested and validated. This characteristic can help reduce development time for a new class in the hierarchy.

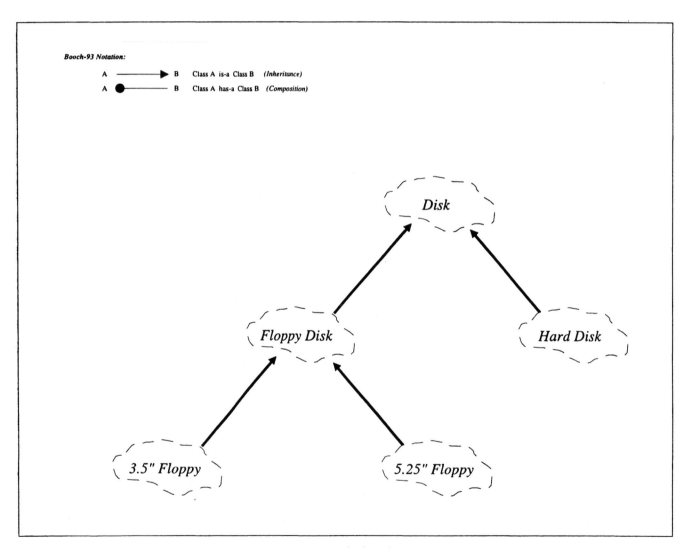

FIGURE 1.9   Disk class diagram.

A design hierarchy forms a *parent-child* relationship between the classes. The *parent* class is referred to as the *base* or *superclass* and the *child* is called the *derived* or *subclass*. In Figure 1.9, *disk* is the base class for the *floppy* and *hard disk* derived classes. Similarly, the *floppy disk* is the base class for *3.5"* and *5.25"* *floppy disk* classes. The *computer* class diagram depicted in Figure 1.6 illustrates design hierarchies for several different types of classes, such as *memory*.

1.2.5 Concurrency

With distributed processing and client/server applications, a software application requires the cooperation of several programs running asynchronously on different platforms/systems. The objects become scattered across hardware boundaries and are no longer contained within the address space of one computer. Figure 1.10 depicts a distributed Graphical On-Line Documentation (GOLD) software application that would maintain aircraft electronic maintenance data across heterogeneous systems [PARTA 1993].

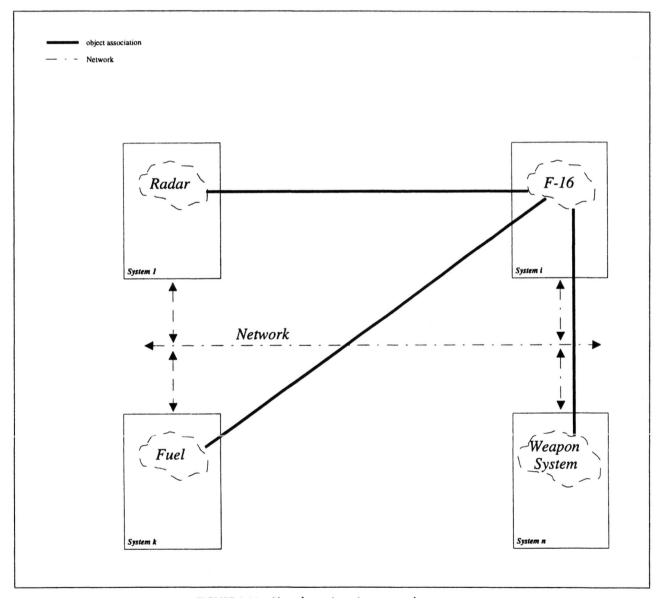

FIGURE 1.10   Aircraft repair maintenance data system.

Like a single process application, the distributed objects must interact with each other in some logical and structured manner. The distributed architecture requires the design to address *concurrency* issues; otherwise the objects will contend for resources, which could result in *deadlocks*. For instance, several objects may invoke operations on another object simultaneously. The requests may conflict with each other and may cause the object to go into an unpredictable state. Unlike a single process application, the requests must be coordinated so that the objects will remain in a predictable state.

Regulation of concurrent processes through mechanisms such as *semaphores* assure an object's state and information are protected. A semaphore is a locking mechanism that regulates access to data by allowing only a single process to access the locked entity within a given time domain. When executing a critical area, the active process activates the lock, thus preventing other processes from accessing the protected entity. Requests by other processes will wait until the lock is released. The object will not be placed into an unpredictable state since access to protected code and data is synchronized.

Object-oriented design views *concurrency* as an optional aspect of the object model [Booch 1994]. However, with distributed architectures and objects, *concurrency* is an integral part of an object-oriented design and must be addressed. Chapter 12 discusses general concurrency issues.

1.2.6 Persistence

In a single platform application, objects are created during the program's execution and, depending on the scope of the object, they are later destroyed. The life span of the objects is directly tied to the lifetime of the program. When the program execution ceases, the objects and their states are permanently lost unless the information is stored in a database. For instance, a *human resource* software application can have *persistence* by using a database to store the employee record objects. The state of the objects will then persist beyond the end of the software execution.

In distributed applications, when a process terminates, certain objects associated with the process cannot be destroyed because other processes running on different platforms may depend on these objects and their information. Thus, these objects must persist independent of the process which they are associated. The *state* of these objects is normally stored in a database or file. Figure 1.11 depicts the graphical user interface (GUI) of the GOLD system [PARTA 1993]. In a distributed architecture, the *F-16 fighter plane* object model may be allocated across several computer systems. For instance, the *radar* object may be maintained on a UNIX-based platform and the *weapon system* object may reside on a Windows-NT-based system. When a user accesses and updates the *F-16 radar* object, the updated radar information must persist. If the updated *radar* object is destroyed at the termination of the user process, the current information would be lost. The reliability of the software application can also be compromised if the state of a distributed object is not maintained. If a second user on another system happened to access the *F-16 radar* object simultaneously, then the destruction of the *radar* object will cause unexpected results. In distributed architectures, the state of objects must transcend through time and space [Booch 1994].

The *persistence* of information for distributed objects is achieved using databases such as object-oriented database management systems (ODBMs). These systems make information storage and retrieval transparent to the client.

1.2.7 Typing

Typing is an optional criterion in OOD and is determined by the programming language. A programming language can provide *weak* or *strong* typing. In a *weakly* typed language, the designer has complete freedom to mix data types in expressions whether it makes sense or not. The following example illustrates an expression that properly mixes built-in types with an instance of a class:

```
Complex z1 = z2 + 3.0 ;  // add a complex number to a real number
```

A *strongly* typed language will not allow the above operation to take place and will result in compilation error. By preventing a design from using mixed data types in expressions, a *strongly* typed language helps to avoid the logical errors caused by implicit conversions. A strongly typed language requires a software developer to specify conversions explicitly. The above operation can then take place through explicit conversions:

```
Complex z1 = z2 + Complex (3.0) ;
         // convert the real number to a complex number and
         // then add the two complex values
```

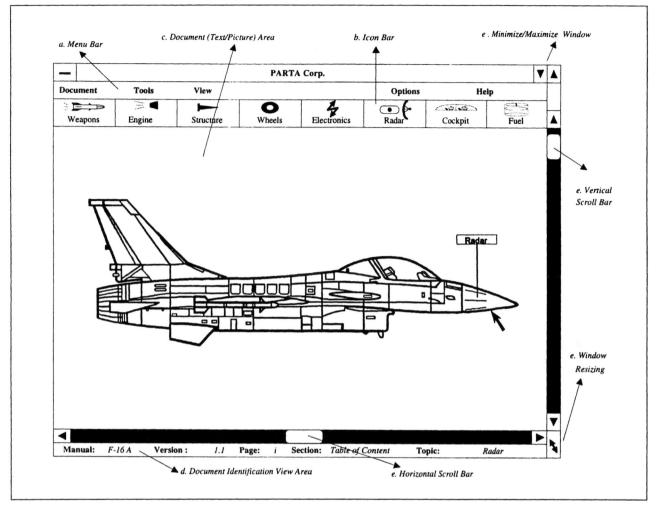

FIGURE 1.11 GOLD software user interface.

A strongly typed language makes the implementation more tedious because it forces the developer to address each type conversion. In addition, changes to the data types in the interfaces would require explicit changes to the client's code due to lack of implicit data conversion.

C++ is neither a *strong* nor a *weakly* typed language and is considered to be between the two. Through implicit conversion, C++ resolves expressions consisting of built-in data types. However, there are restrictions on implicit conversions among objects and built-in data types. Since C++ is not *strongly* typed, a designer is responsible for making sure allowable implicit conversions make sense and provide correct results.

The customer's requirements on typing determine the choice of the object-oriented language that will produce the necessary implementation, such as using Ada 95 for military projects.

1.3 RELATIONSHIPS AMONG OBJECTS

When objects interact with each other, they form relationships. One object becomes a client of another and uses the other object in some capacity. The relationship between the objects can be categorized as the following [Booch 1994]:

1. **Using**: An object uses the resources of another for accomplishing a task. In Figure 1.12, a person uses a car to go to the market. The classes form the *"use-a"* relationship:

        person uses-a car

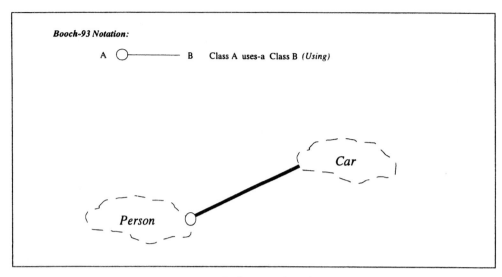

FIGURE 1.12 Car/person class diagram

2. **Composition**: In *composition*, the objects form a *system-subsystem* architecture and the design is broken into aggregated components. In Figure 1.13, the *F-16 radar* class is composed of the *transmitter*, *receiver*, and *antenna* classes. The decomposition simplifies the modeling by breaking a class into several components. In composition, objects form the "**has-a**" relationship:

```
radar has-a receiver, transmitter, and antenna
car has-an engine, body, and wheels
```

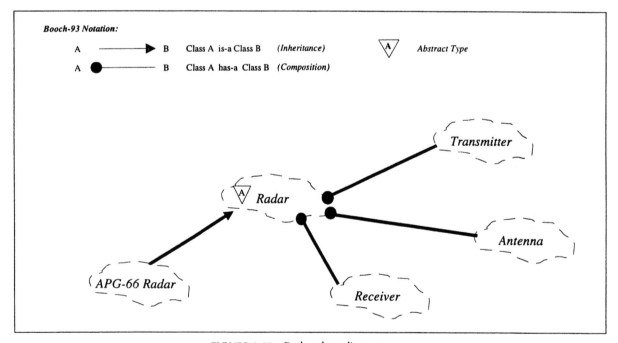

FIGURE 1.13 Radar class diagram.

3. **Inheritance**: A new class is created from an existing class by inheriting its properties. For example, a *laser printer* and *ink jet printer* are created by inheriting the properties of a general *printer* (Figure 1.14). The architecture forms an "**is-a**" relationship:

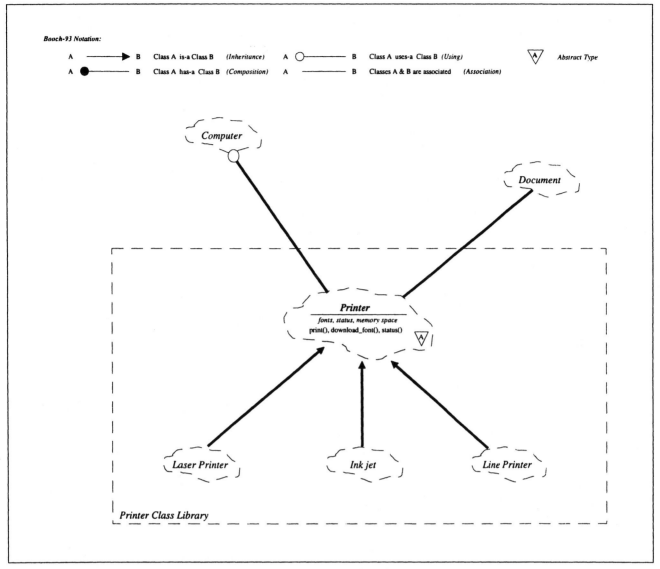

FIGURE 1.14 Printer class diagram

```
laser printer is-a printer
ink jet printer is-a printer
```

Figure 1.15 depicts a design hierarchy for military aircraft. The *airplane* class creates a design umbrella for the different types of military aircraft by identifying them as some type of an airplane. This class is considered *abstract* because in reality there is no generic airplane. In diagrams, the abstract property is highlighted by using the triangular symbol with the letter "A" enclosed in it. This symbol specifies that the *airplane* is an *abstract* class, whereas *F-16* is a real airplane and is referred to as a *concrete* class:

```
F-16 is-a fighter plane
```

An *abstract* class defines the design interface for its *derived* classes, and captures the common operations and attributes between the *derived* classes. An *abstract* class allows a client to operate on any of the *derived* *concrete* classes in a generic way (*polymorphism*). Chapter 10 discusses this property in detail.

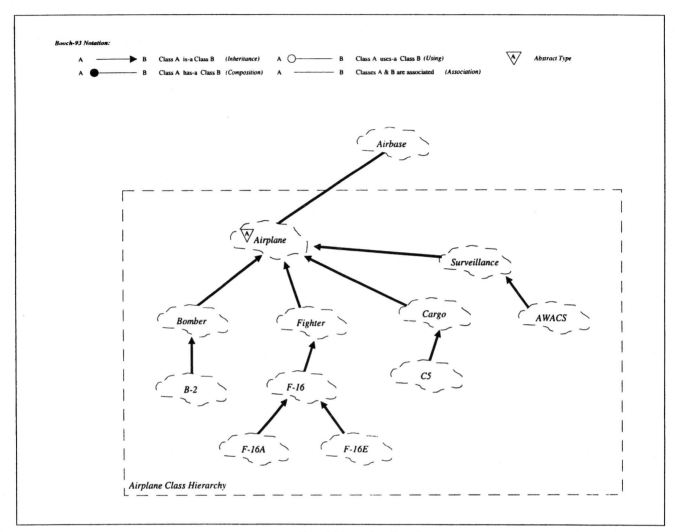

FIGURE 1.15   Aircraft hierarchy class diagram.

4. **Association**: When there is a loose relationship between two objects, they become associated with each other. It is typically used in the early stages of analysis before a more concrete relationship such as "***is-a***" has been defined. For example, a *patent attorney* and a *legal case* are associated with each other. In Figure 1.14, *printer* and *document* form an "*associated*" relationship and in Figure 1.15, *airplanes* are associated with an *airbase*:

```
a document is-associated with a printer
an airplane is-associated with an airbase
```

During the design phase of an object model, relationships such as "***is-a***" are used to describe the association between the classes. The classes in an object-oriented (OO) design must form proper relationships, and the relationships must make sense. Figure 1.16a depicts an incorrect model for a car because *a car **is-not** an engine or a wheel*. The proper design approach would have been to use *composition* and make *engine*, *wheel*, and *body* aggregate components of a *car* (Figure 1.16b). Improper use of relationships leads to OO designs that are hard to maintain.

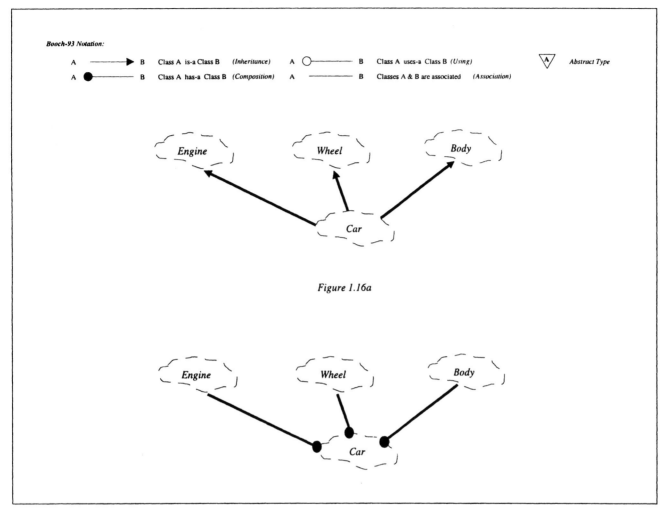

FIGURE 1.16   Improper car class diagram.

1.4 NOTATION

1.4.1 Booch-93 Notation

Graphical presentations help convey design information. For example, the architectural plans for a house presents the architect's vision to the customer before the house is built. The floor plan shows the architecture, room layouts, and sizes. The three-dimensional plan shows the facade and shape of the house. By using different types of diagrams, different information is conveyed to the customer.

Similarly, Booch-93 diagrams depicted in this book convey and describe the design. Booch-93 notation uses different types of diagrams to present different aspects of the object-oriented design, and captures both *static* and *dynamic* aspects of the object model. The system architecture, classes, and their relationships represent the *static* aspects. The *dynamic* behavior describes the interactions between the objects and their states. Figure 1.17 categorizes the following diagrams using the static and dynamic models:

a) Process diagram
b) Category diagram
c) Module diagram
d) Class diagram
e) Class specification

f) Object diagram
g) State transition diagram
h) Interaction diagram

Except for the *process* diagram and *class specification*, this book utilizes all of the Booch diagrams for its presentations. For a complete description of these diagrams, the reader should refer to *Object-Oriented Analysis and Design with Applications* by Grady Booch [Booch 1994].

In typical object-oriented designs, the object models may consist of hundreds of classes. To present these classes using a single class, object, and interaction diagram is not only impractical but counterproductive. The audience will become overwhelmed with the vast amount of information. The purpose of these diagrams is to convey design ideas in a concise and standard manner, and are not to overwhelm the reader. Therefore, different aspects of the design are illustrated using different and multiple diagrams.

Static Model	*Dynamic Model*
Process Diagram Module Diagram Category Diagram Class Diagram Class Specification	State Transition Diagram Interaction Diagram Object Diagram

FIGURE 1.17 Booch-93 Diagrams

1.4.1.1 Module Diagram

The *module* diagram presents a high-level view of the system and partitions a system in terms of *subsystems* and *modules*. A *subsystem* is a collection of *modules* logically grouped together. Similarly, a *module* is a collection of classes logically grouped together in order to perform a specific task in a system. For example, the classes associated to a fax system's *communication* module are responsible for coordinating the transmission of data via the phone line.

In Figure 1.18, a high-level module diagram for the GOLD system is presented [PARTA 1993]. The dependencies between *modules* and *subsystems* are shown, using arrows. The system is partitioned into GUI, multimedia, maintenance log (persistence), airplane repair manuals, and airbase spare parts. The module *specification* and *body* icons are based on Ada's package specification and package body. These icons can be loosely compared to a C/C++ header and source file. These icons are superimposed in the module diagram to denote the association between the declarations and definitions.

The use of a *module* diagram partitions the design along well-defined boundaries by breaking down the system architecture into *subsystems* and *modules*. The logical partitioning of a system into *subsystems* permits the targeted audience to focus on a high-level view of the system.

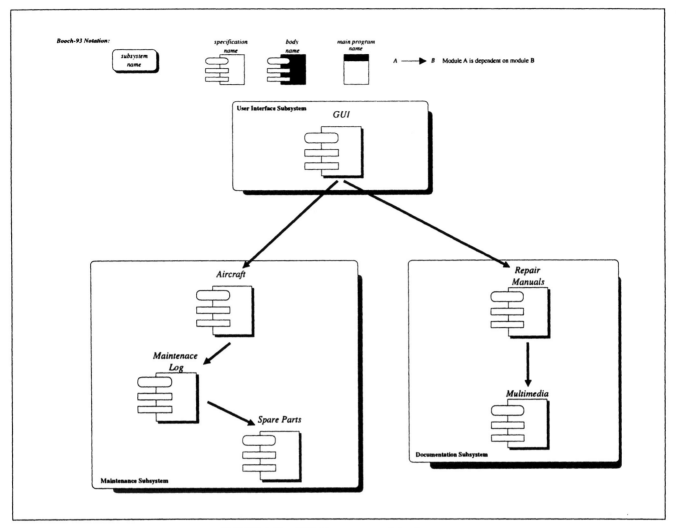

FIGURE 1.18   GOLD system module diagram.

1.4.1.2 Category Diagram

The *category* diagram facilitates the presentation and partitioning of a *subsystem* and *module* into logical and cohesive categories. Each category will consist of its own set of classes. A category organizes a group of classes in a set. In the design of complex modules, a category diagram provides a high-level view of the module's detailed design. The classes associated to category may be documented in the category diagram by listing the classes in the applicable category box. The categories interact with each other through well-defined interfaces.

Figure 1.19 depicts the categories used in the design of the *spare parts* module for the GOLD system [PARTA 1993]. This diagram views the system as a hierarchical (multilayered) architecture by having the higher level categories appear on top.

In the diagram, the categories form a *"using"* relationship. The common and core categories that are used by all or most categories in the diagram are grouped at the bottom of Figure 1.19 and are denoted using the **"global"** keyword. This notation prevents the diagram from becoming too cluttered with the *"using"* relationship lines.

1.4.1.3 Class Diagram

For a detailed view of a module or class category, a *class* diagram is used to show the exact relationships between the classes. A *class* diagram captures detailed information for the static model by identifying the classes and their relationships. Examples of this diagram have been depicted throughout the chapter, such as in Figure 1.15. In addition to relationships, a class diagram may specify other details such as *containment*, *cardinality*, *properties*, and *export controls*:

Booch-93 Notation:

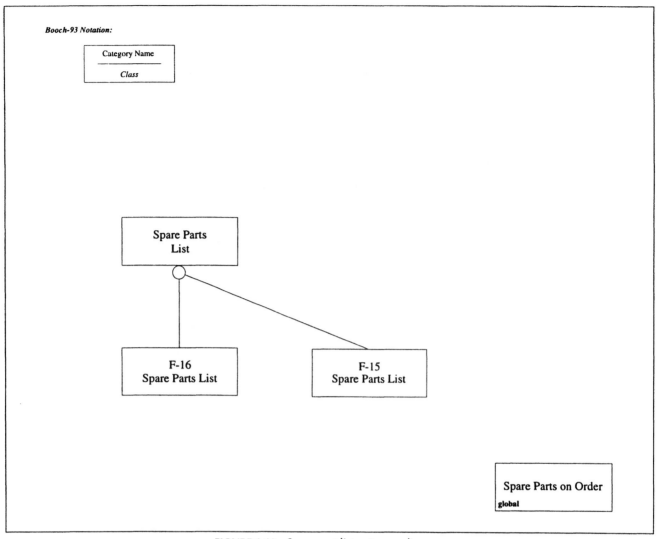

FIGURE 1.19   Spare part list category diagram.

1. **Containment:** Identifies how a system class maintains its subsystem class: *externally* or *internally*. For example, an *F-14 fighter plane* may be modeled on the basis of its structural architecture. Figure 1.20 decomposes this plane and shows the relationship and containment type for some of its parts. For every instance of an *F-14 fighter plane* class, there are two instances of the *engine* and three instances of the *wheel* classes.

   Containment is denoted by the square shape symbols. A darkened square denotes internal containment (value) and a white square denotes external (reference) containment. With *internal* containment, an instance of *F-14* contains three instances of *wheel* objects. The lifetime of *F-14* and its *wheels* are closely coupled. Since an *F-14* contains three instances of *wheel*, when an *F-14* object comes into existence the *wheel* objects are also created, and when the *F-14* object is destroyed, the *wheel* objects are also destroyed. In the case of *external* containment, the above is not necessarily true. *F-14* may create the *engine* objects or they may have been created prior to construction of *F-14*. The lifetime of the two objects becomes an implementation issue. However, *F-14* is basically referencing two *engine* objects, which reside outside of it.

2. **Cardinality**: Specifies the number of instances associated between two classes. In Figure 1.20, for every *F-14* object there are two instances of engines. Therefore, there is a 1-2 cardinality. Booch notation supports one-to-many, many-to-one, or many-to-many cardinality [Booch 1994]:

.Exactly one relationship: 1

.Unlimited number (0 or more):   n

. Zero or more: 0 .. n

. One or more: 1 .. n

. Range: 10 .. 30

.Range and number: 2 .. 4 , 8

Cardinality applies to *composition* and *association* relationships.

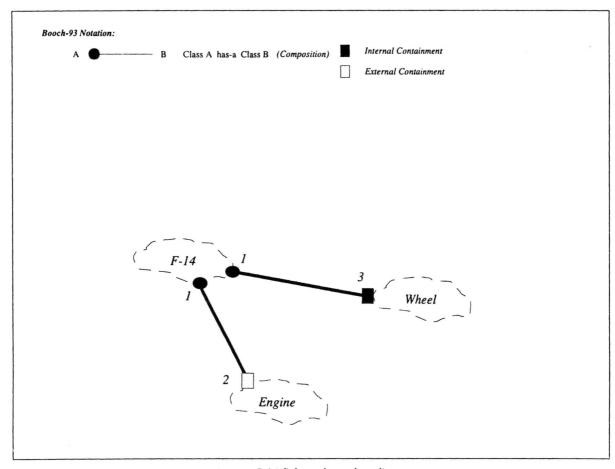

FIGURE 1.20   F-14 fighter plane class diagram.

3. **Property**: A property is enclosed in an upside-down triangle. The following identifies the available properties:

   a. *abstract (A)*: An abstract class is used in the formation of a design hierarchy. In Figure 1.15, a generic aircraft was marked as an abstract class. These types of classes establish a common design interface for their derived classes and cannot have an instance.

   b. *friend (F)*: This property denotes that a class is a friend of another and has access to the internal data members of another class. This property tightly couples design components and eliminates modularity and encapsulation between the two classes. This property should be used sparingly in a design.

   c. *virtual (v)*: The virtual property is used when a class may be inherited indirectly twice or more. Examples of abstract and virtual properties are presented in Chapters 9 and 10 of this book.

d. *static (s)*: This property identifies that the class is a static member of another class and one instance of the class will be shared by all instances of the other class. Static members are described in detail in Chapter 5.

4. **Export Controls**: Identifies the access levels. There are four types of export control: public, protected, private, and implementation. The export controls are depicted using vertical bars on the relationship lines. Examples of this feature are provided in subsequent chapters.

Except for the abstract property, the other properties appear on the line identifying the relationship between two classes. Examples of these properties are provided in later chapters.

1.4.1.4 State Transition Diagram

A *state transition* diagram defines the dynamic behavior of an object by identifying the possible states for an object. This diagram identifies the *events* and *operations* that cause the object to transition from one state to another. In Figure 1.21, the state transition diagram identifies the possible states for the *modem* object: **idle**, **setup**, **transmitting**, **receiving**, **error**, and **termination**. The condition enclosed in brackets identifies the criterion that has caused the state transition.

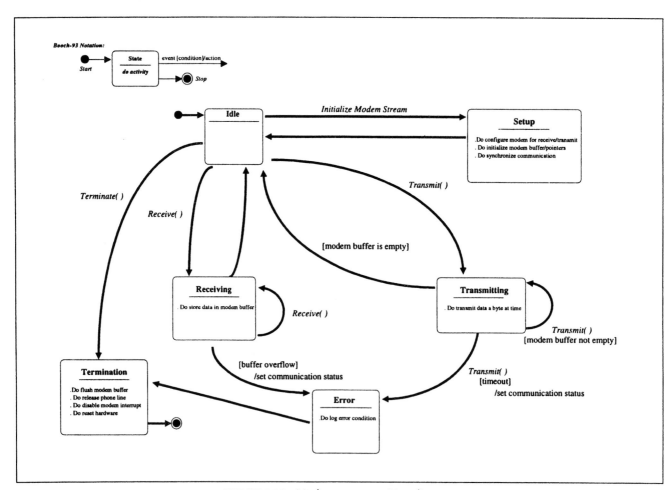

FIGURE 1.21   Modem state transition diagram.

Some of the *events* and *operations* cannot cause the object to transition unless a certain *condition* is met, also known as a *guarded condition*. For instance, a transmit request event causes the **transmitting** state to transition to the **error** state when the modem times out. Since an *event* may cause a state to transition to several other states, the *guarded condition* is used to identify the criterion for the transitioning and makes the state diagram deterministic. In the **transmitting** state, the **transmit()** operation either maintains the object in the same state or transitions it to the *error* state. Without the *guarded condition*, the behavior is not clear. Associated with an *event*, there also may be an *action*. For instance, the communication failure status is set before transitioning from the **receiving** state to the **error** state. An *action* is considered to take zero processing time and cannot be interrupted. The following identifies the sequence for transitioning from an event:

1. An event occurs
2. Guarded condition is evaluated
3. Action is performed
4. State transition takes place

Within a *state*, several activities can take place and are documented by "*do activity.*" In the error state, an activity is to log the error condition. An activity may be interrupted by an event.

A transition diagram may identify entry and exit points denoted by darkened and semidarkened circles, respectively. The entry point identifies the initial state when an object comes into existence. There can be only one entry point in a transition diagram but there can be many exit points (Figure 1.21).

1.4.1.5 Interaction Diagram

The *interaction* diagram traces events within a design and defines the *messages* (events and operations) between the objects. Figure 1.22 illustrates the events and operations associated with the interaction among the personnel

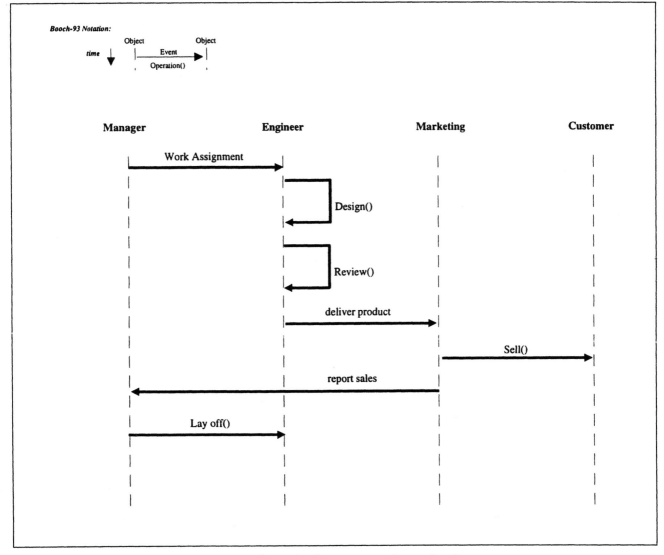

FIGURE 1.22 Software development group interaction diagram.

of a software development company in the 1990s. The *operations* are differentiated from *events* by using parentheses. In this diagram, the company's personnel are viewed as objects. This diagram provides a chronology of events: the company executive provides the Research/Development (R/D) engineer with a statement of work. The engineer designs the product and then reviews the design. Upon product acceptance, the engineer delivers the product to the marketing department, which later sells the product to the customer. Marketing reports the product sales to the management. At the end of the project, the management consolidates the company by laying off the engineer. The order of events is from top to bottom with the time axis pointing downward.

The interaction diagram does not provide many details, making it useful for high- level design. The diagram permits algorithm notes and pseudocode to appear on the left-hand side, explaining the events in greater detail in addition to identifying conditional statements, decisions, and loops.

1.4.1.6 Object Diagram

The *object* diagram presents the same information as the *interaction* diagram except that it shows greater detail. This type of diagram defines the object interactions, synchronization, roles, visibility, data flow, and data direction.

Figure 1.23 uses a new notation to show the event interactions for the software development company depicted in Figure 1.22. Unlike an *event interaction* diagram, the location of interaction lines in the *object* diagram are unimportant. Thus, the events and operations must be numbered in order to identify the sequence of events.

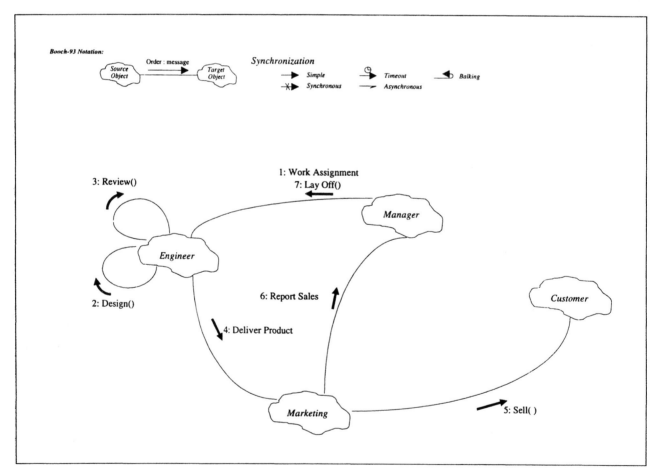

FIGURE 1.23   Software development group object diagram.

The direction of the message is shown by the arrows. The object diagram supports different notation for the messages in order to support real-time applications and concurrency:

1. **Simple**: The standard arrow is used to depict a single thread control from a source to a target object.
2. **Synchronous**: A synchronous message is shown by an arrow with an X mark. This message indicates the operation that takes place after the target object accepts the request. The source object waits until the message is accepted.
3. **Timeout**: The timeout synchronization is shown by the clock above an arrow to indicate that the event or operation must be completed within a specified amount of time. The source object abandons the operation if it is not completed within the allowed time.
4. **Asynchronous**: An asynchronous message is shown by a *modified arrow* (¬). This synchronization scheme is used for multithreaded applications when the source object sends a message to another object and continues its execution without waiting for a response. The *modified arrow* (¬) denotes that the operation is executed asynchronously.
5. **Balking**: The balking synchronization is shown by an arrow that points back to the source object. The message is passed to the target object only if the target object is ready to receive it. The operation is abandoned if the target is not ready.

The above synchronization scenarios are useful for describing the dynamic behavior of distributed objects. Subsequent chapters utilize the above symbols in their object diagram examples.

1.4.2 Function Hierarchy

For classes whose operations form a hierarchy, the function hierarchy diagram is used to illustrate the relationships between the functions. This diagram is useful for low-level design and is not part of the Booch methodology. This book uses this type of diagram to show the relationships between the functions. For example, Figure 1.24 depicts the data transmission function hierarchy for a *Serial Stream* class library. The external operations are denoted by **bold face** characters and are part of the design interface. The operations denoted by nonbold face characters are internal functions to the design of the class. This diagram creates a pictorial representation of the functions and their relationships in a complicated design. In Figure 1.24, the **transmit_packet()** function calls several private and public member functions such as the **transmit_string()** and **receive()** functions.

SUMMARY

The object-oriented design (OOD) methodology focuses on *objects* rather than on processes and algorithms. Objects become abstract representations of the entities in the problem domain. For example, the design of a facsimile (fax) machine will focus on identifying the objects required to represent a fax machine, such as a modem, scanner, keypad, and printer. These objects collaborate with each other and model the operation of a fax machine. Object-oriented design formalizes the definition of an object as "*an entity that has a state, identity, and behavior.*"

In C++, only the memory layout and content (static behavior) of the object can be defined at the source file level, and is known as the *class* definition. A class definition logically groups data and functions. On the basis of the values and settings of the data members, the instance of the class would exhibit a state. The member functions operate on the data elements and perform operations such as initialization and cleanup. These functions give the instance of the class a behavior. Since a class may have many instances, each instance is considered to have a unique identity. *An object is an instance of a class.*

In object-oriented systems, an *object* model is created by analyzing the software requirements. The granularity of the *object* model is enhanced and completed iteratively. Finally, the design is implemented using an object-oriented programming language. An object-oriented design must incorporate and address the *major* elements of the object model's framework:

1. Modularity
2. Encapsulation
3. Abstraction
4. Design hierarchy

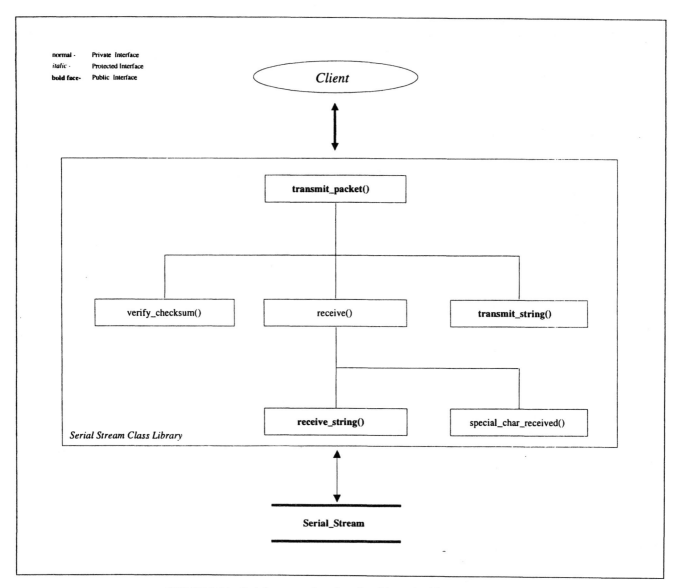

FIGURE 1.24 Serial stream class function hierarchy (data transmission)

The framework is formalized to enhance software maintainability, reliability, and reusability. These elements are required components of the *object* model. Designs lacking the design hierarchy elements are called *object-based* designs instead of *object-oriented* designs.

The object model also has three other *minor* elements that are considered optional:

1. Concurrency
2. Persistence
3. Typing

Concurrency and persistence play an important role in distributed objects where the objects reside across multithreaded and multiprocess environments.

At the time of implementation, the *object model* must identify both dynamic and *static* behaviors:

1. **Static Behavior**: The system's architecture, data representation, interfaces, and relationships among the classes are identified.
2. **Dynamic Behavior**: The state and the interaction among the objects are specified.

To help capture the above information, industry standard notations such as Booch are used. Owing to the graphical nature of the Booch notation, this book uses the Booch-93 notation. The diagrams represent the details and the architecture of design and convey ideas visually, similar to other notations such as the *Unified Modeling Language* [Rational 1996].

GLOSSARY

Abstraction
Hiding the complexity of the design and the underlying processes involved in carrying out the operations on an object

Base class
In inheritance, the *base* class is used to create new classes (*derived*). The *derived* classes inherit the properties and attributes of the existing class (*base*)

Cardinality
Number of instances of a class

Class
A class is a structured set consisting of the declarations of member data with the member functions being the operation on the set. A class identifies the memory layout for an object and specifies the functions that operate on the object

Client
A class becomes a client of another class by using its features in its design. Depending on the relationships and syntax in C++, the clients can be grouped into *is-a, associate, has-a,* and *use-a* relationships

Data encapsulation
The process of hiding the internal architecture of a data structure and the underlying data representation by building a series of functions around the design. The functions act as the gateway by regulating the access of *clients* to the data members

Derived class
By inheriting properties and attributes of an existing class (*base*) and adding additional features, a new class (*derived*) emerges from the design

Inheritance
The ability to inherit the architecture, attributes, and properties of an existing (*base*) class in the design of a new (*derived*) class. Inheritance creates an "***is-a***" relationship between the *base* class and its *derived* class

Modularity
A design that exhibits high cohesion and low coupling

Member function
A function that can operate freely on the data members of a class and is part of the class design. A member function hides the internal architecture and specifies the operations on the class

Method
An Ada term for function. This book uses method, function, and operation interchangeably

Object
An object is an entity that has a **state, behavior,** and **identity**

Object-based
A design that focuses on collaborative effort of objects that are instances of different classes. However, the objects do not form hierarchical architecture

Object-oriented

A design must not only satisfy the *object-based* criteria, but also the classes must form design hierarchies through *inheritance*

OOA

Object-oriented analysis (OOA)

OOD

Object-oriented design (OOD)

Subclass

Another term for the *derived* class

Superclass

Another term for the *base* class

CHAPTER 2

Object Model Development

INTRODUCTION

Based on the principles of object-oriented design, an *object model* characterizes the *static* and *dynamic* behavior of a system. The *static* component describes the system's architecture in terms of classes and their relationships. The *dynamic* component shows the interactions between the objects and describes the objects' behavior. A designer analyzes the requirements and develops an *object model* based on one of the object-oriented design methods, such as the *Object-Modeling Technique (OMT), Booch,* or *Unified Modeling Language (UML)*[1] [Rational 1996]. These methods use graphical diagrams to communicate the design in a concise and clear manner. This book uses Booch-93 notation, which provides a variety of diagrams for capturing the *static* and *dynamic* aspects of both high-level and detailed design (Figure 2.1). The *module* diagram provides a high-level view of the system architecture. The *class category* and *class* diagrams convey the detailed design of the *modules* in the system. Similarly, the *object, interaction,* and *state transition* diagrams illustrate the object interactions and behavior, which specify the *dynamic* behavior of the system.

A system is best designed via a well-balanced effort spread between *strategic* and *tactical* project activities. Analysis and design of an object-oriented project is partitioned into corresponding *macro-development* and *micro-development* processes:

1. **Macro-development Process**: This process concentrates on the *strategic* issues, or the global design issues, such as performance, reliability, external interfaces, and cohesion. The product that emerges from the *macro-development* process is the top-level view (*architecture*) of the system. The architecture describes the system in terms of *subsystems* and *modules* (Figure 2.1).
2. **Micro-development Process**: The day-to-day design activities represent the *tactical* issues that shape the direction and content of the *micro-development* process. The high-level design activities from the *macro-development* process transition into detailed design activities (Figure 2.1).

The system requirements and architecture are the basis of the *micro-development* process. In this stage, classes, their relationships, and interactions are defined. They are then logically grouped into *categories*, and the *categories* into a *module* (Figure 2.1).

---

[1]The *Unified Modeling Language (UML)* integrates the Booch, Object-Modeling Technique (OMT), and Object-Oriented Software Engineering (OOSE) methods. It is the work product of Grady Booch, James Rumbaugh, and Ivar Jacobson.

Architecture   **Booch-93 Notation**

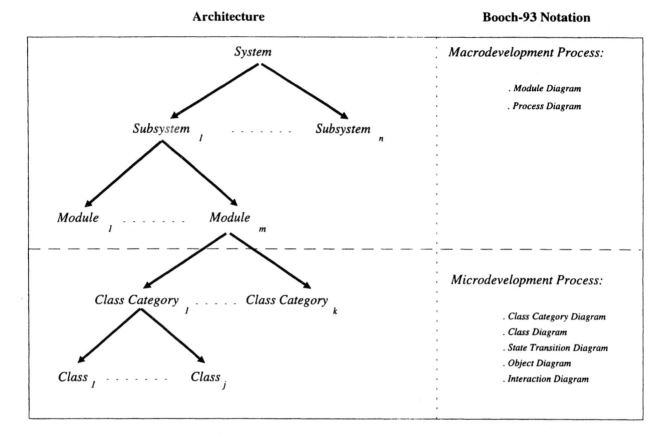

FIGURE 2.1   System development overview.

The *macro-development* process is based on a top-down approach, while the *micro-development* process is a bottom-up approach. They converge at the *module* level.

This chapter describes the incremental specification of an *object model* using the following phases (Figure 2.2):

1. Requirements Definition
2. Analysis and Design
3. Implementation
4. Test and Integration

The discussion primarily concentrates on the *Analysis and Design* phase of a software development project and describes the key activities, deliverables, and teams involved in this process.

2.1 ORGANIZATIONAL INFRASTRUCTURE

The design and implementation of a large modern software system requires the collaboration of different types of teams such as those identified below (Figure 2.3). These teams each have a specific charter and focus. By working closely together, the teams create an appropriate balance between the *strategic* and *tactical* activities:

1. **Systems Engineering Team**: This team collects customer requirements and presents them in a standard and clear fashion using different types of requirements specification documents.
2. **Architecture Team**: After the system requirements have reached a state of maturity and stability, this team analyzes the system requirements and architects a top-level view of the system (*architecture*). This team

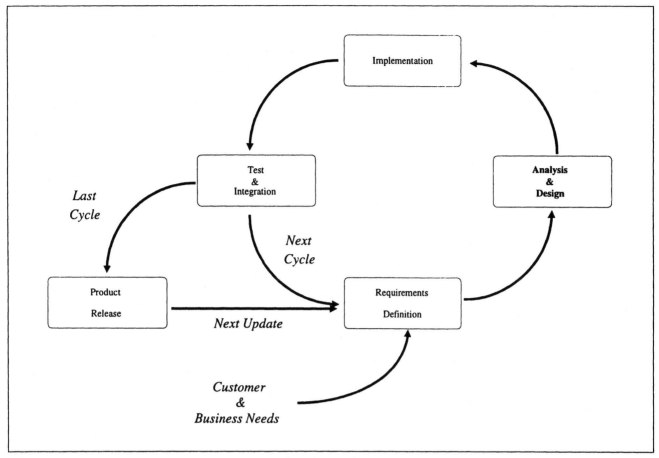

FIGURE 2.2 Object-oriented software life cycle.

focuses on the *strategic* issues and generates the high-level design. This team typically consists of both system and software design engineers.

3. **Development Teams**: The development teams use the *system architecture* developed by the architecture team as the foundation and the framework of their day-to-day design activities. These teams focus on the detailed design of the system. They design the contents of specific *modules* in the system and perform the project's *tactical* activities.

4. **Quality Assurance (QA) Team**: The QA team verifies that the *system architecture* adheres to the system requirements. In addition, this team ensures that the detailed design by the development teams also fulfills the system and software requirements and is consistent with the *system architecture*.

5. **Test Team**: This team uses test drivers and software models to test the *modules*. A formal test process allows this team to verify that the software operation and behavior is consistent with the *dynamic* behavior as specified in the object model.

6. **Support Team**: The support team performs infrastructural activities and takes care of the logistical needs of the entire development organization. Some of the services provided by this team are Software Configuration Management (SCM), training, project library maintenance/release, and an electronic documentation control system.

7. **Management Team**: The management team plans and monitors the project's activities, schedule, and budget. The management team also facilitates the progress of the development teams by making sure that their logistical needs are being addressed and resolved immediately. This team addresses both strategic and tactical management issues.

The name, membership, size, and scope of the above-described teams vary from one organization to another and are dictated by the size of the project and business needs. The succeeding sections discuss the significance and activities of these teams in relation to object model development.

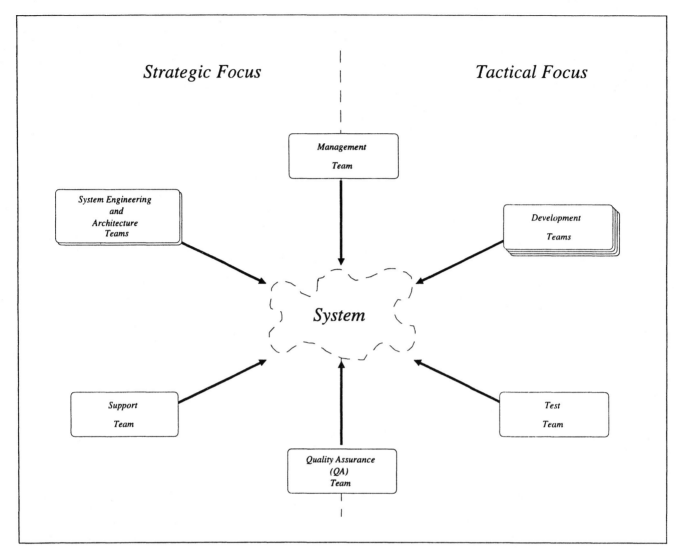

FIGURE 2.3   Software development organizational overview.

2.2 REQUIREMENTS DEFINITION PHASE

Prior to system modeling and analysis, customer requirements are collected and described in a set of requirements documents. In most system development efforts, IEEE standards or military standards (MIL-STD-497) are used to prepare these documents. These standards provide guidelines on content, format, and layout of the documents. In the case of requirements, these standards provide a common and consistent way to collect and present customer requirements. The characteristics of a good requirements specification document are [IEEE 1983]:

1. **Unambiguous**: There can be only one interpretation of the requirements.
2. **Completeness**: The requirements must have reached some level of stability and completeness before software analysis and modeling can start. Even though requirements change during the lifetime of a project and cannot be frozen, a degree of stability is needed. Without a reasonable level of stability and completeness, the system architecture will be equally volatile.
3. **Verifiability**: The software standards also guide a system engineer in preparing *quantifiable* requirements. For instance, the following example illustrates the difference between a quantifiable and nonquantifiable requirement: "*the communication response time shall not exceed 5 seconds,*" versus "*the communication*

response time shall be fast." If a requirement cannot be verified through the design, it is either not well defined or not a requirement.

The verifiability of requirements is important because the test team develops test cases from software requirements.

4. **Consistency**: During the software life cycle, business needs may change. These changes directly affect requirements and subsequently the design. The standards specify outline and contents of requirement specification documents, thus reducing the likelihood of requirement redundancy. Duplication of a requirement in a document causes conflicts when the requirement is changed and the changes are not consistently reflected throughout the document. By avoiding redundancies, changes to the documentation are localized to one place, and the requirements remain consistent.

5. **Traceability**: At the time of analysis and design, correlating requirements to the applicable modules and classes is an important task. This provides *forward* and *backward* traceability. Requirements traceability ensures that the system design adheres to the requirements and facilitates the identification of affected modules and classes when the requirements do change.

To capture the customer's requirements, the following documents are generally produced:

1. System Specification
2. Hardware Requirements Specification (HRS)
3. Software Requirements Specification (SRS)
4. Interface Requirements Specification (IRS)

For example, a *Software Requirements Specification (SRS)* document prepared on the basis of these standards contains the following information [IEEE 1983; DIDs 1988]:

1. **Functional Requirements**: These requirements describe the behavior and operation of the system, and identify how inputs are transformed into outputs.

2. **Performance Requirements**: The performance requirements specify both the *static* and *dynamic* numerical requirements. For example, the number of simultaneous users is a *static* requirement, while the number of transactions within a given time frame is a *dynamic* requirement.

3. **Design Constraints**: These requirements identify the types of constraints imposed on the design:

   a. **Standards**: For instance, the software implementation may be required to follow certain C++ programming guidelines; or the deliverable documentation must be prepared on the basis of the IEEE standards; or the system design must comply with specific electrical and mechanical standards.

   b. **Security**: A system that maintains sensitive information requires protection against external and internal threats. Depending on the security requirements, the design incorporates security measures, such as password protection, different access levels, and encryption algorithms. For example, bank account security requirements identify security protocols and user privileges. A bank teller is given full access to the *credit history* of an *account*, while an *account* holder is only given read permission to the same information, and other users are denied access altogether.

   c. **System Limitations**: A system hardware configuration may place limitations and constraints on the design of the software. For example, the capacity of a local hard disk and random access memory (RAM) may place a limitation on the number of bank transaction records stored locally in an automated teller machine (ATM).

   d. **System Availability**: The design may be required to guarantee different levels of availability to system features and operations in the case of an error. These requirements address the error detection and recovery factors.

4. **External Interfaces**: These requirements capture the user, hardware, software, and communication interface requirements. The user interface (UI) requirements specify the UI characteristics. These characteristics include screen format, reports, help information, and menus. The hardware requirements identify the hardware external interfaces such as the number and types of network interfaces, parallel ports, and serial ports. The communication requirements specify communication protocols and any applicable standards.

5. **Miscellaneous Information**: Other requirements include database operations, backup and recovery, and site adaptation requirements.

Based on the above categories, the system engineering team collects and documents the system requirements.

2.3 ANALYSIS AND DESIGN PHASE

The *Analysis and Design* phase follows the *Requirements Definition* phase. Figure 2.4 provides a more detailed view of this phase from the *strategic* and *tactical* perspectives. This stage is divided into *macro-* and *micro-development* processes. The global design issues are addressed at the *macro-level*, and the *tactical* design issues are handled at the *micro-level*. Analysis, modeling, and design activities in both *macro-* and *micro-development* processes are iterative. During each iteration, the object model is reviewed and is further refined. Through continuous feedback, the system architecture gains a higher degree of granularity, and the design of the system takes on an evolutionary form. The continuous interaction between the *micro-* and *macro-development* levels also ensures that there are no inconsistencies between the *strategic* (global) and *tactical* (local) views of the system. The feedback also helps the designers to uncover design flaws and bottlenecks in the architecture and detailed designs early on in the development process.

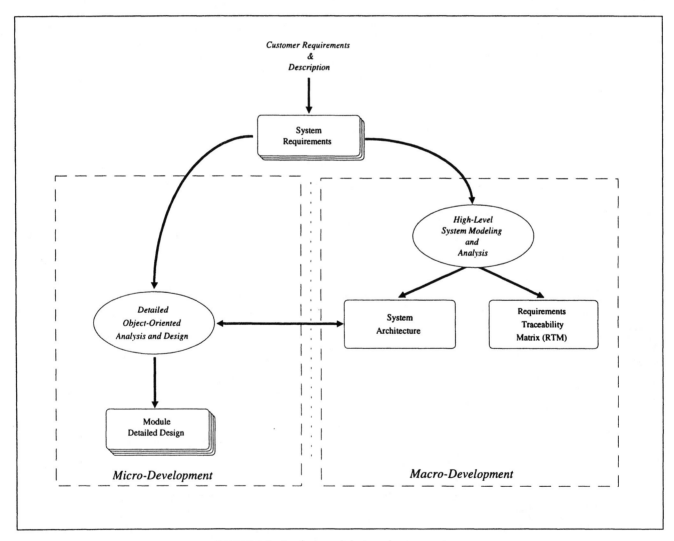

FIGURE 2.4   Analysis and design phase overview.

2.3.1 Macro-Development Process

2.3.1.1 Process and Activities

The architecture team plays the most significant role in the high-level analysis and design of the system architecture. In the *macro-development* process, this team is responsible for the following deliverables in the *Analysis and Design* phase:

1. **System Architecture**: The architecture is similar to the floorplan of a house. Before an architect begins modeling the contents for each room, the architect needs to create a floorplan that depicts the overall layout of the house. The floorplan provides a high-level view of the house by identifying types of rooms, their locations, and size. Most importantly, the floorplan shows how the rooms are interconnected. At this stage, the architect is not interested in the interior and exterior details of the house such as wall paper, paint color, and construction materials. These details are decided at a later stage.

   Similarly, a system architecture defines the system in terms of *subsystem*, *modules*, and their interfaces. This high-level perspective provides a structural view of the system at a *strategic* level. Figure 2.5 depicts a

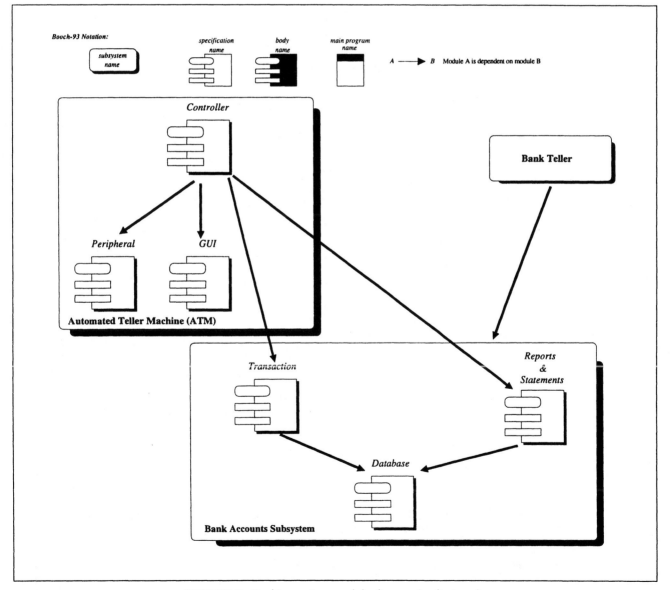

FIGURE 2.5 Banking system module diagram (preliminary).

hypothetical architecture of a banking system. The system is partitioned into *Automated Teller Machine (ATM), Bank Teller,* and *Bank Accounts* subsystems. Each subsystem is then partitioned into specific *modules,* such the *Graphical User Interface (GUI)* module of the *ATM* subsystem.

The design teams use the *system architecture* in the *micro-development* process to create detailed designs. The system architecture is a significant deliverable and is the foundation of the *micro-development* process. The need for a stable architecture cannot be overemphasized. Initiation of detailed design without a stable framework substantially increases development risk. It also leads to quality problems and nonreusable software modules.

2. **Requirements Traceability Matrix (RTM)**: In the design of complex and large systems, the task of verifying that the design is in compliance with the requirements is quite tedious. Manual verification is not feasible, nor it is desirable. Instead, automated databases are used to streamline the *micro-development* process design and validation activities. The system and software requirements are mapped to the appropriate *modules* in the architecture. Using an off-the-shelf database, the partitioned requirements are then documented in the *requirements traceability matrix (RTM)* tables. Typically, an RTM table contains the following information (Figure 2.6):

Module	Scanner Module			
Feature	*Requirement Title & Description*	*Requirement Reference*	*Design Document Reference*	*Source Code Reference*
Line Buffer	Line Buffer Size	FAX SRS Section 3.3.4 (Ver 1.0)	Scanner Design Document Section 4.2 (Ver. 1.1)	/Scanner/line.h (Ver. 1.0)

FIGURE 2.6   Requirements traceability matrix (RTM) sample

a. **Module Name**: This information organizes and relates a set of requirements and features to a specific *module*.

b. **Requirement Title**: The requirement title identifies which requirement is being mapped to the specified module.

c. **Requirement References**: This field identifies the title, section, and paragraph numbers of the requirements specification document. These references provide *backward* traceability. During the design validation, the QA team uses the above information to verify that the design and implementation of the specified *module* complies with the stated requirements.

d. **Design References**: This field identifies the title, section, and paragraph numbers of the software design document. These references provide *forward* traceability. When the requirements change, the database is searched using these references to identify the affected modules.

e. **Source Code References**: This field identifies the C++ header and source file names. These references provide traceability to the implementation level. At times, the program references are left out owing to volatility of source files and to a need to reduce bureaucracy.

2.3.1.2 Method

A system architecture is developed by analyzing data and control flow through the system. This analysis is performed at a high level in order to identify the subsystems, modules, and their interfaces. In the following example, the software requirements for a group 3 facsimile machine are studied, and a data flow model for the transmission of a facsimile is presented. Figure 2.7 illustrates the data flow[2] for transmitting a facsimile using a group 3 fax machine [CCITT 1991]:

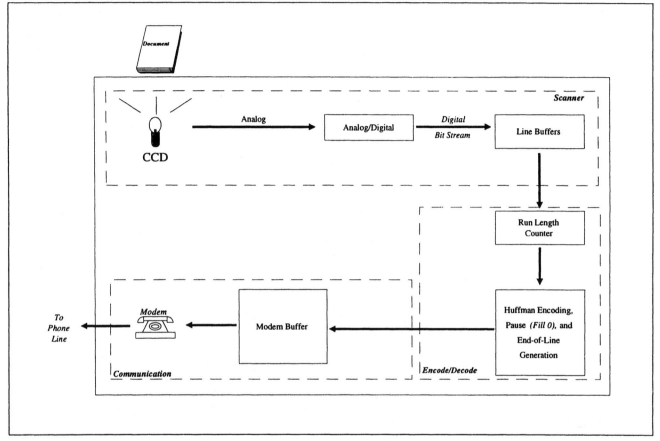

FIGURE 2.7 Facsimile transmission data flow block diagram.

1. **Scanning**: For a facsimile transmission, a page is scanned one line at a time. The analog signal from the charge-coupled device (CCD) is converted to a digital bit stream of zeros (0's) and ones (1's) representing white and black *picture elements (pel)* in the line, respectively. The 0's and 1's are then stored in a line buffer.

2. **Data Compression**: To reduce the volume of data and data transmission time, the scanned lines undergo two levels of data compression by using the *Modified Huffman* encoding scheme (Figure 2.8). In the first stage, the number of consecutive zeros (0's) and ones (1's) in a line is counted. This value is referred to as a *run-length.*

   In the second stage of data compression, the *run-length* values are encoded using the *Modified Huffman* codes. This encoding scheme is based on a probabilistic model in which *run-length*s are given different variable length codes. The most commonly transmitted *run-lengths* use a shorter length code than the least commonly transmitted ones. The CCITT standard specifies the algorithm and the *Modified Huffman* codes for white and black *run-lengths*. For instance, the standard has specified 0111 and 00010011 codes for white *run-length* values of two (2) and thirty-four (34), respectively.

3. **Transmission**: The encoded *run-lengths* in each line are then stored in the modem buffer for transmission. To allow the receiving point to keep up with data transmission, each line must satisfy a minimum

---

[2]Although data and control flow analysis are part of structured design methodology, this book uses the general concepts for high-level analysis. This book intentionally avoids the use of data flow diagrams, and does not combine structured design notations with the OO notations.

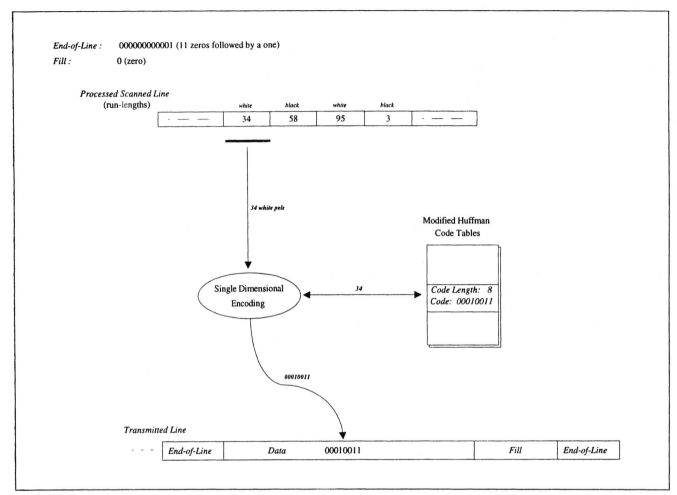

FIGURE 2.8   CCITT group 3 facsimile data encoding block diagram.

transmission time (T_{min}). For lines that are mostly white or black, there may not be a sufficient number of run-lengths to meet T_{min} and the software then pads the encoded line with the appropriate number of fill (0) characters (Figure 2.9).

In addition, an *end-of-line (eol)* character which consists of 11 consecutive 0's and a 1 (000000000001), is also transmitted between lines. The *eol* character represents the end of one line and the start of a new line.

The architecture team designs the system architecture by analyzing the data flow for all possible scenarios: facsimile transmission, receiving a facsimile, and copying a document. Figure 2.10 illustrates the system architecture for the fax machine in terms of the following *modules*:

1. **Controller Module**: This module coordinates the operation of the other modules and monitors them for fatal errors, such as a paper jam detected in the **scanner** module. The system provides deterministic behavior by having the **controller** module schedule system activities. This module is the highest level module and is directly dependent on the **UI** and **Encoder/Decoder** modules.
2. **User Interface (UI) Module**: This module monitors the keypad for user inputs and requests. The UI also handles the display of error messages and system status.
3. **Scanner Module**: This module scans a page one line at a time and stores its digital bit stream representation in the internal line buffers.
4. **Encoder/Decoder Module**: During the transmission of a facsimile, this module encodes the lines by computing run-lengths and then encoding these values using the *Modified Huffman* encoding scheme.

When the fax machine is receiving a facsimile, this module decodes the run-length values and reconstructs each line to its original format. The line is then sent to the **printer** module.

End-of-Line :   000000000001 (11 zeros followed by a one)

Fill :   0 (zero)

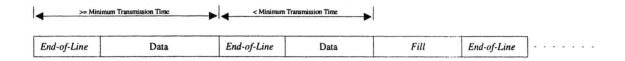

T_{min} = 20 msec (Alternative 1)

T_{max} = 5 sec

FIGURE 2.9   CCITT group 3 facsimile data transmission format.

5. **Communication Module**: This module is responsible for the transmit and receive operations. During a facsimile transmission, it appends *fill* and *eol* characters. The **communication** module controls the modem's hardware and performs the low-level communication tasks.

6. **Printer Module**: This module is responsible for printing a received facsimile transmission or a scanned document. It controls the printer hardware.

Unlike the earlier *bank account* example, the system architecture for the fax machine is defined within a single *subsystem* symbol. The system is not complicated enough to warrant decomposition into *subsystems*. In addition, the object model is not required to span across different hardware platforms.

In addition to the data flow analysis, the architecture team analyzes the system requirements and creates a control flow model for the system. The control flow includes the *timeliness* and *concurrency* issues:

1. **Timeliness**: For instance, the **communication** module must transmit a line within a time window specified by T_{min} and T_{max} (20 msec to 5 sec). The system design needs to encompass the real-time requirements in the high- level design and identify the real-time design requirements for the applicable modules.

2. **Concurrency**: In the case of the fax system architecture, the operations of the modules are made concurrent by employing pipelining (Figure 2.11). While the **scanner** module is scanning a line$_i$, the **encoder/decoder** module is encoding the previous line (line$_{i-1}$), and the **communication** module is busy transmitting line$_{i-2}$. The output of each module is fed into the next stage of the pipeline. Such parallelism streamlines system operation by maximizing system resource use.

Even though data and control flow analysis are based on **structured** analysis, they are valuable tools in creating the object model's framework. Another alternative is to use a technique known as the **use-case** analysis formalized by Jacobson [Jacobson 1992]. This technique analyzes and models a system at a high level by focusing on transactions, or sequences of events, referred to as *scenarios*.

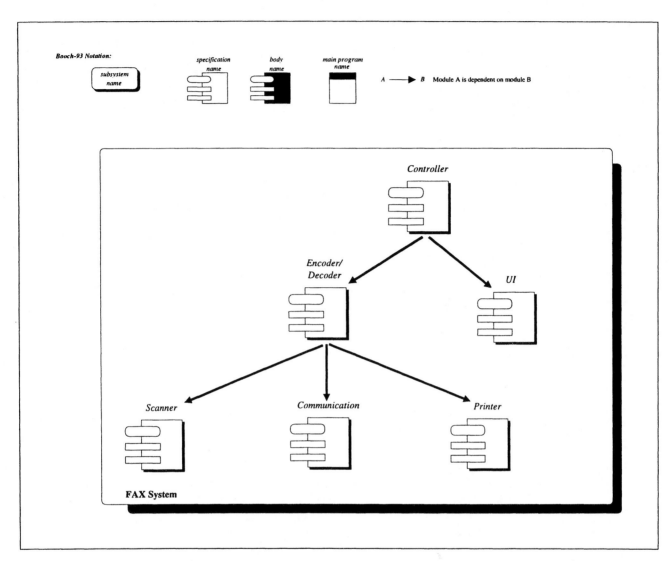

FIGURE 2.10 FAX system module diagram.

The analysis begins by identifying the user who initiates a *scenario*. The user may be a person or another system and is considered an external event. The analysis then describes the scenario in a series of single sentences. Each sentence describes a single *action* or *activity*. For example, a person initiates a *facsimile transmission* scenario by placing a document in the paper tray of a FAX machine, keys in the phone number, and presses the dial button. The facsimile transmission begins when the dial button is pressed. The following events describe a facsimile transmission scenario based on a **use-case** analysis. The ‖ symbol is used to separate multiple actions that are closely coupled in the same sentence:

1. User places pages to be faxed in the paper tray.
2. User keys in the desired phone number ‖ and presses the dial button.
3. FAX machine activates the modem.
4. FAX machine establishes communication with the target FAX machine.
5. Both FAX machines negotiate communication parameters for current page.
6. FAX machine activates the scanner ‖ and encoder.
7. Scanner scans a page one line at a time.
8. Scanner notifies Encoder when it finishes scanning a line.
9. Encoder uses the run-length counter to compute the *run-length* value for the consecutive 0's or 1's in a line ‖ and then encodes each run-length by using the *Modified Huffman* encoding algorithm.

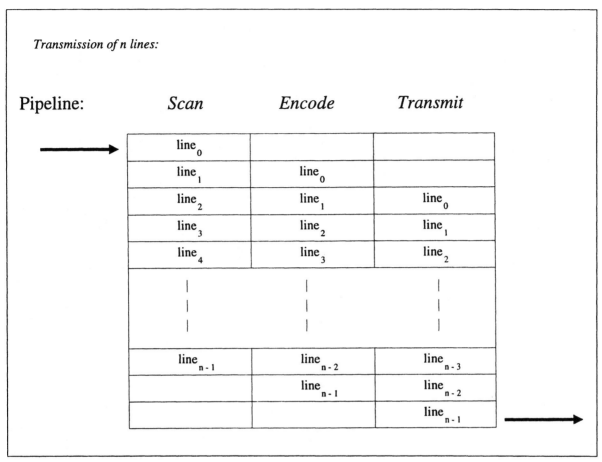

FIGURE 2.11 Facsimile transmission.

10. Encoder stores the encoded line in the modem buffer ‖ and notifies the modem that the line is ready for transmission.
11. Modem then transmits the encoded line.
12. Steps 7 through 11 are repeated for each line in the page.
13. FAX machine shuts down the scanner ‖ and encoder in an orderly fashion.
14. FAX machine repeats steps 5 through 13 while the paper tray is not empty or no error has occurred.
15. FAX machine terminates communication with the interfacing FAX machine.
16. FAX machine shuts down the modem.

The above scenario provides only a high-level view of the facsimile transmission process; some of the details are intentionally left out. For example, step 6 is vague on how the scanner is activated. From the architect's viewpoint, the process of turning on the CCD circuitry and checking the paper tray sensor is irrelevant at this stage of analysis and design. These details will become crucial in the *micro-development* process.

The **use-case** analysis describes the key scenarios in the system. For the FAX system, these scenarios are facsimile transmission, receive, and document copying. Using the results of the analysis, the architecture team represents a FAX system by identifying the modules. For the specified scenarios, some of the *modules* and *subsystems* would be the same. For example, both *facsimile transmission* and *receive* scenarios need the **communication** and **encoder/decoder** modules. However, the *facsimile transmission* scenario does not require the **printer** module, and the *facsimile receive* scenario does not require a **scanner** module. The architecture team studies the similarities and differences, and then consolidates these differences into the system architecture (Figure 2.10).

2.3.1.3 Analysis and Design Issues

To create a stable system architecture, the architecture team must take the following issues into consideration:

1. **Performance**: For real-time systems, the *system architecture* must take *timeliness* factors into consideration. The architecture team must analyze the operation of the system and identify the critical computational and operational needs. The computational needs are additional design requirements that the time-critical *modules* need to address.
2. **Reliability and Error Handling**: When an error occurs, the objects within modules may need to notify objects residing in other modules. The sharing and propagation of errors is part of a module's design interface, which makes error detection and recovery a strategic issue. A cohesive and homogeneous error detection and recovery strategy prevents the development teams from creating unique error-handling schemes and duplicating functionality.
3. **Fault Tolerance**: Depending on the system requirements, the architecture team specifies fault modes and identifies the behavior of the affected *modules* for these modes.
4. **Concurrency**: For a system whose functionality is partitioned across a series of computer systems and/or processes, the object model must address concurrency issues. The model must incorporate strategies for avoiding deadlocks caused by simultaneous access of an object by multiple processes.
5. **Connectivity**: The system architecture may be affected by a network interface. By making data bandwidth and related connectivity considerations part of high-level analysis and design, the architecture team avoids design flaws and shortcomings in the architecture.
6. **User Interface**: Ease of use and a user-friendly interface are key marketing requirements. The design of the user interface starts in the early stages of system development. This approach allows early engagement of the customer who can provide extremely valuable feedback. The system's UI can then evolve and mature before it reaches the market.
7. **System Platform**: In conjunction with system requirements, the architecture team identifies the operating system, hardware platform, development environment, and the Commercial Off-the-Shelf (COTS) tools that have a *strategic* impact on the design of the system modules.
8. **Security**: For applications that need to provide a secured environment, the flow of data within the system may need to be controlled. The security becomes a design issue for the system architecture.

2.3.1.4 Objectives

The top-level view presented by the system architecture and the requirements traceability matrix (RTM) provides the following benefits:

1. **Strategic View**: In the early stages of the development process, a comprehensive and well-defined view of the system allows the development organization to create a systematic and organized path in evolving and developing the system. Many of the teams identified in Section 2.2 are actually the customers of the system architecture:

   a. **Management Team**: This team uses the architecture in planning the micro-development activities. By combining the *spiral development* model described in this book's prologue, the management team distributes the system development activities across several development cycles [Boehm 1988].

   In each cycle, a collection of related modules is designed and implemented. In the design of the fax machine, the *micro-development* can be broken into three cycles: the first cycle handles the facsimile transmission scenario; the second cycle focuses on providing the capability to receive facsimiles; and the third cycle allows the system to use the fax machine as a copier (Figure 2.12).

   Using the system architecture, the management team identifies the modules that need to be developed in a specific cycle. In the first cycle, the **scanner, controller, UI, encoder/decoder,** and **communication** modules are implemented. In the second cycle, the **printer** module is implemented, and the **controller, UI, encoder/decoder**, and **communication** modules are modified to handle incoming facsimiles. This approach allows the system to be developed iteratively, where each cycle builds on the capabilities developed in the previous cycle. By having each cycle focus on specific functionality, the system evolves through time and is refined from one iteration to the next. The integration tests and reviews in each cycle improve the system design for the next cycle. In addition, test and validation efforts are performed in parallel to the development activities and are not sequential activities performed at the end of cycle 3 (Figure 2.12).

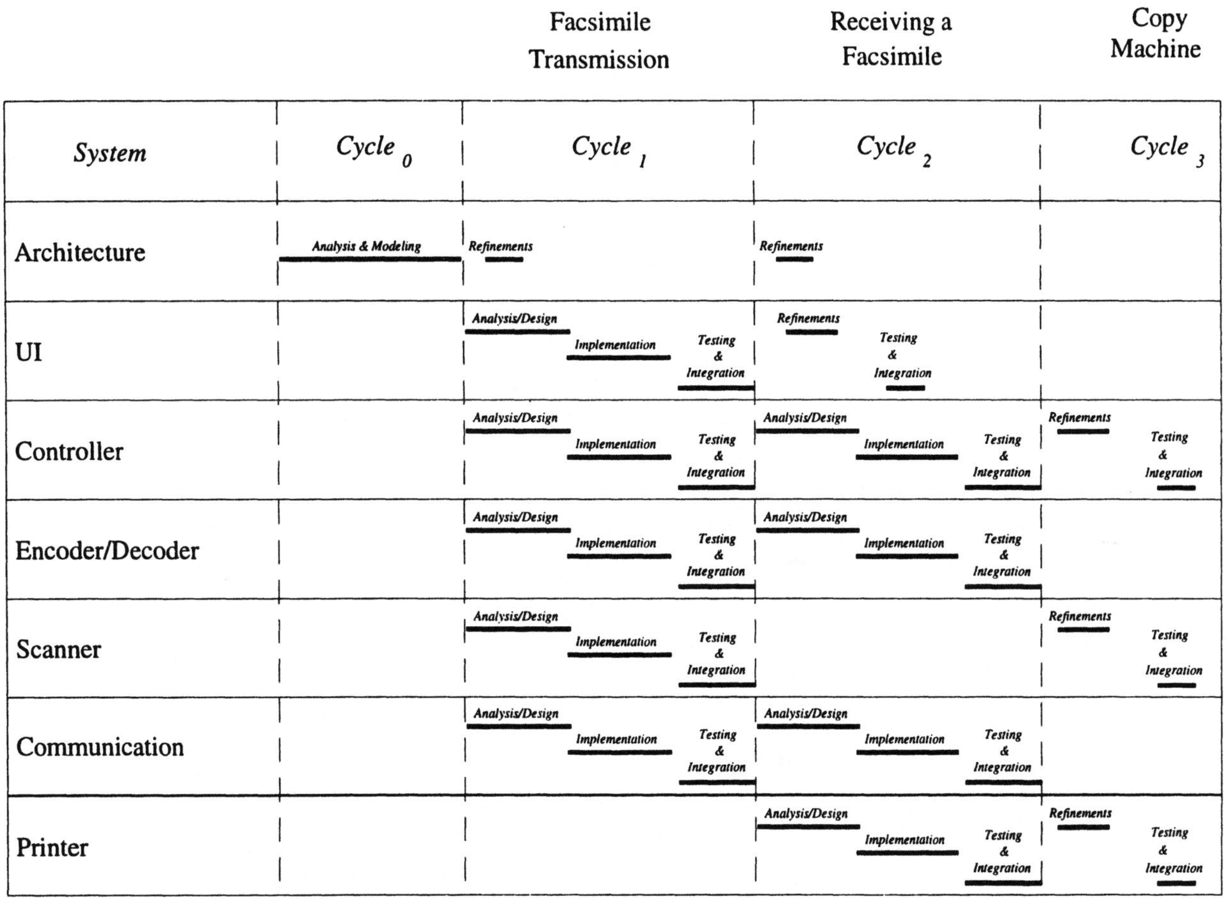

	Facsimile Transmission	Receiving a Facsimile	Copy Machine	
System	*Cycle$_0$*	*Cycle$_1$*	*Cycle$_2$*	*Cycle$_3$*
Architecture	*Analysis & Modeling*	*Refinements*	*Refinements*	
UI		*Analysis/Design* · *Implementation* · *Testing & Integration*	*Refinements* · *Testing & Integration*	
Controller		*Analysis/Design* · *Implementation* · *Testing & Integration*	*Analysis/Design* · *Implementation* · *Testing & Integration*	*Refinements* · *Testing & Integration*
Encoder/Decoder		*Analysis/Design* · *Implementation* · *Testing & Integration*	*Analysis/Design* · *Implementation* · *Testing & Integration*	
Scanner		*Analysis/Design* · *Implementation* · *Testing & Integration*		*Refinements* · *Testing & Integration*
Communication		*Analysis/Design* · *Implementation* · *Testing & Integration*	*Analysis/Design* · *Implementation* · *Testing & Integration*	
Printer			*Analysis/Design* · *Implementation* · *Testing & Integration*	*Refinements* · *Testing & Integration*

FIGURE 2.12 FAX system development cycles.

   b. **Development Teams**: The strategic view provided by the system architecture helps the development teams to better understand the system. By showing the *subsystems*, *modules*, dependencies, and interactions, the development teams understand where their designs fit in the system and how they are being used. The strategic view clears up ambiguities in a complex system by clarifying each module's responsibilities and boundaries. It also streamlines communication among the development teams. By having well-defined interfaces between the *modules*, the development teams can quickly resolve the *tactical* design and interface conflicts.

   In addition, the development teams benefit from additional design guidelines for each module, such as standardized error detection and recovery mechanisms provided by an architecture team.

   c. **QA Teams**: Prior to the micro-analysis and design, the QA team verifies that the system architecture meets the specified requirements.

2. **Early Detection of Design Flaws and Problems**: Since the development of a *system architecture* is an iterative process, the architecture undergoes a series of design reviews, namely preliminary, critical, and acceptance reviews. These reviews are performed by the system engineering, development, and QA teams. The reviews identify bottlenecks and design flaws in the architecture in the early stages of development. Early detection of design flaws and inconsistencies reduces cost overruns and schedule slips. Figure 2.13 compares the cost of discovering and correcting design flaws at various phases of the software life cycle [Stroot 1987].

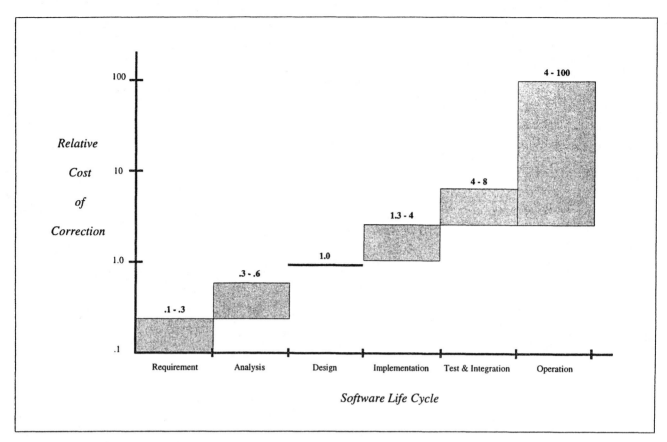

FIGURE 2.13   Relative cost of corrections in the software life cycle.

3. **Partitioning Complexity**: After the architecture is partitioned into a well-defined set of *subsystems* and *modules*, the *requirements traceability matrix (RTM)* specifies the applicable requirements for a module. The *RTMs* reduce the development teams' workload by filtering out irrelevant requirements. Each development team focuses its analysis and design on the applicable requirements for its assigned module(s).

4. **Requirements Traceability**: Since an *RTM* maps a set of requirements to a specific *module* in the system architecture, the electronic documentation (database) of these tables facilitates *forward* and *backward* traceability. A QA team traces requirements through the design and implementation.

2.3.2 Micro-Development Process

2.3.2.1 Process and Activities

When the *system architecture* matures and reaches a stable state, the development teams begin analyzing requirements specific to their *subsystems* and *modules*. Each team then creates a preliminary *object model* for its assigned module. These models provide a *logical* view of the module by specifying the key objects and their behaviors. A *logical* model represents a unique perspective of a development team. At the *strategic* level, the *logical* models developed by the development teams may not be consistent with each other.

To establish design coherency, these *logical models* are reviewed by the system engineering, architecture, and development teams. In these reviews, the common design patterns across several modules are identified. These common patterns are then consolidated into one, and shared by the applicable modules. This approach creates a congruity across modules and avoids duplication of design and implementation. These reviews also help identify off-the-shelf tools and standard class libraries for the implementation of object models, such as using a *container* class from the *Standard Template Library (STL)* instead of creating a custom implementation.

The reviews and refinements change the *logical* views into *development* views. After the appropriate changes are made to the models, the class interfaces are finalized and the implementation phase begins.

2.3.2.2 Method

There are a variety of techniques that a development team may use to develop a detailed design. Some of the techniques concentrate on the *static* aspects of the object model, and others on the *dynamic* behavior. The following is a brief description of some popular techniques:

1. **Classical Approach:** This approach uses a common property or a collection of properties to identify classes and their relationships. A property must be quantifiable. For instance, an *engine block* can be quantified in terms of its size. A 427-cubic inch engine is categorized as a *large engine block*.

   In the *classical* approach, candidate classes are identified on the basis of different selection criteria, some of which are identified below [Booch 1994]:

   a. **Physical and Tangible Things**: In the fax system, the *Scanner*, *Printer*, and *Modem* are selected as classes, because they are tangible and physical objects.

   b. **Roles**: Objects are identified by the role they play in the system. For example, a *Scanner* uses a *Sensor* to detect if there is any paper left in the paper tray. Thus, *Sensor* is viewed as a class. This class plays a supporting role in the operation of the fax machine.

   c. **Structure**: Classes are defined and related by examining the structure of a system. The structure of the system then governs the relationships formed among the classes, such as the "is-a," "has-a," "use-a," and "is-associated" relationships. In the **scanner** module of the fax system, the structure and components of a physical scanner are used to define the appropriate classes (Figure 2.14). The *Scanner* class is composed of a motor, CCD, and its internal buffers. The components of the *Scanner* are kept hidden from the client by using the **private** export control (II). This class also uses an *Alarm* to report paper jams, and *Paper Sensor* to detect the presence of paper in the facsimile transmission tray. The use of *Alarm* and *Paper Sensor* is kept hidden from the clients. They are internal to the implementation of the *Scanner* member functions. The objects in the *Encoder* module would have to use the *Scanner* methods specified in the design interface to obtain a scanned image.

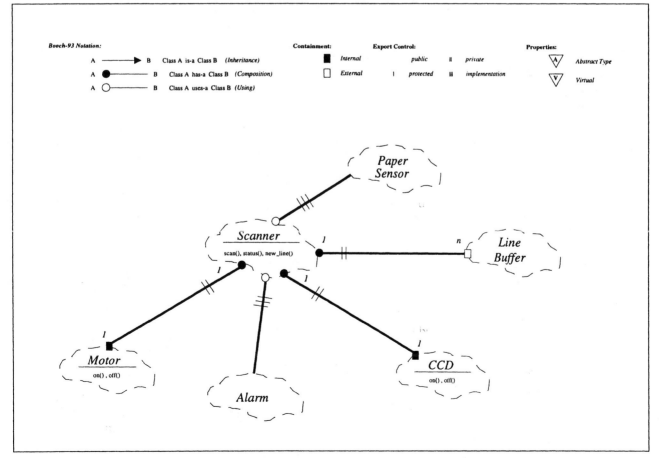

FIGURE 2.14 Scanner class diagram

d. Events: Classes are identified on the basis of events that need to be recorded. For instance, a *Trace Stream* class may be used to capture and record intermediate results transparent to the system user. This class incorporates internal data tracing in the system that is useful for verifying the system operation during the system qualification tests as well as for collecting data when the system has been deployed in the field.

Using the **classical approach**, the classes are identified. The design then proceeded by identifying the static and dynamic behavior of the classes. For example, Figure 2.15 depicts the state transition diagram for the *Scanner* object, which has a complex behavior. The *Scanner* object initially is in the **idle** state. When a **scan( )** request is made, the *Scanner* object transitions into the **scanning** mode and activates the hardware. As it is scanning a page into memory, or if it has already completed the scanning a line, the objects in the *Encoder* module may synchronously obtain a line that has already been scanned by invoking the **next_line()** method of the *Scanner*. This causes the object to transition to the **reading** state. When the requested line has been passed to the client, the object transitions to its previous state, which may have been **idle** or **scanning**. This is denoted by the *History (H)* symbol in Figure 2.15. Incidentally, **idle** and **scanning** are substates of the **active** superstate.

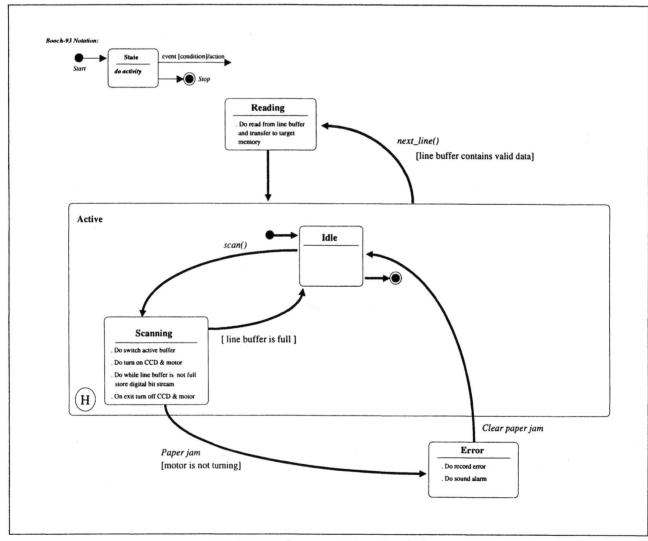

FIGURE 2.15   Scanner state transition diagram

2. **English Description Approach**: Similar to the **classical approach**, this technique focuses on the *static* aspects. This technique extracts classes and applicable operations from the requirements by analyzing the sentences in the requirements specification documents. The nouns in each sentence are underlined as **candidate** classes, and the verbs are underlined as their supporting operations. The list of **candidate** classes with their corresponding operations is then captured in a data dictionary. The data dictionary is then reviewed, and the list is filtered by removing the unwanted classes and operations. In the following example, the data encoding requirement is analyzed using this technique. The **candidate** class and the applicable operation are underlined using single and double lines, respectively:

The run-lengths in each __line__ shall be __encoded__ using the CCITT standard for group 3 facsimile systems.
Class: Line
Operation: encode()

In the above example, *Line* is viewed as a class and **encode**() as an operation on this class.
This approach has some drawbacks associated with it:

   a. **Requirements and Writing Quality**: The quality of the grammar and the completeness of the requirements have a direct impact on the effectiveness of this technique. Poorly written documents or incomplete requirements can nullify this technique's effectiveness.
   b. **Amount of Requirements**: If the volume of the requirements that need to be analyzed is too great (that is, several hundred pages), the task of underlining nouns and verbs becomes laborious and tedious.

   The use of the RTM usually avoids this problem because it narrows the focus of analysis and modeling to a selected number of requirements. The occurrence of this problem even with an RTM is an indication that the module has been assigned with too many responsibilities and should be partitioned into smaller modules.

3. **Use-Case Analysis**: This method provides a systematic and structured approach in analyzing requirements. In addition, use-case analysis is not only applicable for designing an architecture (*macro-development*), but is also an effective tool for detailed design. The scenarios developed in the macro-development process are elaborated on and decomposed into smaller scenarios. By adding detailed information in the use-case models developed by the architecture team, **the *strategic* view of the system architecture naturally flows into the tactical view**.

The action and activities in the macro-level scenarios are expanded to include details for the detailed design of the applicable modules. For example, the detailed use-case scenarios include pertinent information such as exceptions. On the basis of these use-case scenarios, the classes, their roles, responsibilities, and supporting operations are identified. In the following example, the facsimile transmission use-case scenario from Section 2.3.1.2 for scanning a page is expanded on:

   a. Scanner activates the charge-coupled device (CCD) circuitry ‖ and resets its hardware registers.
   b. Scanner starts its motor for feeding the paper through the scanner.
   c. Scanner converts the analog signal from the CCD circuitry to a digital bit stream ‖ and stores 0's and 1's in the active line buffer.
   d. When scanner finishes scanning a line, it notifies encoder module ‖ and switches to another buffer.
   e. While there are more lines on the page to scan and no pending error (no paper, paper jam, or invalid page size), scanner repeats steps 3 through 4.
   f. Scanner shuts down the CCD circuitry.
   g. If no paper jam, the scanner feeds out the paper ‖ and shuts down the paper roll motor.

On the basis of the above use-case scenario, the applicable classes and their operations are identified, such as the one depicted in Figure 2.14. Some of the objects involved in the scenario are hidden objects. For example, step 5 specifies that in the case of no paper, the scanner aborts its operation. This implies that the scanner module needs a *Paper Sensor* for detecting the presence of paper. In this situation, the use-case scenario is incomplete, and details must be added to the use-case model to reflect the involvement of the paper sensor.

The completed use-case scenario is then converted to a graphical representation by using either an *interaction* or *object* diagram. On the basis of the above use case, Figure 2.16 describes the dynamic behavior of the **scanner** module. For a scan request, the *Scanner* object advances the paper one line at a time by using the motor. If there is no paper jam, *Scanner* turns on the *CCD* circuitry and stores the digital bit stream into the active *Line Buffer*.

The *state transition* diagram is used for classes that have complex behavior, such as the one depicted in Figure 2.15 for a *Scanner* object.

An object model gains its details by using a combination of the above techniques in order to identify classes, their attributes, and operations. In addition, the relationships and interactions are defined and quantified. The **use-case** analysis is one of the most popular techniques because it breaks down the analysis task into simple and structured steps. In addition, it is a valuable tool for both *macro-* and *micro-development* processes.

Regardless of the technique used, the dynamic and static models that emerge from the analysis must be consistent with each other. For example, suppose the *Scanner* module class diagram specifies that the *Scanner* class uses a *Paper Sensor* (Figure 2.14), but the interaction diagram does not show any interaction between the two (Figure 2.16). This would be an indication that the static and dynamic models are incomplete and/or inaccurate.

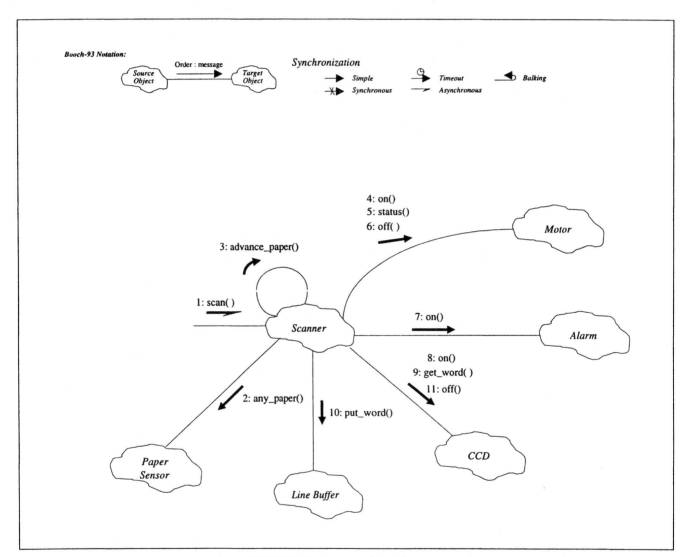

FIGURE 2.16   Scanner object diagram.

To facilitate capturing and maintaining an object model, object-oriented Computer- Aided Software Engineering (CASE) tools, such as *"Software through Pictures"* by Integrated Development Environment (IDE), are used. CASE tools help identify inconsistencies in the dynamic and static diagrams, as in the example described in the previous paragraph.

2.3.2.3 Analysis and Design Issues

The *logical* view evolves into the *development* view as the following issues are taken into consideration:

1. **Design Hierarchies**: Some of the classes across the module boundaries may form an "is-a" relationship and are specific variations of a basic type. Since several teams may be involved in the *micro-development* process of a system, the relationships between classes of the object model may not be explicitly conveyed by the *logical* models. Design reviews uncover common patterns and relationships and provide a systematic path for the consolidation and refinement of the design. In this case, the classes are organized and related through a design hierarchy.

   In designing a hierarchy, the common features and operations among the identified classes are mapped to the *base* class (basic type). These classes then inherit from the *base* class and add features specific to their needs. Thus, the design hierarchy creates a common design baseline for the *derived* classes spanning modules. For example, several bank account development teams that have created and implemented models specific to their accounts will need to review their designs for cohesion and relationships among their *Savings*, *IRA*, and *Checking* account classes. By consolidating the similarities across the bank accounts into an *Account* class, the derived classes share common attributes and operations such as customer's **name**, **address**, and **picture** (Figure 2.17).

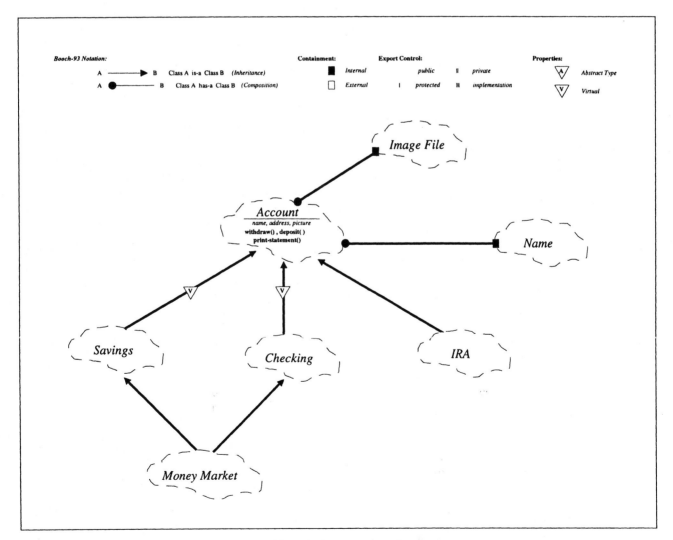

FIGURE 2.17 Account class diagram.

In addition, operations that have the same meaning across the *derived* classes but require different implementations for each of the *derived* classes are declared in the *base* class. For instance, the **print_statement()** operation requires a different implementation based on the type of account because the statement contents varies among the bank account types. The *Checking* account's version contains the information on the checks that have been processed for a given period and includes check numbers, amounts, and dates. Even though the implementation varies across the *derived* classes, the concept is the same. By having the *base* class declare the function's prototype, the *derived* classes will share the same interface. These declarations incorporate *polymorphic* behavior in the hierarchy and standardize the design interfaces across the hierarchy. Through *polymorphism*, data coupling between the clients and the *derived* classes are reduced, and clients can operate on any *derived* object in a generic way. For example, an *ATM's* method operates on different types of bank account and invokes the **print_statement()** operation (Figure 2.17). Depending on the type of account, the applicable **print_statement()** operation at run time is executed.

In addition to minimizing data coupling, each of the bank account development teams can build on a standardized and common baseline. Chapters 9 and 10 discuss application and implementation of a design hierarchy in C++.

2. **Common Classes**: Some of the classes across module boundaries may be identical in operation and behavior. Instead of each team creating its own unique version and implementation, a more general definition for the class can be provided that will be shared by all the affected modules.

   For example, suppose the **scanner** module in the fax machine uses a *Scanner Sensor* class to sense if the scanner tray is empty. The **Printer** module in the fax may also use a *Printer Sensor* class to indicate if the paper tray contains any paper. During the design review, it may turn out that both classes have identical characteristics and behavior. A common *Paper Sensor* class can be designed instead of developing two identical sensor classes in two different modules. This creates a design coherency across the modules and reduces redundancies.

3. **Core Libraries**: By building on the notion of common classes, the low-level objects that are reusable across system boundaries can be moved into core libraries. These libraries will be shared by different modules and projects. For example, a *scanner* class in the fax scanner module may be used for different types of fax systems being designed by the organization.

   Since object-oriented projects are designed and implemented using an iterative approach, the designs of the modules are reviewed against the previously developed class libraries. If an existing class library provides equivalent functionality for some of the classes in the design, this library would then be used as the design and implementation of the applicable classes.

   For an existing class library that provides a partial fit, similarities and differences between the appropriate classes are compared. By using design hierarchies and/or by adding new features to a class, the applicable classes are combined and integrated with the previously developed class libraries. As long as the interfaces of the library are not affected by the changes, the integration of new classes into the existing library has minimal effect. For instance, if a new operation needs to be added to a class library, then the existing clients are probably not affected.

   If the incorporation of new class(es) would require substantial changes to the class library design and interfaces, then the extent of the redevelopment, retesting, and revalidation effort must be assessed. Since the changes have global ramifications on the previously developed and tested modules, the consolidation of the designs may not be feasible.

4. **Standard Class Libraries**: Some of the classes in the model can be implemented by using the standard ANSI C++ class libraries. It is more advantageous from maintainability, testability, reusability, and portability perspectives to use these libraries instead of developing custom implementations.

   For instance, when a model uses a *container* class to maintain a group of objects in a list, an appropriate *container* class from the *C++ Standard Template Library (STL)* is a better alternative than a custom one.

   Standard libraries can also be expanded and extended in the design of a system. A custom class library may use an ANSI C++ class as its baseline. Chapter 10 discusses how the standard ANSI C++ *exception* library can be extended in the design of a custom exception class library (Section 10.7). A C++ program then handles both custom and standard C++ exceptions in a generic and consistent way.

In Chapter 6 (Section 6.3) a custom *Complex* class uses the ANSI C++ *Stream I/O* class library's features to read and write the contents of a *Complex* object to a stream. The use of a standard stream I/O library avoids custom development and promotes extendibility.

5. **Off-the-Shelf Tools**: Off-the-shelf software products and libraries are used to reduce development time and expedite *time-to-market*. In addition, some of the classes in the object model may have special requirements, such as persistence and concurrency, that are outside the scope of product development. In the bank example, the state of the *bank account* classes must be maintained independent of the program's execution (*persistence*). An off-the-shelf object-oriented database management tool should be incorporated into the design of the *bank account* classes to address persistence issues.

6. **Legacy Software**: The use of existing software libraries eases the transition of a development organization into object-oriented methodology. Software can hide the use of a legacy component in the implementation via a *wrapper* or *adaptor* class. A *wrapper* or *adaptor* class does not provide any functionality of its own, except for minor and hidden data transformations that its member functions may perform to accommodate the use of existing products [Gamma et al., 1994]. The *wrapper* class hides the use of an off-the-shelf or legacy library in the design. If the software tool is later replaced by an internal implementation or another vendor's tool, the *wrapper* class prevents the rest of the design from being affected.

The object model that emerges at the end of the development cycle identifies the static and dynamic behavior of the objects of the system at a detailed level. The above activities transform the *logical* view of the module to a *development* view. The consolidation of design patterns systematically combines common designs and creates coherency across the *modules* and *subsystems*. For a detailed discussion of design patterns, the reader is referred to *Design Patterns: Elements of Reusable Object-Oriented Software* [Gamma et al., 1994].

2.3.2.4 Objectives

The object model of the *Analysis and Design* phase must comply with the definition of an object-oriented design. The objects in the model must be *entities with state, behavior, and identity*. The model itself must follow the framework of OOD discussed in Chapter 1:

1. **Encapsulation**: The member functions hide the design of a class by encapsulating the data architecture and its representation. For instance, the **scan()** function hides the data member's type, name, and architecture of the *Scanner* class. By preventing the client from operating on the data members directly, the member functions protect the object from being placed into an unknown state.

2. **Abstraction**: The member functions hide design complexity by abstracting the algorithms and processes associated with the operations of the class. The **scan()** function abstracts the process of scanning a page into memory for the clients of *Scanner*.

3. **Modularity:** The design relationships between the classes should minimize coupling and maximize cohesion. For example, a *module* whose classes form a cyclic topology creates a tight coupling among the classes. Since one class is dependent on another, changes to the architecture may cause a ripple effect throughout the classes. A tightly coupled architecture makes the design less maintainable and extendable.

4. **Design Hierarchies**: The classes within the model should form a hierarchical relationship. The use of a hierarchical architecture makes clients less dependent on specific types used in the hierarchy. In addition, the *derived* classes reuse the features and attributes of their *base* classes.

5. **Timeliness**: The timeliness factor is a component of an OOD and applies to the design of real-time systems. Since a real-time system must respond to an event within a specified time, the object model needs to address *timeliness* requirements. This is one of the major components of the object model in *Real-Time Object-Oriented Modeling (ROOM)* [Selic et al., 1994].

A typical real-time system responds to different types of events within a designated time identified by the *latency* time (T_l) and service time (T_s). The latency time (T_l) is measured from the occurrence of an event to when the event is serviced. The service time (T_s) is the time necessary to process an event.

In the design of the fax machine, the transmission of each line must be completed within 5 sec. This requirement places an upper limit on the combined value of T_l and T_s. Even though the order and occurrence of the events may not be predictable or deterministic, the system design must ensure that the system's behavior is deterministic and predictable.

6. **Concurrency**: For distributed architectures and applications, the object model must take concurrent events and issues into consideration. The required sequences (*threads*) and processes specify the system's behavior by specifying concurrent interactions between the objects that are scattered across different platforms and processes.

Threads interact with each other through shared memory, rendezvous, remote procedure calls (RPCs), and/ or message passing. By specifying the order and timing of execution in the design, the threads are synchronized. In the fax machine, when the *scan sequence* finishes scanning a line, it notifies the *encoding sequence* through one of the supported communication means, such as shared memory.

The concurrent processes may be synchronous or asynchronous. For example, the data transmission of a facsimile is broken into a three-stage pipeline: scan, encode, and transmit (Figure 2.11). This pipeline forms a synchronous architecture, because the operations of each stage are synchronized with the subsequent stage. The design relies on parallel activities. When the pipeline is full, the fax machine will be scanning a line, encoding another line, and transmitting yet another line all at the same time.

7. **Persistence**: Some of the objects in the model cannot be destroyed after their process or threads finish executing, thus requiring the *state of the object to transcend through time and space* [Booch 1994]. Typically, a database is used to maintain the state of a persistent object. For example, after a withdrawal transaction, the state of a *Savings* object must be maintained. Next time the same *Savings* object is accessed, its state must reflect the previous withdrawal operation.

8. **Typing**: The selection of an object-oriented language to implement an object model determines data typing. If internal or customer requirements require strong data typing, Ada 95 is the best choice for implementing the object model. When strong data typing is not an issue, C++ may be preferred. As discussed in Chapter 1, data typing is determined by the object-oriented programming language.

2.4 IMPLEMENTATION PHASE

The design transitions into implementation. The object model is implemented in this phase. For object models that are implemented in C++, the header files for new modules are created and the existing header files that are affected are updated. The header files contain class and member/nonmember function declarations, in addition to **typedefs**, constant definitions, and applicable compiler directives (for example, **#include**). At this stage, the client and the class designer resolve any local discrepancies and finalize the class interfaces.

The functions are then implemented as described in Chapters 3 through 11. These chapters describe the implementation of an object-oriented design in detail and relate them to the applicable C++ features.

2.5 TEST PHASE

In a formal object-oriented test methodology, the software deliverables undergo different types of tests. In the *layered* methodology, the software implementation is tested at different layers (Figure 2.18). Each layer determines the scope of the performed test and verifies different aspects of the software. For example, in the *object* layer the member functions of a class are exercised and tested in isolation. In the higher layers, the objects are tested in conjunction with each other. The scope of the tests broadens as one moves from the *object* layer to the *module* layer. At the same time, the granularity of test decreases.

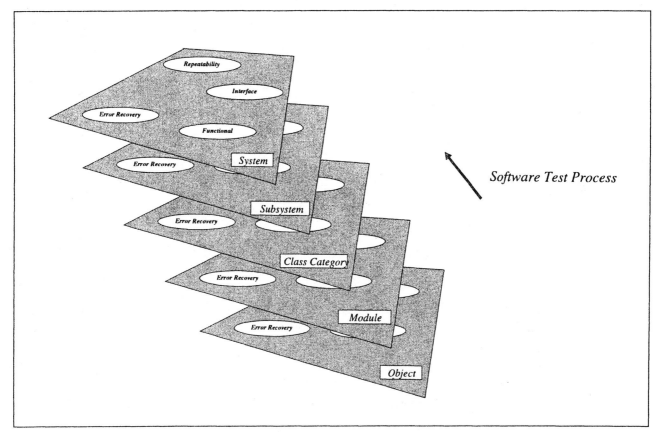

FIGURE 2.18   Layered test methodology.

The layered tests uncover the different types of errors that arise in a software design. For instance, the *subsystem* layer should uncover data flow problems between the modules, and the *object* layer should uncover functionality problems in the implementation of the member functions. The following briefly describes the *layered* test methodology:

1. **Object**: The tests focus on the functionality and error detection capabilities of the member functions. The tests are designed to verify that the object does not transition into an unpredictable state with invalid data or induced errors. In addition, the tests verify that the object model has been correctly implemented, and that the interaction of member functions cannot cause any unpredictable behavior.
2. **Class Category**: This layer broadens the test to a group of objects grouped into a category. By exercising a group of objects together, the tests verify that the object interactions do not cause adverse behavior and that the objects as a group perform the desired task.
3. **Module**: The tests at this level are similar to the *class category* layer. However, the tests are further broadened to encompass objects within the whole module.
4. **Subsystem**: At this layer, the modules are integrated. The tests verify that the collections of objects from different modules operate harmoniously and that there are no improper behaviors or events such as resource collisions or data flow problems between the modules.

5. **System**: The system layer test is performed on a fully integrated system. At this layer, the tests validate the system's overall behavior. Conceptually, functionality problems should have been resolved earlier at the object and class category layers. This layer uncovers performance problems and task overruns and helps identify areas of improvement, such as the user-friendliness of the system.

In each layer, different types of tests are performed to exercise different attributes and aspects of the software:

1. **Functionality Test**: This test verifies that the functional requirements have been properly implemented in the software. Typically, a variety of sample data and inputs are used for this type of test.
2. **Repeatability Test**: Using the same sample data and inputs, the software is tested repeatedly. This test verifies that the software behavior is consistent. Thirty (30) iterations are the normal baseline because statistically, that number provides a high confidence level.
3. **Error Detection/Recovery Test**: The ability of software to detect errors and recovery gracefully is verified by inducing different types of errors and verifying that they are properly detected, that the error information is propagated to the recovery point, and that the applicable recovery operation is performed.
4. **Interface Test**: The software interfaces are verified.

The development and test teams develop *test drivers*, *software models*, and *stubs*. A *software model* provides the key functionalities of the object-under-test and produces the expected results. A *test driver* contains input stimuli and coordinates the test process by interacting with the object(s)-under-test and the software model. Using the test environment, the test driver compares the expected and actual results and logs the test results in a file or a database for further analysis. An object-oriented test environment controls the scope and granularity of the test. In the object layer, the environment will use *stubbed* versions of objects with which the *object-under-test* is interacting. *Stubbed* objects provide either no functionality or a partial functionality and are used to keep the test focused on the object(s)-under-test by satisfying their dependencies on other objects.

The *layered test* methodology formalizes the test process and helps in developing a reliable system. The test software drivers, models, and stubs are reused in future development cycles in order to verify that the changes to the modules did not affect the existing features.

SUMMARY

Analysis and design of a software system is similar to building a house. An architect determines the home owner requirements and creates a model of the house. The architect prepares different types of diagrams, such as a floorplan, three-dimensional views, and a utility plan to capture the design of the house. The architectural drawings and the three-dimensional model depict the architect's vision.

Similarly, a development organization defines, on the basis of its customer requirements and marketing needs, the requirements for a product. The product requirements are typically captured and documented using IEEE or military standards. Using these standards, the following types of requirements are defined and quantified:

1. Functional
2. Performance
3. Design constraints such as security, system limitations, and availability
4. External interfaces
5. Special requirements such as database specifications

The documentation templates specified by the standards guide the preparation and presentation of requirements. They also provide guidelines on developing unambiguous, complete, verifiable, consistent, and traceable requirements.

After the requirements have reached a stable state, an architecture team consisting of system and software design engineers analyzes the system requirements. Using **use-case** analysis, the architecture team describes how the system responds to transactions and events in *scenarios*. The description of the scenario creates a storyboard by identifying the actions taken in response to an event in a series of single sentences. On the basis of the actions, the team creates an architecture for the system. This architecture provides a high-level and structural view of the system in terms of subsystems, modules, and their interfaces.

The architecture team then partitions the system requirements and maps them to the applicable modules in the system. The mapping of requirements is documented in the *requirements traceability matrix (RTM)*.

The development teams then use the architecture team's work products to complete the object model. For each module, the development teams may use the classical approach, **use-case** analysis, English description, and other techniques to identify classes, relationships, behavior, and interactions. The design is then captured using one of the object-oriented standard notations, such as Booch-93. For example, class category and class diagrams are used to document the static behavior, and interaction, object, and state transition diagrams are used to document the dynamic behavior.

The initial model created by these teams is a *logical view* of the system. This model undergoes system-wide reviews for:

1. Requirement compliance
2. Identification of design flaws
3. Creation of coherency and minimization of design redundancies by identifying common patterns

The identification of common design patterns and classes across module boundaries allows the object model to be further refined. This approach leads to the creation of design hierarchies and common libraries. Design hierarchies make the architecture more extendable, while common libraries localize changes to a single implementation. The emerging object model provides the *development view* that is later implemented.

The object model is implemented in several stages. In the initial stage, the header files containing the class definition(s) are developed and reviewed for consistency. In the last stage, the source files containing the function definitions are coded.

Using testing techniques such as the layered testing methodology, the development teams test their deliverables at object, class category, and module layers. These tests verify the software functionality and error detection/recovery. In addition, they verify that the behavior of the software is repeatable. Finally, the programs are integrated and tested at the module, subsystem, and system levels.

The above process is designed to create a well-formed object-oriented architecture that is:

a) Extendable
b) Maintainable
c) Reusable
d) Testable

GLOSSARY

Adaptor class
A class that has no functionality of its own. Its member functions hide the use of a third-party software component, or an object with a noncompatible interface, or a non-object-oriented implementation

CASE tool
Computer-Aided Software Engineering tool

Class category
A close-knit collection of classes that are grouped in a category

Container class
A class that maintains a group of objects

COTS
Commercial Off-the-Shelf

Dynamic model
This model describes the state of the objects, their behavior, and their interactions with each other

Macro-development

The macro-development process focuses on strategic activities such as the design of the system architecture and system-level tests

Micro-development

The micro-development process focuses on tactical issues that are day-to-day activities, such as the detailed design and testing of a class

OMT

Object-Modeling Technique, developed by James Rumbaugh

ROOM

Real-Time Object-Oriented Modeling, formalized by Selic et al. [Selic et al., 1994]

RTM

Requirements Traceability Matrix

Static model

This model defines the system architecture based on classes and the relationships among them. The model identifies other details such as member functions, cardinality, access levels, roles, and responsibilities

STL

Standard Template Library, developed at Hewlett-Packard and adopted into the ANSI C++ standard

Strategic view

The strategic view provides a high-level view of the system and identifies issues that have an impact on the system architecture, such as performance

Stub object

A stubbed class provides little or no functionality. It allows a test environment to narrow the focus of a test on an object by eliminating the behavior of other objects. The stubbed object uses the same interface as the actual implementation but contains partial implementations or predetermined responses

Tactical view

The tactical view focuses on local design issues and provides a narrow and detailed view of part of a system

Wrapper class

Another term for *adaptor* class

CHAPTER 3

Object-Oriented
Programming and C++

INTRODUCTION

Chapter 3 builds on the object-oriented discussion from the previous chapter and follows the outline below to relate C++ features and tools to object-oriented concepts and definitions:

1. **Class**: In C++, the architecture of an object and the operations on an object are defined via the *class* definition. The *class* definition syntax and semantics formalize the relationship between data members and functions (*member functions*). Access levels are added to allow enforcement of *encapsulation* by the compiler. Finally, initialization (*constructor*) and cleanup (*destructor*) functions are introduced for automatic construction and destruction of objects.
2. **Object**: An *object* is an instance of a *class* and comes into existence only when the program is executed. This chapter describes how objects are created, operated on, and destroyed in C++.
3. **Object Model**: Through its features and tools, C++ supports the *major* components of an object model: *modularity, encapsulation, abstraction*, and *design hierarchy*.

This chapter introduces the reader to C++ and object-oriented programming (OOP) and provides a brief overview of key features in C++ such as inheritance and templates. Since these advanced topics require knowledge of C++ semantics and syntax, the preliminary discussion is intentionally kept brief. These topics are discussed in detail in later chapters.

3.1 OBJECT-ORIENTED PROGRAMMING

A program is considered an *object-oriented program* when it meets the following criteria [Booch 1994]:

1. **Design**: Software is viewed as an interacting group of objects. Thus, objects are the centerpieces of the design and functions are operations on the objects.
2. **Types**: Objects are *instances* of classes.
3. **Relationship**: The objects in the design form hierarchies through inheritance.

3.2 CLASS

A *class definition* logically organizes data and functions and allows the designer to assign access levels to them. The access levels are *private*, *protected*, and *public*:

```
class Name
{
        access_level:
                // data element declarations
                type data_member ;

        access_level:
                // function prototypes (declarations)
                return_type function_name( arguments, if any ) ;
} ;
```

A class *definition* identifies the architecture for an instance of the class (object) by specifying the data members and their types. The compiler needs this information to identify the size and type of data stored in the memory space of an object. In addition, the class *definition* contains the member function *prototypes* (declarations). The function declarations (*prototypes*) highlight the functions that can operate on the internal members of the class. They also specify function's name, number and types of parameters, and return value's data type.

A class definition is typically maintained in a *header* file and the function definitions are maintained in a *source* file. Using the **#include** compiler directive, the client includes the contents of the header file and gains access to the *class definition*. The client then declares objects and operates on them using the member functions in the class definition. The separation of the class definition and the function definition encapsulates the class implementation from the client. The client does not need to be concerned with the internal operations of the class maintained in the source file, and only needs the features and operations specified in the design interface of the class maintained in the header file.

In the following example, the *Account* class definition specifies the layout of a bank account object and identifies the member functions (Figure 3.1). In this design, the *Account* class maintains the basic account information such as customer name, address, identification (id), and balance. Clients such as an automated teller machine (ATM) use this class to make simple transactions such as withdrawal and deposit. The **last transaction** date identifies if an account is active or inactive. The **current_balance** and **last_transaction** data members are used to identify the state of the object:

```
//              ACCOUNT.H Header File
typedef    char       Text ;
typedef    float      Currency ;
typedef    int        ID ;
typedef    char       Date ;
typedef    bool       Boolean ;
// bool is a C++ built-in type that takes false and true values (keywords).
// For C++ compilers that still do not support the bool type, and the false
// and true keywords, use the following definition:
//    typedef    enum{ false , true }        Boolean;

class Account
{
        // C++ provides the // symbol for single-line comments
        private:
                // customer_name, customer_address, id, and
                // current_balance, last_transaction components are internal
```

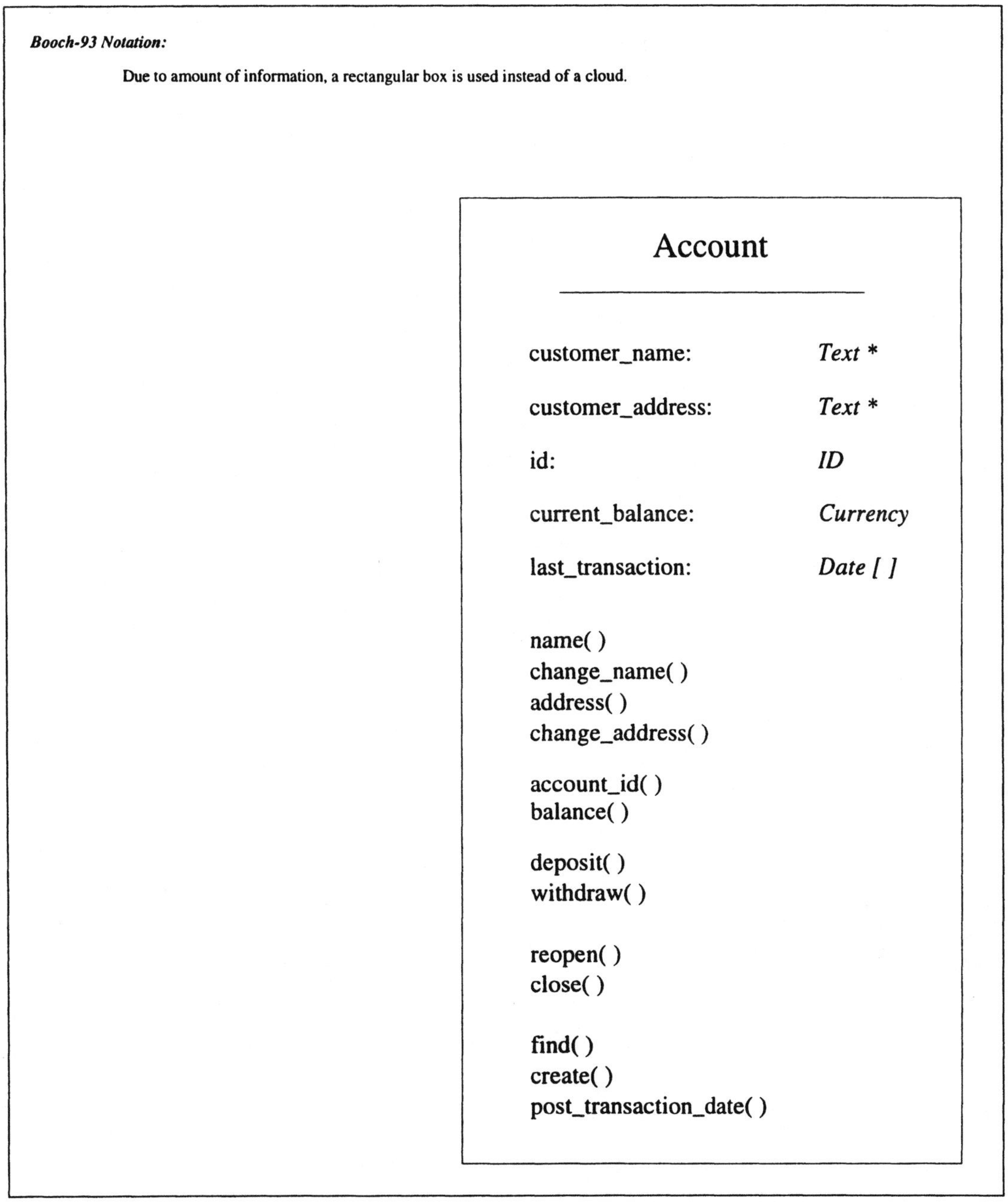

Account	
customer_name:	*Text **
customer_address:	*Text **
id:	*ID*
current_balance:	*Currency*
last_transaction:	*Date [ ]*
name( )	
change_name( )	
address( )	
change_address( )	
account_id( )	
balance( )	
deposit( )	
withdraw( )	
reopen( )	
close( )	
find( )	
create( )	
post_transaction_date( )	

FIGURE 3.1 Account class diagram.

```
// and can only be accessed by the class member functions
Text        *customer_name ;
Text        *customer_address ;
ID          id ;
Currency    current_balance ;
Date        last_transaction[9] ;

// Utility Functions
Boolean find( void ) ;
Boolean create( void ) ;
void post_transaction_date( void ) ;
```

```
public:
        // Access Functions
        Currency balance( void ) ;
        ID account_id( void ) ;
        const Text *name( void ) ;
        Boolean change_name( const Text *new_name ) ;
        const Text *address( void ) ;
        Boolean change_address( const Text *new_address ) ;

        // Processing Functions
        Currency deposit( Currency amount ) ;
        Currency withdraw( Currency amount ) ;
        Boolean reopen( void ) ;
        Currency close( void ) ;

        // public data and functions are accessible
        // to all clients
} ;
```

This section decomposes the discussion on the *class definition* into the following topics:

1. Access levels
2. Data members
3. Member functions
4. Design interface

3.2.1 Access Levels

A software developer **provides** *data encapsulation* through proper analysis and design. Since the developer does not have control over the actions of the client, the enforcement of data encapsulation must be provided by the language. The compiler enforces *data encapsulation* through the use of access levels. In C++, a class may specify an internal interface (**private**) and two external interfaces for its clients (**public** and **protected**). These interfaces identify the visibility of features and attributes to the clients:

1. **public**: The clients of a class have full access to the **public** interface of a class. For example, clients use the **deposit()** and **withdraw()** functions of the *Account* class to operate on the account balance. These public member functions protect the *current_balance* data member from being set to incorrect values by the client:

```
//            ACCOUNT.H Header File
typedef    float      Currency ;
typedef    bool       Boolean ;

class Account
{
      private:
             Currency    current_balance ;

             // Utility Functions
             Boolean find( void ) ;

      public:
             // Processing functions
             Currency deposit( Currency amount ) ;
             Currency withdraw( Currency amount ) ;
             // Other details left out
} ;
```

The designer of a class must be careful in defining public members. Since clients have free access to the public members, these members cannot be removed without affecting the application source code. For example, if the access level of the **deposit()** function is changed to **private**, the clients will be unable to access this function. Therefore, all of the application source files using this function must be updated. Removing and changing public members affects the design interface with the outside world and often requires substantial modifications of the client's source code.

2. **protected**: Used in conjunction with *inheritance*, it gives derived classes access to the **protected** members of a class. However, nonderived classes cannot access the **protected** members. Basically, this access level allows the designer to distinguish between types of clients by providing free access to the inheriting classes while blocking other types of clients from accessing the **protected** members. Chapter 9 discusses the **protected** access level in detail.

   As an analogy, a company may provide different entrances for employees, visitors, and the general public. The employee entrances normally provide access to sensitive areas of the company. With proper escort, visitors have access to selected areas of the company such as conference rooms. The general public is restricted to the building's lobby area (Figure 3.2).

3. **private**: The **private** access level removes data and functions from the design interface by making them invisible to the client, thus encapsulating the data and code. Only the class member functions can operate on private members. In the above example, the **deposit()** and **withdraw()** member functions have access to the private data elements and functions such as **current_balance** and **find()**. Clients use the public member functions to access and operate on the private data.

Through the use of the above access levels, the class designer specifies how the resources of a class are accessed and used by its clients. The compiler uses the same information to detect access violations. Upon detecting access violations by the client, the compiler generates an error message at compile time. By regulating access to the members, the compiler preserves *data encapsulation.*

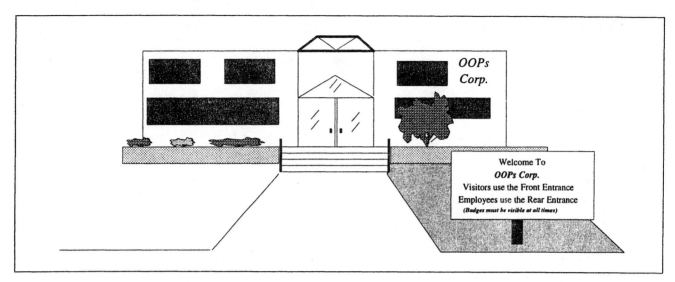

FIGURE 3.2   Access levels.

3.2.2 Data Members

The class definition identifies the memory layout, size, and contents of an instance of the class. For example, the memory layout and content for an *Account* object are depicted in Figure 3.3. This figure provides a logical view

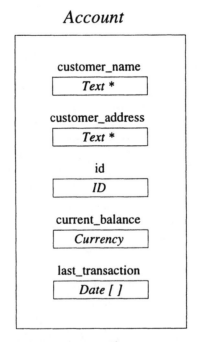

FIGURE 3.3   Account Class Memory Layout

of the memory layout and is not a physical view. The physical locations of the members in the object vary among C++ compilers. For example, a compiler may assign the members on different integer boundaries (32-bit or 16-bit). A C++ program should not rely on the physical layout of the object:

```
//              ACCOUNT.H Header File
typedef     char        Text ;
typedef     float       Currency ;
typedef     int         ID ;
typedef     char        Date ;

class Account
{
    private:
            Text        *customer_name ;
            Text        *customer_address ;
            ID          id ;
            Currency    current_balance ;
            Date        last_transaction[9] ;
    public:
            // Other details left out
} ;
```

To hide the architecture and data representation from the client, data members are normally declared with a **private** access level. Therefore, the clients will not depend on the particular data representation, such as using an integer data type for the *Account* class's *id*. If type of *id* is changed from integer to character string, clients will not be affected by this internal change, and only the *Account* member functions must be updated.

3.2.3 Member Functions

A client uses the class member functions to operate on objects and change their state. The functions hide the data architecture and representation (*encapsulation*), and they also prevent the clients from placing the object into an unknown state, that is, setting the data members to an illegal or nonexistent value.

When the data representation or architecture changes, the changes are localized to the member functions. For example, the *Account* member functions hide the use of external character buffers for maintaining the customer names and addresses. If the class is later changed to use *Name* and *Address* classes for maintaining customer information, the change will impact only the bodies of the *Account* member functions operating on these information.

Member functions also abstract the internal tasks of the class from the client. For example, the client makes deposits to a bank *account* by using the **deposit()** function. This function contains the steps necessary to post a deposit and the process remains hidden from the client.

By incorporating the function declarations (*prototypes*) in the class definition, C++ creates an explicit relationship between *member data* and *member functions*. In the following example, the function declarations (*prototypes*) in the *Account* class definition allow the compiler to differentiate between the member and nonmember functions:

```
//              ACCOUNT.H Header File
typedef     char    Text ;
typedef     float   Currency ;
typedef     int     ID ;
typedef     char    Date ;
typedef     bool    Boolean ;

class Account
{
    private:
            Text        *customer_name ;
            Text        *customer_address ;
            ID          id ;
            Currency    current_balance ;
```

```
            Date              last_transaction[9] ;

            // Utility Functions
            Boolean find( void ) ;
            Boolean create( void ) ;
            void post_transaction_date( void ) ;

    public:
            // Access Functions
            Currency balance( void ) const ;// read-only function
            ID account_id( void ) const ;
            const Text *name( void ) const ;
            Boolean change_name( const Text *new_name ) ;
            const Text *address( void ) const ;
            Boolean change_address( const Text *new_address ) ;

            // Processing Functions
            Currency deposit( Currency amount ) ;
            Currency withdraw( Currency amount ) ;
            Boolean reopen( void ) ;
            Currency close( void ) ;

            // Other member functions declarations left out
} ;
```

The above *member* function declarations tell the compiler that these functions have access to the private members of the class and can operate freely on any data member. By operating on the data members, the member functions handle the initialization, manipulation, and cleanup tasks. The above example has categorized the *Account* class member functions on the basis of their functionality:

1. **Access Functions**: The class provides several access functions such as **balance()** and **account_id()**. These functions regulate access to selected member(s) of a class. The above functions return a copy of the *current_balance* and *id* parts of an *Account* object to the calling function.

    Some of the access functions do not change the contents and the state of the *Account* objects. They are specified as *read-only* by using the **const** keyword at the end of the function declaration.

    To enhance maintainability and readability, the data types used to represent *current_balance* and *id* have been named *Currency* and *ID* using C's **typedef** feature. This feature describes the context in which the built-in data type is being used and avoids the hard coding of the built-in data type. In the case of *Boolean*, **typedef** is used to enhance portability for compilers that do not support the ANSI C++ "*bool*" data type.

2. **Processing Functions**: These functions provide functionality to the class by allowing the clients to perform tasks such as depositing and withdrawing money from an account. For example, the **deposit()** and **withdraw()** functions operate on the account's *current_balance* and return the current *balance*. These operations typically affect the state of the object. For instance, a **withdraw()** operation that causes the balance to become negative leads the object to transition to an **overdrawn** state.

3. **Utility Functions**: These functions are internal to the design of the class and are used for internal tasks. For example, the **find()** function queries the bank account database and loads the specified account information into memory. This function hides the use of a database from the clients and the other member functions, thus hiding the *persistence* property.

4. **Constructors**: These functions perform the initialization tasks and are discussed in later sections. The *Account* constructor will use the **find()** function for querying the bank account database and initialize an account object.

5. **Destructor**: This function performs the cleanup tasks and is also discussed in later sections. For *Account*, destructor deallocates the dynamically allocated memory for a customer's name and address.

Member functions are defined using the following generic syntax:

```
return_data_type  class_name ::  function_name( parameter list, if any )
{
      // function's body
}
```

Except for "*Class_Name::*," member function definitions have the same format as C functions. The class name followed by the *scope resolution* (::) operator is part of the function name and forms its signature. The class name is analogous to a person's last name and explicitly associates the member functions with their class. Nonmember (standalone) functions in C++ are defined using C-Language syntax:

```
return_data_type function_name( parameter definitions, if any )
{
      // function's body
}
```

In the following example, the **ACCOUNT.CPP** source file includes the **ACCOUNT.H** header file definition and provides the implementation of the member functions. The class name in the function definition correlates each member function with the *Account* class.

```
//                    ACCOUNT.CPP Source  File
#include <string.h>        // string library
#include <malloc.h>        // dynamic allocation library
#include <math.h>          // math library
#include "dbase.h"         // Account Database Interface
#include "account.h"       // Account class library

// class access functions:
Currency Account:: balance( void ) const
{
      return( current_balance ) ;
}

ID Account:: account_id( void ) const
{
      return( id ) ;
}

// processing functions: transactions
Currency Account:: deposit( Currency amount )
{
      // if amount is positive => update balance
      if( amount >= 0.0 )
      {
            current_balance += amount ;
            post_transaction_date() ;
                  // update last transaction date
      }
      return( current_balance ) ;
}

Currency Account:: withdraw( Currency amount )
{
      // if withdrawing the specified amount from balance
      current_balance -= fabs( amount ) ;
```

```
        post_transaction_date() ;// update last transaction date

        if( balance < 0.0 )
        {
                // Account is overdrawn and take the appropriate actions
                // such as sending a letter & applying service charge
                current_balance -= SERVICE_CHARGE ;
                // Other details left out
        }
        return( current_balance ) ;
}

// Utility functions
Boolean Account:: find( void )
{
        Boolean record_found = false ;

        // query database using the account name and id
        // if record found then
        // load account information
        // end if
        return( record_found ) ;
}

// Other function definitions are left out
```

A member function automatically gets the address of the current object it is operating on. While generating the executable code, the compiler inserts an additional pointer argument for each member function. For example, the executable version of the **balance()** function actually has a hidden argument known as the "**this**" pointer (a reserved keyword). The compiler hides the incorporation of the "**this**" pointer argument by performing an operation similar to the following C implementation:

```
/*    compiler task for incorporating "this" pointer */
Currency balance( const Account *this )
{
        return( this->current_balance ) ;
}
```

Through the "**this**" pointer, the **balance()** function implicitly obtains the address of the *Account* object when it is called. In the following example, the address of the *customer* object is automatically passed to the **balance()** and **deposit()** member functions via the "**this**" pointer:

```
//                        Test Driver Source File
#include <iostream.h>            // Stream I/O Class Library
#include "account.h"             // Account Class Library

void process_account( Account *customer )
{
        Currency bonus ;

        // prompt the user for the bonus dollar amount
        cout << "Input Amount of Bonus :" << endl ;
        cin >> bonus ; // get amount from the keyboard

        customer->deposit( bonus ) ;  // deposit bonus
```

```
                // display the Account Balance on the display console
                cout << "\n\t Account Balance : " << customer->balance()  ;
                // the address of customer is automatically passed
                // to the above member functions: balance( customer )

                return ;

}
```

3.2.4 Design Interface

Changes to the external interfaces of a class (**public** and **protected**) can adversely affect software maintainability. When the external interface of a software module changes, it directly impacts its client software. Depending on the degree of change, the client software may require substantial modification, retesting, and revalidation. In the following example, the *Account* class design is changed to include branch information. This change affects both the data representation and the class interface. The class architecture must be changed to accommodate the *branch_address*. In addition, some of the member function interfaces must be changed, such as the **Account()** constructor for user-defined values. Most importantly, the interface cannot simply be changed without examining its effect on the previously developed client programs that are dependent on the previous design.

To minimize the addition of parameters in a function's argument list, C++ provides *default arguments* to help soften the impact of changes to the function interface:

```
//                      ACCOUNT.H Header File
typedef       char       Text ;
typedef       float      Currency ;
typedef       int        ID ;
typedef       char       Date ;
typedef       bool       Boolean ;

#define DATE_BUFFER_SIZE       9

class Account
{
        private:
                Text       *customer_name ;
                Text       *customer_address ;
                Text       *branch_address ;    // new feature
                ID         id ;
                Currency   current_balance ;
                Date       last_transaction[DATE_BUFFER_SIZE] ;

        public:
                // constructor functions
                Account( const Text *name, ID account_id ,
                         const Text * branch_addr = NULL ) ;
                        // user-defined values constructor
                Account(); // default constructor

                // class access functions
                Currency balance( void ) const ;
                ID account_id( void ) const ;
                const Text *branch( void ) const ;
                        // note: this is a new feature
                // other function declarations are left out

} ;
```

In the above example, the **Account()** constructor has used a default pointer value of null for the branch address. This feature makes this class backward compatible with the software that does not support branch information. The client programs need only to be recompiled:

```
//                    Test Driver Software
#include "account.h"

void process_account( const Text *name, ID id )
{
        Account customer( name, id ) ;
            // initialize customer using (name, id, (Text *) 0)
            // by using the default value for branch address
        // details left out
        return ;
}
```

The clients using the new interface can override the default value by specifying an explicit value:

```
//                    Test Driver Software
#include "account.h"

void process_account( const Text *name,const Text *branch_address,ID id)
{
        Account customer( name, id, branch_address ) ;
            // initialize customer using the user-defined values
            // override the default values
        // details left out
        return ;
}
```

This technique has limited application and, of course, cannot be used when the function interface is completely redesigned or when data types are changed. Another technique to minimize the impact to the design interface is to use *function overloading* to create new functions using existing names but with different interfaces. *Function overloading* is the ability to define two or more functions using the same name, and is discussed in detail in Chapter 4.

3.3 OBJECTS

In C++, an *object is an instance of a class.* This section describes how an object is created, destroyed, and operated on.

3.3.1 Object Construction

In C, the initialization of variables and an instance of a class has been the application software's responsibility. This can pose reliability issues. If the client does not initialize the variable prior to its use, the program's behavior will be unpredictable. Reliance on the client to initialize the memory space for an instance of *Account* is also not reliable. If the client forgets to perform the applicable initialization, the program will produce erroneous results. In a complex program, this bug can be difficult to find. The lack or improper use of data initialization seriously affects software reliability.

To address object initialization, C++ has become actively involved in the data object *construction process.* A data object is *constructed* by allocating the appropriate memory space for the object. After the memory space is reserved, an initialization function is called automatically to initialize the memory space. This process places the object in a *predictable* and *stable* state. Object initialization can be accomplished by several different methods:

1. **Default Values**: An object is initialized to fixed default values.
2. **User-Defined Values**: An object is initialized using client-defined values.
3. **Copy**: An object is initialized by copying the contents of another object of the same type.

Object construction is automated by connecting the initialization functions to the data definitions. On the basis of the data definition, the compiler incorporates automatic calls to an initialization function in the executable code. During the program's execution, the initialization function is called immediately after the memory space for an instance of the class is allocated. This approach ensures that when an object is created, it is always placed in a predictable state. Even if the application program does not define initial values for a local object, the object will be initialized to default values. This process eliminates unpredictable program behavior due to improper initialization.

C++ has standardized the *constructor* naming convention by using the class name for the constructor functions. Since there are several ways to initialize an object, C++ permits a class to support multiple constructor functions through *function overloading*. For example, the **Account( )** class constructors use the *"Account"* identifier:

```
//              ACCOUNT.H Header File
typedef    char       Text ;
typedef    float      Currency ;
typedef    int        ID ;
typedef    char       Date ;
typedef    bool       Boolean ;


#defined DATE_BUFFER_SIZE        9


class Account
{
    private:
            Text        *customer_name ;
            Text        *customer_address ;
            ID          id ;
            Currency    current_balance ;
            Date        last_transaction[DATE_BUFFER_SIZE] ;

            // Utility functions
            Boolean find( void ) ;
            Boolean create( void ) ;

    public:
            // constructor (initialization) functions
            Account( const Text *name,  ID account_id ) ;
                        // user-defined values constructor
            Account(); // default constructor
            // other function declarations are left out
} ;
```

The above *Account* class declares two constructor functions. The function definitions are included in the following section:

1. **User-Defined Values Constructor**: Initializes the object to client-defined values.
2. **Default Constructor**: Initializes the object to internal default values.

The following provides an implementation for these functions:

```
//                    ACCOUNT.CPP  Source  File
#include <string.h>        // string library
#include <malloc.h>        // dynamic allocation library
#include "dbase.h"         // Account Database Interface
#include "account.h"       // Account class library

// user-defined values constructor : initialize object using user-defined values
Account:: Account( const Text *name,  ID account_id )
{
    // compute name's length in bytes (include the null terminator)
    int name_length = strlen( name ) + 1 ;

    // dynamically allocate memory for name
    customer_name = (Text *) malloc( sizeof(Text) * name_length ) ;

    // if allocation fails => abort & use default values
    if( !customer_name )
    {
            customer_address = (Text * ) 0 ; // set to default values
            id = 0 ;
    }
    else
    {       // copy information into name and address buffers
            strcpy( customer_name, name ) ;
            id = account_id ; // setup account id
    }
    current_balance = 0 ; // no balance
    *last_transaction = '\0' ; // set to null string

    // if no allocation failure
    if( id != 0 && customer_name )
    {
            // query database for the account information.
            // Obtain information such as address and verify name & id.
            // if account information not found => create a new account
            if( !find() )
            {
                    create() ; // create a new record
            }
    }
}

// default constructor : initialize to default values (inactive state)
Account:: Account( )
{
    customer_address = (Text * ) 0 ; // set to default values
    customer_name = (Text * ) 0 ;
    id = 0 ;
    current_balance = 0 ;
    *last_transaction = '\0' ; // set to null string
}
```

Using the above user-defined constructor, a client at an automated teller machine (ATM) will be able to update information in the customer's *account*. On the basis of the customer's requests, the ATM object performs the banking transactions on the *account* object. Figure 3.4 depicts a high-level interaction diagram for a withdrawal transaction by a customer. The pseudocode adjacent to the interaction diagram describes the sequence of events and the associated conditions.

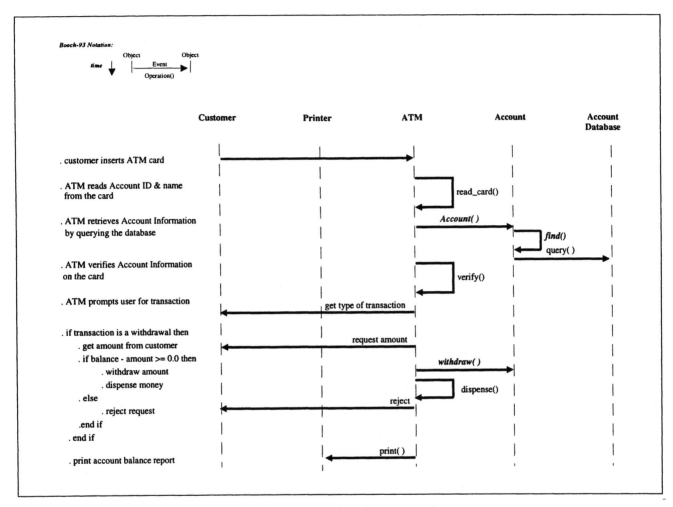

FIGURE 3.4 ATM withdrawal interaction diagram.

In the following example, the compiler connects the local object definitions to the applicable constructor functions for the *Account* class. After the **main()** function is invoked and memory space for *customer1* is reserved on the *stack*, the constructor function is **automatically** called. Since the application has not defined any initialization data for *customer1*, the compiler will use the default constructor. The process for *customer2* is the same, except that the *user-defined values* constructor is called. The object is created using the test driver supplied values (Figure 3.5):

```
//              Test Driver Software
#include <iostream.h>          // Stream I/O Class Library
#include "account.h"           // Account Class Library

int main( int , char ** )
{
    Account customer1 ;
    Account customer2( "Bob Smith", 3000 ) ;
    // customer1 is initialized to default values using Account()constructor
    // customer2 is initialized using the user-defined values constructor
    // other details are left out
```

```
    cout << "Name of Customer 1: " << customer1.name( ) ;
    cout << "Name of Customer 2: " << customer2.name( ) ;

    return( 0 ) ;
}
```

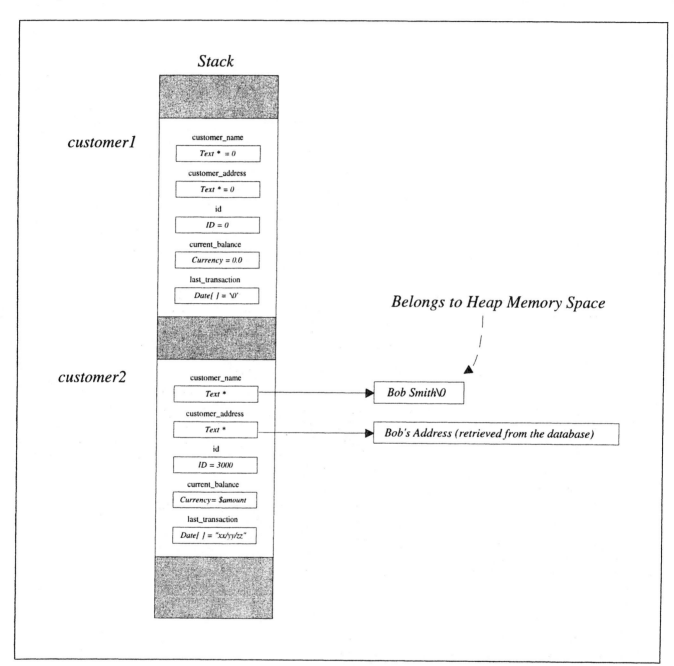

FIGURE 3.5   Construction of account objects.

3.3.2 Object Destruction

The *Account* class uses dynamic memory allocation to allocate buffers for the customer name and address. When an instance of the *Account* class goes out of scope, these buffers must be freed, otherwise the address of these buffers will be permanently lost and the program will never be able to free and reuse the buffer's memory space (*memory leakage*). In the following example, every time the **ATM:: transaction()** function is executed, a *customer* object is constructed. When the function execution returns the control back to the caller, the local *customer* object goes out of scope and its space is freed on the stack. With the current design, the dynamically allocated *name* and *address* buffers are never deallocated:

```
//                    ATM.CPP Source File
#include "account.h"   // Bank Account Class Library
#include "atm.h"        // Automated Teller Machine Library

void ATM:: transaction( const Text *name, ID id )
{
    Account customer( name, id ) ;
              // create an account object

    // other details left out

    return ; // customer goes out of scope
}
```

By not deallocating the buffers, the **transaction()** function causes the program to lose available dynamically allocated memory space (*memory leakage*). If the application software continues to use this function to process accounts, at some point the software will run out of available memory. Software reliability has been compromised.

In a similar fashion to object construction, C++ has implemented object cleanup (*destruction*) by making both the designer of the class and the compiler responsible. For classes whose members reference dynamically allocated memory or file streams, the class should provide a cleanup function referred to as a *destructor*. The designer of the class supplies the *destructor* and the compiler places calls to this function in the appropriate places in the executable code.

The call to the *destructor* is connected to the life span of an *object*. When an instance of a class (*object*) goes out of scope, the *destructor* is called. The *destructor* then performs the necessary cleanup operations, such as closing the file stream or freeing the dynamically allocated memory. When an object goes out of scope, the compiler inserts a call to the destructor in the executable code. By tying the cleanup operations to the lifetime of the object, the destruction is automated during the execution of the program. After the destructor function returns, the object ceases to exist. The object's content is no longer in a *stable* state. At this point, the object is viewed as a block of uninitialized memory.

Unlike a *constructor*, only one *destructor* can be defined. Similar to constructors, the *destructor* uses the same name as the class name, preceded by a tilde (~). The *destructor* does not take any arguments:

```
Class_Name:: ~ Class_Name()
{
    // body of destructor
}
```

In the following example, the *Account* class has been updated to provide both constructor and destructor functions. The reliability issues associated with improper initialization and cleanup of objects have been eliminated in this implementation:

```
//                    ACCOUNT.H Header File
typedef    char      Text ;
typedef    float     Currency ;
typedef    int       ID ;
typedef    char      Date ;
typedef    bool      Boolean ;
```

```
#define DATE_BUFFER_SIZE        9

class Account
{
        private:
                Text        *customer_name ;
                Text        *customer_address ;
                ID          id ;
                Currency    current_balance ;
                Date        last_transaction[DATE_BUFFER_SIZE] ;

                // Class utility functions
                Boolean find( void ) ;
                Boolean create( void ) ;
        public:
                // Constructor functions
                Account( const Text *name,  ID account_id ) ;
                        // user-defined values constructor
                Account(); // default constructor

                // Destructor function
                ~Account( )  ;
                // other function declarations are left out
} ;

//                    ACCOUNT.CPP  Source File
#include <string.h>            // string library
#include <malloc.h>            // dynamic allocation library
#include <math.h>              // Math library
#include "dbase.h"             // Account Database Interface
#include "account.h"           // Account class library

// Account class destructor
Account:: ~Account( )
{
    // if a name buffer exists => deallocate buffer
    if( customer_name )
    {
            free( customer_name ) ;
    }
    // if an address buffer exists => deallocate buffer
    if( customer_address )
    {
            free( customer_address ) ;
    }
}
```

By defining a destructor, the memory leakage problem is resolved. Any time an *Account* object goes out of scope, the destructor is automatically called and the customer address and name buffers are automatically deallocated:

```
//                      ATM.CPP Source File
#include "account.h"        // Bank Account Class Library
#include "atm.h"            // Automated Teller Machine Library

void ATM:: transaction( const Text *name, ID id )
{
        Account customer( name, id ) ;
             // call Account( char *, int ) constructor to create an object


        // other details left out


        return ;
        // when the customer object goes out of scope, the Account ::~Account()
        // destructor is automatically called and the buffers are deallocated.
        // The destructor performs the applicable cleanup task.
}
```

Chapter 5 examines destructor functions in greater detail.

3.3.3 Object Manipulation

When an object comes into existence, it is placed into a *predictable* (*known*) state by the constructor. The member functions are then used to operate on the object. Except for the constructors and destructors, all member functions must be explicitly invoked. To invoke a member function, C++ uses the same notation as C to access the data elements. Member functions are invoked using the *dot* (.) and *arrow* (->) operators:

```
object.member_function( arguments, if any ) ;
object_reference.member_function( arguments, if any ) ;
object_pointer->member_function( arguments, if any ) ;
```

In the following example, the test driver program performs the following:

1. Creates an instance of *Account* on the stack using the supplied name and id.
2. Displays the account information by invoking the applicable access functions.
3. Destructor deallocates the dynamically allocated buffers.

```
//                      Test Driver Source File
#include "account.h"

void process_account( const Text *name, ID id )
{
        Account customer( name, id ) ;
           // define an instance of account

        cout << "Customer Name: " << customer.name() ;
        cout << "Account ID: " << customer.account_id() ;
        cout << "Account Balance: " << customer.balance() ;

        return ;
}
```

Member functions may cause an object to change state. In the bank account example, the account's *current_balance* and *last_transaction* are used to identify the possible states for a *bank account* object (Figure

3.6). The state transition diagram illustrates all the known states and shows how operations such as **deposit()** and **withdraw()** cause the object to transition from one state to another:

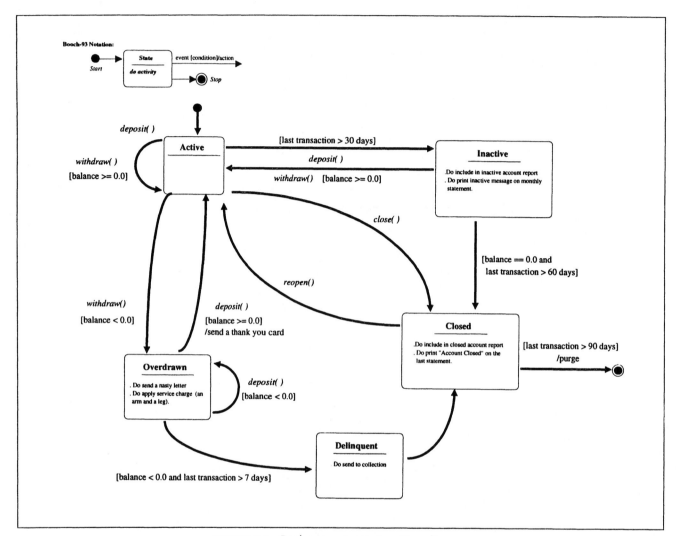

FIGURE 3.6   Bank account state transition diagram.

1. **Active**: In our bank model, an account is considered active if it is in good standing and it is being used regularly. The criteria for this state are as follows:

   ```
   (balance >= 0.0) and (today's date - last transaction date) < 30 days
   ```

2. **Inactive**: When an account is not used for more than 30 days, the account is considered inactive:

   ```
   today's date - last transaction date > 30 days
   ```

3. **Overdrawn**: When the account's *balance* becomes negative, the account is overdrawn:

   ```
   balance < 0.0
   ```

4. **Delinquent**: An account becomes delinquent when its balance remains negative for more than 7 days:

(balance < 0) and (today's date - last transaction date > 7 days)

5. **Closed**: An account is closed when it has been inactive for a long period, or closed by the customer, or after it has been delinquent long enough to go to the collection department.

The state transition diagram identifies the *conditions* that cause a state transition except for the transitioning from **delinquent** to **closed**. In this case, after all of the *activities* in the **delinquent** state are completed, the transition to **closed** takes place automatically.

3.4 OBJECT MODEL

C++ supports the *major* components of the framework of an *object model:*

1. **Modularity**: C++ supports implementation of modular designs through classes and libraries. These features provide the mechanism for partitioning the system's architecture along well-defined boundaries, resulting in the creation of loosely coupled and highly cohesive modules. For instance, a bank accounting system may be partitioned into *subsystems* and *modules*. They are then decomposed into *categories*, and the *categories* into a collection of classes. Figure 3.7 illustrates the *module* diagram for this bank accounting system.

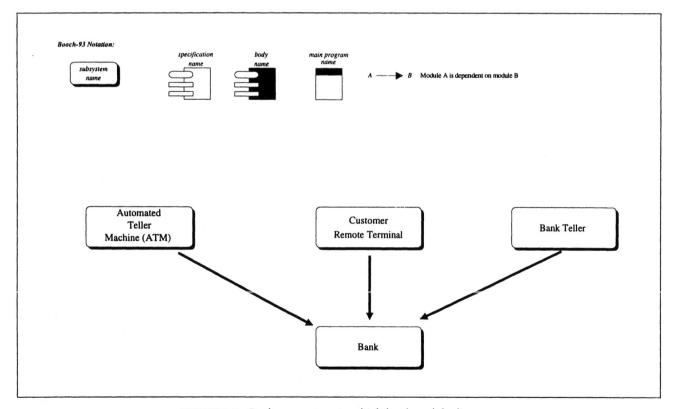

FIGURE 3.7 Bank account system high level module diagram.

In typical C++ applications, the class definitions and functions are logically organized into class libraries. For example, the bank account classes may be grouped into an *Account class* library (Figure 3.8). The automated teller machine (ATM) subsystem will use this library to operate on the customers' accounts (Figure 3.9). The ATM client gains access to the resources of this library by including the "account.h" header file.

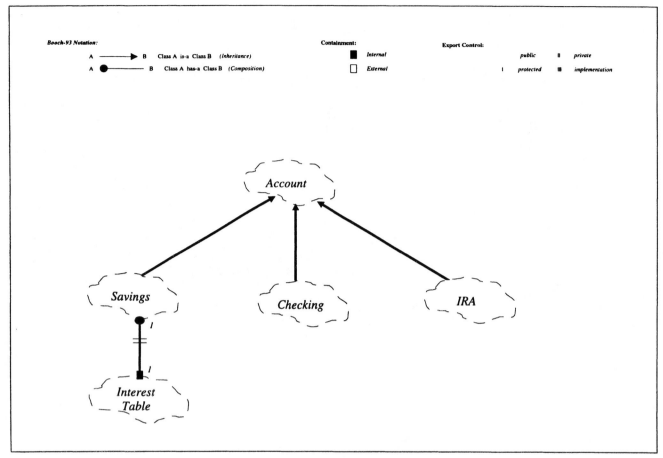

FIGURE 3.8   Account class diagram.

2. **Encapsulation**: C++ hides both design implementation and data architecture. The access levels in the class definition allow the compiler to enforce data encapsulation and to prevent the client from accessing the private data members of a class.

   The design implementation is kept hidden by allowing the declarations and definitions to be separated from each other. Header files are used to maintain class definitions, function declarations (prototypes), and constant definitions. The client accesses this information through the **#include** compiler directive. The function definitions and internal objects (**static** definitions) are maintained in source files that hide the implementation from the client.

3. **Abstraction**: The member functions hide the design complexity, and internal operations are transparent to the client. The client operates on the objects through well-defined interfaces.

4. **Design Hierarchy**: Classes can inherit from each other in C++. The implementation of the design presented in Figure 3.8 is covered in the following sections.

C++ does not explicitly support two *minor* components of the object model:

1. **Concurrency**: Some compilers support *concurrency* through libraries and/or language extensions. However, a library is not considered part of a programming language and language extensions are specific to languages such as C+- (C-plus-minus), whose code is not portable [Seizovic 1994].

   Concurrency can also be achieved to a lesser degree through separate executables in multitasking operating systems such as UNIX.

2. **Persistence**: The developer is responsible for providing *persistence* behavior. For example, the *bank account class* library used a database to maintain the bank account information. This behavior is not built into the language and must be implemented by the developer or adapted from available tools such as a database.

   Chapter 12 provides a more detailed discussion on these two subjects.

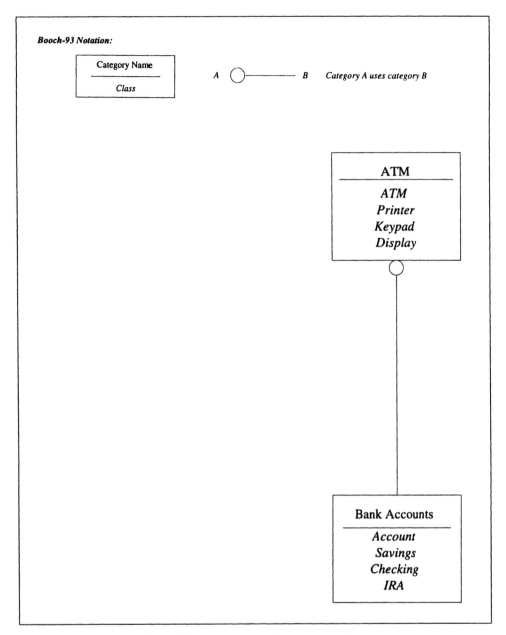

FIGURE 3.9 ATM and account class category diagram.

3.5 INHERITANCE

The examples in this section are designed only to introduce the reader to *inheritance* in C++. Since *Inheritance* is a complex topic, it is discussed in detail in chapters 9 and 10.

The C-Language does not provide syntax that allows the compiler to recognize the "*is-a*" relationships between data structures. The inability to create explicit relationships impedes the reuse of an existing design in new applications. For instance, the designer of a new bank *Account* must copy the source and header files and customize them to design a new *Savings* account from them. The C-Language does not support the designer in relating and reusing the bank *Account* architecture and functions in the new design.

Through inheritance, C++ provides for a class to inherit the properties of another class. In Figure 3.8, *Savings* inherits the data and function members of the *Account* class. Thus, it does not need to reimplement them and the design of the new class builds on the existing design:

```
//              ACCOUNT.H Header File
typedef      char       Text ;
typedef      float      Currency ;
typedef      int        ID ;
typedef      char       Date ;
typedef      unsigned   Days ;
typedef      bool       Boolean ;

#define DATE_BUFFER_SIZE        9

class Account
{
      private:
              Text       *customer_name ;
              Text       *customer_address ;
              Text       *branch_address ;
              ID         id ;
              Currency   current_balance ;
              Date       last_transaction[DATE_BUFFER_SIZE] ;

              // Utility Functions
              Boolean find( void ) ;
              Boolean create( void ) ;
              void post_transaction_date( void ) ;
      public:
              // Constructors
              Account( const Text *name, ID account_id ,
                      const Text * branch_addr = NULL ) ;
                      // user-defined values constructor
              Account();// default constructor

              // Destructor
              ~Account( ) ;

              // Access functions
              Currency balance( void ) const ;
              ID account_id( void ) const ;
              const Text *name( void ) const ;
              Boolean change_name( const Text *new_name ) ;
              const Text *address( void ) const ;
              Boolean change_address( const Text *new_address ) ;
              Days last_posting( void ) const ; // # of days from last posting

              // Processing Functions
              Currency deposit( Currency amount ) ;
              Currency withdraw( Currency amount ) ;
              Boolean reopen( void ) ;
              Currency close( void ) ;
} ;
```

In the following example, *Savings* is derived from *Account* (Figure 3.10). Since *Savings* is inheriting from *Account*, it automatically has access to features and resources of the *Account* class design. A *Savings* object consists of an *Account* and a *Savings* segment. Each segment is maintained by its own class member functions. The *Account* member functions operate on the *Account* data and hide the *Account* design from the *Savings* member functions:

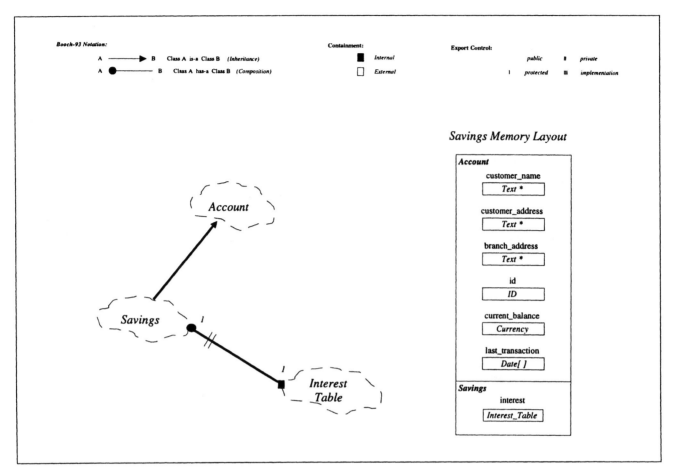

FIGURE 3.10 Savings account class.

```
//              SAVINGS.H Header File
typedef      float       Rate ;

class Interest_Table
{
      private:
            Rate interest_rate ;
            Text start_date[DATE_BUFFER_SIZE] ;
            Days interest_period ;

      public:
            // Constructor
            Interest_Table( Rate new_rate, Text *new_period = NULL ) ;
            // Access functions
            Rate rate( void ) const ;
            Days period( void ) const ;
            Boolean change_rate( Rate new_rate ) ;
} ;

class Savings: public Account
      // Savings is inheriting the properties of Account. The effect
      // of the public keyword is explained in Chapter 9. The public
      // keyword only affects the clients of Savings and not the
```

```
        // Savings member functions.
{
        private:
                Interest_Table interest ;
        public:
                Currency income( void );
                // Other details left out
} ;
```

The *Savings* member functions have access to the **public** and **protected** members of the *Account* class. In the above example, the *Account* class does not provide a **protected** interface. In the following example, the **Savings:: income()** function utilizes the *Account* **public** member function to operate on a *Savings* object:

```
//                      SAVINGS.CPP Source File
#include <iostream.h>          // Stream I/O Class Library
#include "account.h"           // Account class header file
#include "savings.h"           // Savings class header file

Currency Savings:: income( void )
{
        Currency current_income = 0.0 ; // initially, no earnings

        // if last posting was 30 days ago then apply income
        if( last_posting() >= 30 )
        {
                current_income = interest.rate() * balance() ;

                // reflect income in the balance
                deposit( current_income ) ;

                // by inheriting from Account, Savings is
                // using the existing Account class features
                // in its design.
        }
        return( current_income ) ;
}
```

Figure 3.8 depicts the *Account* class diagram and its relationship to other classes. The *Savings* class *"is-an" Account* and its *Account* segment contains a *Name* and an *Address*. In addition, *Savings* has an *Interest Table* class for maintaining the interest rate information.

Inheritance creates a parent-child relationship among the classes. In the above design, the *Account* class is the *base* (parent) class and the *Savings* class is the *derived* (child) class. The design of the *Savings* and *Account* classes conforms to an **"is-a"** relationship. This relationship becomes the primary criterion for the use of inheritance in class designs:

```
Savings is-a Account
```

If the above statement did not hold true, then inheritance would have been a poor choice for creating *Savings* from *Account*.

3.6 TEMPLATES

In C++, *templates* are *generic* definitions and can be used for both classes and algorithms. Since certain applications such as sort algorithms and linked lists can be applied to different data types, a template is used to define a generic algorithm or class definition. In the following example, instead of creating different specific implementations for a **swap()** function, a designer uses a *template* in C++ to specify a generic definition:

```
//              SWAP.H Header File
template <class Generic_Type>
void swap( Generic_Type *data1, Generic_Type *data2 )
{
    Generic_Type temp = *data1  ;
    *data1 = *data2 ;
    *data2 = temp  ;
}
```

The **swap()** template instructs the compiler to create the actual function implementation on the basis of the calling function's data types, that is, float, char, integer, *Account*, *Savings*, and so on. In the next example, the **sort_accounts()** client calls the generic **swap()** algorithm to sort a group of accounts on the basis of name. The compiler uses the data types in the function call and instantiates a **swap()** function for the *Account* class:

```
// An example of a template function and an inefficient sort algorithm!
void sort_accounts( Account list[], unsigned short num_accounts )
{
    unsigned short i , j ;

    // swap in the ascending order
    for( i = 0 ; i < num_accounts - 1 ; i++ )
    {
        for( j = 0 ; j < num_accounts - 1 ; j++ )
        {
            if( strcmp( list[ j ].name() , list[ j+1 ].name() ) > 0 )
                swap( &list[ j ] , &list[ j+1 ] ) ;
                // based on the above function call,
                // the compiler creates a Account
                // implementation for swap()
        }
    }
}
```

To use a class or an algorithm with different data types, the designer relinquishes the right to specify the type of data for a class or function definition. The client can then use the generic definition with an appropriate data type. The compiler instantiates the generic definition by generating type-specific executable code based on the identified data type. In the above example, the designer of **swap()** provided the generic algorithm for swapping the contents of two objects and the **sort_accounts()** client specified the actual type of data for **swap()**.

In OOP, *templates* are mainly used for *parameterized* (generic) classes. A linked list is a suitable application of a *parameterized class*. A generic linked list class definition allows the linked list to be used with a variety of data types, such as a bank account and graphical shape objects (Figure 3.11). The class is instantiated when the client specifies the type of object to be maintained by the list. Based on the type of data specified by the client, the compiler creates a custom implementation of the template class for the specified type. In Figure 3.11, the compiler instantiates two versions of the generic linked list. A *parameterized* class allows a design to be reused for different applications. In addition, changes in the design become localized to only one generic definition. This topic is discussed in detail in Chapter 11.

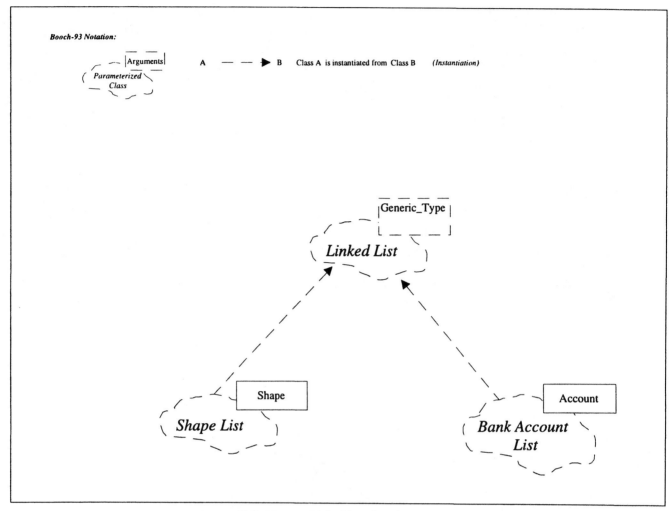

Booch-93 Notation:

FIGURE 3.11   Linked-list class diagram.

SUMMARY

C++ is a modern programming language that has incorporated advanced concepts and features to support the OOD paradigm. C++ features are designed to support OOD in the following areas:

a) Implementing and enforcing *data encapsulation*
b) Automating *object construction* and *destruction*
c) Minimizing changes to the interfaces
d) Enhancing software reusability via *inheritance* and *templates*

A *class* packages related member data and member functions into a standard set. In object-based designs, the member functions hide the internal architecture and representation of data from the clients of the class. This technique is known as *data encapsulation*. Any language that supports data structures can implement the concept of *data encapsulation*. However, to ensure compliance with the design concept, a language must also enforce data encapsulation. In C++, the designer of a class is responsible for the data encapsulation **implementation** and the compiler handles the data encapsulation **enforcement**. By having the C++ compiler enforce the data encapsulation, a designer can implicitly control the actions of his/her clients.

When implementing *data encapsulation*, a design needs to minimize the interaction of external functions with the data members. This is done by building a series of member functions around the class data. To allow a C++ compiler to recognize the member functions, the member function prototypes are incorporated into the data structure's definition.

C++ enforces *encapsulation* by providing three types of *access levels* for the members of a data structure: **private**, **protected**, and **public**. The access levels are specified by the designer. They specify and regulate the *client's* rights. Through the access levels, the C++ compiler detects encapsulation violations by the client. Table 3.1 describes access to the members of a class:

TABLE 3.1   Access Levels and Clients

Access Level	Relationship of Clients
Private	Except for "friend" classes and functions (described in Chapters 5 and 6), other classes do not have access to private members
Protected	Derived classes have access to protected members
Public	The public members can be accessed by a client having any type of relationship: is-a, use-a, has-a, and so on

In C, the initialization and cleanup operations of variables (instances of a structure) have always been the responsibility of the clients. Since the designer of a data structure in C has little control over the actions of the client software, software reliability can be adversely affected owing to improper initialization. If the application fails to initialize the memory space of a variable, software execution behavior may become unpredictable. C++ has addressed the initialization and cleanup issue by making both the compiler and the designer of the data structure responsible for the initialization and the cleanup processes. The designer of a class provides several initialization functions (*constructors*) and a cleanup function (*destructor*) for a data structure. The compiler then automates the data initialization and cleanup processes by associating these functions with the lifetime of the object:

1. **Construction**: The initialization process is linked to the *object* definition. The *constructor* is called when the object comes into scope. The function call automates the object initialization.
2. **Destruction**: When an object goes out of scope, the *destructor* for the class is automatically invoked to clean up the object.

By relieving the client from the construction and destruction tasks, the software reliability is enhanced.

To address software reusability, C++ allows a design to create relationships between classes. For instance, a general bank *Account* class can be directly associated with a *Savings* class. Prior to the advent of C++, the designer of *Savings* had to copy the general bank *Account* header and source files manually and customize them for *Savings* which creates a maintenance nightmare. Through *inheritance*, C++ allows *Savings* to inherit the features of the *Account* class as well as add any unique features for *Savings*. By creating an "*is-a*" relationship, a new design can reuse an already tested design.

C++ provides a basic code generation feature. A design provides a generic definition (*template*) for an algorithm or a class by leaving out the actual data types. The client provides a specific data type and the compiler uses the *template* (*parameterized*) definition to generate an implementation (executable code) based on the specified data type. A *template* is an ideal tool for creating generic sorting and searching routines. By not requiring a unique implementation for every data type, a *template* reduces software development time. Unlike a conventional definition in a library, the *template* definition does not change for new data types because it is independent of the data type. With templates, the software maintainability also improves because changes to the template design are localized to a single template definition.

The C++ features have made this language a far more complex and sophisticated language than C. To use a math analogy, C is to algebra as C++ is to calculus. Even though C++ is commonly referred to as "*a better C*" in the industry, a closer examination shows substantial differences between the two languages. Key C++ features such as inheritance are fundamental in supporting object-oriented software.

GLOSSARY

Access levels

In C++, the **private**, **protected**, and **public** access levels are used to enforce encapsulation by identifying client privileges

Base class

In inheritance, the base class is used to create new classes *(derived)*. The *derived* classes inherit the properties and attributes of the existing class *(base)*

Class

A class is a structured set consisting of data members, and the member functions that can operate on the data members

Constructor

A *member function* that initializes the memory space of an object

Derived class

By inheriting properties and attributes of an existing class *(base)* and adding additional features, a new class *(derived)* emerges from the design

Destructor

A *member function* that performs the internal cleanup operation on an object such as deallocating dynamically allocated memory or closing a file stream. This function is the counterpart of a *constructor*

Member function

A function that can operate freely on the data members of a class and is part of the class design. A member function hides the internal architecture and specifies the operations on the class

Memory leakage

When an object that uses dynamic memory space does not free up its reserved memory space at the time of destruction, the memory space stays reserved. Since the location of the memory space is lost, it cannot be returned to the available memory pool and causes memory leakage

Object

An object is an instance of a class

OOP

An object-oriented program (OOP) consists of a collaboration of objects that are instances of classes. In addition, the objects are based on design hierarchies

Prototype

A function declaration that identifies name, return value's type, number, and types of parameters

Parameterized class

A generic definition, not instantiated until the client provides the needed information. A *parameterized* class is also referred to as a *template* class

Scope resolution

The *scope resolution* operator (::) is used to associate a member to its class by specifying the full signature. The operator appears between the member's name and the class name (example: *Account:: current_balance*)

Template

A generic algorithm or class definition

CHAPTER 4

Basics of C++

INTRODUCTION

In the early 1980s, C++ was developed at AT&T Bell Laboratories by Bjarne Stroustrup. The C programming language was used as the foundation for C++ and is considered a subset of C++ (Figure 4.1). Originally C++ was implemented as a translator (*cfront*), which required that the source files be compiled in two stages. The C++ source files were first translated to C and then compiled using a C compiler. The use of C as the foundation allows previously developed C programs to be reused in C++ software projects. This enables software reuse and makes the transition to C++ smoother. Thus, existing software projects can evolve into C++ and object-oriented programming (OOP).

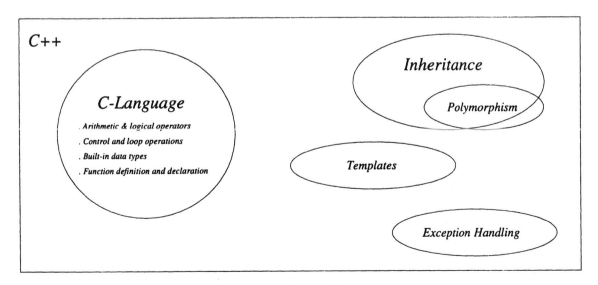

FIGURE 4.1 C++ venn diagram.

To create a basic foundation for the subsequent chapters, this chapter focuses on C++. By assuming the reader is already familiar with C, this chapter provides an overview of the following basic components of C++ and the *Stream I/O class* library:

1. Brief description of the *Stream I/O class* library
2. Description of documentation style and syntax
3. Defining constant "*read-only*" variables as an alternative to **#defines**
4. Using a *reference* data type for simplifying data manipulation
5. Object lifetime and visibility in C++
6. Prevention of name collisions through the use of **namespace**
7. Type-safe casting in C++

For illustrating the above features, this chapter primarily uses a simple *Circle* object. A *Circle* is represented by a **center** and a radius (**r**) (Figure 4.2). The **center** is represented using the *Point* class, which may be based on a *Cartesian* (x,y) or *Polar* (r,theta) coordinate system (Figure 4.3). By using *Point*, the *Circle* class utilizes the features and attributes provided by the *Point* class in representing its **center** instead of implementing them from scratch. The radius (**r**) is a floating point data type (that is, a built-in data type) and therefore does not appear as a class in the diagram. In Figure 4.3, the *Circle* and *Point* classes form a "*has-a*" relationship. *Circle* hides from its clients the use of the *Point* class, which is denoted by the **private** export control. The member functions of *Circle* regulate access to the **center** and radius (**r**) data members and hide the algorithms for computing the area and circumference of *Circle*. Since *Circle* uses one instance of *Point* for representing its **center**, the two classes form a *one-to-one cardinality*: for every instance of a *Circle* there will be one instance of *Point*.

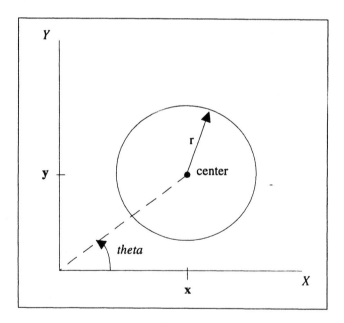

FIGURE 4.2   Circle data representation.

Figures 4.4 and 4.5 depict the contents of *Circle* class header and source files. The class definition and the member function definitions are separated into different files, which underscores the separation of the design interface from the implementation. The header file specifies the design interface for the *Circle* class library (Figure 4.4). Client class libraries use the features described in the **public** interface of the class definition to operate on *Circle* objects. In addition, the C++ compiler uses the class definition to identify the size and usage of memory space for *Circle* objects and to enforce data encapsulation. Figure 4.5 shows the contents of the *Circle* source file, which contains the member function definitions. This implementation hides the details of *Circle* from its clients and also hides the computational algorithm for the **area()** and **circumference()** functions.

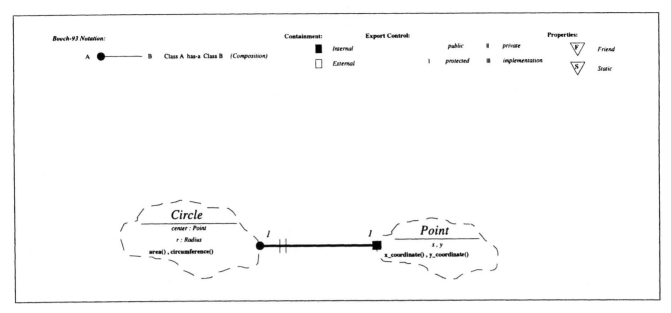

FIGURE 4.3 Circle class diagram.

4.1 STREAM I/O CLASS LIBRARY

The *Stream I/O Class* (**iostream**) library has been introduced with C++ and is a replacement for the *Standard I/O* (**stdio**) library. The new library has numerous features and benefits not supported by its C library counterpart. The new *Stream I/O Class* library supports string, file, and console I/O. This section provides a brief tutorial introduction on the basics of the *Stream I/O Class* library. For a more detailed discussion, the reader should refer to a C++ compiler reference manual.

The *Stream I/O Class* library is similar in concept to the C-Language's *Standard I/O* (**stdio**) library. The *Stream I/O Class* library is based on a buffered I/O scheme and treats the display and keyboard as streams. The class library uses the following names for the standard I/O streams:

1. Standard input: **cin**
2. Standard output: **cout**
3. Standard error (unbuffered): **cerr**
4. Standard error (buffered): **clog**

Data are sent to an output stream, such as a file, by using the *stream output* operator (<<). Data is read from an input stream using the *stream input* operator (>>). Kernighan and Ritchie's famous *"hello, world"* example is reimplemented in C++ by sending the string to the standard output stream (**cout**) [Kernighan and Ritchie 1988]:

```
#include <iostream.h>    // Stream I/O Class Library

int main( int , char ** )

{
        cout << "hello, world \n" ;

        return( 0 ) ;
}
```

Unlike the **stdio** library, the *Stream I/O Class* library is type safe. The compiler invokes the applicable functions for the data type being operated on and relieves the designer from having to specify the data types. For example, the **fprintf()** and **fscanf()** function (Standard I/O) arguments must match the data type definitions in the *data format control strings*:

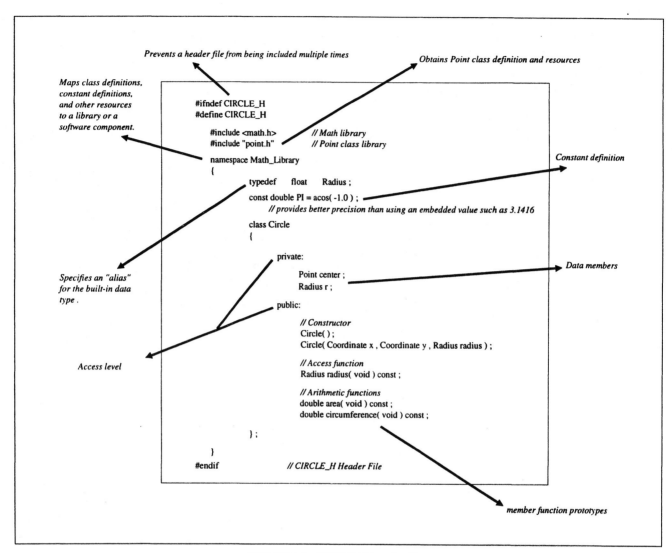

FIGURE 4.4   CIRCLE.H header file.

```
//                 Test Driver Source File
#include <stdio.h>            // Standard Header File
#include "circle.h"           // Math Library

int main( int , char ** )
{
        Circle c1( 1 , 3 , 4.0 ) ;

        printf("\n\t Radius: %f", c1.radius( ) ) ;
                // radius's type and control string ( %f ) have to match

        return( 0 ) ;
}
```

The implementation and interfaces provided by the *Standard I/O* library require the developer to ensure that the built-in data type definitions match the ones specified in the *control string* of the **fprintf()** and **fscanf()** functions. Should the data types change, the programmer must manually search through the *Standard I/O*

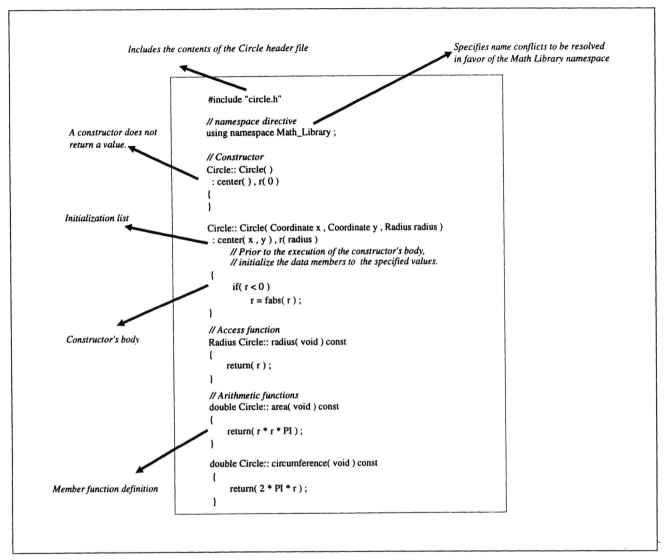

Includes the contents of the Circle header file

Specifies name conflicts to be resolved in favor of the Math Library namespace

A constructor does not return a value.

Initialization list

Constructor's body

Member function definition

```
#include "circle.h"

// namespace directive
using namespace Math_Library ;

// Constructor
Circle:: Circle( )
  : center( ) , r( 0 )
{
}

Circle:: Circle( Coordinate x , Coordinate y , Radius radius )
  : center( x , y ) , r( radius )
    // Prior to the execution of the constructor's body,
    // initialize the data members to the specified values.
{
    if( r < 0 )
        r = fabs( r ) ;
}

// Access function
Radius Circle:: radius( void ) const
{
    return( r ) ;
}

// Arithmetic functions
double Circle:: area( void ) const
{
    return( r * r * PI ) ;
}

double Circle:: circumference( void ) const
{
    return( 2 * PI * r ) ;
}
```

FIGURE 4.5 CIRCLE.CPP source file.

function calls, such as **printf()** and **scanf()**, and modify the control strings to match the new data types. This process is time consuming, tedious, and error prone.

When using the *Stream I/O Class* library, the compiler automatically selects the floating point display function in order to display the value returned by **radius()**, which is of type float. A designer need not worry about checking the data types. In the following example, the character string message is sent to standard output followed by the value returned by **radius()**:

```
cout << "\n\t Radius: " << c1.radius( ) ;
```

The *stream output* operator (<<) sends data to the console in several steps. Initially a string output function is called to output the character string ("\n\t Radius:"). This call is followed by another call to a floating point stream output function. The output operation is broken into several stages and function calls are cascaded.

Input operation is similar to output operation, except that the *stream input* operator (>>) is used instead. In the following example, the program displays an input message string on the console, the program then reads the value entered on the standard input stream (keyboard), converts the data to floating point, and stores it in *radius*. Then an instance of *Circle* is created using the value specified by *radius*. The **Circle:: radius()** access function is then used to send this value to the console:

```
//              Test Driver Source File
#include <iostream.h>           // Stream I/O Class Library
#include "circle.h"             // Math Library

int main( int , char ** )
{
        Radius radius ;

        cout << "\n Input Value of Radius: " ;
        cin >> radius ;

        Circle c1( 0 , 0 , radius ) ;
                // create an instance of Circle located at origin (0,0)
                // using the specified radius
        cout << "\n Radius: " << c1.radius() ;
                // display radius on the console

        return( 0 ) ;
}
```

Using the type of the data, the compiler incorporates a call to the applicable *Stream I/O* function in the executable code. The *Stream I/O* class library's notation is extremely useful when the data types change.

The *Stream I/O* class library provides stream input and output functions for all built-in data types. In C++, the *Stream I/O* operators can also be overloaded for classes, which provides a standard stream I/O notation for both built-in data types and classes. Operator overloading is discussed in detail in Chapter 6.

4.2 COMMENTS

In addition to the /* *comment* */ symbols in C, C++ provides the // symbol for *single-line* comments. The compiler ignores all text beginning with the // symbol to the end of the line. The new comment delimiter simplifies documentation for single comment lines, and enhances debugging by allowing a code block that has nested comments to be commented out without the need of removing the // comment delimiters:

```
//              Test Driver Source File
#include <iostream.h>           // C++ I/O Stream Library
#include "circle.h"             // math library

int main( int , char ** )
{
        /*
        ** The traditional commenting still can be used.
        */
        cout << "\n\t Welcome to C++" << endl ;
                // replacement for formatted output, such as printf()
/*
**   the new comment delimiter allows a commented code block to be
**   commented out during software debugging (nested comments).
        Radius radius ;
        // prompt the user for radius of circle
        cout << "\n\t Input Radius of Circle: " ;
        cin >> radius ;        // obtain radius from console (keyboard)

        Circle c1( 0 , 0 , radius ) ;
        cout << "\n\t PI: " << PI ;  // output results
```

```
                cout << "\n Radius: " << c1.radius() ;
                                  // display radius on the console
                cout << "\n\t Area = " << c1.area() ;
                                  // compute area of the circle
  */
                return( 0 ) ; // Normal termination
  }
```

C++ permits nested comments by allowing a *single-line* comment to be nested within a comment block. In the above example, the *Circle* object manipulation and stream I/O code block have been commented out without any modifications to the existing comment delimiters.

4.3 CLASS DEFINITION

A class is either defined by the **struct** or the **class** keyword. The **struct** keyword is used for compatibility with programs written in C. The **class** keyword allowed C++ to evolve without distorting the C-Language's **struct**. In C++, both keywords may be used for data structures.

Many C programs have been implemented on the basis of design models other than the OOD paradigm. To provide the ability to reuse C libraries in C++ projects, the definitions associated with a **struct** are considered *public* unless another access level (that is, *private* keyword) has been utilized:

```
typedef        float        Coordinate ;
typedef        float        Radius ;
struct Point
{
        Coordinate x , y ;        // members are public by default
} ;

struct Circle
{
        Point center ;           // members are public by default
        Radius r ;
} ;
```

Since C++ has been developed around the OOD paradigm and the **class** keyword is not native to C, it does not need to follow the same logic as **struct** and defaults to the *private* access level to promote data encapsulation:

```
class Point
{
        Coordinate x , y ;        // members are private by default
} ;
```

Since the above *Point* definitions do not explicitly define the member data access levels, the compiler will use the default access levels: **private** for *class* and **public** for *structure*. However, for clarity, access levels should be explicitly defined at all times. In the following example, the *Circle* class explicitly specifies its **private** and **public** design interfaces. By using the **private** access level, the data representation (such as the use of *Point*) has been encapsulated from the client (Figure 4.4). The **public** member functions regulate access to data and abstract their internal algorithms:

```
//            CIRCLE.H Header File
#ifndef CIRCLE_H  // if CIRCLE_H has not been defined then
#define CIRCLE_H  //      define CIRCLE_H and include file contents
                  // prevents Circle header file from being included more than once
```

```
// Include the header files of other libraries necessary for Circle
#include <math.h>           // Math Library: need acos() declaration
#include "point.h"          // Point Class definition: for center

typedef       float          Radius ;
const double PI      =       acos( -1.0 ) ;

class Circle
{
      private:
              Point center ;          // Using Point class
              Radius r ;
      public:
              // Constructor
              Circle( ) ;
              Circle( Coordinate x, Coordinate y , Radius radius ) ;

              // Access function
              Radius radius( void ) const ;

              // Arithmetic functions
              double area( void ) const ;
              double circumference( void ) const ;
      } ;

#endif            // CIRCLE_H Header File
```

In the above example, the **#ifndef** preprocessor directive prevents a header file from being directly or indirectly included more than once. Since the *Circle* class utilizes the resources of the *Math* and *Point* class libraries, the header files for these libraries are being included in the **CIRCLE.H** header file. By automatically including these files, the clients of *Circle* are relieved from including the support files manually in their header and source files. At the implementation level, this approach reduces the coupling of client source files with *Circle's* header files. For example, if the data representation for *Circle* changes and the *Point* class becomes unnecessary, the client's source files remain unaffected when the reference to *Point* and its header file in the **CIRCLE.H** header file is removed.

The *Circle* member functions are implemented in the corresponding **CIRCLE.CPP** source file:

```
//              CIRCLE.CPP Source File
#include "circle.h"              // Math Library

// Access function
Radius Circle:: radius( void ) const
{
      return( r ) ;
}

// Arithmetic functions
double Circle:: area( void ) const
{
      return( r * r * PI ) ;
}

double Circle:: circumference( void ) const
{
```

```
        return( 2 * PI * r ) ;
}

// Constructors
Circle:: Circle( )
    : center( ) , r( 0 )          // initialization list
    // should initialize data members before executing the body of
    // constructor using the applicable initialization function
{
    // do-nothing body: nothing else to do to create a Circle object
}

Circle:: Circle( Coordinate x, Coordinate y , Radius radius )
    : center( x , y ) , r( radius )
{
    // if radius is negative => take absolute value
    if( r < 0 )
    {
        r = (Radius) fabs( r ) ;
    }
}
```

In the above example, the **Circle()** constructor uses an *initialization list* for initializing the data members. For the *user-defined value* constructor, *r* is initialized using the value specified by *radius*. *Center* is initialized by calling the **Point()** *user-defined value constructor* and passing *x* and *y* to it. The interactions between the constructors are illustrated in Figure 4.6. An *initialization list* is used for a variety of reasons:

1. **Predictable State**: The *initialization list* guarantees that data members are in predictable states before the constructor body is executed. This feature becomes extremely important for classes whose constructor must perform complex initialization tasks.

   By having the data members in a predictable state, the constructor can complete the initialization process by using the information stored in them. For instance, the *user-defined value constructor* checks the value of radius supplied by the client to ensure it is not negative.

2. **Composition**: For classes that use *composition* ("*has-a*" relationship), such as *Circle*, the class member functions do not have access to the private data members of their composed data members. For instance, *Circle* does not have access to the **private** members of *Point*: *x, y*.

   The *initialization list* provides an interfacing mechanism between the constructors of *Circle* and *Point*. In the above example, the **Circle()** constructor calls the applicable *Point* constructor to initialize its *center*.

After the initialization list is processed, the constructor's body is executed, as shown in Figure 4.6. Chapter 5 provides a more detailed discussion on a constructor's *initialization list*.

4.4 CONSTANTS

During the software life cycle, constants can change as requirements change. When the value of an embedded constant is changed, a designer must review each source file manually for occurrences of the embedded constant and change the value at the appropriate places. This process is tedious and time consuming. Furthermore, use of embedded constants can lead to reliability problems. For example, if a designer forgets to change one of the occurrences of the embedded constant, the program may not behave as expected. A designer should avoid using embedded constants:

```
area = 3.1416 * radius * radius ; // poor programming practice
```

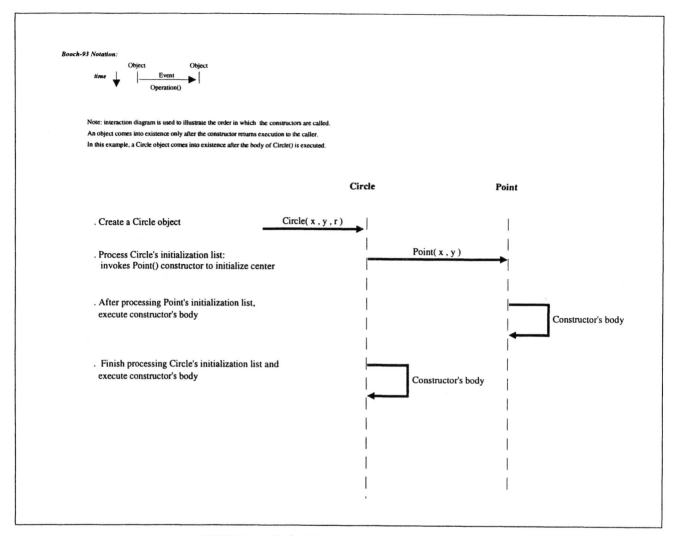

FIGURE 4.6 Circle object creation interaction diagram.

In the above example, the numerical value of PI has been embedded in the source code. If this value is used in many places in the program and the designer wishes to increase the precision of PI, modifying all the occurrences of PI will be time consuming.

The constant definition tools in C++ play an important role in developing maintainable code:

1. **Preprocessor Constant**: A symbolic name is associated with a constant value. The **#define** preprocessor statement is a symbolic definition and is replaced by the actual value during compilation. The compiler replaces the symbolic names by their literal values in the function's body. The literal value becomes part of the executable code and resides in the program memory space. Therefore, a value defined by the **#define** preprocessor is not accessible to a debugger at run-time.

```
#define  PI   3.1416
// PI is symbolic name which is replaced by the specified
// value at compile time.
```

2. **Enumerated Lists**: An enumerated list is a set of constants that are logically grouped together.

```
enum Color
{
```

```
            BLUE, RED , YELLOW
                // BLUE = 0 , RED = 1, YELLOW = 2
    } ;
```

3. Constant Data: C++ provides *constant data* through the **const** keyword:

```
const    data_type    constant_name =    value ;
```

Constant variables are applicable to both built-in data types (for example, float) and classes. The **const** keyword denotes that the object is a constant and its value cannot be changed after it is initialized. Conceptually, a constant object resides in the *read-only* area of memory. The following example uses the constant definition for PI:

```
const     double PI = 3.1416 ;        // a read-only variable
```

Since *constant data* uses the data memory space, it is visible to a debugger. A *constant data* definition is therefore a better alternative to **#define**.

Through the above constant definition tools, symbolic names such as PI are assigned to constants. The symbolic names are then used in the source files instead of the hard-coded values. During compilation, the compiler substitutes the symbolic names with their defined values. Constant definitions are normally placed in header files. If the software evolves and constant values are changed, the changes are localized to the constant definitions in the header files. The source files remain unaffected and need only to be recompiled. The compiler guarantees that the changes to the constants are reflected in the executable code, and the process of updating constants is simpler.

A constant variable is accessed in the same way as a regular variable. In the following example, the **area()** function calculates the area of a circle. PI is evaluated once by calling the arc-cosine function before the execution of the **main()** function. As a programming guideline, define constants using upper case letters and variables using lower case letters. This coding style improves readability by magnifying the distinction between variables and constants:

```
//             CIRCLE.H Header File
#ifndef CIRCLE_H
#define CIRCLE_H

    #include <math.h>        // Math Library: need acos() declaration
    #include "point.h"       // Point Class definition: for center
    typedef     float        Radius ;
    const double PI =  acos( -1.0 ) ;
    // const is better than #define PI acos(-1.0) or #define PI 3.1416

    class Circle
    {
        private:
                Point center ;
                Radius r ;
        public:
                double area( void ) const ;
                double circumference( void ) const ;

                // Other details left out
    } ;

#endif          // CIRCLE_H Header File
```

```
#endif// CIRCLE_H Header File
```

```
//                    CIRCLE.CPP Source File
#include "circle.h"              // Math Library

double Circle:: area( void ) const
{
      return( r * r * PI ) ;
              // at run-time, PI is accessed
}

double Circle:: circumference( void ) const
{
      return( 2 * PI * r ) ;
              // at run-time, PI is accessed
}
```

When **area()** or **circumference()** is called, the function accesses PI (constant variable) to compute the circle's area and circumference. Since the above constant variable has been evaluated only once, the use of constant data improves software performance. If the designer had used the **#define** preprocessor statement instead, the compiler would have replaced each symbolic definition with a call to the arc-cosine function:

```
return( r * r * acos( -1.0 ) ) ;
```

With this implementation, the arc-cosine function would be called every time the functions were executed. Since the arc-cosine function is a floating point arithmetic function, which is time consuming, the performance would be degraded.

In C++, pointers can point to constant data or can be constant pointers themselves (Figure 4.7):

```
char * const logo = "C++ is Cool" ;
          // conceptually, logo resides in read-only memory (logo cannot
          // be reassigned). The data pointed to by logo can be modified.

const  char *header = "C++ is Cool" ;
          // header can be reassigned and the data cannot because
          // it resides in read-only memory space.

const char * const name = "C++ is Cool" ;
          // conceptually, name and data reside in read-only memory space
          // and neither can be changed.
```

4.5 FUNCTION OVERLOADING

C++ supports *function overloading* by allowing multiple functions to use the same name. The compiler distinguishes the appropriate function by examining the number and type of arguments in the function call. Using function overloading, a class can support a series of constructor functions:

```
//                    POINT.H Header File
#ifndef POINT_H
#define POINT_H
```

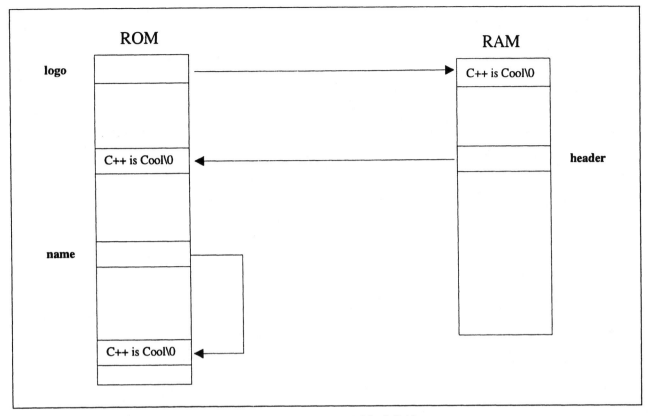

FIGURE 4.7 Constant variable definitions.

```
typedef    float        Coordinate ;
class Point
{
      private:
            Coordinate x , y ;
      public:
            // Constructors
            Point( Coordinate new_x, Coordinate new_y ) ;
            Point( Coordinate new_x ) ;
                          // user-defined values constructors
            Point( ) ;    // default constructor

            // Class access functions
            Coordinate x_coordinate( void ) const ;
            Coordinate y_coordinate( void ) const ;
            // Other function declarations are left out

      } ;

#endif            // POINT_H Header File
```

The above *Point* class declares three constructor functions. The function definitions are included in the following section:

1. **User-Defined Values Constructors**: These two initialize the object to the client-defined values.
2. **Default Constructor**: Initializes the object to default values, for example, (0,0).

types of data in the initialization list to resolve the function calls:

```
//                      Test Driver Source File
#include "point.h"

int main( int , char ** )
{
        Point p1 , p2( 3,4 ) , p3( 1 )  ;
        // p1 is initialized to default values using Point( ) constructor
        // p2 is initialized to (3,4) using
        //    Point( Coordinate,Coordinate ) constructor
        // p3 is initialized to (1,0) using
        //    Point( Coordinate ) constructor

        // other details are left out
        return( 0 ) ;
}
```

For overloaded functions, the arguments must differ in number and/or data type. Functions cannot also be overloaded solely on their return type. The following is an illegal overloading:

```
//          PORT.H Header File
class Port
{
    public:
            short receive( char *buffer, unsigned short buffer_size ) ;
            float receive( char *buffer, unsigned short buffer_size ) ;
                    // illegal overloading, overloaded only on return type
    private:
            // Other details left out
} ;
```

```
//          Test Driver Source File
#include "port.h"
#define MESSAGE_BUFFER_SIZE          100

int test_port( void )
{
        Port port1 ;
        char message[MESSAGE_BUFFER_SIZE];

        port1.receive( message, MESSAGE_BUFFER_SIZE) ;
                    // this is ambiguous!
        // other details are left out
}
```

In the above program, the compiler cannot identify which version of **receive**() should be called. While syntactically legal, the above function call is ambiguous and the compiler will generate an error message.

4.6 FUNCTION PARAMETERS

During a function call, a copy of the object (call-by-value) or its address (pointer) is passed to a function. In addition to call-by-value and call-by-address, C++ provides a call-by-reference.

4.6 FUNCTION PARAMETERS

During a function call, a copy of the object (call-by-value) or its address (pointer) is passed to a function. In addition to call-by-value and call-by-address, C++ provides a call-by-reference.

4.6.1 Call-by-Value

For classes, passing a copy can be a time-consuming operation. In the following example, the *Point* class uses the Cartesian coordinate (x,y) system to represent a data point (Figure 4.8). The implementation of the **add()** function for this class obtains a copy of the passed point object. The original object's content must be copied to the stack (Figure 4.9):

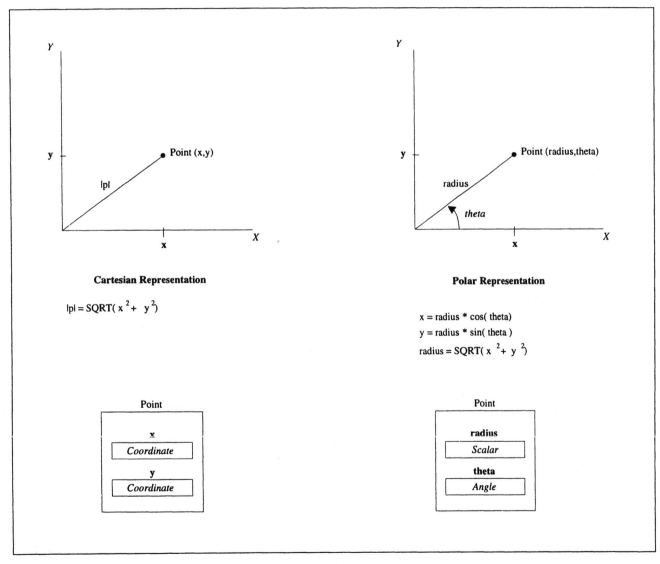

FIGURE 4.8   Point data representation.

```
//        POINT.H Header File
#ifndef POINT_H
#define POINT_H
```

```
        typedef        float          Coordinate ;

        class Point
        {
              private:
                    Coordinate x , y ;

              public:
                    Point() ;            // Default constructor
                    Point(Coordinate new_x, Coordinate new_y) ;
                                         // User-defined value constructor
                    // Access Functions
                    Coordinate x_coordinate( void ) const ;
                    Coordinate y_coordinate( void ) const ;

                    // Arithmetic Functions
                    Point add( Point p ) const ;
        } ;

#endif              // POINT_H Header File


//          POINT.CPP Source File
#include "point.h"

Coordinate Point:: x_coordinate( void ) const
{
      return( x ) ;
}

Coordinate Point:: y_coordinate( void ) const
{
      return( y ) ;
}

// Arithmetic functions: only addition is presented
Point Point:: add( Point p ) const
{
      // add x coordinates of this and p objects
      Coordinate new_x = x_coordinate() + p.x_coordinate() ;

      // add y coordinates of this and p objects
      Coordinate new_y = y_coordinate() + p.y_coordinate() ;

      // store the result in a temporary Point
      Point result( new_x, new_y ) ;
      return ( result ) ; // return result of the Point addition
}

Point:: Point()
      : x( 0 ) , y ( 0 )  // initialize to default values
{
}

// user-defined value constructor
Point:: Point(Coordinate new_x, Coordinate new_y)
      : x ( new_x ) , y( new_y )
{
}
```

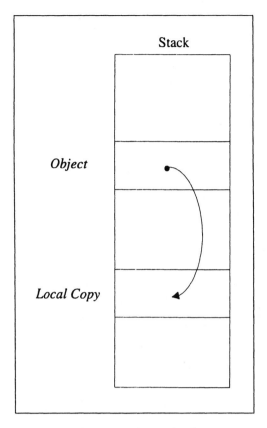

FIGURE 4.9 Access levels.

A copy of a *Point* object is passed to the **add( )** function. In the following example, before this function is called, the contents of *p2* (*x* and *y* data elements) are copied onto the stack, thus creating a copy of it (Figure 4.10). The **add( )** function operates on a copy and cannot modify the original *p2* object. Thus, all operations are local to the copy:

```
//              Test Driver Source File
#include <stdio.h>
#include "point.h"

int main( int , char ** )
{
    Point p1(2,3) , p2 (1,4) , p3 ;
        .
    p3 = p1.add( p2 ) ;
        // make a copy of p2 by using the Point() copy constructor
        // and pass the copy on the stack
}
```

Even though the integrity of the original *p2* is not affected by **add()**, the overhead associated with pass-by-value (copy) for a user defined object can be high. Before the function call, the contents of the object must be copied onto the *stack*, which consumes processing time and memory space. However, *p1* is passed through the "**this**" pointer (Figure 4.10).

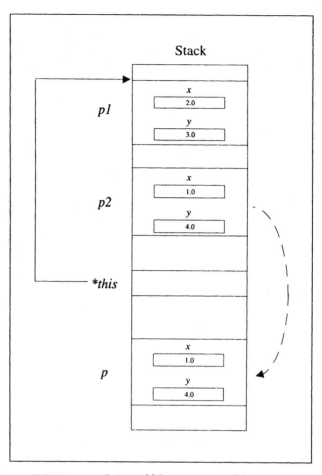

FIGURE 4.10   Point::add () parameter call-by-value.

4.6.2 Call-by-Address

Instead of passing a copy of an object to a function, the address of an object or the beginning of an array can be passed (Figure 4.11). A *pointer* eliminates the overhead associated with passing a copy of the object. When pointers are used the function gets a copy of the object's address from the calling function. For pass-by-address (pointer), a function has access to the original object and therefore has the ability to modify the object.

In the following example, the **add()** function's interface has been changed to use a pointer implementation. The address of the calling function's object is passed to this function:

```
//              POINT.H Header File
typedef         float       Coordinate ;

class Point
{
      private:
            Coordinate x , y ;

      public:
            // Arithmetic Functions
            Point add( const Point *p ) const ;

            // Other details left out
} ;
```

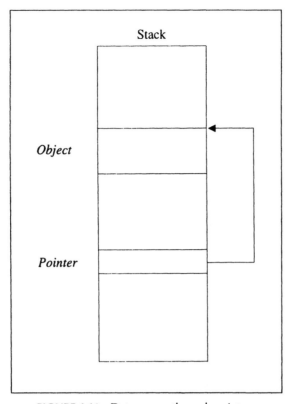

FIGURE 4.11 Data access through pointers.

The **const** keyword is used in the function's interface in order to limit access to the calling function's objects. The function has read-only permission because the data pointed to by *p* has been declared as read-only and cannot be changed (Figure 4.12). In addition, the **const** keyword at the end of the **add( )** function declaration denotes that the "**this**" pointer only has read permission. The use of the **const** keyword ensures that data integrity is maintained. It also tells the client that the above operation does not change the state of the object. Finally, it tells the compiler to detect inadvertent write operations and data access violations.

```
//            POINT.CPP Source File
#include "point.h"

// arithmetic functions: only addition is presented
Point Point:: add( const Point *p ) const
{
      // add x coordinates of this and p objects
      Coordinate new_x = x_coordinate() + p->x_coordinate() ;

      // add y coordinates of this and p objects
      Coordinate new_y = y_coordinate() + p->y_coordinate() ;

      // store the result in a temporary point
      Point result( new_x, new_y ) ;

      return ( result ) ; // return result of the point addition
}

//            Test Driver Source File
#include "point.h"
```

```
int main( int , char ** )
{
          Point p1(2,3) , p2 (1,4) , p3 ;
              .
          p3 = p1.add( &p2 ) ;
                // pass the address of p2 on the stack

}
```

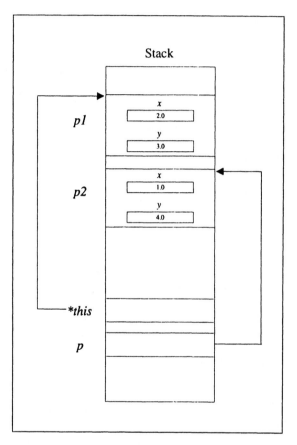

FIGURE 4.12   Point::add() parameter access.

4.6.3 Call-by-Reference

The necessity for explicit pointer referencing and dereferencing has been the main complaint against C by software developers. A designer must use the *reference* operator (&) to get the variable's address, and the *dereference* operator (*) to access the content of a built-in data variable. If the designer does not use the reference (&) and dereference (*) operators properly, the program's behavior will be unpredictable. The continuous referencing and dereferencing operations associated with pointers force a software developer to become familiar with the low-level details of data storage in memory. In addition, functions returning an address cannot be dereferenced on the left-hand side of an *assignment* operator (=) immediately after the function call. Instead, the calling function must store the address being returned in a pointer variable and dereference it in subsequent statements:

```
float * get_record(void) ;
float *temp ;
temp = get_record() ;
      // call function and store the record's address in a temp pointer
*temp = 0 ; // initialize the record to 0
```

```
// the record initialization was a two step process:
// 1. get address
// 2. initialize
```

C++ has expanded the language data access capability by introducing a new data access methodology. The new data access methodology addresses the complexities associated with pointers and is known as the *reference* data type:

```
data_type    &reference_name = data_object ;
```

A *reference_name* is an alias for the *data_object*. For instance, "Jim" is an alias for "James" and both names may be used to refer to the same person. In the following example, the *Point* class has been reimplemented using the reference notation:

```
//              POINT.H Header File
typedef         float        Coordinate ;

class Point
{
        private:
                Coordinate x , y ;

        public:
                // Arithmetic Functions
                Point add( const Point &p ) const ;

                // Other detail left out
} ;
```

When **add()** is called, *p* becomes an alias for the object being passed. Operations on *p* affect the caller's object. The *reference* data type uses the efficiency of pointers with the clear notation of copies. Unlike pointers, the data access and manipulation is transparent to the programmer since the use of *reference* (&) and *dereference* (*) operators has been eliminated. A reference makes the C++ compiler responsible for pointer initialization and manipulation, thus relieving the software developer of these tasks.

```
//              Test Driver Source File
#include "point.h"

int main( int , char ** )
{
        Point p1(2,3) , p2 (1,4) , p3 ;
        .
        p3 = p1.add( p2 ) ;
                // pass the address of p2 to the add() function
}
```

In the following example, the address of the *Point* object is passed to the **add()** function and is similar to the example in the previous section (Figure 4.12). Since *p* has access to the original object, the **const** keyword is again used so that the *Point* reference has read permission only. A reference to a user-defined object allows the programmer to use the *dot* operator (.) to operate on the data elements and, unlike a pointer, a *reference* does not need to be dereferenced and is easier to read:

```
//              POINT.CPP Source File
#include "point.h"
```

```
// arithmetic functions: only addition is presented
Point Point:: add( const Point &p ) const
{
     // add x coordinates of this and p objects
     Coordinate new_x = x_coordinate() + p.x_coordinate() ;

     // add y coordinates of this and p objects
     Coordinate new_y = y_coordinate() + p.y_coordinate() ;

     // store the result in a temporary point
     Point result( new_x, new_y) ;

     return ( result ) ; // return result of the point addition
}
```

C++ applies certain restrictions to a reference. For example, a reference parameter cannot be reassigned within the function: the *p* reference cannot be reassigned to another *Point* object within the **add()** function. A reassignment is an attempt to use an alias for another object. As an analogy, if "Bob" is an alias for "Robert" and is later used for "Bobby" in a conversation, it will be difficult to understand which person is being referred to by "Bob."

A function must not return references to its local objects because the local variables are destroyed after the function returns control back to the caller. If this is done, the program's behavior will be unpredictable. The **add()** function, shown below, returns a reference to *result*, which is a local object. The operation is meaningless and will cause unpredictable behavior since *result* is destroyed after the **add()** function returns control to the calling function:

```
Point & Point:: add( const Point &p ) const
{
     Coordinate new_x = x_coordinate() + p.x_coordinate() ;
     Coordinate new_y = y_coordinate() + p.y_coordinate() ;

     // store the result in a temporary point
     Point result( new_x , new_y ) ;

     return ( result ) ; // will cause unpredictable results
}
```

An ANSI C++ compiler's language reference manual identifies additional restrictions that have been placed on a reference type.

The reference plays an important role in cascading operations. For example, it is used most extensively in the *Stream I/O Class* library. By returning a reference to a nonlocal object back to the calling function, the reference can be used immediately on the left-hand side of the assignment operator or reused in cascaded and pipelined operations. Later chapters examine this property in more detail.

4.7 DYNAMIC MEMORY ALLOCATION

Dynamic memory allocation is used in applications for which the amount of memory required for objects is not known at compile time.

The C compiler handles only static memory allocation for objects. Dynamic memory allocation is handled by the *Dynamic Memory Allocation* (**malloc**) library. A library is not considered part of the language and is a supporting software tool. C++ has taken control over dynamic memory allocation and pulled this process into the language with the **new** and **delete** operators. These operators give C++ full control over memory management. Therefore, both static and dynamic memory allocations have the same characteristics and behavior.

Consider the following program, in **main**(), the size of an array of circles is determined at run time by calling **num_shapes**(). The program then dynamically allocates an array to hold *length* elements (Figure 4.13). The starting location of the array is stored in *list*. After the program completes processing the data, the *Circle* array pointed to by *list* is deallocated.

```
//            Test Driver Source File
#include "circle.h"        // Circle Class Library

// function declarations
unsigned short num_shapes( void ) ;

#define ERROR -1

int main( int , char ** )
{
        int status_code = 0 ;
        Circle *list ;
        unsigned short length ;

        // identify number of current circle shapes
        length = num_shapes() ;
```

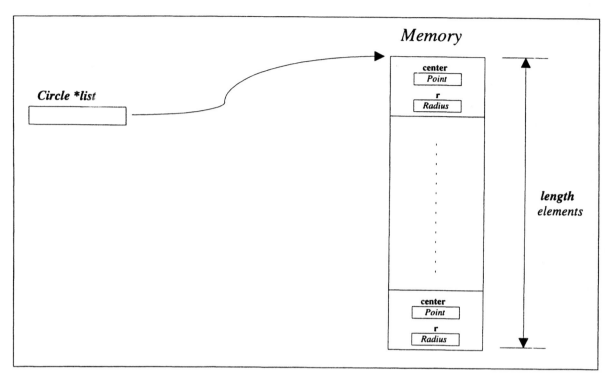

FIGURE 4.13 Data access through pointers.

```
// allocate a Circle array using "length" as dimension
list = new Circle[ length ] ;
if( list ) // if allocation is successful
{
        // operate on list of circles
}
else
{
        status_code = ERROR ; // dynamic allocation failure
}

delete [ ] list ; // call destructor for every element & deallocate list

return( status_code ) ;
}
```

In the above example, the compiler recognizes the dynamic allocation request and incorporates calls to the *default* constructor. At run time, when the program execution reaches the **new[ ]** operator, the memory space for the array is dynamically allocated and the default constructor is called "*length*" number of times to initialize each element of the array. Similarly, prior to deallocation of the array, the destructor is called "*length*" number of times in the reverse order to clean up the *Circle* objects and then the **delete[ ]** operator is used to deallocate the memory space occupied by the array.

Chapter 7 provides a detailed discussion on dynamic memory allocation.

4.8 OBJECT VISIBILITY AND LIFETIME IN C++

In C++, the declaration of an object determines its *visibility* and *lifetime*:

1. **Visibility**: Identifies where an object is accessible in a source file. For example, a local object is visible or accessible in the function in which it is defined.

2. **Lifetime**: Identifies when an object is created and when it ceases to exist. An object is created when its constructor is called and is destroyed when the destructor is called.

An object's *visibility* and *lifetime* in C++ are similar to their counterparts in C:

1. **External Object**: A global (extern) object's *lifetime* is throughout the execution of the program. The object is initialized using a constructor function prior to the execution of the **main()** function. After execution of the **main()** function is complete, and prior to the return of control to the operating system, the global objects are destroyed using their destructor functions.

```
#include "point.h"
Point p1(3,4) ;
        // using user-defined values constructor, initialize p1 prior
        // to execution of main

int main( int, char ** )
{
        // function's body
}
```

In the above example, the lifetime of *p1* begins with its initialization before the execution of the **main()** function. *p1* ceases to exist after the execution of the **main()** function is completed.

A global object is *visible* to all of the source files as long as the functions manipulating the object have access to the object's declaration. In the above example, *p1* is global and is accessible by the source files containing the following declaration:

extern Point p1 ;

2. **Static Objects**: The initialization of static objects depends on where the object is defined. Static objects defined outside a function are global in that source file and are visible only to the functions in that file. These objects are initialized using their constructor functions prior to the execution of the **main()** function. If the static object is defined within a function, the static object is initialized the first time the function is entered, but it is visible only to that particular function.

Static objects are similar to external objects and they cease to exist after the **main()** function's execution is finished. Prior to return of control to the operating system, the destructors are invoked to clean up the static objects.

```
static Point p1(3,4) ;
        // lifetime: construct before main() & destroy after main()
        // visibility: from point of definition to the end of the source file

int process_point_data( void )
{
        static Point p2 ;
        // lifetime:constructed first time the function is entered
        // and destroyed after main() function is exited
        // visibility:from point of definition to the end of the
        // code block, in this case, the
        // process_point_data() function.
}
```

p1 is accessible by all the functions in the source file, but **p2** is accessible only by **process_point_data()**.

3. **Local Objects**: Local objects are initialized by a constructor when the block of code containing the object's definition is entered. After the program's execution leaves a code block (denoted by braces), the local

objects associated with the code block are destroyed. Local objects are visible only in the block of code where they are defined.

```
int process_point_data( void )
{
        Point p1( 2 , 3 ) ;
        // lifetime:constructed at the point of definition
        // and destroyed after the function is exited
        // visibility:from point of definition to the end of the
        // code block (in this case, the function)
        // display the (x,y) values on the display console
        cout << "\n\t p1 (x,y) =  (" << p1.x_position() <<
                    << ',' << p1.y_position() << ")\n" ;
}
```

Table 4.1 summarizes the *visibility* and *lifetime* of objects, based on their definitions.

TABLE 4.1 Object Visibility and Lifetime

Type	Visibility	Lifetime
Extern (global)	As long as the object is declared in the source file, the object is visible in that file	Object is created prior to the execution of **main()** and is destroyed after the execution of **main()**
Static (permanent)	The object is visible from the point of definition until the end of the source file	Object is created prior to the execution of **main()** and is destroyed after the execution of **main()**
Static (local)	The object is visible in the function in which it is defined	Object is created the first time the function is invoked and is destroyed after the execution of **main()**
Local (auto)	The object is visible in the code block in which it is defined	Object is created when the program's execution enters the code block in which it is defined. It is destroyed when the program's execution exits the code block
Dynamic Allocation	The object is operated on by using its address	The object is created when the **new** operator successfully allocates memory. It is destroyed when the **delete** operator is used

The following example demonstrates the *visibility* and *lifetime* of objects in C++. In this example, the *Object* class maintains a message buffer. During object construction, a user-defined message is stored in the buffer. When the object is destroyed, the message is displayed on the screen. By displaying a message during the construction and destruction processes, an object's lifetime for different data types can be visualized:

```
//                  OBJECT.H Header File
class Object
{
    private:
        char message[30] ;
    public:
        Object( const char *new_message ) ; // constructor
        ~Object() ; // destructor
} ;


//                  OBJECT.CPP Source File
```

```
#include <iostream.h>
#include <string.h>
#include "object.h"

Object:: Object( const char *new_message )
{
        strcpy( message, new_message ) ;
        cout << "\t Creating: (" << message << ")\n";
}

Object:: ~Object()
{
        cout << "\t Destroying:  (" << message << ")\n";
}
```

To demonstrate the scope of the objects, the test driver uses a mixture of global, static, and local variables. The *constructor* and *destructor* functions for the objects are called at the appropriate time, based on the object's scope.

```
//                      TEST.CPP Source File
#include <iostream.h>
#include "object.h"

int main( int , char ** ) ;
void test_scope( void ) ;

Object global_data( "Global" ) ; // global variable

static Object permanent_data( "Permanent" ) ; // permanent variable

int main( int , char ** )
{
        cout << "\n\n *** Scope Test: Entering Main Function ***" << endl ;
        cout << "\n ** Calling Scope Function" << endl ;
        test_scope() ;
        cout << "\n ** Exiting Main Function" << endl ;
        return( 0 ) ;
}

void test_scope( void )
{
        Object local1( "Local 1") , local2( "Local 2" ) ;
        static Object plocal_data( "Permanent Local" ) ;

        char user_input ;
        cout << "\n\t Create another local variable (y/n)?" ;
        cin >> user_input ;
        if( user_input != 'n' )
        {
                Object local3( "Local 3" ) ;
        }
        cout << "\n ** Exiting test_scope() function" << endl ;
}
```

Construction takes place by reserving memory space for the object and invoking the constructor to initialize the memory space. The destruction takes place by invoking the destructor function to perform the cleanup operation followed by deallocation of the memory space. The following is the run-time result of the program:

Program Execution Results

```
        Creating: (Global)
        Creating: (Permanent)

*** Scope Test: Entering Main Function ***

** Calling Scope Function
        Creating: (Local 1)
        Creating: (Local 2)
        Creating: (Permanent Local)
        Create another local variable (y/n)? n

** Exiting test_scope() function
        Destroying:  (Local 2)
        Destroying:  (Local 1)

** Exiting Main Function
        Destroying:  (Permanent Local)
        Destroying:  (Permanent)
        Destroying:  (Global)
```

Global (*global_data*) and permanent (*permanent_data*) objects are constructed prior to execution of the **main()** function. The local objects *local1* and *local2* are constructed when the **test_scope()** function is entered. These local objects are destroyed in reverse order after the **test_scope()** function is exited. The static object, *plocal_data*, is created only the first time the **test_scope()** function is entered. The static and global objects are destroyed after the **main()** function is exited in the reverse order of the construction process.

The placement of objects in definitions determines the order of construction and destruction. Objects are constructed on the basis of their placement in the definition from left to right and are destroyed in the reverse order. In **test_scope()**, the *local1* object is constructed before and is destroyed after the *local2* object.

4.9 NAMESPACE

A common occurrence in both C and C++ is to encounter *name collisions* between two or more libraries. In the following example, when the *graphics* and the *math* libraries are used in application software, the definitions in the libraries cause name collisions, specifically, definitions for *Circle* and **PI**:

```
//            GRAPHICS.H Header File
#ifndef GRAPHICS_H
#define GRAPHICS_H

        typedef      short      Radius ;
        typedef      bool       Boolean ;

        const double PI = 3.1415926 ;

        class Circle
        {
                private:
                        Point center ;
                        Radius r ;
                public:
```

```
                        Boolean draw( void ) ;
                        // other details left out
            } ;

#endif                  // GRAPHICS_H Header File

//              CIRCLE.H Header File
#ifndef CIRCLE_H
#define CIRCLE_H

    typedef        float        Radius ;

    const double PI = acos( -1.0 ) ;

    class Circle
    {
            private:
                    Point center ;
                    Radius r ;
            public:
                    float area( void ) const ;
                    // other details left out
            } ;

#endif                  // CIRCLE_H Header File
```

The following program will not compile because there are multiple declarations for **PI**, *Radius*, and *Circle*:

```
//              Test Driver Source File
#include "circle.h"       // math library definitions
#include "graphics.h"     // graphics library definitions

int main( int , char ** )
{
        Circle *list ;     // Compiler error due to name conflicts
        ...
// other details left out
}
```

C++ has incorporated a feature called **namespace** similar to *Ada* "package" names to minimize name collisions in the global name space. This keyword assigns a distinct name (*signature*) to a library, which allows other libraries to use the same identifier names without creating any name collisions. Furthermore, the compiler uses the **namespace** signature for differentiating the definitions. **namespace** is analogous to a person's last name, which differentiates "**James Prell**" from "**James Smith**." Using the last name, there is no confusion about which "**James**" is referenced. The following presents the generic notation for using **namespace**:

```
//              Library Header File
namespace identifier_name
{
        constant, enum, and other library definitions
        class definition
}
```

By incorporating the **namespace** feature in the *graphics* and *math* libraries header files, the name collision no longer exists because the definitions in each library have been assigned a unique signature:

```
//          GRAPHICS.H Header File
#ifndef GRAPHICS_H
#define GRAPHICS_H

        namespace        Graphics_Library
        {
                typedef    short       Radius ;
                typedef    bool        Boolean ;

                const double PI = 3.1415926 ;
                class Circle
                {
                        private:
                                Point center ;
                                Radius r ;
                        public:
                                Boolean draw( void ) ;
                                // other details left out
                } ;
        }

#endif// GRAPHICS_H Header File

//          CIRCLE.H Header File
#ifndef CIRCLE_H
#define CIRCLE_H

        namespace        Math_Library
        {
                typedef    float       Radius ;

                const double PI = acos( -1.0 ) ;

                class Circle
                {
                        private:
                                Point center ;
                                Radius r ;
                        public:
                                float area( void ) const ;
                                // other details left out
                } ;
        }

#endif      // CIRCLE_H Header File
```

In the above header files, the compiler can differentiate the **PI** definitions from each other because one is considered part of the **Math_Library:: PI** and the other as part of the **Graphics_Library:: PI**. The nonmember functions are also part of the namespace. In the **CIRCLE.H** header file, **acos()** is owned by the **Math_Library** namespace. To associate the function's definition with its namespace, the namespace is used explicitly in the definition:

```
double Math_Library:: acos( double angle ) // identifies namespace
{
        // function's body
```

```
}
```

Similarly, the member function definitions for the *Circle* class in the math library will use the corresponding namespace definition:

```
//                CIRCLE.CPP Source File
#include "circle.h"

float Math_Library:: Circle:: area( void ) const
{
        float current_area ;

        current_area = PI * r * r ;

        return( current_area ) ;
}
```

As a programming guideline, abbreviations, acronyms, and common names should not be used as the **namespace** *identifier*. The possibility of name collision may be reintroduced. It is analogous to two people with the same first and last name, which makes references ambiguous and confusing. By using meaningful names for the *identifier*, the likelihood of name collision between namespaces is minimized. For source files using a **namespace**, long **namespace** names may be abbreviated by using an *alias*:

```
namespace alias_name = identifier_name ;
```

In the following example, *MathLib* is used as an alias for the *Math_Library* library.

```
//                Test Driver Source File
#include <iostream.h>        // Stream I/O Library
#include "circle.h"          // math library definitions

namespace MLib = Math_Library ;
                // using an alias for a namespace

int main( int , char ** )
{
        cout << "PI: " << MLib:: PI ;
                // using Math_Library:: PI definition

        return( 0 ) ;
}
```

However, aliasing makes source files difficult to read because the software developers in a large project may use different aliases for the same **namespace**. The names used should be standardized by the development group, or else this feature should be avoided altogether.

An application source file uses a name defined through a **namespace** by either specifying a *using directive* or a *using declaration*. A *directive* will cause the whole **namespace** to be imported into the application source file, while a *declaration* limits the import to a single explicit entity in the **namespace**.

In the following example, the application uses the **namespace** *directive* to access the resources provided by the *math* library in **main()**:

```
//                Test Driver Source File
#include <iostream.h>        // Stream I/O Library
#include "circle.h"          // math library definitions
```

```
#include "graphics.h"          // graphics library definitions
using namespace Math_Library ;
                     // using directive to use the math library globally
                     // this directive instructs the compiler which Circle and PI
                     // definitions are being used

int main( int , char ** )
{
        Circle *pie = new Circle(1,3,4) ;
                     // using math library's definition
        cout << "Area:" << pie->area() ;
                     // using Math_Library:: Circle:: area()
        cout << "PI: " << PI ;
                     // using Math_Library:: PI definition
        delete pie ;

        return( 0 ) ;
}
```

The *using declaration* is less inclusive than the *using directive* and causes a specific name from a **namespace** to be imported into the application source file. The scope of the declaration is within the block in which it is used. In the following example, the application uses a **namespace** *using declaration* to use specific features from the *math* and *graphics* libraries:

```
//                 Test Driver Source File
#include "circle.h"          // math library definitions
#include "graphics.h"        // graphics library definitions

int main( int , char ** )
{
        using Math_Library:: acos ; Graphics_Library:: PI ;
                     // using declarations for PI and acos()

        cout << "PI: " << acos( -1.0 ) ;
                     // using Math_Library:: acos()
        cout << "PI: " << PI ;
                     // using Graphics_Library:: PI Library's definition

        return( 0 ) ;
}
```

Even with **namespace**, ambiguities may result with overloaded functions that have identical arguments in two different namespaces. If one function is introduced through a *using declaration* and the other through a *using directive*, the compiler defaults in favor of the one introduced by a *using declaration*. If the compiler is unable to resolve an ambiguous call, it will generate an error message.

namespace is an important addition to C++ because it solves name collision problems, especially for large-scale software development. Since this feature is not incorporated in all C++ compilers, this book has deferred examples that illustrate this feature for later editions.

4.10 C++ CAST CONSTRUCTS

In C, explicit data conversion is performed by using a **cast construct**:

```
variable = (Type) (expression) ;
```

The above cast instructs the compiler to convert the result of the expression to the specific *Type*. In the following example, the sum of *radius1* and *radius2* is converted from integer data to floating point data. Since both radii are short integers, the division operation would always give a zero (0) result without the *floating point cast*:

```
double intensity ;
short radius1 , radius2 ;
.
intensity = 1 / (float) (radius1 + radius2) ;
```

The above addition is performed as integer addition and the result is then converted to floating point representation. The division then occurs as a floating point operation. The final result is converted to the *intensity* variable's type (double). The contents and types of *radius1* and *radius2* are not affected by the cast.

By defining explicit keywords for cast constructs, the ANSI committee has expanded and formalized casting in C++:

1. **Static Cast**: A **static_cast** construct performs the same operation as its C counterpart. The compiler will resolve data conversions in the expression at compile time, based on the specified data type:

```
variable = static_cast<Type> (expression) ;
```

The previous C example is implemented by using the **static_cast** construct:

```
double intensity ;
short radius1 , radius2 ;
    .
  intensity = 1 / static_cast<float> (radius1 + radius2) ;
```

This cast construct is a better alternative than its C counterpart only because it is easier to locate a C++ cast construct in a source file. Using an off-the-shelf search tool such as Unix's *grep*, the source files can be searched for the occurrence of "_cast." Therefore it becomes easier to locate and fix data conversion errors.

2. **Dynamic Cast**: A **dynamic_cast** construct is usually used for converting pointers and references to *derived* objects in design hierarchies. In the following example, this cast converts a *base* class pointer or reference to a *derived* class pointer or reference:

```
Derived_Type *ptr = dynamic_cast<Derived_Type *> ( base_pointer );
```

The data conversion is performed at run time on the basis of the actual type of *derived* object. Since *dynamic casting* is applicable to class hierarchies, Chapter 10 examines this topic in detail.

3. **Reinterpret Cast**: A **reinterpret_cast** instructs the compiler to force a data conversion whether it makes sense or not. This makes it the least type-safe cast:

```
variable = reinterpret_cast<Type> (expression) ;
```

A **reinterpret_cast** is used for bit manipulation. A developer needs to exercise caution when using this cast because it can easily lead to data corruption. In some digital signal processing applications, it may become necessary to extract the sign, mantissa, and exponent of a floating point number (Figure 4.14). Since the C++ binary operators (such as the *and* [&] operation) cannot be used for noninteger data types, a **reinterpret_cast** is used to treat a floating point variable as an unsigned long variable, thus allowing the program to operate on the floating point components. In the following example, the *IEEE_32* class is used to extract and store the sign, exponent, and mantissa of a floating point number:

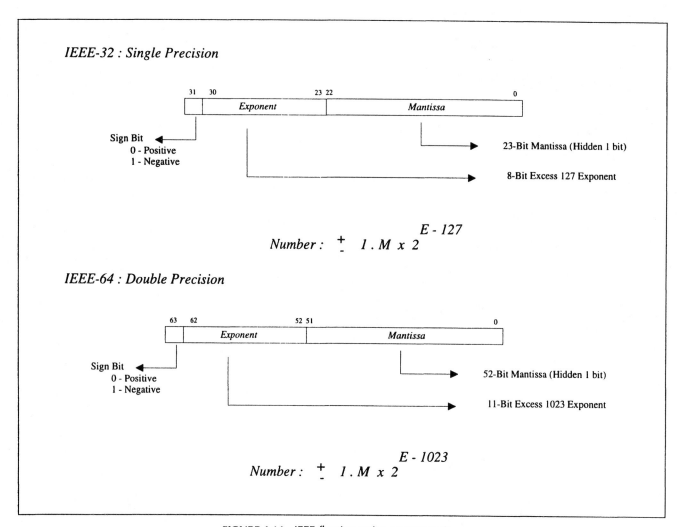

FIGURE 4.14 IEEE floating point representation.

```
//      IEEE_32.H Header File
#ifndef IEEE_32_H
#define IEEE_32_H

        //IEEE-32 Floating Point Format
        #define MASK_SIGN         0x80000000
        #define MASK_MANTISSA     0x007fffff
        #define MASK_EXPONENT     0x7f800000

        typedef     bool      Boolean ;

        class IEEE_32
        {
              private:
                     Boolean positive_value ;
                     unsigned long current_mantissa ;
                     unsigned short current_exponent ;
```

```
                    public:
                            // Constructors
                            IEEE_32() ;
                            IEEE_32( float number ) ;

                            // Access Functions
                            unsigned long mantissa( void ) const ;
                            unsigned short exponent( void ) const ;
                            Boolean is_positive( void ) const ;

                            // Processing Functions
                            float value( void ) const ;
          } ;

#endif// IEEE_32_H Header File
```

In the following example, the **IEEE_32()** constructor extracts the mantissa, exponent, and sign of an IEEE-32 floating point number, and the **value()** function uses the **reinterpret_cast** to put together the floating point value:

```
//      IEEE_32.CPP Source File
#include "IEEE_32.h"        // Math Library

IEEE_32:: IEEE_32( float number )
     : positive_value( false ) , current_mantissa( 0 ) ,
     current_exponent( 0 )
{
     // treat the floating point value as a 32-bit binary pattern
     unsigned long *data_point  =
            reinterpret_cast<unsigned long *> ( &number ) ;
                    // The number is treated as an integer.

     // The following isolates the sign bit
     if( (*data_point & MASK_SIGN) )
     {
            positive_value = false ; // number is negative
     }
     else
     {
            positive_value = true ; // number is positive
     }

     // extract exponents and mantissa
     current_exponent =
            (*data_point & MASK_EXPONENT) >> 23 ;
     current_mantissa =
            (*data_point & MASK_MANTISSA ) ;
}

unsigned long IEEE_32:: mantissa( void ) const
{
     return( current_mantissa ) ;
}

unsigned short IEEE_32:: exponent( void ) const
{
```

```
                return( current_exponent ) ;
        }


        Boolean IEEE_32:: is_positive( void ) const
        {
                return( positive_value ) ;
        }

float IEEE_32:: value( void ) const
{
        float number ;

        // treat the floating point value as a 32-bit binary pattern
        unsigned long *data_point  =
                reinterpret_cast<unsigned long *> ( &number ) ;
        *data_point = 0 ; // clear all bits

        // if number is negative => update sign bit
        if( !positive_value )
        {
                *data_point = MASK_SIGN ;
        }


        // incorporate exponent & mantissa in the number
        *data_point |=
                static_cast<unsigned long> (current_exponent) << 23 ;

                *data_point |= current_mantissa ;

        return( number ) ;
}
```

In the following example, the test driver uses the *IEEE_32* class to operate on a floating point item and displays its exponent, mantissa, and sign:

```
//       Test Driver Source File
#include <iostream.h> // Stream I/O Library
#include "IEEE_32.h"  // Math Library

int main( int , char ** )
{
        IEEE_32 number( 3.0 ) ;

        cout << "\n\t is Positive (True/False) ?"
        << number.is_positive();
        cout << "\n\t Exponent: " << hex << number.exponent() ;


        cout << "\n\t Mantissa: " << hex << number.mantissa() ;
        cout << "\n\t Value    : " << number.value() << endl ;

        return( 0 ) ;
}
```

4. Constant Cast: The **const_cast** construct is used to access and modify the type of **const** or **volatile** data:

```
Type *pointer = const_cast<Type *> ( & constant_data ) ;
```

In the following example, the **strcpy_special()** function copies a *source* text string into a *target* text string until a *special* character in the *source* string is found, or the end-of-string (*source* text string) has been reached, or the maximum number of characters (specified by *max_char*) has been copied. The calling function can include the *special* character in the *target* buffer through the use of the *include_flag* parameter:

```
char *strcpy_special(char *target, const char *source, char special,
                Boolean include_flag, unsigned max_char)
{
      unsigned i ;

      // While the # of characters defined has not been copied
      // and the null termination has not been encountered
      // copy a character from the source to the target buffer
      for( i = 0 ; i < max_char && *source != NULL_CHAR ; i++ )
      {
            // If special character is encountered
            if( *source == special )
            {
                  // if include flag is set
                  //      copy the special char into the target buffer
                  if( include_flag )
                  {
                        *target++ = *source++ ;
                  }
                  break ;
            }
            // copy normal characters into target
            *target++ = *source++ ;
      }
      *target = NULL_CHAR ; // Null-terminate target string

      return( const_cast<char *> (source) ) ;
}
```

Since the *source* buffer is not affected by the function, it is defined as a read-only pointer through the **const** keyword. The above function returns the location of the character in the *source* buffer that has not yet been processed. Since the return value is a regular character pointer, the **const_cast** cast must be used for converting the read-only *source* pointer to a nonconstant pointer. The **const_cast** statement highlights the conversion that is being performed on constant data.

A **reinterpret_cast** or **const_cast** carelessly used may lead to data corruption. Since the potential for misuse is high, the use of **reinterpret_cast** and **const_cast** is usually discouraged.

SUMMARY

By using the C-Language as its baseline, C++ began with the features of an existing language. Additional tools have been incorporated to transform C++ into an object-oriented programming language. The following basic features have been added to make the compiler responsible for more of the low-level details and implementations, thus relieving the developer of these chores:

1. **Constant Variables**: Constant variables are introduced to allow an object to be treated as read-only. A *constant variable* is an alternative to **#define**. Unlike a **#define**, a *constant variable* is mapped to the data memory segment and is accessible to a debugger.

2. **Function Overloading**: C++ permits multiple functions to use the same name. The compiler differentiates them by matching the number and types of arguments in the function calls. C++ requires the overloaded functions to be different by at least one argument, and the functions cannot be overloaded when differing only in return type. The compiler uses the entire function declaration to identify which implementation to call.

3. **Reference Type**: In addition to pointers, objects can be accessed and manipulated by using a *reference* type. A *reference* is an *alias* for a variable or object. The compiler may or may not assign storage for a reference type. A reference hides the referencing and dereferencing of the addresses by making the compiler responsible for the pointer manipulation. References are useful in function interfaces. A reference can be used on the left-hand side of an *assignment* operator (=) and allows operations to be cascaded and pipelined. The flexibility and importance of references becomes evident in subsequent chapters.

4. **Dynamic Allocation**: Through the use of the **new** and **delete** operators, C++ has full control over dynamic memory allocation. The use of the **new** operator tells the compiler that at run time the program will attempt to allocate memory dynamically. The C++ compiler incorporates calls to the applicable constructor in the executable code for initializing the memory space after the allocation takes place.
   The **delete** operator tells the compiler that a dynamically allocated object (or variable, or array) is being deallocated. At the point of deallocation, the compiler incorporates calls to the destructor in the executable code in order to clean up the internal memory space of the object prior to deallocation.

5. **Object Declarations**: The object declarations in C++ not only convey the memory space requirements and usage to the compiler but also associate a *constructor* to the definition. This property makes the definitions part of the executable statement. By automating the construction and destruction process, objects are created and destroyed automatically on the basis of their scope:

   a. **Construction**: Global (**extern**) and **static** objects defined outside a function are initialized by their constructors prior to the execution of the **main()** function. Local objects are initialized in the code block where they are defined. **Static** objects that are defined within a function are initialized once when the function in which they are defined is called.

   An object can be initialized with user-defined values, or by copying another object, or by using default values. To handle the variance in the initialization process, the language allows the class to support multiple *constructor* functions. The compiler selects the applicable *constructor* function by matching the initialization values specified in the object definition to the *constructor* prototype.

   If an object definition does not provide initialization values, the compiler will use the data structure's *default constructor*. This mechanism ensures that local objects are always in a *predictable* state and eliminates the reliance on manual initialization of the data object prior to manipulation of the object.

   b. **Destruction**: When execution exits a code block, local objects in the code block go out of scope. At such times, the *destructor* functions are automatically called to clean up the objects. The *destructors* for global and permanent objects are called when the **main()** function is exited and before control is returned to the operating system or calling process.

6. **Namespace**: To reduce and eliminate name contention and collision among libraries, the **namespace** keyword assigns a unique signature to the definitions within the library. It is similar to a person's last name, which gives an explicit identification to a person.

7. **Casts**: C++ offers **static_cast**, **dynamic_cast**, **reinterpret_cast**, and **const_cast** operators, which simplify the identification of explicit data conversions in source code. They also provide additional capability over the C counterparts.

GLOSSARY

Constant variable
   A read-only variable. After being initialized, a constant variable's content cannot be changed

Function overloading
   The ability to define multiple functions with the same name but different signatures (declaration)

Dynamic allocation
   Allocation of memory at execution time from the free store or heap memory space

Lifetime
   The duration between the creation and destruction of an object

Namespace
   A unique signature assigned to definitions in a library

Visibility
   Identifies where in the code an object is accessible

Reference
   An alias for an object

CHAPTER 5

Class

INTRODUCTION

A *class* definition defines the data attributes and operations of an *object* and is similar to the blueprint of a house (Figure 5.1). Similar to a house floorplan, that identifies the size, type, and location of each room, the *class* definition specifies the memory storage requirements for the instances of the class (*objects*), identifies the types of data mapped to this memory space, and specifies the member functions and their interfaces. This information is used by the compiler to enforce data encapsulation, which prevents external functions from manipulating the internal data members.

Using the *class* definition, the client defines instances of the class (*object*). In object-oriented design (OOD), an *object* is defined as an entity that has an ***identity, state***, and ***behavior*** [Booch 1994]. For instance, a *house* object satisfies the stated properties (Figure 5.1):

1. **Identity:** Even though a group of tract houses has the same blueprint, the houses are different because various materials such as paint, bricks, shingles, and other materials are used to give each its own identity. The interior decoration, exterior facade, and street address make each house unique.
2. **State:** Each home has a *state*. Some are occupied and some unoccupied. In addition, a home may be in the process of being repainted, which puts it into a different state, that is, the repaired state.
3. **Behavior:** There are operations associated with a home that will cause its state to be changed. For instance, the **paint()** and **clean()** operations change the *state* of the home.

The *class* definition creates an abstracted representation of the entity being modeled. For example, a *laser printer* class would abstract the internal operations of the printer from other class libraries and software packages. The class *member* functions hide the architecture and data representation from other classes (*encapsulation*). Furthermore, the *member* functions *abstract* the internal processes from the other classes (clients). For example, the client of the *laser printer* would "print" a PostScript document without having to worry about the internal printing operations that translate PostScript to the formatted text.

This chapter describes the class definition by partitioning it into *data members* and *member* functions. The *data members* are partitioned into static and regular data members. Similarly, the *member* functions are categorized into constructor, destructor, regular, and static member functions.

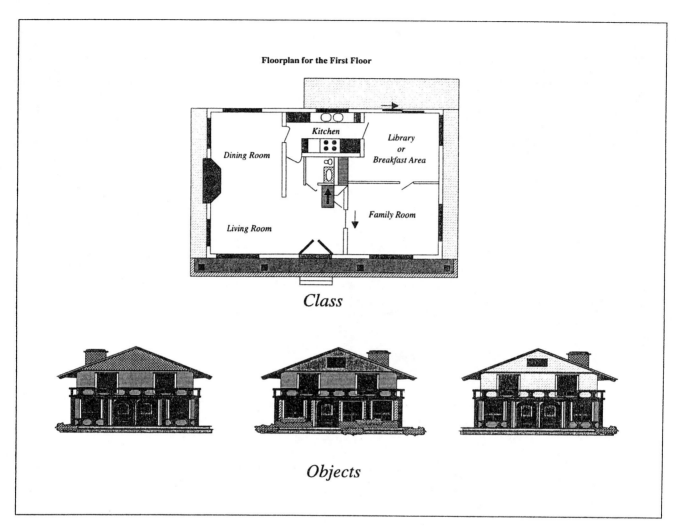

Floorplan for the First Floor

Kitchen

Dining Room

Library
or
Breakfast Area

Family Room

Living Room

Class

Objects

FIGURE 5.1 House floor plan and its instances.

5.1 CLASS DATA MEMBERS

A *class* definition identifies the memory layout, attributes, and operations of an object and is the object's "blueprint." Using the definition, the compiler knows how much memory space is needed for each instance of the class and how the types of data are mapped within this memory space.

In C++, a data member can either be unique for every instance of the class (*regular data member*) or shared by all the instances of the class (*static data member*). This section discusses the basic architecture of a class in terms of regular and static data members.

5.1.1 Regular Data Members

The class definition specifies the composition of an object by identifying the information maintained by that object. In the following example, the *Savings* account class maintains the customer, branch, and account information. The design relies on both built-in data types and classes, namely *Name*, *Address*, and *Picture* classes (Figure 5.2):

```
//          SAVINGS.H Header File
#ifndef SAVINGS_H
#define SAVINGS_H
```

```
#include "picture.h"      // Picture class library: customer's picture
#include "name.h"         // Name class library
#include "address.h"      // Address class library

typedef      long      ID ;
typedef      float     Currency ;
typedef      float     Rate ;
typedef      char      Text ;

class Savings
{
    private:
            Picture      customer_picture ;
            Name         customer_name ;
            Address      customer_address , branch_address ;
            ID           id ;
            Currency     balance ;
    public:
            // Other details left out
    } ;
#endif          // SAVINGS_H Header File
```

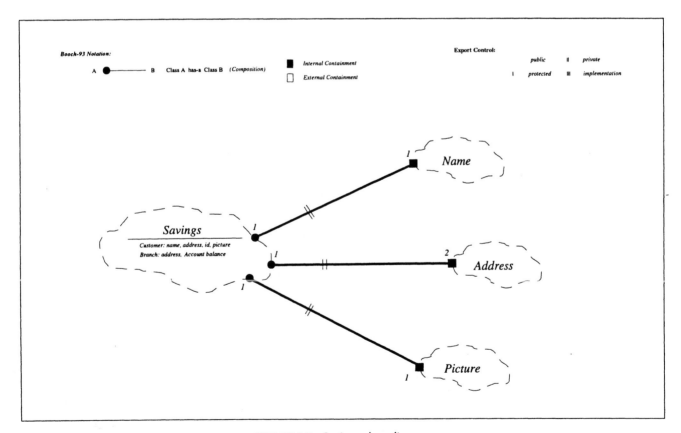

FIGURE 5.2   Savings class diagram.

The above implementation of *Savings* is based on *internal containment* (Figure 5.2), where the customer and branch information are maintained within the object. In C++, the design can also be implemented in terms of *external containment* (Figure 5.3), in which the member data are stored external to the class. The class references the external object through a pointer or a reference. The following example demonstrates a mixture of the two:

```
//          SAVINGS.H Header File
#ifndef SAVINGS_H
#define SAVINGS_H

    // Other details left out

    class Savings
    {
        private:
                Picture        customer_picture; // internal containment
                Name           *customer_name; // external containment
                Address        *customer_address , *branch_address ;
                ID             id  ;       // internal
                Currency       balance ;   // internal
        public:
                // Other details left out
    } ;

#endif             // SAVINGS_H Header File
```

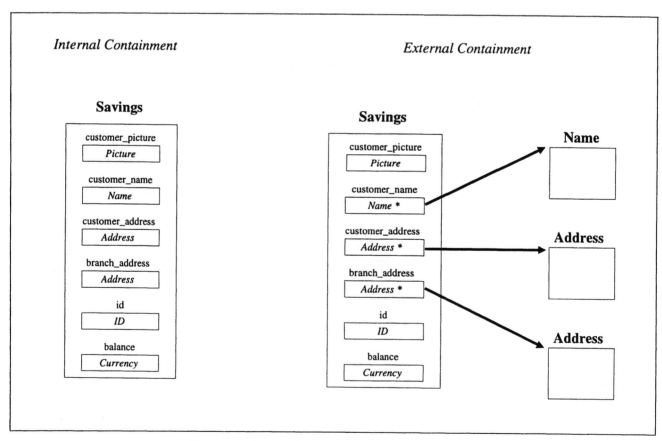

FIGURE 5.3   Savings class representations and architectures.

Both the *internal* and *external* implementations have benefits and drawbacks, and specific design requirements will govern which implementation is better for a specific class. In the case of *internal containment*, there is a close coupling between the lifetime of the *system* and *subsystem* objects. In the above example, whenever a *Savings* object is created, a *Picture* object is also created because the customer's *Picture* resides within the *Savings* object. In addition, when a *Savings* object is destroyed, the *Picture* object is destroyed as well. For *external containment*, the *subsystem* object resides outside of the *system* object and is linked through a reference or a pointer. Thus, the lifetimes of the *system* and *subsystem* objects are not tightly coupled. With *external containment*, a *subsystem* object may be created prior to the *system* object and its reference passed to the *system* object's constructor. *External containment* provides more flexibility when the number of *subsystem* objects is not known at design time. For instance, if the *Savings* class must handle both single and joint accounts, one or more *Name* objects need to be associated with each instance of *Savings*. By allowing the *Savings* constructor to determine the type of account, the constructor can then dynamically create the number of *Name* objects needed. In the case of *internal containment*, the *Savings* class specifies a predefined *Name* array. This limits the maximum number of *Name* objects associated with a *Savings* object and wastes memory space for *Savings* objects that need only one instance of *Name*. Through *external containment*, *Savings* can provide a more flexible design:

```
class Savings
{
    private:
            int num_account_holder ;
            Name *customer[2] ;        // external containment
    public:
            // single or joint account constructors
            Savings( Text *customer ) ;
            Savings( Text *customer1, Text *customer2 ) ;

            // other details left out
} ;
```

Creating copies of objects that are based on designs using *external containment* is an important C++ implementation issue. In these designs, the default object copy operation provided by the language causes the source object's content to be copied into the target object (Figure 5.4). Since only the references to the external objects are copied, the two *system* objects end up sharing the same *subsystem* objects. This is referred to as a *shallow copy*.

In C++, a shallow copy causes serious reliability issues for designs based on *external containment*. In Figure 5.4, the target *Name* reference is lost during the copy operation. This leads to memory leakage since the original *Name* object is never destroyed. Since the two *Savings* objects share the same resources, any operations on the *Name* objects affect the shared information, which may lead to data integrity problems. Finally, when the destructor for one of the *Savings* objects is called, their common *Name* objects are destroyed. This causes the other *Savings* object to be placed in an unpredictable state because it no longer has a *Name* object associated with it. Sections 5.2.3 and Chapter 6 address the problems associated with *shallow copies* by discussing proper implementation strategies for constructors and the assignment operator.

In OOD, *encapsulation* is one of the four key components of an object model [Booch 1994]. The data members are typically defined as **private** data members. The **private** access level reduces design coupling between the classes and allows the compiler to enforce *data encapsulation*. In the above examples, the *Savings* class, a client of the *Name* class, must use the **public** member functions of *Name* to operate on the **private** data members of *Name*. This approach minimizes the design dependencies between *Name* and *Savings*, and the underlying internal data representation of *Name* is kept hidden. The **private** access level for the composed elements are highlighted in Figure 5.2, using the *export control* feature in the class diagram. *Data encapsulation* increases data processing time owing to higher overhead but, in general, this is a small price to pay for improved software maintainability and reusability.

5.1.2 Static Data Members

At times, it is desirable for the objects in a design to share common information. For example, the interest rate for a basic *Savings* may be the same for all instances of *Savings*. One approach is to have each instance of a class store the interest rate.

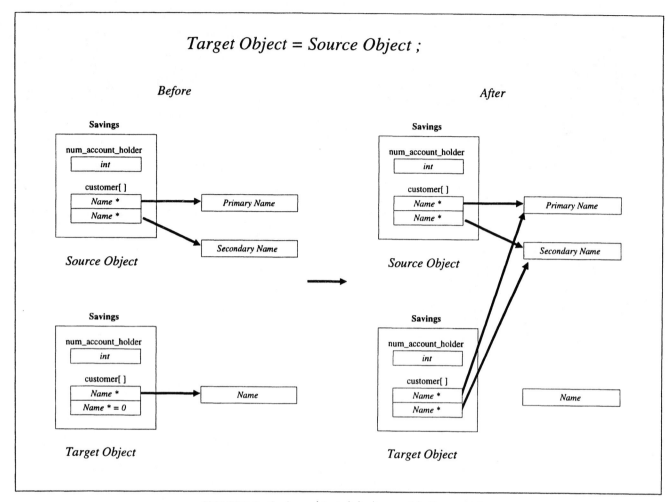

FIGURE 5.4 Savings object default copy (shallow copy).

```
//              SAVINGS.H Header File                        -
#ifndef SAVINGS_H
#define SAVINGS_H

    #include "picture.h"    // Picture class library
    #include "name.h"       // Name class library
    #include "address.h"    // Address class library

    #define DATE_BUFFER_SIZE        9   // buffer's length
    #define DEFAULT_INTEREST_RATE  .06  // default rate

    typedef     long      ID ;
    typedef     float     Currency ;
    typedef     float     Rate ;
    typedef     char      Text ;
    typedef     int       Days ;

    class Interest_Table
    {
        private:
            Rate interest_rate ;
```

```
                    Date start_date[DATE_BUFFER_SIZE] ;
                    Days interest_period;
            public:
                    Interest_Table( Rate new_rate,
                            const Date *start = static_cast<Date *> ( 0 ),
                            Days duration = 30 ) ;
                    Rate rate( void ) const ;
                    Days period( void ) const ;
    } ;


    class Savings
    {
            private:
                    Picture             customer_picture ;
                    Name                customer_name ;
                    Address             customer_address,
                                        branch_address ;
                    ID                  id ;
                    Currency            balance ;
                    Interest_Table      interest ;
            public:
                    // other details left out
      } ;
#endif               // SAVINGS_H Header File
```

In the above bank example, if the interest rate is the same for any *Savings* customer, this implementation would increase the memory space requirement and processing time for the class. Every time an object is constructed, the same value for the interest rate must be stored in the new object. In addition, when the interest rate is changed, the software somehow must search through all *Savings* objects and update the interest rates. It is more desirable to have all instances of the *Savings* class share the same interest rate. The shared interest table should then exist outside of any object.

By building on the concept of **static** data, C++ incorporates a method of associating external data with instances of a class. External data are logically related to a class by being designated as a *static* member. By using the **static** keyword, all *Savings* account objects will share the same interest rate. Instead of each *Savings* object holding this information, the common account information is maintained apart from the objects (Figure 5.5).

```
//           SAVINGS.H Header File
#ifndef SAVINGS_H
#define SAVINGS_H

    // Other details left out

    class Savings
    {
            private:
                    Picture             customer_picture ;
                    Name                customer_name ;
                    Address             customer_address ,
                                        branch_address ;
                    ID                  id ;
                    Currency            balance ;
                    static Interest_Table       interest ;
                            // resides outside of any Savings object
            public:
                    Currency income( void ) const ;
```

```
                    // other details left out

         } ;

#endif                   // SAVINGS_H Header File
```

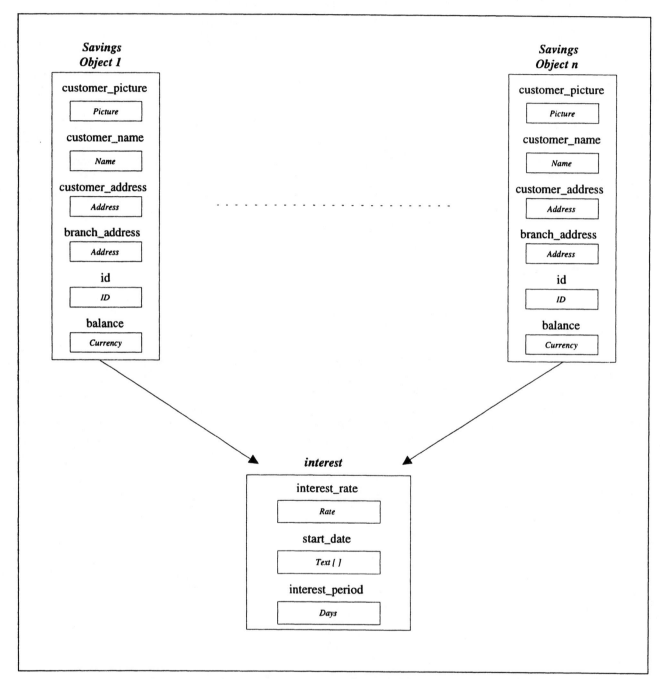

FIGURE 5.5   Static class member.

Static class elements are external yet accessible by all of the instances of the class. The compiler creates only one instance of a static element. The above **interest** member is common to all of the Savings objects and is shared by all of them. These members are denoted in the class diagram by a triangular symbol with the letter "S" enclosed in it (Figure 5.6).

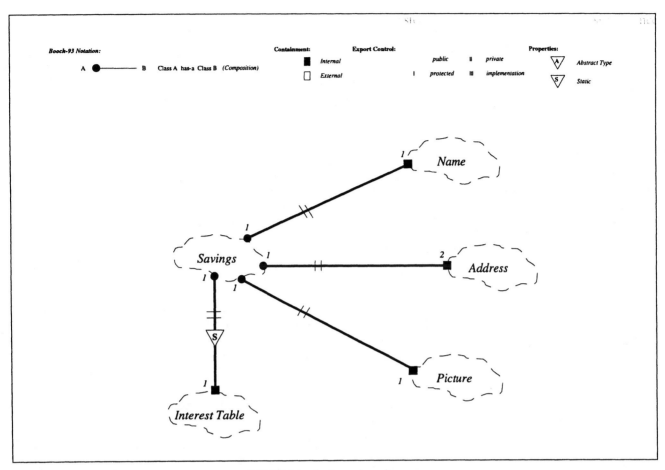

FIGURE 5.6   Savings class diagram.

A static element's lifetime is the same as the program's lifetime and *the static element exists even if no objects of the class are instantiated.* The ***interest*** data member is constructed prior to the execution of the **main()** function and exists even if no instances of the *Savings* class are ever created.

Because the lifetime of a **static** element is separate from the instances (objects) of the class, the **static** element must be explicitly initialized in one of the source files, otherwise the linker will generate an error message. The initialization statement must be placed in a source file and not in a header file, since the header file may be included several times, which will cause the compiler to generate a multiple declaration error message. Good programming practice dictates that the initialization statement should occur in the source file containing the class member functions. A static member is defined and initialized using the same syntax as a global variable:

```
type class_name :: static_element = initial_value ;
```

In the following example, ***interest_rate*** is initialized to the default value (6 percent) in the **SAVINGS.CPP** source file:

```
//              SAVINGS.CPP Source File
#include "savings.h"

Interest_Table Savings:: interest( DEFAULT_INTEREST_RATE ) ;

// Savings member and non-member function definitions
```

The static element initialization should **not** take place within the class constructor because there is only one occurrence of a *static* member in memory. If the initialization is performed in the constructor, every time an object is created the value of the static element is reset.

```
Savings:: Savings() // default constructor
      : interest( DEFAULT_INTEREST_RATE )
                // poor technique: every time an object is constructed,
                // the shared interest_rate is reset
{
}
```

   Access to a *static* member is governed by the access level assigned to the member in the class definition. A private *static* element is accessible only to the member functions. A public *static* element is part of the design interface and is accessible to both the clients and member functions of the class.
   Static members can be accessed and manipulated by using the following syntax:

```
object_name.static_element
object_reference.static_element
object_pointer->static_element
class_name:: static_element
```

   In the following example, the **Savings:: income()** function operates on *interest*, which is a static data member. Since this function does not have access to the private data members of the *interest* object, it must invoke the **Interest_Table:: rate()** function to obtain interest rate information. Figure 5.7 illustrates the interaction and data flow between these objects:

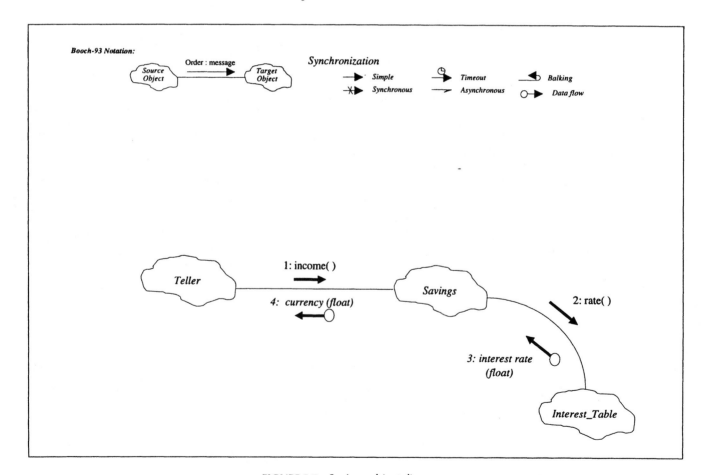

FIGURE 5.7   Savings object diagram.

```
//                  SAVINGS.CPP Source File
#include "savings.h"

Interest_Table Savings:: interest( DEFAULT_INTEREST_RATE ) ;

Currency Savings:: income( void ) const
{
        Currency current_income = balance * interest.rate( ) ;
        // or can be defined using the following syntax:
        // Currency current_income = balance * Savings:: interest.rate( ) ;
        return( current_income ) ;
}
```

5.2 CLASS MEMBER FUNCTIONS

Member functions can be organized in terms of their tasks and operations with respect to their class:

1. **Construction:** A *constructor* function initializes memory space for the data members and places their contents in a *predictable* (*known*) state.
2. **Destruction**: A *destructor* function is called to carry out cleanup operations on an object, such as deallocating dynamically allocated memory.
3. **Regular Member Functions**: These functions use the information stored in data member(s) to accomplish a task. For example, the above **income()** function computes the income generated for the specified period.
4. **Static Member Functions**: Usually *static* data members are maintained and operated on by *static* member functions of a class. Since a *static* data member's lifetime is separated from the *instances of the class (objects)*, these functions provide access to these members independent of an object.

5.2.1 Class Constructor Functions

To create an *object*, the memory space for an instance of a class must be reserved and then initialized by placing it in a *predictable* state. The compiler and the designer of the class are both responsible for the initialization process. Access levels in C++ prevent clients from accessing the data members directly. A designer provides a series of *constructor* functions for the class. For every object instantiation, a call to the applicable *constructor* function is incorporated in the executable code. The compiler guarantees that the initialization process is consistent and uniform for all instances of that class.

Constructors resolve the invalid data initialization issues and enhance software reliability. By regulating access to data, a *constructor* can verify the application defined values, (for example, it can check boundary conditions) and can prevent the objects from being created in unknown or invalid states. Since the construction is applied consistently to all instances of the class, a *constructor* ensures that all objects will be placed in a *stable* (*predictable*) state upon creation.

During the *construction process* the following activities are performed with respect to the object's memory space:

1. **Reserve Memory Space**: On the basis of the definition in the source code, the memory space for an object is reserved on the stack, in the permanent memory space, or in *free store* (dynamic allocation memory space).
2. **Initialize Memory Space**: The *constructor* function is then called to initialize the memory space.

Constructor definition syntax is as follows:

```
Class_Name :: Class_Name ( list of arguments, if any )
      : initialization_list (optional)
{
        // constructor body: boundary checks & other initialization statements
}
```

5.2.1.1 Constructor Identifier

A *constructor* must be a *member* function and must use the same name as the class name. A *constructor* cannot have a return value, and may not even use the "void" keyword.

In the following example, a *Name* class is designed to represent a person's identity. The *Name* class is composed of first, middle, and last names. This information can be maintained in either internal character buffers (*internal containment*) or external buffers (*external containment*). Figure 5.8 depicts the memory layout for both implementations. The type of *containment* is not important to the client but it is an important implementation issue. The following design is based on *external containment* (Figure 5.8):

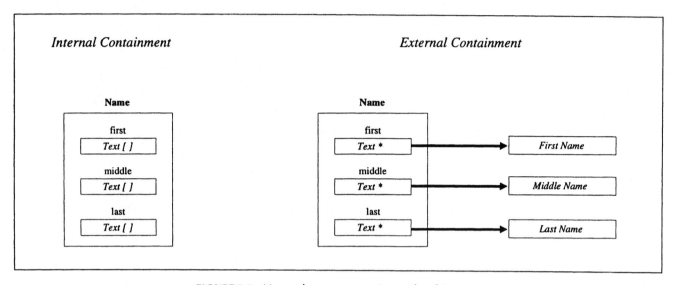

FIGURE 5.8   Name class representation and architecture.

```
//           NAME.H Header File
#ifndef NAME_H
#define NAME_H

     typedef      char      Text ;

     class Name
     {
          private:
               Text *first , *middle , *last ;
               // store name's components in external buffers
          public:
               Name( const Text *current_name =
                          static_cast<Text *> ( 0 ) ) ;
                    // default (no arguments) and user-defined
                    // values constructors merged into one
               // other details left out
     } ;

#endif
```

For the construction process, the *Name* class has explicitly provided a single constructor that initializes the components of a name object using the application defined name. In the absence of a user-defined value, the compiler will use the fixed default values (the null address) for the **Name()** constructor's argument and the constructor will then behave as a *default* constructor (no arguments):

```
//              Test Driver Source File
#include "name.h"
int main( int , char ** )
{
     Name customer1( "Bob Smith" ) , customer2 ;
          // initialize customer1.Name( "Bob Smith" ) ;
          // initialize customer2.Name( static_cast<Text *> (0) ) ;
     return( 0 ) ;
}
```

5.2.1.2 Constructor Initialization List

Before the body of the *constructor* is executed, the *data members* can be placed into a predictable state by using the *initialization list* in the constructor. Since the *initialization list* guarantees that data members are in a predictable state, the constructor body can then complete the initialization process by using the information stored in them. In the following example, the *first*, *middle*, and *last* members are initialized to null values before the execution of the **Name()** constructor's body:

```
//              NAME.CPP Source File
#include "name.h"

Name:: Name ( const Text *current_name )
     :  last(  static_cast<Text *> ( 0 ) ) , middle( static_cast<Text *> ( 0 ) ) ,
        first(  static_cast<Text *> ( 0 ) )
                         // initialize composed elements to default values
{
     // other details left out
}
```

The order of initialization is determined by the class definition and **not** by the order in the *initialization list*. Even though the *last* data element appears first in the above *initialization list*, the *first* data member is initialized first, followed by the *middle* and then *last* data members (refer to the *Name* class definition).

In addition, the *initialization list* provides a simple interface between the *constructors* of classes. Since a class may use other classes in its implementation, it will not have access to the private members of these classes. The *initialization list* allows the *Savings* constructor to interact with the *Name* and *Address* constructors before its body is executed. In the following example, the *Savings* class uses the *Name* class to represent its customer information (Figure 5.2). The *Savings* constructor uses the *Name* and *Address* constructors to initialize its **customer_name** and **customer_address** data members, respectively:

```
//              SAVINGS.H Header File
#ifndef SAVINGS_H
#define SAVINGS_H

     #include "picture.h"       // Picture class library
     #include "name.h"          // Name class library
     #include "address.h"       // Address class library
     #include "interest.h"      // Interest Table library

     typedef     long      ID ;
     typedef     float     Currency ;

     class Savings
     {
          private:
                    Picture        customer_picture ;
```

```
             Name            customer_name ;
             Address         customer_address ;
             Address         branch_address ;
             ID              id  ;
             Currency        balance ;
             static Interest_Table interest ;

      public:
             Savings( ) ;
             Savings( const Text *name , const Text *address,
                    ID account_id );
             // other details left out
   } ;


#endif         // SAVINGS_H header file
```

Since the *Savings* class does not have access to the private members of the *Picture*, *Name*, and *Address* classes, it must interface with the appropriate constructors in those classes. This interface keeps the design of *Savings*, *Name*, and *Address* separate and minimizes data coupling between them. Through an *initialization* list, the *Savings* constructor invokes the *Name* constructor to initialize the **customer_name** before the *Savings* constructor body is executed:

```
//          SAVINGS.CPP Source File
#include "savings.h"

Interest_Table Savings:: interest( DEFAULT_INTEREST_RATE ) ;

Savings:: Savings(const Text *name, const Text *address, ID account_id)
     : customer_name( name ), customer_address( address ),
       id( account_id ), balance( 0 )
{
     // other details left out
}
```

Use of an *initialization list* is optional. If the constructor does not contain an initialization list, the *default* constructors for the data members will be called prior to executing the constructor's body. In the above example, the **branch_address** data element is not explicitly initialized in the *initialization list*. During compilation, the compiler incorporates a call to the *Address* default constructor to initialize this element. By placing the **branch_address** in a predictable state before executing the body of **Savings()**, the code in the **Savings()** constructor will complete the initialization process using valid data.

An *initialization list* supports the following initialization processes:

1. **Composition**: A class may use other classes as members. The class constructor cannot directly initialize the private data members of its composed members and needs to use an *initialization list* to invoke their constructor functions (refer to the above *Savings* example).
2. **References**: C++ requires a *reference* data member to be initialized via an *initialization list*. A *reference* is an alias and must be initialized when it is defined.
3. **Inheritance**: An *initialization list* is used by a *derived* class (child) to initialize its *base* (parent) segment by invoking the *base* class constructor function. This usage is discussed in Chapter 9.

Even though use of an *initialization list* is optional, it is good programming practice and is strongly recommended.

5.2.1.3 Constructor Body

After the *initialization list* is processed and the applicable constructors for the data members are invoked, the data members are placed in known states. At this point, the constructor's body is executed in order to complete the initialization process. In the following example, the ***current_name*** parameter is copied into a dynamically allocated buffer. The supplied name is then partitioned into the first, middle, and last name fields by using the **parse_name()** utility function (Figure 5.9):

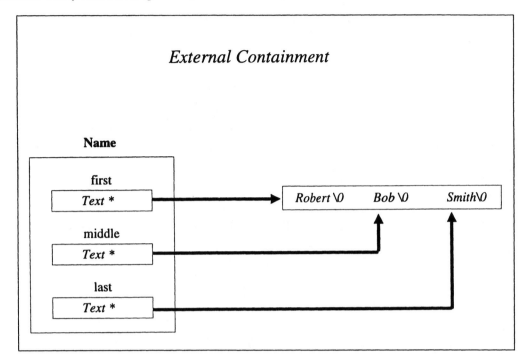

FIGURE 5.9 Construction of a name object

```
//              NAME.H Header File
#ifndef NAME_H
#define NAME_H

    #define NAME_FIELD_SEPARATOR' '
    #define NULL_CHAR'\0'

    typedef     char     Text ;
    typedef     bool     Boolean ;

    class Name
    {
        private:
                Text *first , *middle , *last ;
                Boolean parse_name( void ) ;
                // class utility function (internal to design)
        public:
                Name( const Text *current_name =
                        static_cast<Text *> ( 0 ) ) ;
                // other details left out
    } ;

#endif// NAME_H Header file

//              NAME.CPP Source File
```

```
#include <string.h>
#include "name.h"

Name:: Name ( const Text *current_name )
    : first( static_cast<Text *> ( 0 ) ), middle( static_cast<Text *> ( 0 ) ),
      last( static_cast<Text *> ( 0 ) )
                    // initialize composed elements to default values
{
    // if supplied name exists => use this name to construct object
    if( current_name != static_cast<Text *> (0) )
    {
        size_t length = strlen(current_name) + 1 ;
                // compute string length and add an additional byte
                // for null terminator

        first = new Text[length] ; // allocate buffer for storing name
        // if dynamic allocation successful
        if( first != static_cast<Text *> (0)  )
        {
            // copy user-defined name into buffer
            strcpy( first, current_name ) ;

            // partition name into components
            if( !parse_name( ) )
            {
                // recovery code for invalid name
            }
        }
        else
        {
            // recovery code for dynamic allocation failure:
            // eg. using C++ exception handling
        }
    }
}
```

The **parse_name()** function is a private member function and is used internally by the constructor function to partition a name into the first, middle, and last name fields. This function scans through the name looking for the name field separator (blank space):

```
Boolean Name:: parse_name( void )
{
    Boolean valid_name = true ;
    Text * marker = first ;        // point to beginning of the name

    if( marker != static_cast<Text *> ( 0 ) ) // if no name => abort
    {
        // while not end of name
        while( *marker != NULL_CHAR )
        {
            // if name field separator found then
            //partition & mark the fields
            if( *marker == NAME_FIELD_SEPARATOR )
            {
                *marker++ = NULL_CHAR ;
                    // null terminate current field
```

```
                            // if middle name not found yet then
                            if( middle == static_cast<Text *> ( 0 ) )
                            {
                                    middle = marker ;
                                    // mark beginning of the middle name
                            }
                            else
                            {
                                    last = marker ;
                                    // mark beginning of the last name
                                    break ; // all components found
                            }
                    }
                    else
                    {
                            ++marker ; // point to next character
                    }
            }

            // if middle and last markers never initialized
            if( (middle == static_cast<Text *> ( 0 )) &&
            (last == static_cast<Text *> ( 0 ) ) )
            {
                    valid_name = false ;
            }
            else if( last == static_cast<Text *> ( 0 ) ) //no last name found
            {
                    last = middle ; // indicates no middle name
                    middle = static_cast<Text *> ( 0 ) ;
            }
    }
    else
    {
            valid_name = false ;
    }

    return( valid_name ) ;
}
```

5.2.1.4 Types of Constructors
Since the initialization process can vary, C++ allows the definition of multiple constructors for a class. These constructors are categorized as:

1. **Default Constructor**: A constructor with no parameter list. It initializes the class members to default values.
2. **User-Defined Values Constructor:** Initializes the members to the values defined in the constructor's parameter list. A class may have multiple user-defined values constructors.

   Note: By using default parameters, the *default* and *user-defined* constructors can be merged into one function (refer to the *Name* example in 5.2.1.3), and the *user-defined constructor* can behave as a *default* constructor.
3. **Copy Constructor:** This constructor is used to copy the contents of an object to the newly created object of the same class. For example, when an object is passed by-value to a function, the copy constructor is called to create a copy of the object.

In the following example, the above constructor types are defined for the *Name* class:

```
//              NAME.H Header File
#ifndef NAME_H
#define NAME_H

    #define NAME_FIELD_SEPARATOR        ' '
    #define NULL_CHAR                   '\0'
    typedef     char            Text ;
    typedef     bool            Boolean ;

    class Name
    {
        private:
                Text *first , *middle , *last ;
                // class utility function (internal to design)
                Boolean parse_name( void ) ;
        public:
                Name( ) ;
                    // default constructor
                Name( const Text *current_name ) ;
                    // user-defined value constructor
                Name( const Name &source) ;
                    // copy constructor
        } ;

#endif          // NAME_H Header file
```

When the **Name()** *default* constructor creates a name object, it initializes the text pointers to null. The **Name (const Text *)** *user-defined values* constructor uses the length of the client-defined name to allocate memory dynamically, copies the client-defined string to this memory space, and parses the name into three fields (Figure 5.9).

The **Name(&)** *copy* constructor creates a *Name* object by allocating duplicate memory space dynamically and copying the **source** object's contents into this memory space (Figure 5.10). The new and **source** objects contain the same information. However, they have their own unique buffers. This copying operation is referred to as a *deep copy*.

```
//              NAME.CPP Source File
#include "name.h"

// default constructor
Name:: Name ( )
    : first( static_cast<Text *> ( 0 ) ), middle( static_cast<Text *> ( 0 ) ),
      last( static_cast<Text *> ( 0 ) )
{
    // since there is no error checking, the constructor's body
    // does not contain any code.
}

 // user-defined values constructor
Name:: Name( const Text *current_name )
    : first( static_cast<Text *> ( 0 ) ), middle( static_cast<Text *> ( 0 ) ),
      last( static_cast<Text *> ( 0 ) )
{
    // refer to previous implementation in Section 5.2.1.3
}
```

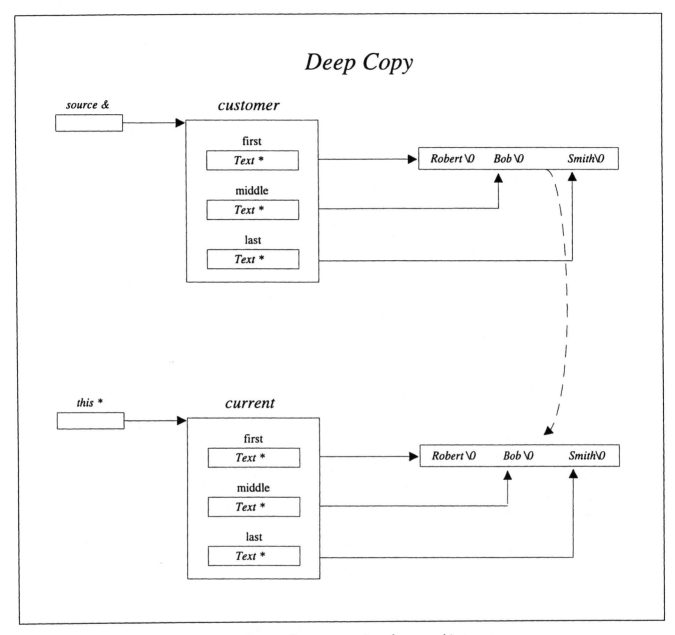

FIGURE 5.10 Copy construction of a name object.

```
// copy constructor
Name:: Name( const Name & source )
     : first( static_cast<Text *> ( 0 ) ), middle( static_cast<Text *> ( 0 ) ),
     last( static_cast<Text *> ( 0 ) )
{
     if( ( source.first != static_cast<Text *> ( 0 ) ) &&
         ( source.last != static_cast<Text *> ( 0 ) ) )
     {
          // if source object contains a valid name
          short length = strlen( source.first ) + strlen( source.last ) + 2;
                             // add 2 bytes for two null terminators
          // if a middle name exists
          if( source.middle != static_cast<Text *> ( 0 ) )
```

```
                {
                        length += strlen( source.middle ) + 1 ;
                }
                first = new Text[length] ; // allocate buffer for storing name

                // if dynamic allocation successful
                if( first != static_cast<Text *> ( 0 ) )
                {
                        // copy user-defined name into buffer
                        strcpy( first, source.first ) ;

                        // if source object has a middle name
                        if( source.middle != static_cast<Text *> ( 0 ) )
                        {
                                // copy name to new object
                                middle = first + strlen(first) + 1 ;
                                strcpy( middle, source.middle ) ;
                                last = middle + strlen(middle) + 1 ;
                        }
                        else
                        {
                                last = first + strlen(first) + 1 ;
                        }
                        strcpy( last, source.last ) ;
                }
                else
                {
                        // recovery code for dynamic allocation failure:
                }
        }
        else
        {
                // recovery code for invalid name
        }
}
```

The above *deep copy* implementation for the *copy* constructor avoids the problems associated with a *shallow copy* because "**this**" object maintains its own copy of information.

5.2.1.5 Explicit Call to a Constructor

If a constructor is called explicitly, the program will create an object with no name, known as a *temporary object*. The lifetime of the *temporary object* is within the defining expression and is destroyed afterward:

```
//              Test Driver Source File
#include "name.h"

int main( int , char ** )
{
        process_customers( Name("Robert Bob Smith") ) ;
                // create a temporary object
}


process_customers( const Name & current )
{

}
```

Temporary objects have limited applications but are useful for intermediate data processing and provide a way for data conversions. The above explicit constructor call causes a temporary *Name* object to be created. After the **process_customers()** function call is completed, the *temporary object* is destroyed.

5.2.2 Class Destructor Functions

A *destructor* is the counterpart of a *constructor* and performs cleanup operations for the class. A *destructor* has the following format:

```
class_Name :: ~class_Name ( )
{
    cleanup statements ;
}
```

Similar to *constructors*, C++ requires the *destructor* to use the same name as the class name and must be preceded by the tilde (~) sign. The above notation standardizes the destructor naming convention.

When an object goes out of scope or a dynamically allocated object is deleted, it is destroyed by the following *destruction process*:

1. **Cleanup Task**: The *destructor* function is called to perform any cleanup operations.
2. **Memory Deallocation**: At this point the object does not exist and is considered to be uninitialized memory space, and the memory space containing the object is deallocated.

A destructor is used for classes that contain pointers and/or references to external data or streams. Prior to destroying an *instance of a class (object)*, the *destructor* is called to clean up the object, closing the stream pointed to by the object. In the following example, since the design of *Name* is based on *external containment* and the name buffer is dynamically allocated, the class must provide a destructor that will deallocate the memory:

```
//          NAME.H Header File
#ifndef NAME_H
#define NAME_H

    #define NAME_FIELD_SEPARATOR        ' '
    #define NULL_CHAR                   '\0'

    typedef     char        Text ;
    typedef     bool        Boolean ;

    class Name
    {
        private:
            Text *first , *middle , *last ;
            Boolean parse_name( void ) ;
            // class utility function (internal to design)

        public:
            // constructor functions
            Name( const Text *current_name =
                    static_cast<Text *> ( 0 ) ) ;
            Name( const Name &source ) ;

            // destructor function
            ~Name() ;
            // other details left out
```

```
    } ;

#endif              // NAME_H Header file
```

Without a *destructor*, the external buffer will not be deallocated and the program will tie up memory resources that could otherwise be made available. When the object goes out of scope there will be *memory leakage*, and the program may eventually run out of free memory.

The ~**Name**() destructor function has no parameters and cannot return a value. The following *destructor* deallocates the external buffer:

```
//            NAME.CPP Source File
#include "name.h"

Name:: ~Name()
{
    // if dynamically allocated buffers exist => deallocate them
    delete[ ] first ;

    // Erase markers
    first       = static_cast<Text *> (0) ;
    middle      = static_cast<Text *> (0) ;
    last        = static_cast<Text *> (0) ;
}
```

The following application software benefits from automatic initialization and cleanup. It is no longer responsible for either initialization or cleanup operations:

```
//            Test Driver Source File
#include "name.h"

void process_customers( const Text *current_name )
{
    Name customer( current_name ) ;
        // After the memory space for customer is reserved on the
        // stack, the customer object is initialized by calling
        // the Name(const Text *) user-defined value constructor.
    ...
        // function's body
    ...
    return ;
        // when the customer object goes out of scope, the ~Name()
        // destructor is automatically called to clean up the
        // dynamically allocated buffers
}
```

Assuming the initialization string points to "Robert Bob Smith," the constructor will allocate buffers for the *customer* first, middle, and last name elements (Figure 5.9). The ~*Name()* destructor for the *customer* is automatically called at the end of the **process_customers**() function when the object goes out of scope. The *destructor* performs the cleanup operation and deallocates the name buffers.

A *destructor* is invoked under the following conditions:

1. A destructor is tied to an object's lifetime. When an object goes out of scope, the *destructor* is automatically invoked to perform the cleanup operation. For local objects, the *destructor* is called after the program's execution exits the code block in which the object is defined. After the program's execution ends, the destructors are called to clean up the permanent (**static**) and global (**extern**) objects.

2. A *temporary object* is destroyed after the evaluation of an expression.

```
//              Test Driver Source File
#include "name.h"

int main( int , char ** )
{
        process_customers( Name("Laura Cetto") );
        // the explicit call to the Name constructor creates a
        // temporary object which is destroyed after the
        // program's execution returns from the
        // process_customers() function
}
```

3. A *destructor* can be called explicitly. The explicit function call is typically used for custom memory management. An explicit call to a destructor is defined below:

```
object_name.Class_Name::~Class_Name() ;
object_reference.Class_Name::~Class_Name() ;
object_pointer->Class_Name::~Class_Name() ;
```

4. When a dynamically allocated object is deallocated by using the **delete** operator, the destructor is invoked automatically prior to invocation of the **delete** operator.

5.2.3 Compiler-Generated Member Functions

Constructor and *destructor* functions are optional member functions, and the compiler provides default ones in the absence of explicit definitions. This capability provides backward compatibility with programs developed in C because data structures developed using C do not support constructors. In the following example, the *Name* class specifies a *default* and a *user-defined values* constructor.

```
//              NAME.H Header File
#ifndef NAME_H
#define NAME_H

    #define NAME_FIELD_SEPARATOR       ' '
    #define NULL_CHAR                  '\0'

    typedef    char           Text ;
    typedef    bool           Boolean ;

    class Name
    {
        private:
                Text *first , *middle , *last ;

                // class utility function (internal to design)
                Boolean parse_name( void ) ;
        public:
                // default constructor
                Name( ) ;

                // user-defined value constructor
```

```
                    Name( const Text *current_name ) ;

                    // destructor function
                    ~Name() ;
                    // other details left out
        } ;
```

```
#endif       // NAME_H header file
```

The compiler creates a *copy constructor* for a class in the absence of an explicit copy constructor. In the previous example, the *Name* class did not define a copy constructor. Therefore, the compiler will create a default *copy* constructor:

```
// compiler will generate a copy constructor similar to the following
Name:: Name( Name &source )
        : first( source.first ) , middle( source.middle ) , last( source.last )
{
}
```

The compiler-generated *copy* constructor copies the content of an existing object to the new object (*shallow* copy). In the above example, the content of the object referenced by **source** is copied into "**this**" object (Figure 5.11).

For classes whose implementation is based on *external containment*, a *shallow* copy may cause serious problems. A *shallow* copy creates a memory image, and the new object will point to the same entities as the original object. If either of the objects is destroyed, the destruction may cause the program to execute incorrectly. In the following example, the **customer** object is copied into the **current** object by using the *default* **Name(&)** *copy constructor*. The *shallow* copy causes both objects to share the same name buffers (Figure 5.11). Therefore, any operations on the **current** object directly affect the **customer** object as well.

Furthermore, when the **current** object goes out of scope, its destructor is automatically called. The **~Name()** destructor deallocates the **current** object's name buffer, which is also the **customer** object's buffer. When the **process_customer()** function returns to the caller, the **customer** object's buffer is no longer valid and the program's behavior will become unpredictable.

```
//            Test Driver Source File
#include "name.h"

int main( int , char ** )
{
        Name customer( "Robert Bob Smith" ) ;

        process_customers( customer ) ;
                // use compiler-generated default copy constructor
}

process_customers( Name current )
{

} // the current object goes out of scope and ~Name() destructor is called
```

In *external containment* implementations, the compiler-generated copy constructor leads to programs that are difficult to understand and maintain. As a programming practice, always define constructors and avoid giving the compiler the option of creating a *default copy* constructor, especially when the implementation is based on *external containment*. The explicit definition of constructors prevents future problems. In the case of the *Name* class, the copy constructor defined in Section 5.2.1.4, which creates a *deep* copy, avoids the problems associated with *shallow* copies.

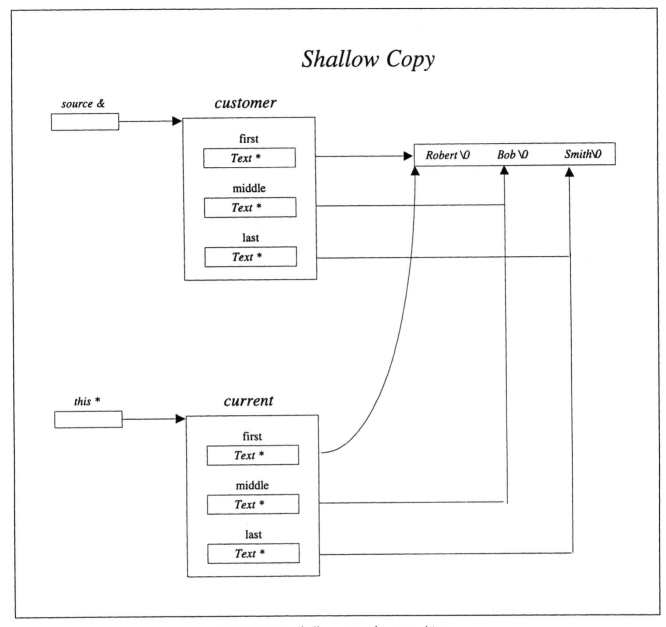

FIGURE 5.11 Shallow copy of a name object

Similar to constructors, the compiler generates a *do-nothing destructor* in the absence of an explicit destructor. For classes that are based on *internal containment* and whose data are built-in data types, for example, the *Point* class, an explicit destructor function is not necessary. The class does not have any pointers to dynamically allocated memory space or open file streams. When a class does not specify a destructor function, a *do-nothing* destructor is logically created for the class by the compiler:

```
typedef        short          Coordinate ;

class Point
{
     private:
          Coordinate x , y ;
     public:
```

```
                Point( Coordinate new_x = 0 , Coordinate new_y = 0 ) ;
                // no destructor defined
} ;

Point:: ~Point()
{
       // do-nothing destructor. Note: this function is created only in a
       // logical sense and the compiler does not place calls to this
       // function in the executable code.
}
```

5.2.4 Regular Member Functions

The regular member functions manipulate and operate on the class members. They keep the internal architecture of a class hidden. For example, the **full_name()**, **size_of_name()**, and **parse_name()** member functions operate on a *Name* object. The public member functions such as **full_name()** keep the internal parts of *Name* hidden from the application by manipulating on and maintaining *Name* data members.

```
//            NAME.H Header File
#ifndef NAME_H
#define NAME_H

    #define NAME_FIELD_SEPARATOR         ' '
    #define NULL_CHAR                    '\0'


    typedef     char        Text ;
    typedef     short       Length ;
    typedef     bool        Boolean ;

    class Name
    {
         private:
               Text *first , *middle , *last ;

               // Utility (internal) function
               Boolean parse_name( void ) ;
         public:
               // default & user-defined value constructor
               Name( const Text *current_name =
                        static_cast<Text *> ( 0 ) ) ;
               // copy constructor
               Name( const Name &source );

               // destructor function
               ~Name() ;

               // access functions
               Length size_of_name( void ) const ;

               // process functions
               void full_name( Text *current_name ) const ;
               // other details left out
    } ;
```

```
#endif    // NAME_H header file
```

In the following example, the **full_name()** function copies the name stored in the object into a client-defined buffer.

```
//              NAME.CPP Source File
#include <stdio.h>       // Standard I/O Library
#include "name.h"        // Name class library

void Name:: full_name( Text *current_name ) const
{
      // if name is valid
      if( ( first != static_cast<Text *> (0) ) &&
        ( last != static_cast<Text *> (0) ) )
      {
            // copy name's component
            if( middle != static_cast<Text *> (0) )
            {
                  sprintf(current_name,"%s %s %s",first,middle,last);
            }
            else   // if no middle name, just use first & last
            {
                  sprintf(current_name,"%s %s",first, last);
            }
      }
      else
      {
            *current_name = NULL_CHAR ; // use null string
      }
}


Length Name:: size_of_name( void ) const
{
      Length length = 0 ;

      // if name is valid
      if( ( first != static_cast<Text *> (0) ) &&
        ( last != static_cast<Text *> (0) )  )
      {
            // Add length of first & last names' length.
            // Also include a byte for spaces between names
            length = strlen( first ) + strlen( last ) + 2 ;

            // if person has a middle name =>
            // add in middle name and one byte for a space
            if( middle != static_cast<Text *> (0) )
            {
                  length += strlen( middle ) + 1 ;
            }
       }
      return( length ) ;
}
```

C++ employs the same notation as used in C to access the data elements. The member functions are invoked through the *dot* (.) and *arrow* (->) operators:

```
object.member_function( arguments, if any ) ;
object_reference.member_function( arguments, if any ) ;
object_pointer->member_function( arguments, if any ) ;
```

The application operates on a Name object by using the supplied public member functions:

```
//              Test Driver Source File
#include <iostream.h>        // Stream I/O Class Library
#include "name.h"            // Name class library

process_customers( const Name &current )
{
        // allocate memory to obtain customer's full name
        Text *name = new Text[ current.size_of_name() ] ;

        if( name ) // if dynamic allocation is successful
        {
                current.full_name( name ) ; // obtain full name
                ...
                // other details left out
        }
        delete[] name ;         // deallocate intermediate buffer
}
```

5.2.5 Static Member Functions

A *private* static data member can be accessed by any regular member function. However, there is a drawback when using a regular member function to access a static data element. Member functions must be invoked in conjunction with an object and cannot be invoked independently. To access a private static data member, a program must define an object regardless of whether the object is needed:

```
//              SAVINGS.H Header File
#ifndef SAVINGS_H
#define SAVINGS_H

    #include "name.h"            // Name class library
    #include "address.h"        // Address class library

    #define DATE_BUFFER_SIZE       9   // buffer's length
    #define DEFAULT_INTEREST_RATE .06  // default rate

    typedef     long        ID ;
    typedef     float       Currency ;
    typedef     float       Rate ;
    typedef     char        Text ;
    typedef     int         Days ;

    class Interest_Table
    {
        private:
                Rate interest_rate ;
                Date start_date[DATE_BUFFER_SIZE] ;
                Days interest_period;

        public:
```

```
                        Interest_Table( Rate new_rate,
                                const Date *start = static_cast<Date *> ( 0 ),
                                Days duration = 30 ) ;
                        Rate rate( void ) const ;
                        Days period( void ) const ;
        } ;


   class Savings
   {
        private:
                        Picture        customer_picture ;
                        Name           customer_name ;
                        Address        customer_address,
                                       branch_address ;
                        ID             id ;
                        Currency       balance ;
                        static Interest_Tableinterest ;
                                // resides outside Savings objects
        public:
                        // Processing functions
                        Currency income( void ) const ;

                        // Access functions
                        Rate interest_rate( void )  ;
                        void change_interest_rate( Rate new_rate ) ;
        } ;

#endif                  // SAVINGS_H Header File

//                      Test Driver Source File
#include <iostream.h>    // Stream I/O Class Library
#include "savings.h"     // Savings class


small_bank()
{
   Savings customer ;

     .
   cout << "\n\t Interest Rate:" << customer.interest_rate() ;
}
```

In the above example, a dummy *customer* object has been defined in order to obtain the current *interest* (Figure 5.5). Using this object, the **interest_rate()** member function can be used to access the private static *interest*. Without this object, the application is unable to obtain the interest rate because **interest_rate()** is a regular member function and can be invoked only in conjunction with an object.

To allow a client to access static elements without having to define an object, a special member function is required. C++ provides *static member* functions, whose only purpose is to access static members and can be invoked in the absence of an object. *Static member* functions are defined using the same notation as other member functions except that they are preceded by the **static** keyword.

```
//                      SAVINGS.H Header File
#ifndef SAVINGS_H
#define SAVINGS_H

      #include "name.h"      // Name class library
      #include "address.h"    // Address class library
```

```
#define DATE_BUFFER_SIZE                    9   // buffer's length
#define DEFAULT_INTEREST_RATE              .06  // default rate

typedef     long        ID ;
typedef     float       Currency ;
typedef     float       Rate ;
typedef     char        Text ;
typedef     int         Days ;

class Interest_Table
{
        private:
                Rate interest_rate ;
                Date start_date[DATE_BUFFER_SIZE] ;
                Date final_date[DATE_BUFFER_SIZE] ;

        public:
                Interest_Table( Rate new_rate,
                    const Text *start = static_cast<Text *> ( 0 ),
                    const Days duration = 30 ) ;
                Rate rate( void ) const ;
                Rate change_rate( Rate new_rate ) ;
                Days period( void ) const ;
} ;
class Savings
{
        private:
                Picture             customer_picture ;
                Name                customer_name ;
                Address             customer_address,
                                    branch_address ;
                ID                  id ;
                Currency            balance ;
                static Interest_Table interest ;
                        // resides outside Savings objects
        public:
                // Processing functions
                Currency income( void ) const ;
                // class access function
                static Rate interest_rate( void )  ;
                static void change_interest_rate( Rate new_rate ) ;
} ;

#endif           // SAVINGS_H Header File




//            SAVINGS.CPP Source File
#include "savings.h"     // Savings class definition

Rate Savings:: interest( DEFAULT_INTEREST_RATE ) ;
    // Initialize the interest object to the default interest rate. For
    // the other data members, default parameters are used (refer
    // to the Savings( ) constructor declaration).
```

```
Currency Savings:: income( void ) const
{
    Currency current_income = balance * Savings:: interest.rate() ;

    return( current_income ) ;
}

Rate Savings:: interest_rate( void )
{
    return( Savings:: interest.rate() ) ;
}

void Savings:: change_interest_rate( Rate new_rate )
{
    // if new rate within limits => change rate for everybody
    if( new_rate > 0.0 && new_rate < MAX_INTEREST_RATE )
    {
        Savings:: interest.change_rate( new_rate ) ;
    }

    return ;
}

//              Test Driver Source File
#include <iostream.h>    // Stream I/O Class Library
#include "savings.h"     // Savings class

int main( int , char ** )
{
    cout << "\n\t Interest Rate:" << Savings:: interest_rate() ;
}
```

A static member function can be invoked by using any of the following notations:

```
object.static_member_function( arguments, if any ) ;
object_reference.static_member_function( arguments, if any ) ;
object_pointer->static_member_function( arguments, if any ) ;
class_name:: static_member_function( arguments, if any ) ;
```

Unlike the regular member functions, static functions do not need to be associated with objects of the class. In the preceding example, **interest_rate()** is a *static member* function and can be invoked whether an object exists or not. Since a *static member* function can be invoked in conjunction with or without an object, C++ restricts a *static member* function from obtaining the "**this**" pointer. The compiler does not incorporate the additional "**this**" argument for *static member* functions. This restriction causes the following behavior:

1. **Member Access**: The *static member* functions can only access the static members because these functions do not get the address of an object. Thus, a *static member* function is unable to distinguish which instance of a defined class to operate on.

   The above **interest_rate()** and **change_interest_rate()** functions are unable to operate on *customer_name* and *id* elements of the *Savings* class because they do not get the object's address (**this**).
2. **Member Function**: Without an object to refer to, the static member function cannot call a regular member function of the same class. A regular member function implicitly expects the "**this**" pointer, but a static function does not obtain the "**this**" pointer and cannot supply it implicitly to a regular member function.

   However, the above restriction is unidirectional, and a regular member function may call a static member function or operate on a static member.

158   Class   Chapter 5

```
//            SAVINGS.CPP Source File
#include "name.h"
#include "address.h"
#include "savings.h"

Currency Savings:: income( void )
{
    Currency current_income ;

    current_income = balance * Savings:: interest.rate() ;
    /*
    ** the function can also use the following notation:
    **current_income = balance * interest.rate() ;
    */

    return( current_income ) ;
}
```

In the above example, **income()** is a regular member function and can freely call the static member functions.

As a good programming practice, invoke *static member* functions by using the class name and the *scope resolution* (::) operator. If an object is used to invoke a *static member* function, the function call gives the false impression to the reader that it is operating only on the current object:

```
//            Test Driver Source File
#include <iostream.h>
#include "savings.h"

small_bank()
{
    Savings customer1( "Bob Smith"), customer2("Mary Jane");

    // the interest rates for all of the Savings objects are being
    // affected, not just customer1
    customer1.change_interest_rate( .07 ) ;
}
```

The above notation gives the false impression that the interest rate only for the *customer1* object is affected, even though in reality the interest rate for all of the objects is changed. The following notation explicitly indicates that the interest rate for all of the *Savings* objects has been affected:

```
Savings:: change_interest_rate( .07 ) ;
      // invokes Savings class static function
```

C++ does not permit a static member function to have the same name as a nonstatic member function.

5.3 FRIEND CLASSES

Through the **friend** keyword, a class can become a "friend" of another class. This means the member functions of the **friend** class gain access to private members of the other class. Thus, the member functions of the **friend** class do not need to use the member functions of the other class to operate on the private data members. The designation of **friend** creates tight coupling between the designs of the involved classes and should be used sparingly. In Figure 5.12, the *Savings* class member functions can directly operate on the private members of *Interest Table*:

```
class Savings
{
      private:
              Interest_Table interest ;
      public:
              // Other details left out
} ;

#define DATE_BUFFER_SIZE        9

typedef      float     Rate ;
typedef      char      Date ;

class Interest_Table
{
      private:
```

```
        Rate interest_rate ;
        Date start_date[DATE_BUFFER_SIZE] ;
        Date end_date[DATE_BUFFER_SIZE] ;
public:
        friend class Savings ;
                // member functions of Savings have access
                // to private members of Interest Table
        // Other details left out
} ;
```

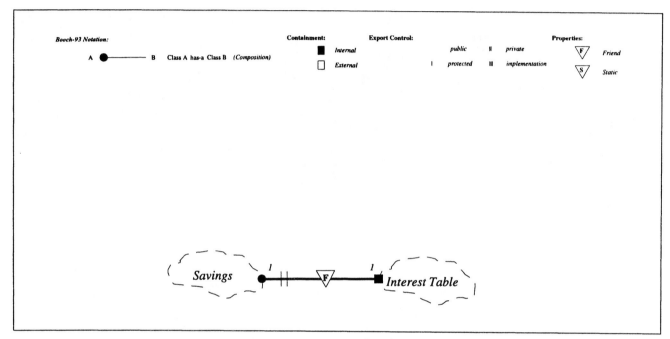

FIGURE 5.12 Savings class diagram.

Since *Savings* can operate directly on the private members of *Interest Table*, the member functions of *Savings* are tightly coupled to the data representation of *Interest Table*. Whenever the *Interest Table* data representation is changed, the *Savings* member functions are also affected. In addition, the *Savings* class member functions must ensure that they do not change the *Interest Table* data to invalid states (for example, setting **interest_rate** to a negative value), which would cause the object to be placed in an unpredictable state. Class libraries based on friend classes forego some of the major components of object-oriented design: *modularity, encapsulation, abstraction*. The design coupling between the classes leads to maintainability and reliability problems. Thus, the use of friend classes in object-oriented (OO) designs is typically discouraged.

SUMMARY

A *class* definition logically organizes data into a set, and the class functions are the operations on the set. From the perspective of C++, data members are either viewed as regular or *static* members. Regular data members reside in an object, whereas *static* members are external to the object and are only logically associated with it. This property allows external data members to be shared by all instances of the class (objects).

Static members are ideal for classes whose objects will need to share the same information, such as look-up tables that are the same for all objects. The *static* members exist independently of the instances of the class. A static member's life span is during the execution of the entire program. The *static* member is created prior to the execution of the **main**() function and is destroyed prior to the return of control to the operating system.

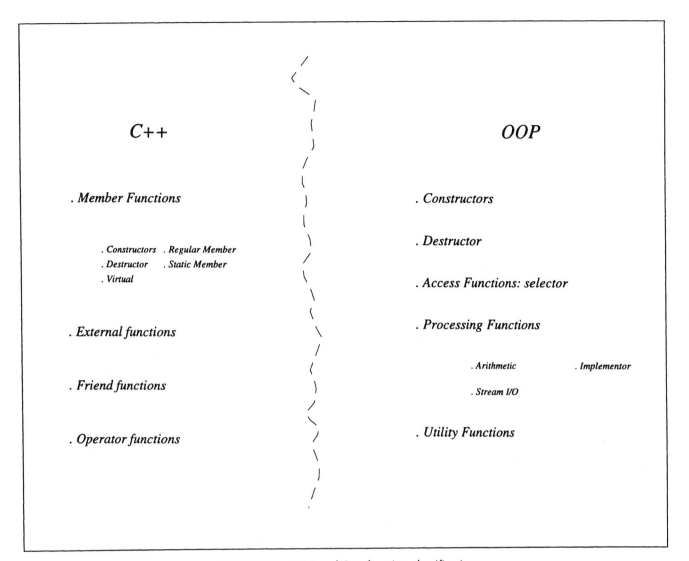

FIGURE 5.13   OOP and C++ function classification.

Application (client) software uses *member* functions to access and operate on the class data members. The *member* functions keep the class design hidden and prevent the client from operating on the data members directly. The *member* functions act as gateways for the clients and result in an object-based design that supports *encapsulation* and *abstraction.* The *member* functions operate on and change the *state* of an object.

In C++, member functions can be partitioned into the following groups, based on their syntax:

1. **Constructors**: These functions initialize the memory space for an instance of a class. For an object to come into existence, the memory space for it must be reserved and placed into a predictable state.
2. **Destructor**: This function is the counterpart of a constructor. This function performs cleanup operations. It is used to destroy dynamically allocated space and close any file streams associated with an object.
3. **Regular**: These functions allow the client to operate on objects after they are created. A client makes requests via these functions.
4. **Static**: These functions are designed to allow the client to operate on the internal static data members of the class.
5. **Virtual**: These functions allow a design hierarchy to support polymorphic behavior and are discussed in Chapter 10.

From an object-oriented perspective, functions can be grouped into the following types (Figure 5.13):

1. **Constructors**: Functions that create an object.
2. **Destructor**: A function that destroys an object.
3. **Access Functions**: Through these functions, a client obtains a controlled view to selected member(s) of a class. For example, the **Savings:: interest_rate()** function provides information on the *Savings* interest rate (refer to Section 5.2.5). An access function is also referred to as a *selector*.
4. **Processing Functions**: This category of functions performs the actual work for a class such as stream I/O, arithmetic operations, and so on. For example, the **Savings:: income()** function computes the account's income (refer to Section 5.2.5).
5. **Utility Functions**: These functions are private member functions that perform internal tasks. For instance, the **Name:: parse_name()** function partitions a name into several fields and is used internally by other member functions (refer to Section 5.2.4).

GLOSSARY

Constructor

The initialization member function

Destructor

The cleanup member function

Deep copy

Using the contents of one object to create another instance of the same class. In a deep copy, the two objects may contain the same information but the target object will have its own buffers and resources. The destruction of either object will not affect the remaining object

External containment

The data members in a class are stored externally and are referenced only through a pointer or reference

Free store

The dynamic memory allocation space is referred to as the *free store* and is operated on by the **new** and **delete** operators. *Free store* is different from *heap*, which is maintained by the *malloc* library

Internal containment

The data members of another class are maintained within an instance of the class

Initialization list

The body of a constructor is preceded by an initialization list. This list allows the data members to be placed in a predictable state prior to the execution of constructor's body

Memory leakage

Loss of free memory space due to a programming error. This condition is caused when a dynamically allocated memory space for an object or array is never deallocated even after the applicable code block finishes using the object or the array

Shallow copy

Copying the contents of one object into another instance of the same class, thus creating a mirror image. Owing to straight copying of references and pointers, the two objects will share the same external resources. The destruction of one object and its external resources causes the externally contained contents of the other object to be unpredictable

Static data member

A data member that is common to and shared by all instances of a class

Temporary object

An explicit call to a constructor creates a nameless object that is destroyed after the expression in which it was created is evaluated.

CHAPTER 6

Functions

INTRODUCTION

The previous chapter focused on the definition of a class and its associated member functions. In addition to member functions, C++ supports other types of functions. This chapter continues the discussion by organizing functions on the basis of their syntax and relationship to a class (Figure 6.1), and describes how they are used in the design of a class:

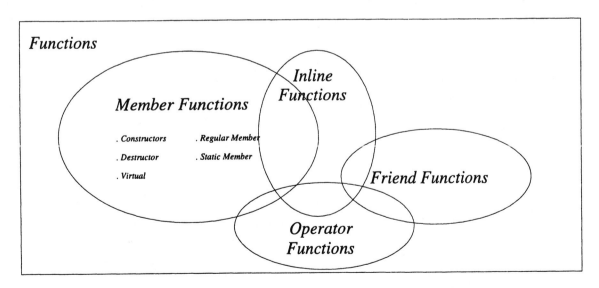

FIGURE 6.1 Types of functions in C++.

1. **Class Member Functions**: On the basis of the member functions' behavior, they are further separated into constructor, destructor, static, and regular member functions.
2. **Inline Functions**: An *inline* function instructs the compiler to embed the function's body in the calling function. These functions improve software performance by eliminating the function call overhead. An *inline* function is typically small in size (several C++ statements).
3. **Operator Functions**: C++ allows most of the existing operators to be overloaded for a class. At times an *operator* function is more intuitive and creates better *data abstraction* by hiding the internal operations. For instance, the *addition* (+) operator may be overloaded to add two *complex* numbers. The addition operator *abstracts* the specific arithmetic operations associated with complex numbers. The expression "*z1* + *z2*" is more readable than "*z1.add(z2)*."
4. **Friend Functions**: These are privileged nonmember functions that have access to the internal members of a class.
5. **Virtual Functions**: These are used in conjunction with *inheritance* to create *polymorphism* and are discussed in Chapter 10.

At the end, this chapter briefly describes several of the ANSI C++ class libraries that use operator overloading and friend functions. The main focus of this chapter is on **operator** functions, and the *Complex* number is an easy and versatile example for describing and illustrating operator overloading. A *Complex* number is represented as an ordered pair (x,y) consisting of *real (x)* and *imaginary (y)* parts [Kreyszig 1983]. Figure 6.2

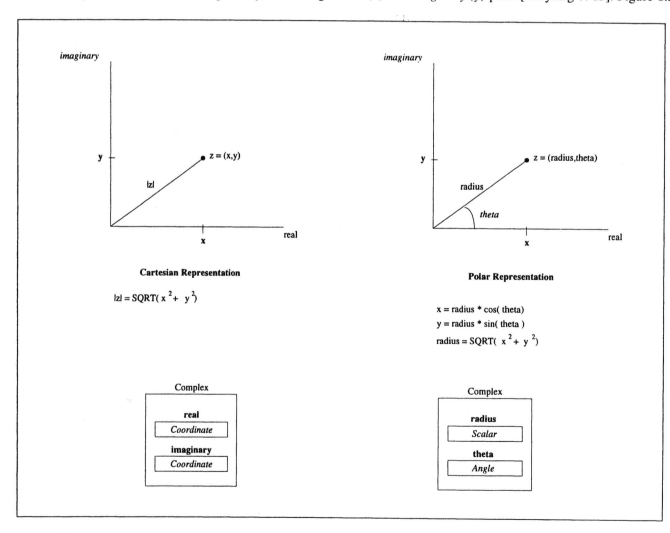

FIGURE 6.2 Complex number representation.

depicts a geometrical representation of a complex number on a *complex* plane. Figure 6.2 illustrates both Cartesian and Polar representation of a complex number. Complex numbers are used in advanced mathematics and engineering applications, such as signal processing and circuit analysis.

6.1 INLINE FUNCTIONS

When functions with few lines of code are called frequently, the function call overhead can degrade the performance of the software. When a function is called, the contents of the processor registers are pushed onto the stack; the passed parameters are copied onto the stack; the function is called; the function retrieves the data off the stack; and the body of the function is executed. When the **return** statement is executed, the return value is pushed onto the stack; the calling function retrieves the return value off the stack; and, the previous contents of the processor registers are restored. These operations affect software performance especially when small-size functions are called within a loop.

In C, macros can be used to eliminate function call overhead since the compiler expands simple pseudofunction. However, macros have subtle problems associated with their use. At times, macros also are inefficient, can cause data conversion problems, and may create unpredictable behavior. C++ has resolved problems associated with macros by introducing *inline* functions.

Using the **inline** keyword on a function, the compiler is instructed to embed the inline function's body in the calling function. An inline function eliminates function call overhead. In the following example, several of the *Complex* class member functions are inlined:

```
//              COMPLEX.H Header File
#ifndef COMPLEX_H
#define COMPLEX_H

     typedef      float         Coordinate ;

class Complex
{
     private:
          Coordinate current_real , current_imaginary ;
     public:
          // constructor (with default values)
          inline Complex( Coordinate x = 0 , Coordinate y = 0 );

          // class access functions
          inline Coordinate real( void ) const ;
          inline Coordinate imaginary( void ) const ;
} ;

// user-defined constructor
inline Complex:: Complex( Coordinate x , Coordinate y )
          : current_real( x ) , current_imaginary( y )
{
}

// class access functions: return real/imaginary components
inline Coordinate Complex:: real( void )  const
{
          return( current_real ) ;
}

inline Coordinate Complex:: imaginary( void ) const
{
```

```
                    return( current_imaginary ) ;
        }

#endif               // COMPLEX_H Header File
```

Since an **inline** definition is actually a function, the expressions in the function call are evaluated before the function's body is executed. Therefore, the problems associated with macros are not encountered with an **inline** function. In addition, the modularity provided by a normal function is maintained while the performance is optimized. In the following example, the bodies of the **Complex()** constructor and access functions are embedded within the calling **main()** function:

```
//              Test Driver Source File
#include <iostream.h>        // I/O Stream Class Library
#include "complex.h"         // Complex Class Library

int main( int , char ** )
{
        Coordinate x1 = 2 , x2 = 3 ;
        Coordinate y1 = 4 , y2 = -8 ;

        Complex z1( x1 + x2 , y1 + y2 ) ;
            // expand the constructor's body instead of calling it
            // compiler will perform the following:
            //      z1.current_real = x1 + x2 ;
            //      z1.current_imaginary = y1 + y2 ;

        cout << "\n\t Real( z1 ) : " << z1.real() ;
            // expand  to:  cout << "Real( z1 ) : " << z1.current_real ;

        cout << "\n\t Imaginary( z1 ) : " << z1.imaginary() ;
            // expand  to:
            //cout << "Imaginary( z1 ) : " << z1.current_imaginary ;

        return( 0 ) ;
}
```

To embed an inline function in the calling function, the compiler needs the inline function's definition. Therefore, the inline function definition (body) should be in either the header file (*see the preceding example*) or the source file where the inline function is being called.

Since the compiler inserts the inline function's body instead of calling it, the inline functions can give rise to executable code that is larger. As a rule, functions with more than three basic C++ statements should not be *inlined*. This is a break-even point [Murray 1993]. The function call overhead becomes negligible as the number of operations in a function increases. Furthermore, if the function is performing time-consuming operations such as floating point operations, the function call overhead becomes negligible. In this type of situation, the use of inline functions produces a larger executable code size with no real savings in execution time. Most compilers provide benchmark tools that allow a designer to determine the performance savings involved in using an inline function.

When a *member* function is defined within the class definition, the compiler treats the function as *inline*:

```
//              COMPLEX.H Header File
#ifndef COMPLEX_H
#define COMPLEX_H

        typedef      float        Coordinate ;
```

```
class Complex
{
    private:
            Coordinate current_real , current_imaginary ;
    public:
            // inlined constructor
            Complex( Coordinate x = 0 , Coordinate y = 0 )
                : current_real( x ) , current_imaginary( y ) {} ;

            // inlined access function
            Coordinate real( void ) const
                { return( current_real ) ; } ;
            Coordinate imaginary ( void ) const
                { return( current_imaginary ) ; } ;
} ;
```

```
#endif       // COMPLEX_H Header File
```

Even though the language permits this seemingly convenient style, definition of functions in the class definition is difficult to read and maintain. The client of a class is only interested in the external design interfaces, which include the **public** and **protected** members and the associated function declarations. For source code readability, include only the function declarations (prototypes) in the class and define the function body outside the class. In the original *Complex* class example, the inline member function definitions were separated from the class definition by using the **inline** keyword and presenting the definitions in a later section of the header file.

The inlining operation is simply a request to the compiler, and the compiler may elect to ignore an inline function definition in certain situations. In such an event, the function is treated as a normal function call (an "*outline*" function). Possible conditions that may force an inline function to be treated as a function call (*outline*) by most compilers are as follows:

1. **Loops**: If an **inline** function contains a **for, while,** or **do-while** loop. The time complexity associated with the loop makes the function call overhead savings negligible:

```
inline long factorial(long n)
{
    long answer = 1 ;
    for( register long i = 1 ; i <= n ; i++)
            answer = answer * i ;
    return (answer) ;
}
```

2. **Recursiveness**: An inline function cannot be recursive because the compiler is unable to determine the number of recursion levels needed to insert into the body of the calling function.

```
inline long factorial(long n)
{
    long answer ;

    if ( n == 1 )
            answer = 1 ;
    else
            answer = factorial(n-1) * n ;
    return( answer ) ;
}
```

3. **Address of a Function:** The address of an *inline* function cannot be obtained. To obtain an address, the compiler must treat the call to the *inline* function as a normal function call and forces it to be an *outline* function.

When an application accesses an inline function's address, the compiler immediately creates an *outline* version of the function. For normal calls, the function is inserted as *inline*. For calls using the address, the function (*outline* version) is actually called. The program ends up using the inline function as both *inline* and *outline*, which introduces a *schizophrenic* behavior for the function [Davis 1993]. As a good programming practice, do not define a function as *inline* if it will later be called as a normal function.

During the software test and integration phase, a complicated inline function should be tested in both outline and inline modes [Davis 1993]. Most compilers provide an option for enabling and disabling the inline feature. For example, the Microsoft C++ compiler uses the *Ob* flag to force an inline function to be treated as an outline function. Since a designer does not have full control over the actions of the clients using the class, the dual testing strategy guarantees the application's behavior is the same under both circumstances.

6.2 OPERATOR OVERLOADING

C++ permits most of the existing operators to be overloaded. When applied properly, operator overloading improves design clarity. For some applications, an operator provides a better representation than a function. For the *Complex* class, "*z1 + z2*" is more intuitive than **add()**. The following paragraphs discuss some popular applications for operator overloading:

1. **Arithmetic Operations:** A math library may overload the arithmetic operators for a user-defined class, as in the *Complex* example.
2. **Stream I/O for User-Defined Types:** By overloading the *Stream I/O* operators (<< and >>), the *Stream I/O Class (iostream)* library can be customized for other classes, creating a type-safe and standard I/O format for all data types:

```
cout << "\n\t Radius:" << radius ;
     // compiler uses the function that matches radius's type
```

The *Stream I/O Class* library has more overhead than its C counterpart (the *Standard I/O* library), because stream I/O is performed through multiple function calls. However, the designer is relieved of the burden of data type checking. This chapter demonstrates extending the *Stream I/O Class* library for the *Complex* class.
3. **Dynamic Allocation:** For a data class, the *dynamic memory allocation/deallocation* operators (**new** and **delete**) may be overloaded to create custom memory management operations. Chapter 7 provides examples of custom memory management.
4. **Array Boundary Error Checking:** Neither C nor C++ checks for array boundary conditions, and memory overrun is a common problem. The *array index* operator ([ ]) may be overloaded to do boundary checking for software testing and debugging purposes. When an application accesses an element in the array, the overloaded *array index* ([ ]) operator will be invoked to check the array indices before operating on an element. If an array index exceeds the array's size, the *array index* function would initiate some type of error recovery. Chapter 11 presents a generic *Array* class (*parameterized type*) that monitors accesses to an array of any data type.
5. **Deep Copy:** The built-in *assignment* operator (=) copies the contents of one object to another object, creating a *shallow copy*. For classes that use *external* containment, such as the *Name* class in Chapter 5, *shallow copies* can create design problems. Basically, the problem associated with the default *copy* constructor also applies to the *assignment* operator (=). For classes that use *external* containment, the impact of the *default copy constructor* and the built-in *assignment* operator must be evaluated. When applicable, the design must provide explicit implementations for both the copy constructor and assignment operator. The overloaded operator would create *deep copies* of objects (Figure 6.3).

6. **Multi-Dimensional Lists**: For multi-dimensional lists such as a *Matrix* class, the *parenthesis* operator is overloaded in order to allow a client to traverse and access the elements of the list. For instance, *matrix(i,j) = expression;*.

Table 6.1 depicts the C++ operators that can be overloaded.

TABLE 6.1 C++ Operators

Description	Operators			Application/Comment
Data Access	->	[ ]		*Arrow* (->) is used to implement smart pointers *Index* ([ ]) is used to hide topology and architecture of a list class. It is also used to detect array boundary violations (Chapter 11)
Parenthesis	( )			Parenthesis is used as an *accessor* for hiding access to the members of a multi-dimensional list class
Increment/Decrement (postfix & prefix)	++	--		For classes such as date and time, they are used to provide increment and decrement capability. The following identifies the signatures of the overloaded *prefix* (++object) and *postfix* (object++) operators for a class, respectively: Class & Class:: operator ++(void) ; Class Class:: operator ++(int) ; The above integer argument is a dummy argument and allows the compiler to distinguish the *prefix* operator from the *postfix* operator
Complement/Not	~	!		For logical negation on a class
Dynamic Allocation	new delete new[ ] delete[ ]			Custom memory management (Chapter 7)
Member Access	->*			
Arithmetic	* / % + -			For math libraries such as the Complex class (Chapter 6)
Binary Shift	<< >>			Stream I/O applications (Chapters 6 and 9)
Relational	< <= > >= == !=			Comparison of objects. The ANSI C++ string class library uses these operators (Chapter 6)
Binary	& ^ |			Math libraries
Logical	&& ||			
Operator/Assignment	= *= /= %= += -= <<= >>= &= |= ^=			For math libraries such as the Complex class (Chapter 6)
Comma				

To overload an operator, a function must be associated with the operator. The following specifies the general syntax for an overloaded operator function:

```
return_type   operator  symbol( parameter list )
{
        function's body ;
}
```

The operator function name consists of the word "operator" followed by the operator symbol. In the following example, the *addition* (+) operator and the *minus* (-) operator are overloaded to add and subtract two complex numbers instead of defining and using the **add()** and **minus()** functions (Figure 6.4). In addition, *relational* operators, such as the *equal* (==) operator, have also been overloaded in order to compare complex numbers:

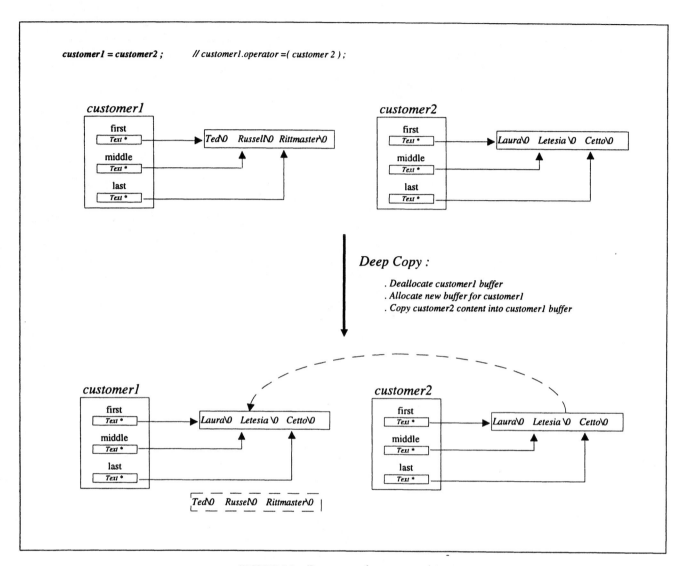

FIGURE 6.3 Deep copy for a name object.

```
//              COMPLEX.H Header File
#ifndef COMPLEX_H
#define COMPLEX_H

        typedef      float       Coordinate ;
        typedef      float       Scalar ;
        typedef      bool        Boolean ;

        class Complex
        {
                private:
                        Coordinate current_real , current_imaginary ;
                public:
                        // constructor (with default values)
                        inline Complex( Coordinate x = 0 , Coordinate y = 0 );

                        // class access functions
                        inline Coordinate real( void ) const ;
```

```
                              inline Coordinate imaginary( void ) const ;

                              // class arithmetic functions
                              Complex conjugate( void ) const ;
                              Scalar magnitude( void ) const ;
                  } ;


             // Arithmetic operator function declarations (prototypes)
             Complex operator +( const Complex &z1, const Complex &z2 ) ;
             Complex operator -( const Complex &z1, const Complex &z2 ) ;
             Complex operator *( const Complex &z1, const Complex &z2 ) ;
             Complex operator /( const Complex &z1, const Complex &z2 ) ;


             // Relational operator functions
             Boolean operator ==( const Complex &z1 , const Complex &z2 ) ;
             Boolean operator !=( const Complex &z1 , const Complex &z2 ) ;


             // user-defined constructor
             inline Complex:: Complex(Coordinate x , Coordinate y )
                         : current_real( x ) , current_imaginary( y )
             {
             }


             // class access functions: return real/imaginary components
             inline Coordinate Complex:: real( void )  const
             {
                           return( current_real ) ;
             }


             inline Coordinate Complex:: imaginary( void ) const
             {
                           return( current_imaginary ) ;
             }


#endif                 // COMPLEX_H Header File
```

Since the arithmetic functions are nonmember functions, they rely on the access and constructor functions for accessing the **private** data members. Therefore, the constructor and access functions have been *inlined* to improve performance while encapsulating the design.

Since a binary arithmetic operator requires both left and right operands, the operator function must take two *Complex* arguments. The left and right operands of the arithmetic operators are denoted by the $z1$ and $z2$ references, respectively. The references have been made constant because they do not affect the contents of the left and right operands (a programming guideline). The preceding arithmetic operator functions return the result of the *Complex* operations.

```
//              COMPLEX.CPP Source File
#include <math.h>         // Math Library
#include <stdlib.h>       // Standard Library
#include <stdio.h>        // Standard I/O Library
#include "complex.h"      // Complex Class Library

// Complex Conjugate: z' = ( x + y i )' = x - y i
Complex Complex:: conjugate( void )  const
{
      return( Complex( real() , -imaginary() ) ) ;
```

```
}

// Magnitude (scalar):  |z| = Sqrt( x² + y² )
Scalar Complex:: magnitude( void )   const
{
      Scalar r = sqrt( real() * real() + imaginary() * imaginary() ) ;

      return( r ) ;
}


// overloaded operator +() function for complex arithmetic
Complex operator +( const Complex &z1 , const Complex &z2 )
{
      // add real parts of the complex objects
      Coordinate real = z1.real() + z2.real() ;

      // add imaginary parts of the complex objects
      Coordinate imaginary = z1.imaginary()+ z2.imaginary() ;

      // return result of the complex addition
      return ( Complex( real, imaginary ) ) ;
}

Complex operator -( const Complex &z1 , const Complex &z2 )
{
      // subtract real parts of the complex objects
      Coordinate real = z1.real() - z2.real() ;

      // subtract imaginary parts of the complex objects
      Coordinate imaginary = z1.imaginary() - z2.imaginary() ;

      // return result of the complex subtraction
      return ( Complex( real, imaginary ) ) ;
}
```

// compute: $z_1 * z_2 = (x_1 + y_1\ i\ ) * (x_2 + y_2\ i)$
```
Complex operator *( const Complex &z1 , const Complex &z2 )
{
```
      // real part: $x_1 * x_2 + y_1 * y_2\ i^2 = x_1 * x_2 - y_1 * y_2$
```
      Coordinate real = z1.real() * z2.real() -
                        z1.imaginary() * z2.imaginary() ;
```

      // imaginary part: $(x_1 * y_2 + y_1 * x_2\ )\ i$
```
      Coordinate imaginary = z1.real() * z2.imaginary() +
                        z1.imaginary() * z2.real() ;

      // return result of the complex multiplication
      return ( Complex( real, imaginary ) ) ;
}
```

// compute: $z_1\ /\ z_2 = (z_1 * z_2'\ )\ /\ |z_2|^2$
```
Complex operator /( const Complex &z1 , const Complex &z2 )
{
      Complex z ; // use default values for the result
```

      // compute $|\ z_2\ |^2$

```
         Scalar divisor = z2.magnitude() * z2.magnitude() ;

         if( divisor != 0.0 )// avoid divide by zero
         {
                  // compute z₁ * z₂'
                  z = z1 * z2.conjugate() ;
                          // z = operator *( z1 , z2.conjugate() ) ;

                  // compute (z₁ * z₂' )/ | z₂ |²
                  z = z * (1/divisor) ;
                          // z = operator *( z , Complex( 1/divisor, 0 ) ) ;
         }

         // return result of the complex division
         return( z ) ;
}


// Relational comparison function: z1 == z2
Boolean operator ==( const Complex &z1 , const Complex &z2 )
{
      Boolean equal = true ;
      char buffer[30] ;

      Coordinate x1, x2 , y1 , y2 ;

      // round off real and imaginary components to 5 decimal places
      // and treat any values less than .000005 as zero.
      // This algorithm will prevent comparison of small numbers
      sprintf( buffer,"%.5f", z1.real() ) ;
      x1 = static_cast<Coordinate> (atof( buffer )) ;
      sprintf( buffer,"%.5f", z2.real() ) ;
      x2 = static_cast<Coordinate> (atof( buffer )) ;

      sprintf( buffer,"%.5f", z1.imaginary() ) ;
      y1 = static_cast<Coordinate> (atof( buffer )) ;
      sprintf( buffer,"%.5f", z2.imaginary() ) ;
      y2 = static_cast<Coordinate> (atof( buffer )) ;

      // compare real and imaginary parts of the complex objects
      if( x1 != x2 || y1 != y2 )
      {
                  equal = false ;
      }

      // return result of the comparison
      return( equal ) ;
}


// Relational comparison function: z1 != z2
Boolean operator !=( const Complex &z1 , const Complex &z2 )
{
      Boolean not_equal = true ;

      // This function uses the above ==( ) operator function:
      //if( operator ==( z1 , z2 ) )
      if( z1 == z2 )
```

```
        {
                            not_equal = false ; // if they are equal then negate result
        }

        // return the result of the comparison
        return( not_equal ) ;
}
```

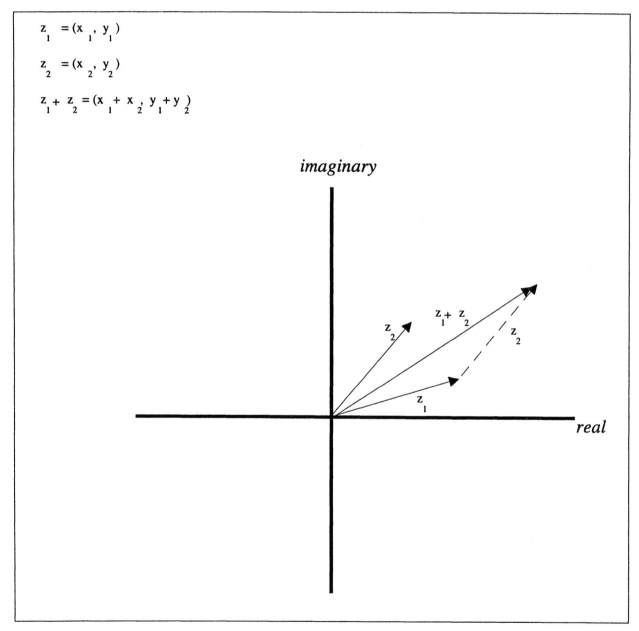

$$z_1 = (x_1, y_1)$$

$$z_2 = (x_2, y_2)$$

$$z_1 + z_2 = (x_1 + x_2, y_1 + y_2)$$

FIGURE 6.4 Complex addition.

The *Complex* operator functions have been defined as nonmember functions. Nonmember functions cannot access private data members and need to use the class access and constructor functions to operate on the data elements. The *Complex* class access and constructor functions encapsulate the class data representation and storage. If the complex representation is changed from *Cartesian* to *polar* representation, only the low-level functions such as the *access* functions are affected. Since the arithmetic functions are independent of the data storage and representation, the

Complex library is more maintainable and the changes are localized. Figure 6.5 depicts the *Complex* library's functional hierarchy and illustrates this independence. The **operator +**() function uses the access functions to obtain the real and imaginary components, and the **operator /**() function utilizes the other *Complex* functions such as the **operator ***() function for implementing the division operation.

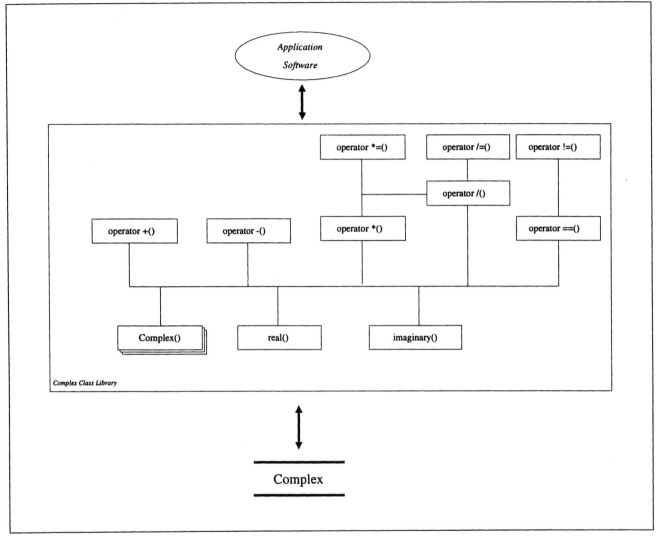

FIGURE 6.5   Complex class function hierarchy.

The application software uses the overloaded arithmetic operators to operate on instances of the *Complex* class (*objects*). The complex arithmetic details and functional hierarchy are transparent to the client. The compiler resolves the calls to the operator functions and uses the left and right operands as the arguments.

```
//           Test Driver Source File
#include "complex.h"

int main( int , char ** )
{
    Complex z1( 1 ) ,  z2( 3,4 ) , z3 ;
        // initialize z1 = (1,0), z2 = (3,4), and z3 = (0,0)

        // add z1 and z2 and store result in z3
        z3 = z2 + z1 ;
```

```
          // z3 = (4,4)
          // the compiler treats the above as a function call:
          //     z3 = operator +( z2, z1 ) ;

     z1 = z2 - z3 ;
          // z1 = (-1,0)
          // compiler treats the expression as
          //     z1 = operator -( z2, z3 ) ;

     z1 = z3 / z2 ;
          // z1 = (1.12, -.16)
          // compiler treats the expression as
          //     z1 = operator /( z3, z2 ) ;

     return( 0 ) ;
}
```

6.2.1 Implicit Conversion

C++ has evolved implicit conversion from the C implementation. C++ not only supports the built-in data conversion of C but the language also allows a built-in data type to be implicitly promoted to an instance of a class in order to evaluate an expression or assignment. The compiler uses the appropriate class constructor to create a *temporary object* on which it performs the implicit data conversion. In the following example, the test driver adds a real number to a *Complex* object ($z2$). The *Complex* class has only one version of the *addition* operator (+) function, which takes two complex arguments. To evaluate the preceding expression, the compiler will apply an implicit conversion. The compiler examines the class constructors and uses the applicable constructor to create a *temporary object*.

```
//                    Test Driver Source  File
#include "complex.h"

int main( int , char ** )
{
     Complex z2( 3 , 4 ) ;

     Complex z1 = 8 + z2 ;
          // compiler treats it as z1 = operator +( Complex(8,0) , z2 ) ;
          // z1 = (11,4)

     return( 0 ) ;
}
```

Through the use of the *temporary object*, the expression can be evaluated. In the above example, the program implicitly calls the *Complex* class constructor. A default value for the imaginary component is passed to the *user-defined values* constructor and the constructor creates a temporary *Complex* object. The temporary object contains (8,0) for its real and imaginary parts. $z2$ and the temporary object are then passed to the addition operator function.

The implicit conversion associated with operator overloading provides flexibility. As shown for the *Complex* class, the client can easily mix real and complex numbers. On the downside, the overhead associated with implicit conversion will degrade performance. The loss in performance is directly dependent on the constructor's and destructor's time requirements and the frequency of calls to these functions.

A designer can take certain steps to reduce the overhead associated with implicit conversion. The simplest solution is to prevent the compiler from applying implicit conversion by prohibiting it from using constructors for creation of temporary objects. In the following example, the *Complex* class constructors do not use default values; instead, distinct implementations for the *default* and *user-defined values* constructors are provided:

```
//                      COMPLEX.H Header File
class Complex
{
        private:
                Coordinate current_real , current_imaginary ;
        public:
                // constructors have been separated
                inline Complex( ) ;
                inline Complex( Coordinate x, Coordinate y ) ;

                // other details left out
} ;
```

The new definition prevents the compiler from applying implicit conversion and the following statements will not compile:

```
z1 = 8 + z3 ;
z1 = z3 + 4.0 ;  // compiler is unable to create temporary object
```

By eliminating the default argument values for the *Complex* constructor function, the design ensures that the compiler cannot apply implicit conversion in the overloaded operator expressions. The above described *Complex* class prevents its clients from knowingly or unknowingly using implicit conversion to mix real and complex number arithmetic. The *Complex* class and its functions will operate only on complex objects, so the application's freedom has been restricted. For classes whose reliability or performance is affected by implicit conversion, the preceding method may be utilized to prevent implicit conversion.

In ANSI C++, the constructor may be proceeded by the **explicit** keyword which denotes that the constructor may not be used for implicit data conversions:

```
//              COMPLEX.H Header File
class Complex
{
        private:
                Coordinate current_real , current_imaginary ;
        public:
                // has been declared as non-converting constructor
                explicit inline Complex( Coordinate x = 0 , Coordinate y = 0 );

                // other details left out
} ;
```

Implicit conversion increases software overhead due to automatic calls to constructors and destructors. This overhead can be reduced without restricting the client's freedom. The designer of the class must become more involved by incorporating the additional features that implicit conversion would otherwise provide. For instance, the *Complex* class may be designed to incorporate different permutations of complex number arithmetic. The additional functions permit an application to mix real and complex objects without adversely affecting the performance. This more elaborate design minimizes data conversion and overcomes the degradation in software performance.

```
//              COMPLEX.H Header File
typedef     float        Coordinate ;
typedef     float        Real ;

class Complex
{
```

```
        private:
                Coordinate current_real , current_imaginary ;
        public:
                // User-Defined Value Constructor with default values
                inline Complex( Coordinate x = 0 , Coordinate y = 0 ) ;

                // Access functions: read-only functions
                inline Coordinate real( void ) const ;
                inline Coordinate imaginary( void ) const ;
} ;


Complex operator +( const Complex &z1, const Complex &z2 ) ;
Complex operator +( Real x, const Complex &z2 ) ;
Complex operator +( const Complex &z1, Real x ) ;
```

The preceding *Complex* class provides three types of addition operator functions. The addition functions eliminate the need for temporary objects for complex addition by supporting all three permutations of complex addition: complex + complex, complex + real number, and real number + complex.

```
//                   Test Driver Source File
#include <iostream.h>              // Stream I/O Class Library
#include "complex.h"               // Complex Class Library

int main( int , char ** )
{
        Complex z1( 3,4 ) , z2 , z3 ;
            // z1: initialize data elements: real = 3 & imaginary = 4
            // z2 & z3: initialize to default values (0,0)

        // process as operator ==( z1 + z2 , z2 + z1 ) ;
        if( z1 + z2 == z2 + z1 )
        {
                cout << "\n\t Addition is commutative" ;
        }

        z2 = z1 + 4 ;
            // process as z2 = operator +( Complex, float) ;
        z2 = 3 + z1 ;
            // process as z2 = operator +( float, Complex ) ;
        z3 = z1 + z2 ;
            // process as z3 = operator +( Complex , Complex ) ;
}
```

The compiler evaluates the preceding expressions transparently to the application software by calling the applicable **operator +**() functions. No temporary complex objects are created and the preceding application program will run faster than its predecessor. The improved performance has come at a certain expense: The designer of the *Complex* class must provide the additional resources.

6.2.2 Binary Operators

A binary operator function may be implemented as a *member* or a *nonmember* function. In the previous examples, the arithmetic binary operators for the *Complex* class were implemented as nonmember functions.

The compiler treats the use of an overloaded operator differently for member implementations and nonmember implementations:

```
A = B op C ;              // where op is an overloaded operator function
                          // B and C are left and right operands
```

1. If implemented as a *nonmember* function, the above statement translates to:

```
A = operator op( B , C ) ;
```

2. If implemented as a *member* function, the left operand represents an object and the right operand becomes the argument to the operator function:

```
A = B.operator op( C ) ;
```

For most programmers, the choice between a member and nonmember implementation is confusing. To identify a better alternative, let's examine two different implementations for complex addition:

1. **Nonmember Implementation**: The *Complex* library implementation in the previous sections has been based on a nonmember implementation.

```
//          COMPLEX.H Header File
typedef     float           Coordinate ;

class Complex
{
    private:
            Coordinate current_real , current_imaginary ;
    public:
            Complex( Coordinate x = 0 , Coordinate y = 0 ) ;
            // details left out
} ;
```

```
Complex operator +( const Complex &z1, const Complex &z2 ) ;
```

As discussed previously and shown below, the use of default values for the *Complex* class constructor's arguments allows the compiler to resolve the "8 + z3" expression. The compiler implicitly calls the constructor and creates a *temporary Complex object*. The *temporary object* and *z3* are passed to the complex **operator +()** function. After the expression is evaluated, the *temporary object* is destroyed. The nonmember implementation is flexible and handles the addition of complex and real numbers.

```
//                Test Driver Source  File
#include "complex.h"

int main( int , char ** )
{
        Complex z1( 1 ) , z2( 3,4 ) , z3 ;

        z3 = z1 + z2 ;
                // treated as z3 = operator +( z1 , z2 ) ;
                // z3 = (4,4)
        z1 = z3 + 8 ;
                // treated as z1 = operator +( z3 , Complex(8,0) ) ;
                // z1 = (12,4)
        z1 = 8 + z3 ;
                // treated as z1 = operator +( Complex(8,0) , z3 ) ;
                // z1 = (12,4)
```

```
            return( 0 ) ;
      }
```

2. **Member Implementation**: For the member implementation, the left operand is treated as the object and the right operand as a parameter to the function. The member function implementation gets the left operand through the "**this**" pointer and the right operand through the argument list. Therefore, the member function interface is completely different from the nonmember implementation.

```
//                       COMPLEX.H Header File
typedef     float         Coordinate ;

class Complex
{
      private:
            Coordinate current_real , current_imaginary ;
      public:
            // constructor with default values
            Complex( Coordinate x = 0 , Coordinate y = 0 );

            // class arithmetic function
            Complex operator +(const Complex &z2) ;
} ;

//      COMPLEX.CPP Source  File
#include "complex.h"

Complex Complex:: operator +( const Complex &z2 )
{
      // left operand is passed to this function through the
      // "this" pointer
      Coordinate x = real() + z2.real() ;
      Coordinate y = imaginary()+ z2.imaginary() ;

      return ( Complex(x, y) ) ;
}
```

The member function implementation requires the left operand to be of the same type as the class, thus placing a constraint on the left operand. Even though "z3+8" is mathematically equivalent to "8+z3" (*commutative property*), the following example, "8 + z3," will not compile.

```
//                    Test Driver Source  File
#include "complex.h"

int main( int , char ** )
{
      Complex z1(1) , z2( 3,4) , z3 ;
      z3 = z1 + z2 ;
            // treated as z3 = z1.operator +( z2 ) ;
            // z3 = (4,4)
      z1 = z3 + 8 ;
            // treated as z1 = z3.operator +( Complex(8,0) ) ;
            // z1 = (12,4)
      z1 = 8 + z3 ;
            // treated as z1 = 8.operator +( z3 ) ;
            // illegal, since left operand is not a Complex object
```

```
                        // and we are trying to perform 8.operator( z3 ) !!!
                        // The above will not compile.

            return( 0 ) ;
}
```

For the *Complex* class library, the preceding nonmember implementation is better because of the commutative property of addition.

As a general design guideline, the implicit conversion applied to the **left-side** operand determines the type of the operator function. If neither operand is affected by the operation and the implicit conversion is applicable to and desirable for the class, the operator function should be implemented as a **nonmember** function [Murray 1993]. Otherwise, the member implementation would be a better choice because it associates the function directly with the class instead of the logical association created by a nonmember implementation. For classes that will be used in design hierarchies (inheritance), the member implementation is a better choice. Therefore, implicit conversion applied to the left operand and the effect of the operator on the right and left operands can be used as the primary criteria in choosing between a member or nonmember implementation.

6.2.3 Unary Operators

Since a unary operator operates on just one object, as a programming guideline the implementation should be as a member function. For the *Complex* class, the unary *minus* (-) operator is overloaded as a member function.

```
//              COMPLEX.H Header File
#ifndef COMPLEX_H
#define COMPLEX_H

        typedef        float           Coordinate ;
        typedef        float           Scalar ;
        class Complex
        {
                private:
                        Coordinate current_real , current_imaginary ;
                public:
                        // Constructor (with default values)
                        inline Complex( Coordinate x = 0 , Coordinate y = 0 );

                        // Access functions
                        inline Coordinate real( void ) const ;
                        inline Coordinate imaginary( void ) const ;


                        // Arithmetic functions
                        Complex conjugate( void ) const ;
                        Scalar magnitude( void ) const ;
                        Complex operator -( void ) ;
                                // unary minus operator
        } ;

#endif              // COMPLEX_H Header File

//              COMPLEX.CPP Source File
#include "complex.h"

Complex Complex:: operator -( void )// member function
{
```

```
        // object is passed through the "this" pointer
        // negate real and imaginary components of "this" object
        // and store result in temporary variables
        Coordinate x = -real() ;
        Coordinate y = -imaginary();

        return ( Complex(x, y) ) ;
}

//                      Test Driver Source  File
#include "complex.h"

int main( int , char ** )
{
        Complex z1(1) , z2( 3,4) , z3 ;
            // initialize z1 = (1,0), z2 = (3,4), and z3 = (0,0)

        z3 = -z1 ;
            // compiler treats the expression as z3 = z1.operator -( ) ;
            // z3 = (-1,0)

        return( 0 ) ;
}
```

6.2.4 Operator/Assignment

In C and C++, when a variable appears on both sides of an assignment, the following shorthand notation can be used:

```
variable operator= expression ; example: x += 3 ;
```

which is **logically** equivalent to:

```
variable = variable operator expression ;example: x = x + 3 ;
```

The *operator/assignment* operates on the left operand. It is good programming practice is to implement the operator function as a **member** function:

```
//                  COMPLEX.H Header File
#ifndef COMPLEX_H
#define COMPLEX_H

        typedef     float       Coordinate ;
        typedef     float       Scalar ;

        class Complex
        {
            private:
                    Coordinate current_real , current_imaginary ;
            public:
                    // constructor (with default values)
                    inline Complex( Coordinate x = 0 , Coordinate y = 0 );

                    // class access functions
```

```
                    inline Coordinate real( void ) const ;
                    inline Coordinate imaginary( void ) const ;


                    // class arithmetic functions
                    Complex conjugate( void ) const ;
                    Scalar magnitude( void ) const ;


                    void operator *=( const Complex &z ) ;
                            // multiplication/assignment operator

        } ;


        // Complex Arithmetic Function
        Complex operator *( const Complex &z1,const Complex &z2 ) ;


#endif          // COMPLEX_H Header File
```

The above *Complex* class provides a unique implementation for both the multiplication and multiplication/ assignment operator functions. The *multiplication/assignment* operator function calls the *multiplication* operator function instead of repeating the same operations. Figure 6.5 depicts the function hierarchy.

```
//                   COMPLEX.CPP Source File
#include "complex.h"

void Complex:: operator *=( const Complex &z )
{
        // use the complex multiplication operator (*) function to implement
        // multiplication/assignment (Figure 6.5)
        *this = *this * z ;
                // compiler treats the expression as *this = operator *( *this,z) ;
}


// compute: z₁ * z₂ = (x₁ + y₁ i ) * (x₂ + y₂ i)
Complex operator *( const Complex &z1 , const Complex &z2 )
{
        // real part: x₁ * x₂ + y₁ * y₂ i²  = x₁ * x₂ - y₁ * y₂
        Coordinate real = z1.real() * z2.real() -
                        z1.imaginary() * z2.imaginary() ;

        // imaginary part: (x₁ * y₂ + y₁ * x₂ ) i
        Coordinate imaginary = z1.real() * z2.imaginary() +
                            z1.imaginary() * z2.real() ;

        // return result of the complex multiplication
        return ( Complex( real, imaginary ) ) ;
}


//                   Test Driver Source File
#include "complex.h"

int main( int , char ** )
{
        Complex z( 2 , 3 ) , z2( 3 , 5 ) ;

        z *= z2 ; // is treated as z. operator *= ( z2 ) ;

        return( 0 ) ;
}
```

6.2.5 Operator Overloading Restrictions

Several restrictions for *operator overloading* prevent the misuse of the language and its features. They are described in the following subsections.

6.2.5.1 Illegal Operator Overloading

The following operators cannot be overloaded for user-defined data types:

1. **Conditional Expression Operator (?:):** The conditional operator (compact-if) is a ternary operator while the other operators use at most two operands. Requiring C++ compilers to handle an overloaded ternary operator function was deemed unnecessary and impractical.

   ```
   min = ( x < y ) ? x : y ;
           // compact-if cannot be overloaded for user-defined objects
   ```

2. **Class Member (.) Operator:** The meaning of the class *member access* (.) operator cannot be changed by a C++ programmer.
3. **Pointer to Member (.*) Operator:** The meaning of this operator cannot be affected, either.
4. **Scope Resolution (::) Operator:** The left operand of a *scope resolution* (::) operator is associated with a data type and cannot be overloaded in the same sense as the other binary operators whose left operand is an actual data object.
5. **sizeof:** The **sizeof()** function is a compile time function.

6.2.5.2 Operator Overloading and Built-in Data Types

C++ operators cannot be overloaded for built-in data types because it would allow an operator's meaning for a built-in data type to be changed. The following function changes multiplication behavior for floating point data:

```
float operator *( float x, float y )
                // illegal, cannot overload for built-in data type
{
      return ( x / y ) ; // change meaning of multiplication to division!
}
```

This restriction prevents a programmer from misusing operator overloading for built-in data types. For floating point data, the preceding function would change the meaning of multiplication to division. Distorting the meaning of operators for built-in data makes programs difficult to maintain. Therefore, C++ compilers require at least one of the arguments for an overloaded operator function to be a user-defined data type (class):

```
Complex operator +( Coordinate real, const Complex &z2 ) ;
// one argument is a floating point and the other is a complex number
```

6.2.5.3 New Operators

New operators cannot be created via *operator overloading*. For instance, an exponent (**) operator equivalent to FORTRAN's exponent (**) operator cannot be created in C++.

```
Complex operator **( const Complex &z, int n ) ;
// z^n: illegal operator overloading. Cannot create a new operator
```

The complexity associated with allowing a designer to create new operators in C++ outweighed the benefits. Such a capability would have made compiler design difficult. A software designer would have had to define the precedence and associativity of the new operator, and somehow convey this information to the compiler. The opportunity to abuse this capability was too easy.

6.2.5.4 Precedence and Associativity

Operator overloading does not alter an operator's precedence and associativity. In C++, an overloaded operator function follows the same precedence and associativity guidelines as those for built-in data.

In the following example, the $\wedge$ operator is overloaded for exponentiation of a complex number: $\mathbf{z}^n$.

```
Complex operator ^( const Complex &z, int n ) ;
```

Unfortunately, this exponent operator function will not work properly because the $\wedge$ operator's precedence is lower than that of arithmetic operators and the exponent operation takes place after that of the arithmetic operations:

```
//                   Test Driver Source File
#include "complex.h"

int main( int , char ** )
{
        Complex z1(2,5) , z2(1,3) , z3 ;
        z3 = z1 ^ 5 + z2 ;
                // z1^5 + z2 will not be performed because the addition (+)
                // operator has higher precedence than the exponent (^)
                // operator. Instead z1^(5 + z2) will be performed
        return( 0 ) ;
}
```

Mathematically, exponentiation has a higher precedence than multiplication. However, the above design fails because the $\wedge$ operator has a lower precedence than the multiplication operator (*) in both C and C++. Therefore, the selection of the $\wedge$ operator for exponentiation was not appropriate.

6.2.5.5 Unary Operations

Except for the *minus* (-) operator, C++ precludes unary operators from being overloaded to handle binary operations. In the following example, the one's complement operator (~) is illegally overloaded for a binary operation:

```
Complex operator ~( const Complex &p1, const Complex &p2) ;
        // illegal because ~ operator is a unary operator and must
        // operate on only one operand

//                   Test Driver Source File
#include "complex.h"

int main( int , char ** )
{
        Complex z1(2,5) , z2(1,3) , z3 ;
        z3 =  z1 ~ z2 ;// illegal overloading
        return( 0 ) ;
}
```

Since the *minus* (-) sign is used for both unary and binary operations, it can also be overloaded for binary and unary operations for a class. In the *Complex* class, the *minus* (-) operator is overloaded to support both unary and binary point arithmetic (refer to Sections 6.2 and 6.3). The unary minus has been implemented as a member function and binary subtraction as a nonmember function.

6.2.5.6 Default Argument Values

An operator function cannot have default values for its arguments:

```
Complex operator +( const Complex &p1, Real x = 0 ) ;
                // illegal, x argument is using a default value
```

The compiler is unable to evaluate the overloaded expressions if default arguments are used.

6.2.5.7 Member Operators

In C++, the following operators can be overloaded only as *member* functions:

1. Array index operator: [ ]
2. Assignment operator: =
3. Parenthesis operator: ( )
4. Object reference operator: ->

6.2.6 Guidelines for Operator Overloading

The effective use of *operator overloading* in conjunction with the class structure hides the complexity of internal operations (*abstraction*). For instance, the *division* (/) operator function hides the algorithm used to divide two complex numbers. The client of the *Complex* class is unaware of the detailed operations performed by the arithmetic operator functions. In addition to being intuitive, the software becomes more maintainable and reusable.

Unfortunately, the flexibility of *operator overloading* can introduce subtle problems and hidden dangers. *Operator overloading* is a powerful feature of C++ but can easily be abused. The restrictions described in the previous sections are to protect the language's built-in data types from incorrect overloading. The classes can be protected through the use of programming guidelines and good design.

The operator overloading used in a design should not lead to ambiguous designs. An operator should be overloaded only if the meaning of the operation is clear to the clients. For instance, a *container* class that maintains a group of objects may overload the *array index* operator ([ ]) to hide the topology used for maintaining the list of objects (Figure 6.6). The overloaded operation hides from the client the internal search operation of

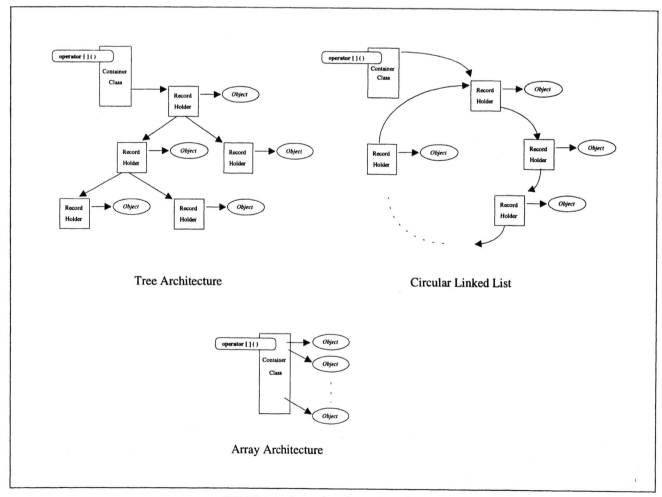

FIGURE 6.6 Examples of container classes.

finding an object (*abstraction*), and is a good example of operator overloading. But an overloaded relational operator (for example, <) in a *Text File* class may create ambiguity, since it is not clear if the file comparison is based on size or content. Ambiguous operations cause unreadable and unmaintainable code. The primary criterion in overloading an operator for a data class is whether the operation is logical and unambiguous to the *clients of the class*.

6.3 FRIEND FUNCTION

Friends have access to private information.

Similar to a *friend* class (*refer back to Chapter 5*), a *friend* function is a privileged external (nonmember) function associated with a class. This type of function is given the same access capabilities as member functions and has access to the **private** and **protected** members of the class.

A *friend* function may be a member of another class or a non-member function. As a non-member, it is defined and invoked using the same notation as for a C function. In the following example, the *Stream I/O* operators are overloaded for the *Complex* class (Figure 6.7). As denoted by the **friend** keyword, the **operator** <<() function is implemented as a *friend* of the *Complex* class. The *Complex* class access levels have no effect on the *friend* declaration. For clarity, these functions are declared in the **public** segment of the *Complex* class. Without the **friend** declaration, the compiler will generate an error message since the **operator** <<( ) function operates on the **private** members of the *Complex* class:

```
//COMPLEX.H Header File
#ifndef COMPLEX_H
#define COMPLEX_H
```

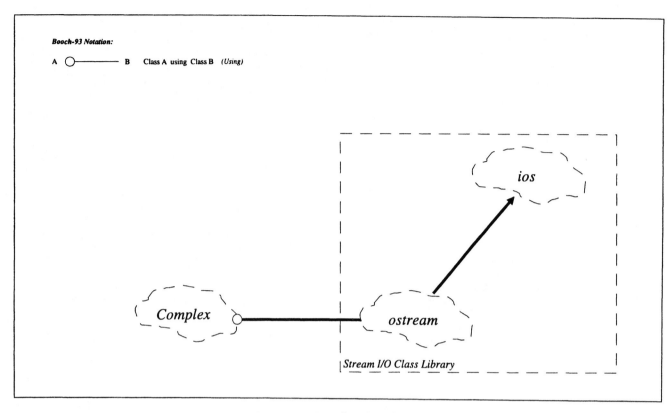

Booch-93 Notation:

A ◯————— B   Class A using Class B   *(Using)*

ios

Complex ○━━━━━━━━ *ostream*

Stream I/O Class Library

FIGURE 6.7 Complex class diagram.

```
typedef      float        Coordinate ;
typedef      float        Scalar ;
typedef      float        Real ;
typedef      bool         Boolean ;

class Complex
{
        private:
                Coordinate current_real , current_imaginary ;
        public:
                // constructor (with default values)
                inline Complex( Coordinate x = 0 , Coordinate y = 0 );

                // class access functions
                inline Coordinate real( void ) const ;
                inline Coordinate imaginary( void ) const ;

                // Stream I/O functions
                friend ostream & operator <<( ostream &os,
                        const Complex &z) ;
                friend istream & operator >>( istream &is, Complex &z) ;

                // class arithmetic functions
                Complex conjugate( void ) const ;
                Scalar magnitude( void ) const ;
                Complex operator -( const Complex &z ) ;
                void operator +=( const Complex &z ) ;
                void operator -=( const Complex &z ) ;
                void operator *=( const Complex &z ) ;
```

```
                    void operator /=( const Complex &z ) ;
          } ;

          // Arithmetic operator declarations (prototypes)
          Complex operator +( const Complex &z1, const Complex &z2 ) ;
          Complex operator -( const Complex &z1, const Complex &z2 ) ;
          Complex operator *( const Complex &z1, const Complex &z2 ) ;
          Complex operator /( const Complex &z1, const Complex &z2 ) ;

          // Relational operator declarations (prototypes)
          Boolean operator ==( const Complex &z1, const Complex &z2 ) ;
          Boolean operator !=( const Complex &z1, const Complex &z2 ) ;

#endif                    // COMPLEX_H Header File

//                       COMPLEX.CPP Source File
#include <iostream.h>             // I/O Stream Library
#include <math.h>                 // Math Library
#include "complex.h"              // Complex Library

ostream & operator <<( ostream & os, const Complex &z )
{
          // if a pending error exists and it is not serious then
          if( os.fail() && !os.bad() )
          {
                    os.clear( os.rdstate() & ~ios:: failbit ) ;// clear failbit flag
                         // the above operation obtains the current
                         // stream state and resets the fail bit flag.
                         // The other flag bits remain unchanged.
          }

          // if an error is not pending then continue,
          // otherwise abort output operation
          if( !os.fail() )
          {
                    // obtain current width
                    int width = os.width() ;
                    os << setw( width ) << z.current_real ;

                    // based on sign of the imaginary part => format output
                    if( z.current_imaginary < 0.0 )
                    {
                              os << " - " << setw( width )
                                      <<    -z.current_imaginary << "i" ;
                    }
                    else
                    {
                              os << " + " << setw( width )
                                      <<    z.current_imaginary << "i" ;
                    }
          }

          return( os ) ;
}
```

In the above example, the overloaded *output stream* operator (<<) checks for pending errors before writing to the output stream. If an error has occurred and it is not considered serious, the function clears the soft failure flag (*ios::*

failbit) and initiates the stream output operation. The function identifies the field length requirements which may have been specified by an earlier client call to the **ios:: setw()** manipulator (*refer to the following example*). The **setw()** manipulator works for only one stream output insertion. Without taking the field width requirements into consideration for both the *real* and *imaginary* components, the data format would become inconsistent. Therefore, the **width()** function is called to identify the field lengths for both the *real* and *imaginary* components before the field specification is reset to the default setting. The **setw()** manipulator is used to output the *real* and *imaginary* components of the *Complex* object using a specified field length:

```
cout << setw( 12 ) << z1 ;
        // output contents of z1 using a 12-character field for both real and
        // imaginary components
```

In the following example, the C++ compiler breaks the stream output statement into several calls. Since the operator's associativity is from left to right, the content of *z1* is sent to the output stream followed by *z2*. The stream output function returns a reference to the output stream that was passed to it from the calling function (*refer to the preceding stream I/O function declarations*). The returned reference is used for another stream output function call, allowing the output stream calls to be *cascaded*:

```
cout << z1 << z2 ;
        // treated as: operator <<( operator <<(cout,z1) , z2 ) ;
        // which is equivalent to:
        // operator << ( cout, z1)
        // operator<<( cout, z2 )
```

Had the *Complex* stream output function not returned a reference to the output stream, the cascading operation would not have been possible and the compiler would have generated an error message for the above statement.

The design of the *stream input* operator (>>) is similar to the *stream output* operator (<<). The input function should check for failures before attempting a read operation. In case of a failure, this function initializes the referenced *Complex* object to default values prior to returning control back to the caller. This function should also check for end-of-stream conditions by calling the **eof()** function:

```
istream & operator >>( istream &is, Complex &z )
{
        Boolean read_error = false ;

        // if a pending error exists and it is not serious then
        if( is.fail() && !is.bad() )
        {
                is.clear( is.rdstate() & ~ios:: failbit ) ;// clear failbit flag
        }

        // if there is no pending error and no end-of-stream then continue,
        // else abort the read operation
        if( !is.fail() && !is.eof() )
        {
                // during the read operation, skip over white space
                long last_state = is.setf( ios:: skipws ) ;

                // call the input prefix function and skip over white space
                is.ipfx() ;
                is >> z.current_real ; // read real component
                        // since operator >> ( ) operates on the private
                        // data members, this function must be a friend.
```

```
                    is.isfx() ; // call the input suffix function

                    // if not end-of-stream => read imaginary part
                    if( !is.eof() )
                    {
                            if( is.fail() )
                            {
                                    // if there is a pending read error on the real
                                    // component then
                                    //    clear real component and reset flag
                                    read_error = true ;
                                    z.current_real = 0 ; // clear real component
                                      is.clear(is.rdstate()& ~ios::failbit );//clear flag
                            }

                            // call the input prefix function to skip over white space
                            is.ipfx() ;
                            is >> z.current_imaginary ; // read imaginary component
                            is.isfx() ; // call the input suffix function

                            // if there is no pending read error on the imaginary
                            // component then
                            //    clear imaginary component and reset flag
                            if( is.fail() )
                            {
                                    read_error = true ;
                                    z.current_imaginary = 0 ;
                                            // clear imaginary component
                                    is.clear(is.rdstate()&~ios::failbit );//clear flag
                            }
                    }
                    else
                    {
                            z.current_imaginary = 0 ; // use default for imaginary part
                            read_error = true ;
                    }

                    // if unable to read the real or imaginary components
                    if( read_error )
                    {
                            // set fail bit to indicate a data format problem
                            is.clear( ios:: failbit ) ;
                    }

                    // restore previous state
                    is.setf( last_state ) ;
            }
            else // use default values
            {
                    z.current_real = z.current_imaginary = 0 ;
            }

            return( is ) ;
    }
```

Prior to and after each read operation, the *input stream* operator (>>) should call the input prefix and suffix functions: **ipfx()** and **isfx()**, respectively. If the *ios:: skipws* flag has been enabled, the **ipfx()** function skips over the leading *white spaces* (tabs or blanks) prior to a read operation.

The **friend** keyword basically bypasses data encapsulation and opens up the architecture to the nonmember functions. Since a *friend* function is given *Read/Write* capability on the private members of a class, this attribute causes a **friend** function to become dependent on the class architecture and data representation. Whenever the architecture of a class changes, friend functions are also affected. To create maintainable software, friend functions should be used sparingly, such as in the case of *stream input* function for the *Complex* class. A better implementation for the *stream output* function for the *Complex* class is to implement it as purely external and use the class access functions: **real()** and **imaginary()**. This implementation minimizes data dependencies:

```
//                    COMPLEX.H Header File
class Complex
{
     private:
            Coordinate current_real , current_imaginary ;
     public:
            // details left out
} ;


// Stream I/O functions
ostream & operator <<( ostream &os, const Complex &z) ;

//            COMPLEX.CPP Source File
#include <iostream.h>      // I/O Stream Library
#include <math.h>          // Math Library
#include "complex.h"       // Complex Library

ostream & operator <<( ostream & os, const Complex &z )
{
     // if a pending error exists and it is not serious then
     if( os.fail() && !os.bad() )
     {
            os.clear( os.rdstate() & ~ios:: failbit ) ;// clear failbit flag
     }

     // if an error is still pending then abort output operation
     if( !os.fail() )
     {
            // obtain current width
            int width = os.width() ;
            os << setw( width ) << z.real() ;

            // based on sign of imaginary part => format output
            if( z.imaginary() < 0.0 )
            {
                   os << " - " << setw( width ) <<  -z.imaginary() << "i" ;
            }
            else
            {
                   os << " + " << setw( width ) <<  z.imaginary() << "i" ;
            }
     }

     return( os ) ;
}
```

6.4 STANDARD C++ CLASS LIBRARIES

Many of the standard C++ class libraries such as the *Stream I/O* class library, the *complex* class, and the *String* class utilize the operator overloading feature in order to provide an intuitive and consistent interface. This section briefly reviews the design interface for each of the following libraries and classes:

1. *Stream I/O* class library
2. *complex* class
3. *string* class

For additional detail, the reader may refer to a C++ compiler reference manual.

6.4.1 Stream I/O Class Library

The *Stream I/O* library overloads the *binary shift* operators (>> and <<) for its stream I/O operation:

```
//                        iostream.h Header File
// output stream class
class ostream: public ios
{
    public:
            // Stream I/O functions for built-in data types
            ostream & operator <<( void * )  ;
            ostream & operator <<( char )    ;
            ostream & operator <<( char *)   ;
            ostream & operator <<( short )   ;
            ostream & operator <<( long )    ;
            ostream & operator <<( int )        ;
            ostream & operator <<( float )    ;
            ostream & operator <<( double );
            ostream & operator <<( long double );

            // other details left out

    private:
            // data member definitions and utility functions
} ;

// input stream class
class istream: public ios
{
    public:
            // Stream I/O functions for built-in data types
            istream & operator >>( char & ) ;
            istream & operator >>( short & )  ;
            istream & operator >>( long & )   ;
            istream & operator >>( int & )        ;
            istream & operator >>( float & )   ;
            istream & operator >>( double & );
            istream & operator >>( long double & );

            // other details left out
    private:
            // data member definitions and utility functions
} ;
```

The preceding overloaded operators provide a type-safe I/O capability for the built-in data types. In addition, the direction of the symbols conveys the flow of data to and from a stream, which is illustrated in the following example:

```
cout << z ;      // data flows to output stream
cin >> z  ;      // data flows out of the input stream
```

The *binary shift* operators were originally selected because their precedence is low relative to most of the other operators supported by the language, and their associativity is from left to right. These properties made them the natural choice for the *stream I/O* operators.

For classes that need to support stream I/O capability, this library can be extended by overloading the *stream output* (<<) and *stream input* (>>) operators. For these classes, these operators must be implemented as nonmember functions (external or friend) because the left operand is of type *istream* or *ostream*, and not as the members of class. The following is a generic scenario illustrating how *stream I/O* overloading takes place:

```
//         Client Header File
class Type
{
      public:
         friend ostream & operator <<( ostream & , const Type & ) ;
         friend istream & operator >>( istream & , Type & ) ;
} ;
```

Unlike the *Complex* class design, other classes may not provide the necessary access functions that provide indirect access to their data members. In this situation, functions such as the *stream I/O* functions that are within the class design domain must be implemented as **friend** functions.

The following is a generic scenario illustrating how *stream I/O* operators are used by the application software:

```
//              Client Source File
#include <iostream.h>
#include "Type.h"

function_name()
{
      Type object ;
      .
      cout <<  object ;
        // cannot be member of Type because the
        // compiler cannot treat the above as :
        //      cout.operator << ( object )
        // Since cout is an output stream, Type must be
        // treated as:
        //      operator <<( cout , object )
}
```

6.4.2 Complex Class Library

The standard math library provides a *complex* class (**complex.h**) with an interface similar to the *Complex* class already presented in this chapter. The following code specifies the public interface of the standard *complex* class:

```
//                        complex.h Header File
class complex
{
```

```
    public:
            // constructor (with default values)
            complex( float re = 0 , float im = 0 );

            // class access functions
            float real( void ) const ;
            float imag( void ) const ;

            // class arithmetic functions
            complex conj( void ) const ;    // conjugate
            // Other details left out
} ;

// Arithmetic operator declarations (prototypes)
complex operator +( const complex &z1, const complex &z2 ) ;
complex operator -( const complex &z1, const complex &z2 ) ;
complex operator *( const complex &z1, const complex &z2 ) ;
complex operator /( const complex &z1, const complex &z2 ) ;
        // Declarations for functions that handle complex and real number
        // arithmetic are left out, and are similar to the ones specified
        // in Section 6.2.1.

// Relational operators
int operator ==( const complex &z1 , const complex &z2 ) ;
int operator !=( const complex &z1 , const complex &z2 ) ;
        // Declarations for functions that handle complex and real number
        // comparison are left out.
```

The ANSI *complex* class supports float, double, and long double data types.

6.4.3 String Class Library

The *string* class maintains a character string. The constructor dynamically allocates memory for a character string and initializes it on the basis of the type of constructor called. The destructor deallocates the character string memory space. Through regular member functions such as **compare()**, this class provides the basic string operations of comparison, copy, append, and search. In addition, the *string* class overloads the relational, stream I/O, array index ([ ]), and addition operators to provide an intuitive and flexible design interface:

```
//        cstring.h Header File
class string
{
    public:
            // Array Index operator
            char & operator [ ]( size_t char_position ) ;
            char operator [ ]( size_t char_position ) const ;
                // accesses a character within the string

            // Deep copy assignment operator
            string & operator =( const string &source ) ;

            // Relational Operators
            friend int operator ==( const string &s1, const string &s2 ) ;
            friend int operator ==( const string &s, const char *str ) ;
            friend int operator ==( const char *str, const string &s );
```

```
friend int operator !=( const string &s1, const string &s2 ) ;
friend int operator !=( const string &s, const char *str ) ;
friend int operator !=( const char *str, const string &s );

friend int operator >( const string &s1, const string &s2 ) ;
friend int operator >( const string &s, const char *str ) ;
friend int operator >( const char *str, const string &s );

friend int operator <( const string &s1, const string &s2 ) ;
friend int operator <( const string &s, const char *str ) ;
friend int operator <( const char *str, const string &s );

// Stream I/O Operators
friend ostream & operator <<( ostream &os, const string &s );
friend istream & operator >>( istream &is, string &s ) ;

// Destructor
~string( ) ;

// Constructors
string( ) ;
string( const char *new_str ) ;
string( const string &source ) ;

// Other details left out
} ;
```

The *string* class provides a variety of constructors; only a selected few are shown in the preceding example:

1. **Copy**: The copy constructor and the *assignment* operator (=) provide deep copy capability.
2. **Array**: Through the *array index* operator ([ ]) functions, the string object can be treated as an array. The function that returns a reference provides "read/write" capability on a character within the string, and the other one returns a copy of the specified character ("read" operation).
3. **Comparison**: The *relational* operators compare *string* objects with each other or a *string* object with a character string (**char ***). Similar to the design of the *Complex* class in Section 6.2.1, different implementations of a relational operator avoid the implicit conversion overhead.
4. **Stream I/O**: The *string* class uses the *Stream I/O* class library to support stream I/O capability for *strings*.

In the design of this class, the C++ *friend* and *operator* functions are used effectively in conjunction with each other.

SUMMARY

A class design should keep data members hidden by making them internal to the class (private). On the basis of *data encapsulation*, the *member* and supporting *friend* functions hide the internal architecture of the class and act as gateways. The client of the class must access and operate on the internal parts of a class, using the member functions.

Object-oriented Programming (OOP) has a higher overhead than procedural programming due to its reliance on the member functions. At times, the design of a class can affect software efficiency. Prior to implementing member functions, the class features and operations should be studied to identify any performance issues. For example, the frequently called functions such as initialization functions may need optimization. By embedding functions at the calling locations, the *inline* feature eliminates function call overhead, maintains function modularity, and still hides the algorithm from the application software. In addition, an *inline* function avoids the problems associated with macros. An inline function is typically a small function (three C++ statements or less).

Operator overloading in C++ is the ability to associate a function with an ***existing*** operator. When the C++ compiler encounters an overloaded operator, it will place a call to the applicable function. By allowing a designer to overload an ***existing*** operator for a class, the internal operations are abstracted from the client. To protect the language from abuse, C++ has placed several restrictions on operator overloading. C++ prevents changing the behavior of an operator for built-in data types by overloading an operator using built-in data types as arguments. Furthermore, an operator's associativity and precedence cannot be changed, which effectively prevents a designer from creating new operators.

When used properly, operator functions allow a designer to keep a process and task completely transparent to the application. The changes to a process or task are localized to the operator functions and the class. Hence, the application software remains unaffected by the changes.

C++ does not protect against misuse of operator overloading for classes. Such a misuse causes software to be ambiguous, incorrect, and unmaintainable. Since the language and the compiler provide very little protection against misuse, proper operator overloading fails becomes the responsibility of the designer. An operator function should be used to create abstraction. If the abstraction leads to design obscurity, then it is no longer serving its purpose. As a general guideline, an operator should be overloaded only when the operation is easily understood by *other designers*. Table 6.2 identifies the guidelines pertaining to operator overloading for user-defined data types:

TABLE 6.2   Operator Function Table Usage

Operator	Usage and Type
?: . .* ::	Cannot overload (C++ rule)
[ ] = ( ) ->	Must be a member function (C++ rule)
Operator=, such as +=	Use as member (guideline)
Unary operator, such as -	Use as member (guideline)
Other binary operators	Member or nonmember (guideline)

Binary operators are normally implemented as nonmember functions when the left and right operands remain unaffected by the operator and implicit conversion is desirable for the left operand. Otherwise the member implementation is a better alternative.

The implicit data conversion associated with operator functions should not be ignored since it can severely affect software performance. The impact of implicit data conversion should be carefully assessed. The designer of the class may instead incorporate multiple implementations of a feature to support all permutations of an operation. Or, if it becomes too difficult to provide several different implementations, constructor functions can be designed using C++ explicit keyword such that the compiler is prevented from applying implicit conversion.

C++ is a flexible language in that it allows nonmember functions to have direct access to the private and protected elements of a class. These functions are known as *friend* functions and are external to the class. Friend functions bypass the data encapsulation concept and are coupled with the internal design and architecture of the class. *Friend* functions should be used sparingly in a design since any changes to the internal architecture of the class affects them as well. As shown in Section 6.4, several of the ANSI C++ libraries effectively combine friend and operator overloading in their designs.

GLOSSARY

Cartesian coordinate
Using (x,y) or (x,y,z) to represent a point in a two- or three-dimensional coordinate system

Container class
A container class is a list and maintains a group of objects. The class hides the topology used for maintaining the objects in memory

Deep copy

Using the contents of one object to create another instance of the same class. In a deep copy, the two objects may contain the same information but the target object will have its own buffers and resources. The destruction of either object will not affect the remaining object

Friend function

A nonmember function that has access to the private and protected members of a class

Inline function

An inline function instructs the compiler to embed the function's body where it is called

Operator function

A function that has been associated with one of the available operators in C++

Outline function

A function that is executed through a function call. This is in contrast to an inline function, whose body is embedded where it is called

Polar coordinate

Using the radius and angle of a point to represent its location in a coordinate system

Parameterized class

A template class, which is a generic class definition. Based on the client supplied data type, the compiler instantiates an implementation for the class and its member functions

Shallow copy

Copying the contents of one object into another instance of the same class, thus creating a mirror image. Due to straight copying of references and pointers, the two objects will share the same external resources. The destruction of one object and its external resources causes the externally contained contents of the other object to be unpredictable

CHAPTER 7

Dynamic Memory Allocation

INTRODUCTION

At run time, objects are created and destroyed in different memory spaces. Depending on where the object is declared in the code, it is created in different memory spaces as depicted in Figure 7.1. During compilation, the compiler examines the local, static, and global definitions and determines the required memory type for the objects, variables, and arrays. Depending on the scope of data, the objects are either assigned to permanent or stack memory spaces. For instance, **static** and global (**extern**) objects are assigned to fixed locations in the memory for the duration of the program's execution. However, local objects are mapped to the stack, and their locations on the stack vary depending on when the function is called.

At times, the actual data storage requirements for a list or an array of objects cannot be determined until run time. A designer in this position may embed a dimension larger than necessary in the program. At run time, if the program does not fully use the array, this approach will cause poor utilization of memory resources. On the other hand, if the array becomes full and the program requires more space to store data, then the program will not be fully functional. A better and more flexible solution is to allocate the objects at *run time* when the actual number of objects can be determined. With *dynamic memory allocation*, the software determines the memory requirements for the object(s) and reserves adequate memory space as the need arises. For instance, an inventory program allocates memory space for its records as it reads the records from an inventory database.

Memory is reserved at run time by interacting with *dynamic memory allocation* tools. These tools are provided either by the language or by a library. In C, *dynamic memory allocation* is performed by the *memory allocation (malloc)* library. C++ uses the **new** and **delete** operators to support dynamic memory allocation. This chapter describes the dynamic memory allocation process. The *malloc* library is used as a precursor to the C++ dynamic memory allocation operators **new** and **delete**. This chapter also describes overloading these operators for custom memory management.

7.1 OVERVIEW OF DYNAMIC MEMORY ALLOCATION

The *dynamic memory allocation* tools obtain a memory block(s) from the operating system and manage this space. Memory management and caching schemes vary among operating systems and compilers and are transparent to the application software.

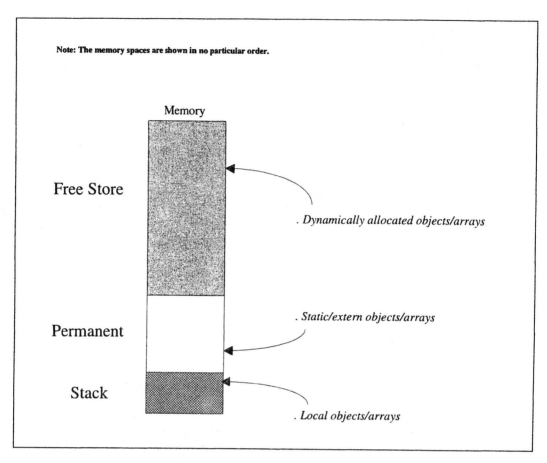

FIGURE 7.1   C++ Object mapping in the memory space.

On the basis of a dynamic memory allocation request made by the application software (Figure 7.2), the *dynamic memory allocation* tools either reserve and free up the memory space that they manage. These tools are not concerned with the type of data maintained in the allocated memory space; the application software has control over the memory's contents.

When a memory allocation request is made, the *dynamic memory allocation* tool searches through the free memory space for a contiguous area large enough to satisfy the memory allocation request (Figure 7.2). Upon locating the memory space, the allocation tool reserves the memory space by updating an internal table associated with the memory space and returns the starting address of the memory space to the requesting program. The memory allocation and search process/algorithm vary among compilers and libraries. **First-fit** or **best-fit** algorithms are common.

If the allocation tool is unable to find adequate free memory to satisfy the request, it notifies the calling software about the allocation failure by returning a null address (Figure 7.3). This condition may occur when none of the free regions between the allocated blocks are large enough (*memory fragmentation*). The application software needs to handle dynamic allocation failures caused by memory fragmentation and lack of memory space. When an allocation failure occurs, the software should take appropriate steps to recover gracefully.

The memory allocation process described above is transparent to the application software and is handled internally by the *dynamic memory allocation* tools. When using dynamic memory allocation, the application software is responsible for performing the following operations:

1. **Memory Space**: The application determines the size of an array or number of objects needed and makes a request to the allocation tool. The tool dynamically allocates memory space (Figure 7.2). How the application software identifies the number of objects or the dimension of an array at run time is application dependent and may involve interaction with a user, data from an external source, or calculations done by an internal process.

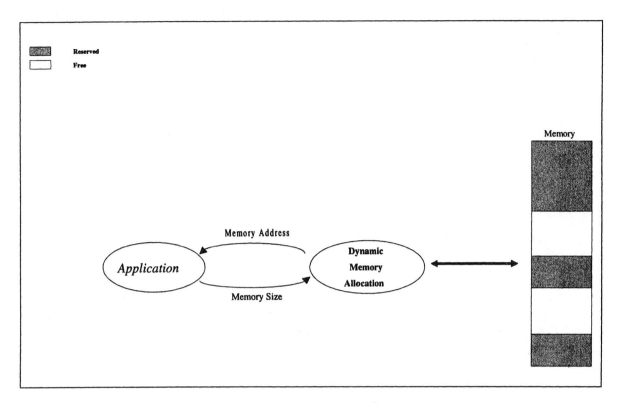

FIGURE 7.2 Dynamic memory allocation.

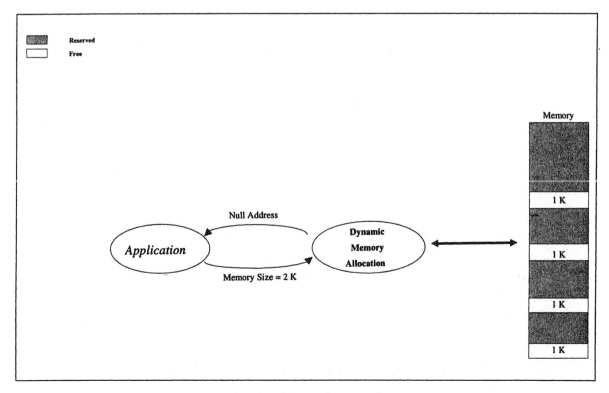

FIGURE 7.3 Memory fragmentation.

2. Data Storage: After the memory space is allocated, the application becomes responsible for the initialization, manipulation, and management of the memory space. The application software has full control over the storage of any type of data in the allocated memory space.

Since an allocated memory region may have been used previously for another dynamic allocation request, the program should initialize the memory space before operating on it.

3. Memory Deallocation: An allocated memory space remains reserved until the software requests the *dynamic memory allocation* tools to free up the memory space, or the program's execution ends and control is returned to the operating system.

7.2 DYNAMIC MEMORY ALLOCATION LIBRARY

In C, the memory allocation (*malloc*) library performs the dynamic memory allocation operations. Since libraries are not part of a language, the C-Language cannot be involved with the allocation or the initialization process. The *malloc* library manages the *heap* memory space. The following identifies some of the common functions supported by this library:

1. **void * malloc (size_t length):** Allocates a block of memory from *heap* memory using the requested *length*. Upon successful allocation, the function returns a pointer to the starting location of the block of memory. In case of allocation failure, the function returns a null pointer:

```
#include <malloc.h>
char *get_page( unsigned short page_size )
{
        char *page = (char *) malloc( page_size * sizeof(char) ) ;
                /* allocate a char string buffer of length page_size */
        return( page ) ;
}
```

The **get_page()** function dynamically allocates a character string buffer to hold *page_size* characters.

2. **void * realloc (void *begin, size_t length):** The **realloc()** function reallocates an existing block of memory identified by *begin* to the requested *length*. The **realloc()** function first attempts to resize the buffer in its existing location. However, if the memory space underneath the requested block is already reserved, **realloc()** will search for a new memory block large enough to satisfy the requested *length*. In such an event, **realloc()** transfers the contents of the original memory block to the new location (Figure 7.4) and deallocates the original memory block. The data transfer operation is transparent to the application software.

Upon successful reallocation, the function returns the *current* address of the buffer. In case of reallocation failure, the function returns a null address. In the following example, the **resize_page()** function reallocates an existing buffer. In case of dynamic allocation failure, it notifies the user:

```
char *resize_page( char *page, unsigned short new_page_size )
{
        /* if current page exists and page size is valid */
        if( page && new_page_size > 0 )
        {
                char *temp ;
                /*reallocate the existing buffer by using the
                ** new page_size
                */
                temp = (char *) realloc( page,
                                    new_page_size * sizeof(char) ) ;
                if( temp )/* if buffer successfully resized */
```

```
                    {
                            page = temp ; /* point to new block */
                    }
                    else   /* for allocation failures: notify user */
                    {
                            printf("\n\t ** Unable to resize buffer **") ;
                    }
            }
            return( page ) ; /* return current address of the page */
    }
```

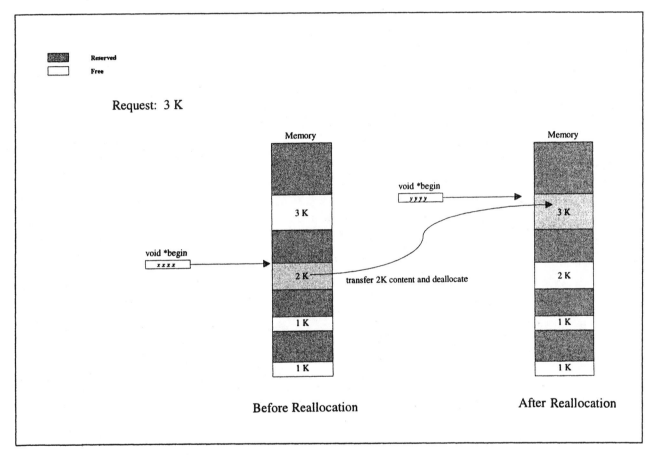

Request: 3 K

Before Reallocation   After Reallocation

FIGURE 7.4 Dynamic memory reallocation.

3. **void free(void *begin):** The **free()** function frees the block of memory previously allocated by **malloc()** or **realloc()**. The memory area is returned back to the *heap* and is available for future allocation requests.

```
void free_page( char *page )
{
        if( page )/* if page exists => deallocate page */
        {
                free( page ) ;
        }
}
```

In the above example, the **free_page()** function deallocates the character string buffer referenced by page. To ensure proper deallocation, the **free_page()** function checks the address for a null value prior to calling **free()**.

If the **free()** function is called using an incorrect address, the behavior of the software will be unpredictable. In C, the application must manually initialize the memory space after every allocation. When the memory space contains pointers to other allocated memory blocks, the application must clean up the space prior to deallocation. If the initialization and cleanup tasks are accidentally omitted by the application, the software's behavior is unpredictable.

7.3 C++ AND DYNAMIC MEMORY ALLOCATION

C++ incorporated dynamic memory allocation into the language with the **new** and **delete** operators. These operators provide the following benefits:

1. **Language Feature**: Both C and C++ determine the memory space requirements for data definitions in a program at compile time. Even though the objects declared in the program and the ones created dynamically at run time are conceptually the same except for the mapping of the memory space, C-Language cannot become involved with dynamic memory allocation because it does not have any built-in tools to recognize and support dynamic memory allocations. For consistency, a language should be responsible for both *static* and *dynamic* allocations.

2. **Object Initialization**: By making dynamic memory allocation part of the language, the compiler is able to recognize dynamic allocation requests and manual initialization can be avoided. The compiler inserts calls to the applicable constructor functions in the executable code after a dynamic allocation request. With the use of the **new** and **delete** operators, the C++ compiler creates a uniform behavior for objects that are declared in a program and the objects that are dynamically allocated.

3. **Object Cleanup**: Similar to the initialization process, the C++ compiler incorporates a call to the destructor in the executable code before a deallocation request is made. An object deallocated with the **delete** operator is automatically destroyed prior to deallocation.

4. **Reliability**: By making dynamic memory allocation part of the language, error-prone manual initialization and cleanup operations can be avoided. In addition, some implementations of the **free()** function in the

malloc libraries are not null safe. When the **free**() function is called with a null address, the program's behavior may be unpredictable and can result in the loss of free memory (*memory leakage*). In C++, the **delete** operator can be used with a null address without any negative side effects.

7.3.1 Memory Allocation

Instances of built-in data types or classes are allocated at run time using the **new** operator. The dynamic memory allocation operators manage the *free store* memory space. The following statements identify the syntax used to allocate memory:

```
Type *object= new    Type( initialization_list ) ;
Type *array = new    Type[size]  ;
Type (*multi_array) [M] = new    Type[n][M] ;
// where n is a variable and M must be a constant
```

After the dynamic allocation, a constructor is automatically called to initialize the memory space. In the following example, the **new** operator allocates a memory area large enough to hold a floating point variable and then initializes the memory space to zero (0.0) (Figure 7.5):

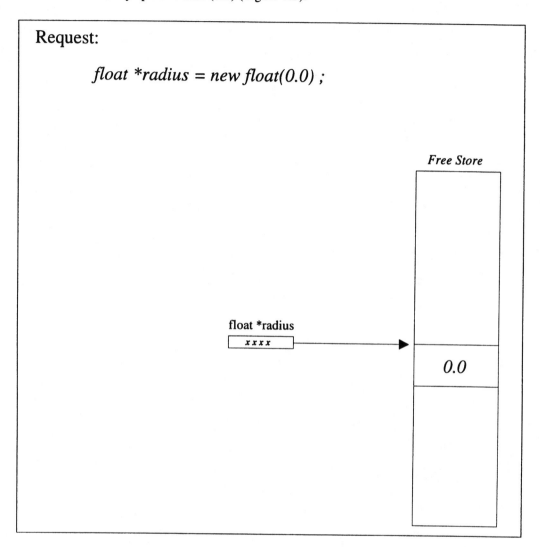

FIGURE 7.5   Grade object dynamic memory allocation.

```
float *radius =  new float(0.0) ;
        // call :: operator new ( ) to allocate sizeof(float) bytes
        // if( allocation for floating point data successful ) then
        //         initialize *radius to 0.0 ;
```

In C, the application software must compute the number of bytes for the object and must convert the pointer returned by **malloc()** to the correct data type. Furthermore, the memory space must be manually initialized. In C++, the **new** operator relieves the programmer of performing these operations. The following example demonstrates the difference between **malloc()** and **new** by reimplementing the preceding example using the **malloc()** function:

```
float *radius =  (float *) malloc( sizeof(float) ) ;
if( radius )/* if allocation successful => initialize memory space */
{
```

```
            *radius = 0.0 ;
}
```

The C++ compiler evaluates the dynamic allocation requests and places the applicable calls to the **new** operator and a constructor function. The compiler also handles the pointer conversion and memory space computation.

```
Type *array= new    Type[length]  ;
        // treat as:
        // Type *array = static_cast<Type *>
        //      ( :: operator new ( sizeof(Type) * length ) ) ;
        // if( array != static_cast<Type *> (0 ) )
        //      for( int i = 0 ; i < length ; i++ )
        //              call default constructor for array[i]
```

The **new** operator searches through *free store* for a block of memory large enough to satisfy the allocation request. If the **new** operator locates a block of memory large enough to satisfy the request, it will return the starting address of the memory space. The constructor is then invoked to initialize the memory space and to complete the object's construction. However, if the **new** operator fails to allocate any memory space, the **new** operator returns a null address and the initialization step is bypassed.

In the following example, the *Name* class uses the **new** and **delete** operators to allocate memory space for its name string buffer (Figure 7.6). Since the class uses external containment to store a person's name, the *copy constructor* and the *assignment* operator (=) have been overloaded to avoid problems with *shallow* copies. These functions create *deep* copies by also allocating unique string buffers for their objects.

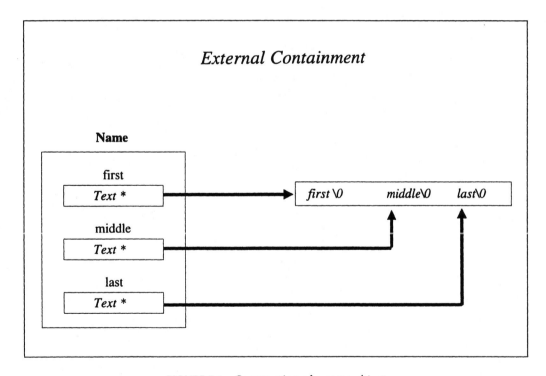

FIGURE 7.6 Construction of a name object.

```
//                      NAME.H Header File
#ifndef NAME_H
#define NAME_H
```

```
#define NAME_FIELD_SEPARATOR        ' '
#define NULL_CHAR                   '\0'

typedef     char        Text ;
typedef     bool        Boolean ;

class Name
{
      private:
            Text *first , *middle , *last ;

            // Utility functions
            Boolean parse_name( void ) ;
            Boolean copy_name( const Name &source ) ;
      public:
            // Constructor
            Name( const Text *current_name =
                        static_cast<Text *> ( 0 ) ) ;
            Name( const Name &source ) ;
            Name & operator =( const Name &source ) ;

            // Destructor
            ~Name( ) ;
                        // other details left out
} ;

#endif              // NAME_H Header file
```

Since the algorithm for both the *copy constructor* and the *assignment* operator (=) functions are the same, the **copy_name()** utility function is used to create a common baseline between the two functions. The **copy_name()** function allocates memory space for **this** object and copies the contents of the **source** object into the *"this"* object buffers. The main difference between the *assignment* and *copy constructor* is that the *"this"* pointer for the *copy constructor* points to uninitialized memory space and the *"this"* pointer for the *assignment* operator (=) points to an existing object. Therefore, the *assignment* operator (=) must destroy its existing object buffer before it can replace the object's content with new data. In addition, the *assignment* operator must verify that the *"this"* pointer and the passed **source** object reference do not point to the same location (*self-assignment*).

```
//              NAME.CPP Source File
#include <string.h>      // String library
#include "name.h"        // Name class library

// copy constructor
Name:: Name ( const Name &source )
    : first( static_cast<Text *> ( 0 ) ), middle( static_cast<Text *> ( 0 ) ),
      last( static_cast<Text *> ( 0 ) )
                        // initialize composed elements to default values
{
    if( !copy_name( source ) ) // use utility function to copy name
    {
            // recovery code for invalid name or dynamic allocation failure
    }
}


Name & Name:: operator = ( const Name &source )
{
```

```
        // if this pointer and source reference do not point to same object then
        // copy name (avoids self assignments)
        if( this != &source )
        {
                delete [ ] first ; // destroy existing name, if any exists

                // erase markers
                first = static_cast<Text *> ( 0 ) ;
                middle = static_cast<Text *> ( 0 ) ;
                last = static_cast<Text *> ( 0 ) ;

                if( !copy_name( source ) )
                {
                        // recovery code for invalid name or
                        // dynamic allocation failure
                }
        }

        return( *this ) ; // allow cascading, e.g. name1 = name2 = name3
}

Boolean Name:: copy_name( const Name & source )
{
    Boolean name_copied = true ;

    // if source object contains a valid name
    if( (source.first != static_cast<Text *> ( 0 )) &&
        (source.last  != static_cast<Text *> ( 0 )) )
    {
            // compute the length of source object's name
            short length = strlen( source.first ) + strlen( source.last ) + 2;
                    // add 2 for null terminators
            // if a middle name exists, then add in middle name
            if( source.middle != static_cast<Text *> ( 0 ) )
            {
                    length += strlen( source.middle ) + 1 ;
            }

            first = new Text [ length ] ; // allocate buffer for storing name

            // if dynamic allocation successful
            if( first != static_cast<Text *> ( 0 ) )
            {
                    // copy user-defined name into buffer
                    strcpy( first, source.first ) ;

                    // if source object has a middle name
                    if( source.middle != static_cast<Text *> ( 0 ) )
                    {
                            // copy name to new object
                            middle = first + strlen(first) + 1 ;
                            strcpy( middle, source.middle ) ;
                            last = middle + strlen(middle) + 1 ;
                    }
                    else
                    {
```

```
                               last = first + strlen(first) + 1 ;
                       }
                       strcpy( last, source.last ) ;
               }
               else
               {
                       name_copied = false ;
               }
       }
       else
       {
               name_copied = false ;
        }


       return( name_copied ) ;
}
```

Similar to the *copy* constructor, the *user-defined values* constructor allocates memory space for its name buffer; it copies the contents of the initialization string into this buffer; and it uses the **parse_name**() utility function to initialize the memory space.

```
//              NAME.CPP Source File
#include <string.h>      // String library
#include "name.h"        // Name class library

Name:: Name ( const Text *current_name )
    : first( static_cast<Text *> ( 0 ) ), middle( static_cast<Text *> ( 0 ) ),
      last( static_cast<Text *> ( 0 ) )
                    // initialize composed elements to default values
{
    // if supplied name exists => use this name to construct object
    if( current_name != static_cast<Text *> ( 0 ) )
    {
            size_t length = strlen(current_name) + 1 ;
                    // compute string length and add an additional byte
                    // for null terminator
          first = new Text [ length ] ; // allocate buffer for storing name

            // if dynamic allocation successful
            if( first != static_cast<Text *> ( 0 ) )
            {
                    // copy user-defined name into buffer
                    strcpy( first, current_name ) ;

                    // partition name into components
                    if( !parse_name( ) )
                    {
                            // recovery code for invalid name
                    }
            }
            else
            {
                    // recovery code for dynamic allocation failure:
                        eg. using C++ exception handling
            }
    }
```

```
      }

Boolean Name:: parse_name( void )
{
      Boolean valid_name = true ;
      Text * marker = first ;// point to beginning of the name

      if( marker  != static_cast<Text *> ( 0 ) )// if no name => abort
      {
            // while not end of name
            while( *marker  != NULL_CHAR )
            {
                  // if name field separator found then
                  // partition & mark the fields
                  if( *marker == NAME_FIELD_SEPARATOR )
                  {
                        *marker++ = NULL_CHAR ;
                              // null terminate current field
                        if( middle  == static_cast<Text *> ( 0 ) )
                        {
                              middle = marker ;
                              // mark beginning of the middle name
                        }
                        else
                        {
                              last = marker ;
                              // mark beginning of the last name
                              break ; // all components found
                        }
                  }
                  else
                  {
                        ++marker ; // point to next character
                  }
            }

            // if middle and last markers never initialized
            if( (middle == static_cast<Text *> ( 0 )) &&
               (last == static_cast<Text *> ( 0 )) )
            {
                  valid_name = false ;
            }
            else if( last  == static_cast<Text *> ( 0 ) ) // no last name found
            {
                  last = middle ; // indicates no middle name
                  middle = static_cast<Text *> ( 0 ) ;
            }
      }
      else
      {
            valid_name = false ;
      }

      return( valid_name ) ;
}
```

The compiler uses the supplied *initialization list* in the dynamic memory allocation request to resolve the call to the constructor:

```
Class_Name *pointer  = new Class_Name(initialization_list);
          // use the initialization list to identify the constructor
```

Using the *Name* class design interface, the clients can then create an instance of *Name* dynamically or as a normal object definition. In the following example, the **main()** function allocates memory space for several *Name* objects. For each of the dynamic allocation requests in the **main()** function, the **new** operator reserves memory space from the free store and the constructors are later called to initialize each of the memory blocks of the *Name* objects. In addition, the constructors also call the **new** operator to allocate memory for their name buffers (Figure 7.7).

```
//              Test Driver Source File
#include "name.h"        // Name Class Library
int main( int , char ** )
{
        Name *customer1 = new Name( "Ted Russell Rittmaster" ) ;
            // allocate a Name object and initialize its dynamically
            // allocated Name string with supplied string

        Name *customer2 = new Name ;
            // allocate a Name object and use the default constructor

        Name *customer3 = new Name ( *customer1 ) ;
            // allocate Name object and use the copy constructor


}
```

If an *initialization list* has not been defined, the compiler will use the *default constructor* to initialize the memory space. In the previous example, *customer2* is initialized using the default constructor. When a dynamic memory allocation request fails, the expressions within the *initialization list* may or may not be resolved:

```
Name *customer = new Name( read_buffer() ) ;
            // allocates a Name object and uses return value from
            // read_buffer to initialize the Name object
```

In case of an allocation failure, the call to **read_buffer()** may not occur. The evaluation of the preceding expressions varies among different platforms and compilers. As a design rule, do not use operators or perform operations that modify the state of an object or a process in the *initialization* list (for example, ++data). If the allocation fails, the state is not deterministic.

When an array is dynamically allocated, the array must be initialized using the default constructor. An application cannot define an *initialization list* similar to the one used for statically declared arrays. In the following examples, every element of the **customers** array is initialized by using the *Name* class *default* constructor:

```
Name *customers = new Name[n] ;
            // allocates an array of Name objects of size n and
            // invokes the default constructor for each element
```

An object dynamically allocated by using the **new** operator remains in existence until either the object is deallocated by a call to the **delete** operator or the program is terminated. In the following example, the *Name* object is allocated and deallocated in different functions. The lifetime of the dynamically allocated object is not dependent on the function where the allocation takes place but is based on where the object is destroyed by using the **delete** operator.

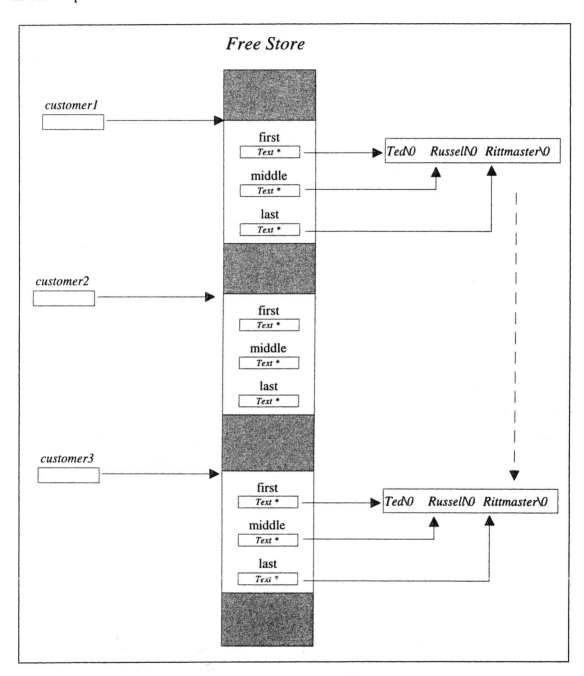

FIGURE 7.7 Deep copy for a name object

```
//              Test Driver Source File
#include "name.h"

int main( int , char ** )
{
        Name *customer = create_customer() ;
```

```
            ...
            destroy_customer( customer ) ;
    }

Name *create_customer( void )
{
            Text first_name[20] , last_name[20] , full_name[40] ;

            // obtain client's name
            cout << "Input first name: \n" ;
            cin >> first_name ;
            cout << "Input last name: \n" ;
            cin >> last_name ;

            // combine first and last name
            sprintf( full_name, "%s %s", first_name, last_name) ;

            Name *current_customer = new Name( full_name )  ;
                // allocate a Name object and initialize its dynamically
                // allocated Name string with supplied string

            return( current_customer ) ;
    }

void destroy_customer( Name *customer )
{
            delete customer ;          // destroy the customer object
    }
```

7.3.2 Memory Deallocation

A dynamically allocated object is deallocated by using the **delete** operator. The **delete** operator frees up the memory space and returns it to the available memory pool in the *free store*. The memory area is reused for other allocation calls by the **new** operator.

The following identifies the generic syntax used to deallocate an object and an array:

```
delete  object_pointer ;       // deallocate object
delete [ ] array_pointer ;     // deallocate array
```

To destroy an object, the destructor function (if any) is called to perform the necessary cleanup operations. The **delete** operator is then called to deallocate and return the object's memory space to the free store. In the following example, the ~**Name**() destructor cleans up the object by destroying its string buffer. Since *first* points to an array, the **delete** statement includes the *array index ([ ])* operator to provide this fact to the compiler:

```
//                NAME.CPP Source File
#include <string.h>
#include <name.h>

Name:: ~Name( )
{
    delete [ ] first ;// deallocate name string buffer
    first = static_cast<Text *> ( 0 ) ;// erase markers
    middle = static_cast<Text *> ( 0 ) ;
    last = static_cast<Text *> ( 0 ) ;
}
```

Since allocation and deallocation of a memory block may occur in different functions and source files (*refer to the preceding example*), at compile time it cannot be determined whether the pointer used with the **delete** operator is a pointer to an array or a pointer to a single object. In the above example, the *first* pointer specifies only the starting location of a memory block containing a string and the compiler cannot determine if the memory is being used to store one or several characters. By using the *array index* operator ([ ]) in the **delete** statement, the designer explicitly tells the compiler that *first* points to an array. The compiler then places the appropriate provisions into the code to handle the cleanup operation for an array. At run time, the size of the array is determined and the destructor for each of the elements is explicitly called in the reverse order of construction. By virtue of the explicit notation, an object or an array can be properly destroyed. The use of the *array index* operator ([ ]) in the **delete** statement is important to ensure software reliability. The program may behave unpredictably when an array of objects is deallocated without using the *array index* operator ([ ]). This situation is especially critical for objects that reference external data. In the following example, an array of *Name* objects is deallocated. The program will cause *memory leakage* (Figure 7.8)

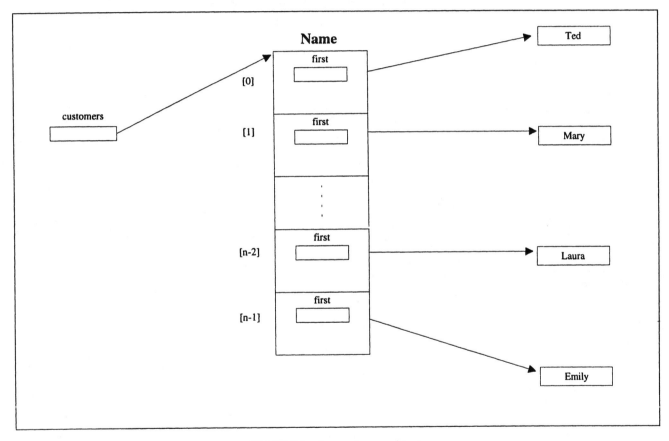

FIGURE 7.8   Array of name objects.

```
Name *customers = new Name[n] ;
...
delete customers ;
      // poor programming habit: instead use delete [ ] customers
```

In the above example, the destructor for only the first element in the array is invoked. Therefore, only the name buffer containing "*Ted*" is destroyed and the name buffers of the other elements are never deallocated. The designer must take the necessary steps to ensure reliable and predictable behavior within the design.

Correspondingly, a program should **not** use the *array index* operator ([ ]) for single objects because, again, it may cause unpredictable behavior. The following example allocates a single *Name* object and later deallocates it as if it were an array of *Name* objects.

```
Name *customer = new Name( "Ted Russell Rittmaster" );
.
delete [ ] customer ; // bad operation
```

In C++, the **delete** operator is null safe and can safely operate on a null address without any side effects. This characteristic relieves software developers from having to check for null addresses prior to deallocating a memory space:

```
delete buffer ;
        // even if buffer contains a null address,
        // the delete will behave properly
```

The operation of the *dynamic memory allocation* (**malloc**) library is independent of the **new** and **delete** operators. The library operates on the *heap* and the C++ operators use the *free store*. These memory pools are conceptually independent of each other. As a guideline, memory allocated through a call to **malloc()** should not be deallocated using the **delete** operator. Similarly, memory allocated using the **new** operator should not be deallocated using the **free()** function. In both scenarios, the behavior of the software will not be deterministic:

```
Name *customer = new Name ;
.
free( customer ) ;   // may cause unpredictable behavior
```

7.4 DYNAMIC ALLOCATION FAILURE AND RECOVERY

C++ provides additional flexibility by allowing the **new** operator to interact with a user-defined error handler when an allocation failure occurs. The following algorithm[1] specifies how the **new** operator dynamically allocates memory:

```
. Allocate block of size n
. if allocation is not successful then
        . if user-defined error handler exists then
                . call user-defined error handler()
                . goto allocation (above) and reattempt allocation
        . else
                . use null address
        . end if
. end if
. return address
```

Prior to an allocation request, the application software may install an error handler. The error handler function should attempt to obtain additional free memory, possibly by deallocating any non critical objects being used by the software. Either by obtaining additional memory or by freeing memory, the error handler allows the **new** operator to reattempt the allocation process in order to satisfy the allocation request. Application software installs an error handler using the **set_new_handler()** function (*new.h* library file), which is an ANSI standardized library function. This function takes the address of a user-defined error recovery function as its argument and returns the previous error handler's address.

In the following example, prior to making allocation requests, **create_customer()** installs the **recover()** function, which is the user-defined error handler. In addition, the **create_customer()** function backs up the previous error handler's address returned by the **set_new_handler()** function. By storing the old error handler's address, every module in the software can support its own unique recovery function and can cycle between them:

---

[1]For simplification, this algorithm leaves out available C++ exception handling.

```
//              Test Driver Source File
#include <new.h>

void recover( ) ;
                // user-defined dynamic allocation error recovery function
int main( int , char ** )
{
        Name *customer = create_customer() ;
        ...
        destroy_customer( customer ) ;
}


Name *create_customer( void )
{
        void (*previous_handler) ( ) ;

        previous_handler = set_new_handler( recover ) ;
                // install recover() function and save the
                // address of the previous handler.

        Text first_name[20] , last_name[20] , full_name[40] ;
        cout << "Input first name: \n" ;
        cin >> first_name ;
        cout << "Input last name: \n" ;
        cin >> last_name ;

        sprintf( full_name, "%s %s", first_name, last_name) ;

        Name *current_customer = new Name( full_name )  ;
                // allocate a Name object. On dynamic allocation failures
                // call the recover() function.

        set_new_handler( previous_handler ) ;
                // restore previous error handler

        return( current_customer ) ;
}

void destroy_customer( Name *customer )
{
        delete customer ;// destroy the customer object
}

void recover( )
{
        // obtains additional memory: e.g. deallocates unnecessary buffers
        // if unsuccessful then
        //    throw an exception of type bad_alloc or use exit() or abort() to
        //    terminate program's execution
        return ;
}
```

If the **new** operator is unable to allocate memory, the operator calls the **recover()** function automatically. If the **recover()** function does not terminate the program and obtains additional memory through deallocation, the **new** operator can reattempt the allocation operation. The above **recover()** function's prototype is based on the

ANSI C++ standards, which require the error handler not to return any data (*void* type). The **recover()** function must provide the following behavior:

1. **Memory Allocation**: If the **recover()** function obtains additional memory space, perhaps by deallocating noncritical buffers, it will then return the control back to the **new** operator, which reattempts the allocation operation.

   If the function fails to obtain additional memory space, it cannot return the control back to the **new** operator. This restriction will prevent the program from going into infinite loops. If the **recover()** function returns, **new** will reattempt the allocation process, which would fail again, then the **new** operator would call the error handler again, and the process would continue to cycle.

2. **Program Termination**: When the **recover()** function fails to obtain additional memory, it may call the **exit()** and **abort()** functions to terminate the program's execution. Since this approach does not rely on graceful degradation and is a hard recovery, in most applications this solution is not viable.

3. **Exception**: When the **recover()** function fails to obtain additional memory, the **recover()** function may raise an exception by throwing an instance of the *bad_alloc* class, which is an ANSI standardized class library. This approach is a better alternative than program termination because it provides a graceful recovery process. Chapter 8 revisits this topic in its discussion of C++ exception handling and standardized exception libraries.

By default, the error-handling mechanism is disabled in C++. If it becomes enabled, an application can always reset and disable the error handler by passing a null function pointer address to the **set_error_handler()** function:

```
set_new_handler( NULL ) ;
          // reset to default mode and disable error handler for new
```

7.5 GARBAGE COLLECTION

During the dynamic allocation and deallocation process, memory can become fragmented. At some point, the memory fragmentation may become so severe that the free memory blocks are smaller than the application's requests. Some systems use *garbage collection* to defragment the dynamic memory space. *Garbage collection* is the process of grouping the free memory blocks together by moving the allocated spaces around. Garbage collection is an effective method in memory management but it has a high overhead due to the swapping of memory blocks. When garbage collection takes place, the program's execution is suspended. After memory is defragmented, the program's execution resumes.

Garbage collection needs to take place when the dynamic allocation tools cannot satisfy an application request even though there is enough fragmented memory to satisfy the request. At such time, the dynamic allocation tools defragment the memory. Since the allocated memory blocks are shuffled around, the application and the dynamic allocation interface become more complicated (Figure 7.9).

For an allocation methodology that uses garbage collection, the application cannot maintain the physical addresses because these addresses may change and become invalid. Normally the dynamic allocation tools use an intermediate table that remains fixed in memory in order to interact with the applications. The table contains the physical addresses of the allocated memory blocks (Figure 7.10).

The application would access the dynamic memory blocks using the current addresses stored in the table. The table is updated by the dynamic allocation functions when the memory is defragmented. This mechanism requires the application to go through *multiple indirection* to access an allocated memory region.

The dynamic allocation operators (**new** and **delete**) and the C-Language's *dynamic memory allocation* (**malloc**) library do **not** perform or support garbage collection. Since both return the physical addresses of the dynamically allocated memory space to the application, the application directly accesses the memory and any garbage collection would have an adverse effect on the application.

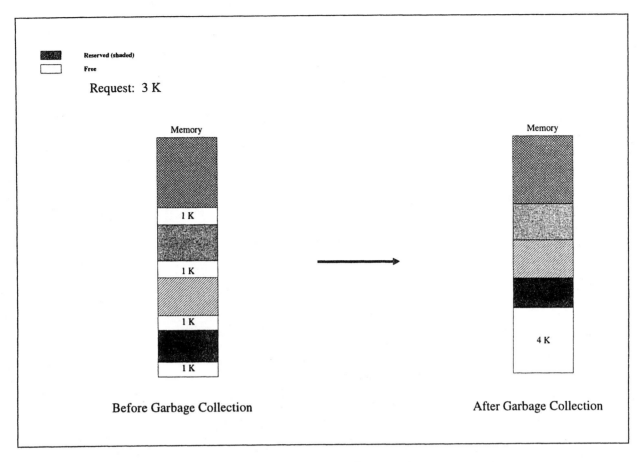

FIGURE 7.9 Memory unfragmentation.

7.6 CUSTOM MEMORY MANAGEMENT

At times when there is a hardware dependency, a design may need to provide custom memory management for instances of a class (objects). This would require the class to overload the **new** and **delete** operators. Custom memory management is used when instances of a class (objects) are mapped to a specific address space (Figure 7.11). For instance, I/O ports such as a serial port are typically mapped to specific addresses. For such architectures, the I/O port can be treated as an object. By designing a class library for the I/O port, the library would encapsulate the internal hardware control and operation from the rest of the software. The design of the class library would be different than a typical class library since there is a restriction on the number and location of the objects. The objects must be mapped to specific locations in memory. The class would need to overload the **new** and **delete** operators, which will hide the address dependencies from its clients, and will simplify the portability and maintainability of the software.

In the following example, the *Serial Port* class is used in the design of the *Serial I/O Communication* class library. This library will allow two devices such as two embedded computers to interact via their RS-232 serial interfaces[2] (Figure 7.12). An RS-232 interface transmits a data byte over a single wire 1 bit at a time. To help the receiving side identify a data byte, data bits are enclosed within *start* and *stop* bits. Thus, each data frame consists of 10 bits: a data byte, and start and stop bits. The data transmission is asynchronous and the transmission rate is determined by the number of bits transmitted per second (*baud rate*)[3].

---

[2]RS-232 is an EIA standard and is applicable to computer and modem interfaces. The standard specifies the requirements for transmission of serial binary digital data.

[3]In most cases, the baud rate is equivalent to the transmission rate of bits per second.

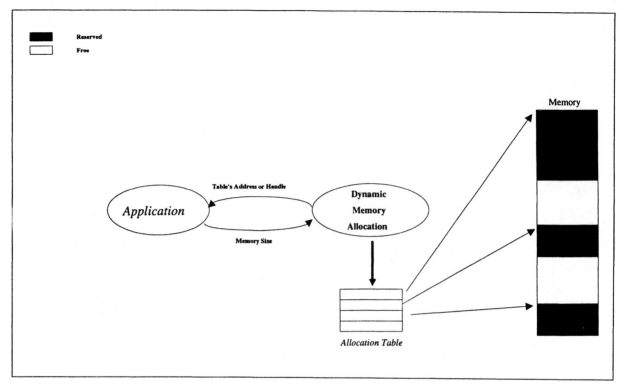

FIGURE 7.10 Dynamic memory allocation with garbage collection.

The serial communication is interrupt driven and the interface provides unique transmit (TXD) and receive (RXD) data lines. The two data lines allow the systems to transmit and receive serial data simultaneously (*full duplex*).

Serial communication provides error detection through the optional *parity* feature. Parity is either "even" or "odd." The number of "1" data bits is used to calculate an *even* or *odd* parity bit. For example, the "00010010" data word has an even number of "1" bits in the number. For the even parity case, the parity bit will be "0" because there is an even number of ones in the data word. For the odd parity case, the parity bit will be "1." The parity bit is incorporated within the data field in the 10-bit frame. When the parity feature is used, only the first 7 bits of data are transmitted and the last bit is used as the parity bit. To transmit the full 8 bits in a data byte, the parity feature can be disabled in serial communication.

The *Serial I/O Communication* library operates on the serial I/O ports and its associated interrupt vector tables. The clients of this library receive and transmit information without being concerned about the details of the serial communication at the hardware level. Figure 7.13 depicts the class diagram for this library. This section focuses on the design of the *Serial Port* class, and the other classes are discussed in the next chapter. The *Serial Port* class hides the operation, location, and internal details of the serial port from its clients by providing the following features:

1. **Construction:** The class provides a user-defined values constructor that initializes the hardware to specify data transmission rate and settings:

```
//              SERIAL_PORT.H Header File
class Serial_Port
{
     // other details left out
     public:
          // Constructors
          Serial_Port( Baud_Rate rate,
               Word_Length length = EIGHT_BIT,
               Parity parity = NO_PARITY,
               Stop_Bits stop_bits = ONE_STOP_BIT ) ;
} ;
```

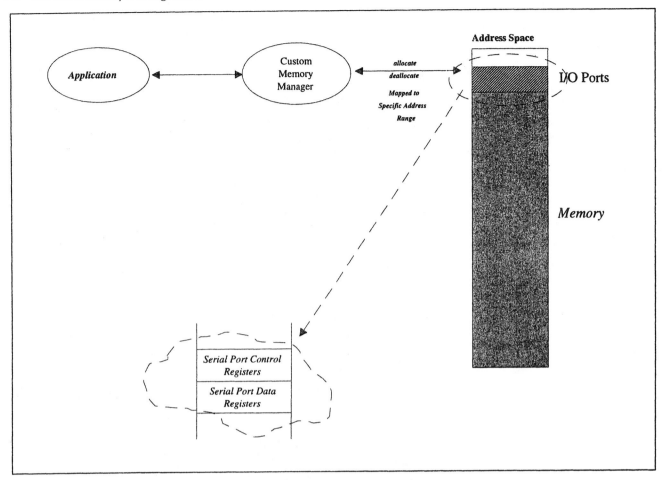

FIGURE 7.11 Custom memory management.

Since there are a limited number of unique ports, the objects cannot be copied. This makes the class *copy* constructor and *assignment* operator useless and potentially dangerous. To prevent the client from using these features inadvertently, they are removed from the design interface by making them **private** members:

```
//                    SERIAL_PORT.H Header File
class Serial_Port
{
        private:
                // ** Note **: Remove following functions from
                // the design interface
                Serial_Port( const Serial_Port & ) ;
                Serial_Port & operator =( const Serial_Port & ) ;
                // other details left out
} ;
```

In addition, the *default* constructor has not been defined because without knowing the serial interface settings this feature is useless. The preceding declarations tell the compiler that these functions are private and prevent the client from performing any of the following operations:

```
// will cause compilation error
Serial_Port port1 ; // attempt to use the default constructor
Serial_Port port2 ( port1 ) ; // attempt to use the copy constructor
port2 = port1 ; // attempt to use the assignment operator
```

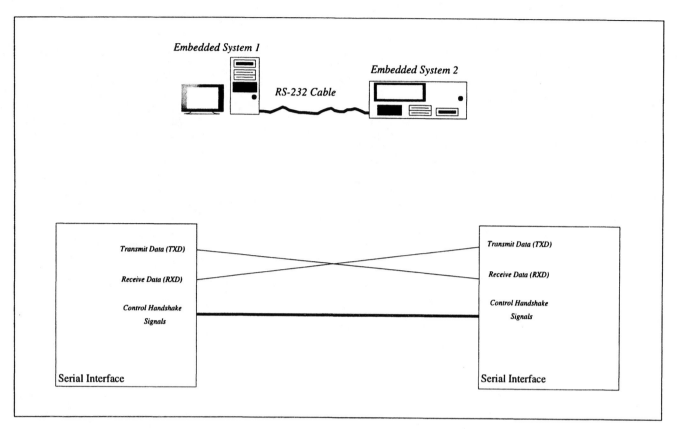

FIGURE 7.12   Embedded systems serial communication block diagram.

2. **Destruction**: The destructor disables the interrupts and the hardware registers and updates the serial port tables to indicate the port is available.

3. **Objects**: The number of serial interfaces in the embedded system is limited and are normally mapped to specific locations within the system's address space. Therefore, the class has overloaded the **new** and **delete** operators to provide a transparent mapping of the instances of the *Serial Port* class.

```
//              SERIAL_PORT.H Header File
class Serial_Port
{
    public:
        // Memory management functions
        static void * operator new( size_t size ) ;
        static void operator delete( void *block ) ;

        // Other details left out
} ;
```

The *Serial Stream* class reads and writes data bytes to a *Serial Port* (Figure 7.13). Since the number of serial ports is limited and the locations are hardware dependent, the *Serial Stream* class must use external containment and the *Serial Port* object must be created dynamically. The *Serial Stream* constructor performs this task and associates the physical serial interface to the serial stream:

```
//              SERIAL_STREAM.H Header File
#ifndef SERIAL_STREAM_H
#define SERIAL_STREAM_H
```

```
#include "buffer.h"        // buffer class
#include "serial_port.h"   // serial port class

class Serial_Stream
{
        private:
                // Serial I/O Interface
                Serial_Port *port ;

                // Internal I/O Buffers
                Buffer input_buffer , output_buffer ;
        public:
                // Constructor
                Serial_Stream( Baud_Rate rate ) ;

                // Destructor
                ~Serial_Stream( ) ;

                // Other details left out
        } ;


#endif            // SERIAL_STREAM Header File
```

Serial Stream uses the overloaded **new** and **delete** operators to create instances of the *Serial Port* class. The overloaded functions overshadow the built-in operators. The *Serial Stream* class creates an instance of a *Serial Port* object in its constructor. The *Serial Stream* object transmits and receives data bytes via this I/O interface. At the completion of the communication session, the *Serial Stream* destructor destroys the *Serial Port* object:

```
//               SERIAL_STREAM.CPP Source File
#include "serial_stream.h"// Serial I/O Communication class library

Serial_Stream:: Serial_Stream( Baud_Rate rate )
{
     Serial_Port *port = new Serial_Port( rate ) ;
          // invoke Serial_Port:: operator new( sizeof(Serial_Port) ) ;
          // if( port != static_cast<Serial_Port> (0) )
          //invoke Serial_Port( ) constructor
     // if serial port object is created =>
     //      complete the initialization process
     if( port )
     {
          // details left out
     }
     else
     {
     // capture & record error condition
     }
}


Serial_Stream:: ~Serial_Stream( )
{
     // close I/O stream
     delete port ;// Destroy serial I/O stream
          // invoke ~Serial_Port() destructor
          // invoke Serial_Port:: operator delete( (void *) port ) ;
}
```

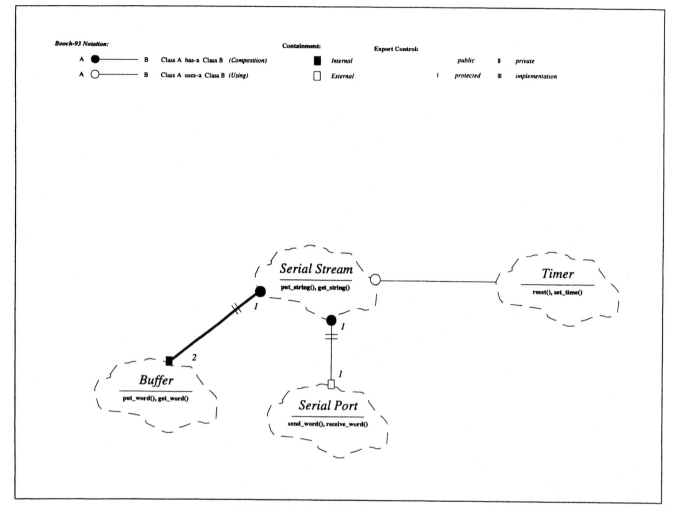

FIGURE 7.13 Serial I/O class diagram.

The syntax and usage of the overloaded operators is identical to the built-in **new** and **delete** operators, which makes the process transparent to the above class.

4. **Port I/O**: The communication functions send and receive data words (8 bits or 7 bits) from the serial port and hide the hardware interaction. The **send_word()** and **receive_word()** functions directly operate on the hardware registers. These functions will be called by the *Serial Stream* interrupt handler. The serial stream interrupt handler needs to perform its task as quickly as possible. Therefore, these functions are **inlined** to eliminate function calls:

```
//              SERIAL_PORT.H Header File
typedef         unsigned char    Word ;

class Serial_Port
{
       public:
               // Data Transmission function
               inline void send_word( Word data ) ;

                    // Data Receive function
                    inline Word receive_word( void ) ;

                    // Other details left out
       } ;
```

5. **Control Information**: Similar to any other class, the *Serial Port* class library will need to provide *access* functions, which allow *Serial Stream* to examine the state of a serial port:

```
//                  SERIAL_PORT.H Header File
class Serial_Port
{
    public:
            // Serial Port State access functions
            inline Baud_Rate transmission_rate( void ) const ;
            inline Stop_Bits num_stop_bits( void ) const ;
            inline Word_Length word_length( void ) const ;
            inline Parity parity_type( void ) const ;
            inline Boolean empty( void ) const ;
            inline Port_Status status( void ) const ;

            // Other details left out
} ;
```

The following is an overall picture of the *Serial Port* class library:

```
//                  SERIAL_PORT.H Header File
#ifndef SERIAL_PORT_H
#define SERIAL_PORT_H

    typedef     unsigned char     Word ;

    #define NUM_SERIAL_PORTS 2 // # of available serial ports

    // Type of interrupt request: transmit or receive data
    enum Mode
    {
        TRANSMIT , RECEIVE
    } ;

    // Data transmission rate
    enum Baud_Rate
    {
        B_2400 = 2400, B_4800 = 4800, B_9600 = 9600,
        B_19200 = 19200, B_38400 = 38400
    } ;

    // Bit error correction mode
    enum Parity
    {
        NO_PARITY , EVEN_PARITY , ODD_PARITY
    } ;


    // # of stop bits for the serial data transmission
    enum Stop_Bits
    {
        ONE_STOP_BIT , TWO_STOP_BITS, NO_STOP_BITS
    } ;

    // size of word length: 8-bits or 7-bits
    enum Word_Length
```

```
        {
            EIGHT_BIT , SEVEN_BIT
        } ;

        //  Serial Port Error Conditions
        enum Port_Status
        {
            NO_SERIAL_ERROR , PARITY_ERROR ,
            OVERRUN_ERROR , FRAMING_ERROR
        } ;

        class Serial_Port
        {
            private:
                    static void *port_address[NUM_SERIAL_PORTS];
                    static Boolean port_usage[NUM_SERIAL_PORTS];

                    // ** Note **: Remove following functions from
                    // the design interface
                    Serial_Port( const Serial_Port & ) ;
                    Serial_Port & operator =( const Serial_Port & ) ;

            public:
                    // Constructors
                    Serial_Port( Baud_Rate rate,
                            Word_Length length = EIGHT_BIT ,
                            Parity parity = NO_PARITY,
                            Stop_Bits stop_bits = ONE_STOP_BIT ) ;

                    // Destructor
                    ~Serial_Port() ;

                    // Memory management functions
                    static void * operator new( size_t size ) ;
                    static void operator delete( void *block ) ;

                    // Communication functions
                    inline void send_word( Word data ) ;
                    inline Word receive_word( void ) ;

                    // Serial Port State access functions
                    inline Mode mode( void ) const ;
                    inline Baud_Rate transmission_rate( void ) const ;
                    inline Stop_Bits num_stop_bits( void ) const ;
                    inline Parity parity_type( void ) const ;
                    inline Boolean empty( void ) const ; // no data available
                    inline Boolean error( void ) const ;
                            // parity or overflow error
                    inline Port_Status status( void ) const ;
                    void enable( void ) ; // enable interrupt
                    void disable( void ) ; // disable interrupt
        } ;

#endif                  // SERIAL_PORT_H Header File
```

7.6.1 Overloaded New Operator

For custom memory management, C++ has placed restrictions on the dynamic allocation operators. Both the **new** and **delete** operators must be implemented as *static member* functions, which implies *"this"* pointer is not implicitly passed to them. The initialization of an object occurs only after the memory space for the object has been allocated. Therefore, when the **new** operator function is called, an object does not yet exist and the overloaded **new()** function is simply allocating raw memory space, and there is no object. After the **new()** function returns, the applicable *constructor* is then called to initialize this memory space.

The following is the generic syntax for the overloaded **new** operator:

```
void * Class_Name:: operator new( size_t ) ;
```

The first argument of the **new** operator must be of type *size_t* (an integer typedef). It identifies the number of bytes required for an instance of the class. The return type is a *void* pointer to the beginning of the memory block because the memory has not been initialized yet. When the allocation fails, the function returns a null address or throws a **bad_alloc** exception, which is discussed in Chapter 8. In the following example, the operator **new()** function for the *Serial Port* class library scans through its internal table and reserves the first available port. In case all ports are used, it returns a null address:

```
//                    SERIAL_PORT.CPP Source File
#include "serial_port.h"

// static members initialization statements
void * Serial_Port:: port_address[NUM_SERIAL_PORTS] =
{
        // serial port addresses
} ;

Boolean Serial_Port:: port_usage[NUM_SERIAL_PORTS] =
{
        false , false
} ;

void * Serial_Port:: operator new( size_t )
{
        void *port = static_cast <void *> ( 0 ) ; // assume no available port

        // scan through the port usage table
        for( int i = 0 ; i < NUM_SERIAL_PORTS ; i++ )
        {
                // if a port is not being used then reserve port
                if( !port_usage[i] )
                {
                        port_usage[i] = true ; // reserve port
                        port = static_cast<void *> ( port_address[i] ) ;
                                // store address
                        break ; // abort search
                }
        }

        return( port ) ;
}
```

In this example, the **new()** function does not use the passed memory size parameter. Therefore, the name for the parameter is not specified.

The **new** operator function normally takes only one argument but through the use of *placement arguments* the application may define additional arguments. The following is the generic syntax identifying the implementation of placement arguments for a custom *Name*:: **new()** function:

```
class Name
{
    public:
            static operator new( size_t , placement_argument(s) ) ;
            // other details left out
} ;
```

The application uses the new operator function using the following syntax:

```
Name *pointer = new (placement argument(s)) Name(initialization list) ;
```

The compiler translates the preceding to a call to the operator **new()** function:

```
Name *pointer = Name:: operator new( sizeof(Name),
                        placement argument(s) ) ;
```

For example, the client of *Serial Port* may specify a preference for a serial port by passing the serial port's id to the **new()** function:

```
class Serial_Port
{
    public:
            void *operator new ( size_t num_bytes ) ;
            void *operator new ( size_t num_bytes , int port_id );
            // other details left out
} ;

        Serial_Port *port = new (2) Serial_Port( B_9600 ) ;
        // is treated as port = Serial_Port::
        // operator new( sizeof(Serial_Port) , 2 );
        // if ( port )
        // port->Serial_Port( B_9600,
        //              NO_PARITY , NO_STOP_BITS )
```

The *placement arguments* are used for applications that not only need the memory space requirements but also need additional information such as a hardware dependency. **As a design guideline,** *placement arguments* **should be avoided because they eliminate the standard and generic interface of the new operator.** The syntax tells the client explicitly that the design has overloaded the **new** operator and the operation is no longer transparent to the client and increases design coupling.

7.6.2 Overloaded Delete Operator

During an object destruction, the destructor is called first to perform the cleanup operation. After the destructor call, the memory space for the object is freed. In dynamic deallocation, when the **delete** operator is called to deallocate the memory space, the object has already been destroyed. Therefore, the **delete** operator may be overloaded for a class as a *static member* function. The **delete()** operator function cannot return any data and its first argument must be a void pointer:

```
void Class_Name:: operator delete( void * ) ;
```

In the following example, the **delete()** function for the *Serial Port* class updates its internal table and returns the port back to its available resource pool:

```
//              SERIAL_PORT.CPP Source File
#include "serial_port.h"

// static members initialization statements
void * Serial_Port:: port_address[NUM_SERIAL_PORTS] =
{
        // serial port addresses
} ;

Boolean Serial_Port:: port_usage[NUM_SERIAL_PORTS] =
{
        false , false
} ;

void Serial_Port:: operator delete( void *port )
{
        // if port's address exists (not null)
        if( port != static_cast<void *> (0) )
        {
                // scan through the port usage table
                for( int i = 0 ; i < NUM_SERIAL_PORTS ; i++ )
                {
                        // if port is assigned then free up port
                        if( port == port_address[i] )
                        {
                                port_usage[i] = false ; // free up port space
                                break ; // abort search
                        }
                }
        }

        return ;
}
```

To maintain compatibility with the built-in **delete** operator, the custom **delete** function must be null safe. The function should ignore deallocation requests for null address values (*refer to the preceding example*).

7.6.3 User-Defined Error Handling

A drawback of custom memory management is that standard error handling supported by the global new operator cannot be called in case of memory allocation failure.

When it is applicable, a class with overloaded **new** and **delete** operators should provide an error handling scheme similar to the one used by the built-in **new** and **delete** operators (refer to Section 7.4). This approach would streamline the design and would make the design compatible with the built-in dynamic allocation capability.

7.6.4 Custom Array Allocation and Deallocation

When the **new** and **delete** operators are overloaded for a class, the design must address not only allocation of single objects, but also handling of arrays for the specified class. To handle dynamic allocation and deallocation of arrays properly, the **new [ ]** and **delete [ ]** operators should be overloaded. In the following example, the *Serial Port* class overloads the **new** and **delete** operators to handle both unique instances and arrays:

```
//              SERIAL_PORT.H Header File
class Serial_Port
{
      public:
              // Constructor
              Serial_Port() ; // need this for arrays

              // Custom memory management
              static void * operator new [ ] ( size_t array_size ) ;
              static void * operator new ( size_t object_size ) ;

              static void operator delete [ ] ( void * array ) ;
              static void operator delete ( void *object_address ) ;
       // Other details left out
} ;
```

These operators are used instead of the built-in operators when the client dynamically allocates and deallocates an array:

```
Serial_Port *ports = new Serial_Port[n] ;
      // allocate n serial ports using Serial_Port:: operator new[ ]
      // if allocation is successful then
      // call default constructor n times
      ...
      ...
delete [] ports ;
      // deallocate using Serial_Port:: operator delete [ ]
      // call destructor n times (in the reverse order) to clean up the objects
```

Without the overloaded array definitions, the built-in array operators **new [ ]** and **delete [ ]** would have been used instead. The overloaded **Serial_Port:: new** operator allocates an object at a specific address. However, the built-in **new [ ]** operator would allocate the array from the *free store* pool, which would have caused unpredictable behavior for *Serial Port* arrays. In the case of *Serial Port* design, custom handling of arrays does not really make sense because there are only a few ports available. To prevent the client from using the built-in version, the **new [ ]** operator is removed from the design interface by declaring it private:

```
//              SERIAL_PORT.H Header File
class Serial_Port
{
      private:
              // ** Note **: Removed from the design interface
              static void * operator new [ ] ( size_t array_size ) ;

      public:
              // Custom memory management
              static void * operator new ( size_t object_size ) ;
              static void operator delete ( void *object_address ) ;

              // Other details left out
} ;
```

The preceding class definition permits the client only to allocate single instances of the *Serial Port* class, while preventing the client from allocating arrays of this class. For the *Serial Port* class, the preceding private **new [ ]** declaration is optional because there is no *default constructor* to initialize multiple instances of *Serial Port*. Without the *default constructor*, the compiler generates compilation errors for dynamic allocation of *Serial Port* arrays. With a *default constructor*, the preceding private **new** declaration would have been necessary. As a defensive programming technique, the **new [ ]** operator has been removed from the design interface.

7.6.5 General Notes

Since the overloaded versions of **new** and **delete** supersede the built-in versions, the client can access the built-in versions by using the scope resolution (::) operator:

```
Serial_Port *port = ::new Serial_Port( B_9600 ) ; // use built-in new
    ...
    ...
::delete port ; // use built-in delete
```

In this example, the specified operation would cause unpredictable behavior because the built-in and overloaded versions use different memory pools and the operation is meaningless for the *Serial Port* class.

SUMMARY

In C++, objects can be defined at compile time or dynamically created at run time. Run time allocation is used for applications that cannot determine the amount of required memory for arrays or objects at compile time. This type of application determines the size of the required memory at run time and allocates the necessary memory using the *dynamic memory allocation* tools. The C++ language has incorporated *dynamic memory allocation* into the language by using the **new** and **delete** operators.

C++ treats dynamically allocated objects in a fashion similar to regular object definitions. It also ties the calls to constructor and destructor functions to the memory allocation and deallocation requests. After each allocation request that uses the **new** operator, the applicable constructor for the object is called to initialize the memory space. Similarly, prior to deallocation of an object using the **delete** operator, the destructor for the object is called to clean up. After the cleanup operation is completed, the memory space is deallocated.

C++ has incorporated a user-defined error handler in order to allow custom error recovery from allocation failures. The error handler is a recovery function and is used by the **new** operator. When the **new** operator is unable to allocate additional memory, this operator calls the error handler. Depending on the application's design, the recovery function can perhaps deallocate some non critical data and allow the **new** operator to reattempt the allocation process. The error handler is an optional feature and by default is disabled.

The **delete** operator is "null safe" and the application does not need to worry about passing a null address to the **delete** operator. However, the **delete** operator relies on valid addresses for proper deallocation and software reliability.

C++ still supports the C-Language's dynamic memory allocation (**malloc**) library. Since constructors and destructors cannot be called in conjunction with this library, a designer should avoid using this library for basic object allocation and deallocation. This library, is however, still useful for creation of custom memory management capabilities.

The operators **new** and **delete** can be overloaded in the design of custom memory managers. Custom memory management is used for specific applications, such as when the allocation is hardware dependent and needs to be performed in a specific address range.

GLOSSARY

Dynamic allocation
    Allocating memory space for an object or an array at run time

Free store

The memory space used by the new operator for dynamic allocation

Garbage collection

The process of defragmenting memory space in order to optimize the memory usage

Heap

The memory space maintained by the malloc library for dynamic allocation

Memory leakage

The loss of available memory in the free store memory space due to improper handling of the memory space

Placement arguments

Additional arguments that can be passed to the new() operator function

Static Allocation

The compiler uses an object or array definition in the program to determine the memory space requirement at compile time.

CHAPTER 8

Error Detection and Recovery

INTRODUCTION

Reliability plays a central role in the design of a system. Since systems do not always work as expected, the design of an object model needs to take unexpected situations (*exceptions*) into consideration. At the object level, the state of the object(s) within a system must remain predictable when an *exception* occurs. When a fatal error occurs, a system should gracefully transition to a degraded state by properly shutting down the affected subsystems. The software process should terminate in an orderly fashion. By incorporating error detection/recovery mechanisms in the object model, recovery from exceptions prevents uncontrolled failures and maintains the system in a deterministic state at all times. In C++, error detection for a class is designed using one of the following approaches:

1. **Passive Approach**: The class uses status flag(s) to indicate error conditions. When a member function detects an error condition, the function captures and records the error by using the internal status flag (data member). Since this approach does not provide for automatic exception condition notification, the clients must query the objects for status. For example, the clients of the *Stream I/O* class library use the **fail()** member function to detect error conditions associated with a stream after a read (>>) or write (<<) operation.

2. **Active Approach**: With *active* error handling, clients do not need to query objects for their status. At the point of detection, the function automatically notifies the recovery function by *throwing* an exception. Associated with the exception, the function detecting the error provides information such as an error code and message. The exception is automatically propagated and *caught* at a higher level by the function doing the recovery. This concept is similar to a football game: a *quarterback* (function detecting the error condition) throws the *football* (error information) to the *receiver* (function performing the error recovery). The *football* may be intercepted by other *players* (functions) in the path of the ball (partial recovery).

C++ provides a built-in mechanism for capturing and reporting errors through the **throw, try,** and **catch** keywords. When a lower level function detects an exception, it uses the **throw** keyword to report the error condition to the calling functions. The **throw** statement causes the *error code* (built-in data type) or *error object* (an instance of a class) to be propagated to a higher level function. The function that contains the **try-catch** clauses for the specified exception then catches the *error code* or *object* and performs the applicable recovery operation. As long as an exception does not occur, the client operates on the objects in a normal fashion.

Chapter 8 continues the design of the *Serial I/O Communication* class library from the previous chapter and incorporates both *active* and *passive* error detection/recovery mechanisms into the design. With the focus on error handling, this chapter partitions the *Serial I/O Communication* class design discussion into:

1. Capturing and recording exceptions
2. Identifying exception handling in the class interfaces
3. Detecting and reporting exceptions
4. Handling exceptions

At the end, this chapter provides an overview of the ANSI *exception* class library.

8.1 SERIAL I/O COMMUNICATION CLASS LIBRARY OVERVIEW

The *Serial I/O Communication* class library hides the internal details of serial communication such as hardware configuration, interrupt management, and data buffering from its clients. In Figure 8.1, a PC system uses the RS-232 serial port to communicate with an embedded system. The *communication* module is responsible for transmitting information between the two systems. In addition, it encapsulates and abstracts the communication protocol and hardware/software interactions from the rest of the software.

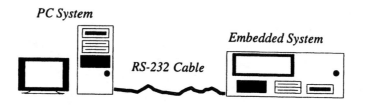

FIGURE 8.1   PC communication block diagram.

In Figure 8.2, the *Terminal* class category is responsible for the communication protocol used in transmitting and receiving a file through the RS-232 interface. *Terminal* uses *Stream I/O* for reading or writing the contents of the file to the disk. The file contents are transmitted and received using the *Serial I/O* class category. The *Serial I/O* class category stores data in its intermediate buffers and when a hardware interrupt occurs, data are transferred from/to the serial port register to/from the internal buffers. For data transmission, the hardware serializes data bytes and transmits them over a single wire (refer back to Chapter 7).

During data transmission, a variety of errors may occur, ranging from communication protocol errors to serial I/O failures. The software must be able to handle such exceptions. For example, *Serial I/O* uses *Timer* to prevent the software from waiting indefinitely for data when the interface is disconnected. When the timer expires and the requested serial I/O event is still not completed, the serial I/O function aborts.

The *Serial I/O Communication* class library views the RS-232 interface as a stream (Figure 8.3). Figure 8.3 depicts the architectural view of the *Serial I/O Communication* library. This library is based on the interaction of several objects with *Serial Stream* as the focal point. The *Serial Stream* coordinates serial I/O operation by interacting with the *Serial Port*, *Serial Exception*, and *Buffer* classes.

Since data flows in both directions asynchronously, the *Serial Stream* class needs two *Buffers* for temporary storage of incoming and outgoing data (Figure 8.4). The class diagram depicts the existing cardinality for the *Serial Stream* and *Buffer* classes (Figure 8.3). The *Timer* class is used to detect communication timeouts by the *Serial Stream* member functions. The *Timer*, *Serial Port*, and *Buffer* classes are used internally in the design of this library and are denoted by the **implementation** and **private** *export controls*. The client uses this library by interacting only with *Serial Stream*.

To maximize system performance and utilization, serial communication is asynchronous relative to the client's read and write operations. For example, a client uses the **Serial_Stream:: put_string()** function to write

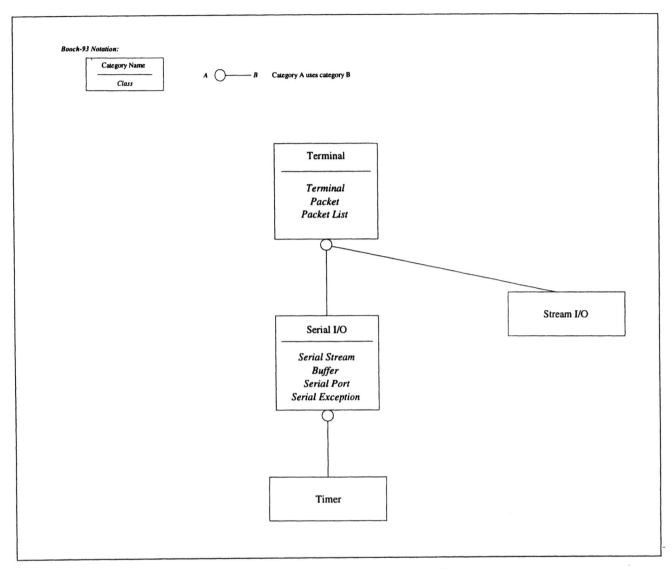

FIGURE 8.2   Communication module category diagram.

a string to the serial stream (Figure 8.3). This function could transmit a string 1 byte at a time by polling on the *Serial Port* object. However, the polling approach forces the program to wait for the serial port (a slow device), which degrades performance and is an inefficient utilization of the processor's bandwidth. Instead, the program should be interrupt driven.

Figure 8.5 depicts the *Serial Stream* state transition diagram, which shows the state transitions caused by interrupts and regular stream I/O requests. The **Serial_Stream:: put_string**() function uses the *Buffer* class to store the string in an output buffer and returns control back to the client. While the software performs other operations, the string is transmitted asynchronously from the output buffer. When a serial interrupt occurs, the interrupt handler examines the direction of data flow to determine transmit or receive mode (Figure 8.5). When transmitting, the interrupt handler reads a data word from the output buffer by using the **Buffer:: get_word**() function and sends it to the *Serial Port* hardware by calling the **Serial_Port:: send_word**() function (Figure 8.3). The **send_word**() function transfers the data word to the serial I/O data register. After the interrupt handler services the interrupt, the program execution resumes. At this point, the object transitions to its previous state prior to the interrupt, and this is denoted by the *History* (H) symbol in Figure 8.5. The hardware asynchronously serializes the data and transmits it 1 bit at a time.

Figure 8.6 illustrates the object interaction for data transmission. Since the data byte transmission is asynchronous, the asynchronous symbol is used to denote the operation. The **put_string**() function provides a

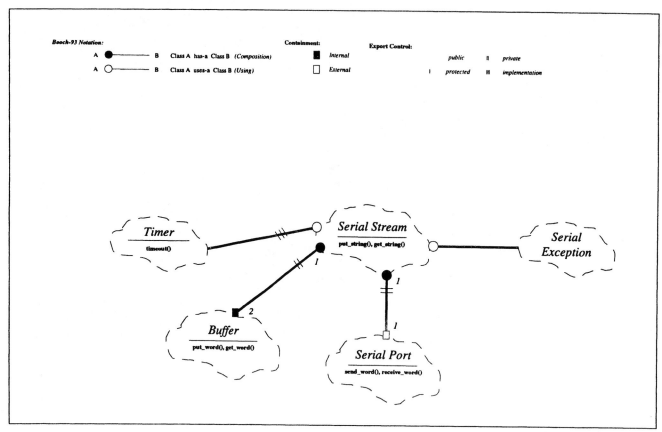

FIGURE 8.3 Serial I/O communication class diagram.

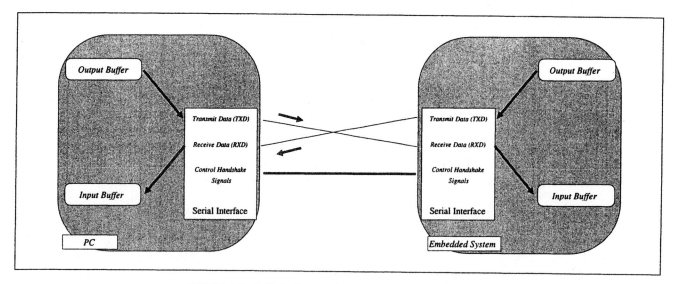

FIGURE 8.4 Full-duplex serial communication block diagram.

timeout feature, which is denoted by the clock symbol above the arrow sign. When the output buffer is full and the serial port is not transmitting, the function uses the *Timer* object to abort the transmission event. In addition, the function aborts on a buffer overflow condition.

When an interrupt occurs and the **Buffer:: get_word**() function is called, the function returns a word from the buffer, which is then sent to the *Serial Port* object via **send_word**(). When the output buffer is empty, the **get_word**() function ignores the request. Since the **get_word**() function is not ready at this time, it aborts by returning a null character (zero), which is transmitted by the **Serial_Port:: send_word**() function.

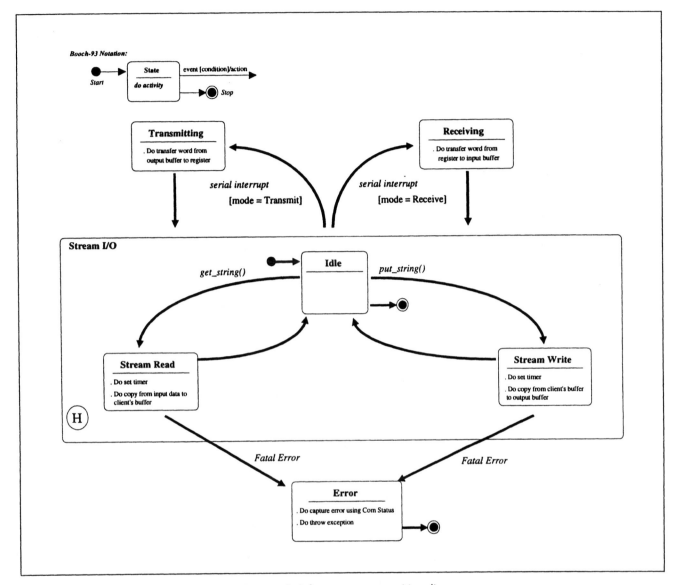

FIGURE 8.5 Serial stream state transition diagram.

For receiving data, the **Serial_Stream:: get_string**() function waits until *Serial Port* receives the applicable number of words. The function uses *Timer* to abort the read operation when data do not arrive within the specified time. Figure 8.7 depicts the object interactions for receiving a string. The **get_string**() function also provides a timeout feature. The *Timer* allows the *Serial Stream* functions to recover when the communication interface is severed.

8.2 SERIAL I/O EXCEPTIONS

The *Serial I/O Communication* library's functions may encounter the following errors:

1. **Serial Port Errors**: The *Serial Port* object operates on the hardware. During data transmission and receive operations, the hardware can detect RS-232 communication failures such as parity, frame, and interrupt overrun errors. For instance, an RS-232 interrupt may not be serviced before another data byte arrives, which would overwrite the previously received byte. Error conditions like these are captured in the hardware status register(s).

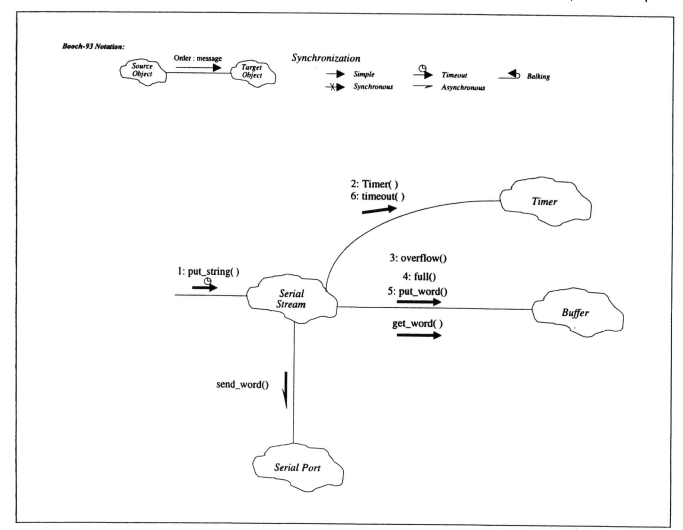

FIGURE 8.6 Data transmission object diagram.

Using a design similar to the *Serial Port* class in Chapter 7, the following is based on a *passive* approach and the *Serial Stream* class must query the *Serial Port* object for status by using the **status()** and **error()** member functions:

```
//              SERIAL_PORT.H Header File
class Serial_Port
{
        public:
                // Serial Port State access functions
                Boolean error( void ) ; // parity, frame, or overflow error
                Port_Status status( void ) ;
                // other details left out (refer back to Chapter 7)
} ;
```

These functions operate on the hardware's status register, which indicates pending error conditions.

2. Buffer Overflow: If the data flow rate is not controlled properly, the *Serial Stream* buffers may overflow. Therefore, the *Buffer* class needs to address this situation. In the following example, the *Buffer* class provides status flags that allow the client to detect an overflow or dynamic allocation failure condition (*passive* mechanism):

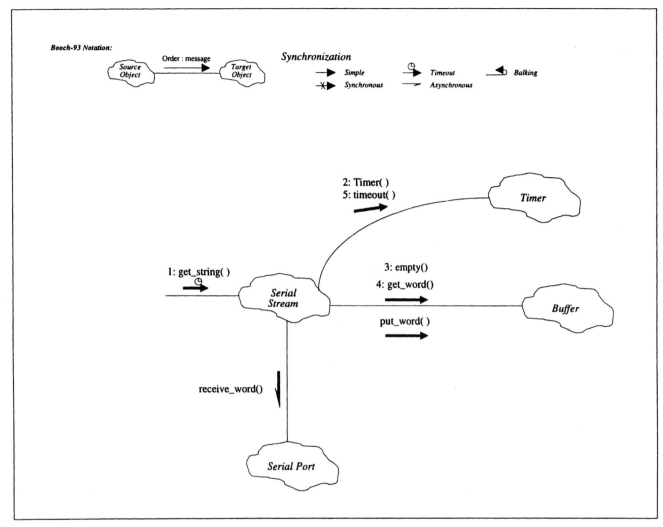

FIGURE 8.7 Data receive object diagram.

```
//              BUFFER.H Header File
#ifndef BUFFER_H
#define BUFFER_H

        typedef         unsigned char          Word ;
        typedef         bool                    Boolean ;
        typedef         unsigned int            Boolean_Bit ;
        typedef         unsigned short          Length ;

        class Buffer
        {
                private:
                        // Buffer information
                        Word  *begin            ; // beginning of the buffer
                        Length current_length ; // length of buffer

                        // Read/Write pointers
                        Word *read_ptr , *write_ptr ;
```

```
                        // Buffer status flags
                        Boolean_Bit buffer_full: 1      ;
                        Boolean_Bit buffer_empty:1      ;
                        Boolean_Bit buffer_overflow :1 ;
                        Boolean_Bit buffer_reserved:1  ;
                            // allocation successful or failed

                        // Note: removed from the design interface
                        Buffer( const Buffer & ) ;
                        Buffer & operator =( const Buffer & ) ;
            public:
                        // Constructors
                        Buffer( Length new_length ) ;

                        // Destructor
                        ~Buffer( ) ;

                        // Access functions
                        inline Length length( void ) const ;
                        inline Boolean full( void ) const  ;
                        inline Boolean empty( void ) const ;


                        // Status functions
                        inline Boolean overflow( void ) const ;
                        inline Boolean fail( void ) const ;

                        // Buffer I/O functions
                        inline Boolean put_word( Word data ) ;
                        inline Word get_word( void ) ;

                        // Buffer Flush & Reset functions
                        void flush( void ) ;
                        void clear_overflow( void ) ;
            } ;

inline Boolean Buffer:: put_word( Word data )
{
        Boolean word_saved = true ;

        // if buffer is not full and no overflow then
        // proceed with storing data word to buffer
        // & update status flags
        // else
        //     indicate overflow
        if( buffer_overflow )
        {
                word_saved = false ;
        }
        else if( !buffer_full )
        {
                *write_ptr++ = data  ; // store data word

                // if end of buffer has been reached
                if( write_ptr == &begin[current_length] )
                {
```

```
                    write_ptr = begin ; // reset to beginning
            }

            // if write pointer has reached read pointer then
            // buffer is full
            if( write_ptr != read_ptr )
            {
                    // buffer is not full
                    buffer_full = static_cast<Boolean_Bit> ( false );
            }
            else
            {
                    // buffer is full
                    buffer_full = static_cast<Boolean_Bit> ( true ) ;
            }
            // buffer is not empty
            buffer_empty = static_cast<Boolean_Bit> ( false ) ;
    }
    else
    {
            // indicate overflow
            buffer_overflow = static_cast<Boolean_Bit> ( true ) ;
            word_saved      = false ;
    }

    return( word_saved ) ;
}

inline Word Buffer:: get_word( void )
{
    Word data = 0 ;

    // if buffer is not empty then
    //    retrieve a data word from buffer
    // else
    //    indicate overflow
    if( !buffer_empty )
    {
            data = *read_ptr++ ; // retrieve data word

            // if end of buffer has been reached
            if( read_ptr == &begin[current_length] )
            {
                    read_ptr = begin ; // reset to beginning
            }

            // if read pointer has reached write pointer then
            // buffer is empty
            if( write_ptr != read_ptr )
            {
                    // buffer is not empty
                    buffer_empty = static_cast<Boolean_Bit> (false);
            }
            else
            {
                    // buffer is empty
```

```
                        buffer_empty = static_cast<Boolean_Bit> (true);
                }
                // buffer is not full
                buffer_full = static_cast<Boolean_Bit> ( false ) ;
        }

        return( data ) ;
}

inline Boolean Buffer:: empty( void ) const
{
        return( static_cast<Boolean> ( buffer_empty ) ) ;
}

// other inline function definitions left out

#endif           // BUFFER_H Header file
```

The *Buffer* class treats its cache buffer (***begin***) as a *circular* buffer (Figure 8.8). The class maintains read and write pointers to identify the start and end of an unprocessed block of data. The ***read_ptr*** pointer always points to the next buffer location from which to retrieve a data word, and the ***write_ptr*** pointer identifies the next location to write a data word to. Whenever one of these pointers reaches the end of the buffer, it is reset to the beginning, thus creating the *circular* property (refer to the preceding **put_word()** implementation). When ***write_ptr*** reaches ***read_ptr***, the buffer is full. Any further write attempt is considered an overflow situation and the **put_word()** function balks at writing the word to the buffer, causing the supplied data word to be lost. Similarly, when ***read_ptr*** reaches ***write_ptr***, the buffer is empty. Any further read attempts would cause the buffer to underflow since there are no more valid data words in the buffer. In this case, the **get_word()** function returns a zero. The *access* functions such as **empty()** and **full()** allow the client to detect and guard against these conditions.

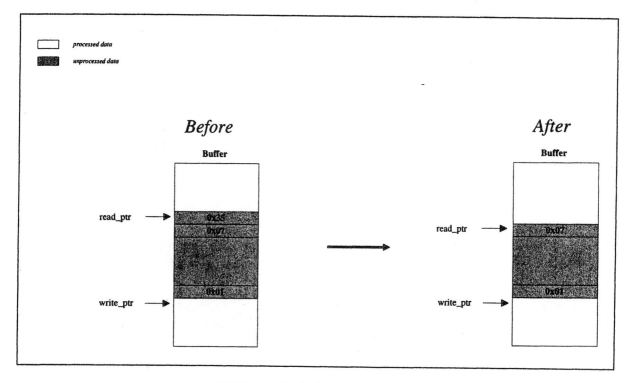

FIGURE 8.8 Circular buffer block diagram.

Since the interrupt handlers call the *access* and *buffer I/O* functions, these functions have been inlined.
3. **Timeout**: This condition occurs when one of the *Serial Stream* read or write functions is waiting for data. If the request is not satisfied within a specified time limit, the functions will abort (Figures 8.6 and 8.7). The timeout prevents the client from waiting indefinitely for an I/O event. The *Timer* object provides this capability (Figures 8.3, 8.6, and 8.7).

Since the interrupt handler operates on the *Buffer* and *Serial Port* objects, these classes must use passive error handling and their member functions cannot throw exceptions from within an interrupt handler. For other types of classes, *passive* error handling is used when their performance must be finely tuned and the overhead of C++ exception handling is not desired.

The regular *Serial Stream* read and write operations are not as time critical as the above classes. In addition, the *Serial Stream* is unable to handle fatal errors at its level and the recovery points are separated by layers of function calls. Therefore, the design of *Serial Stream* is based on *active* error handling. When the member functions of this class detect a fatal error associated with a serial communication operation, they report the error condition to the client by throwing exceptions.

8.3 ERROR CAPTURING

The *Serial Stream* class uses the *Serial Exception* class to capture and record information about an error condition (Figure 8.3). This class maintains a raw error code (*id*) and an *error message*. The *error_message* data element identifies the name of the function, the condition that caused the exception, and any additional information useful to the clients. The class associates the raw error code (*id*) with a high-level *description* of the error condition via the *descriptions* table.

```
//              SERIAL_EXCEPTION.H Header File
#ifndef SERIAL_EXCEPTION_H
#define SERIAL_EXCEPTION_H

    #define NUM_COM_ERRORS      8

    typedef    char       Text ;

    enum Com_Error
    {
         OVERFLOW_ERROR ,
         BUFFER_SETUP_ERROR,
         STREAM_SETUP_ERROR ,
         TIMEOUT_ERROR ,
         PORT_PARITY_ERROR ,
         PORT_OVERRUN_ERROR ,
         PORT_FRAMING_ERROR
    } ;

    class Serial_Exception
    {
         private:
              Text *error_message ;
                   // to identify function & additional info
              static const Text *descriptions[NUM_COM_ERRORS];
                   // description of errors
              Com_Error id ; // error id code
         public:
              // constructors
              Serial_Exception( Com_Error error_code,
```

```
                        const Text *message )  ;
            Serial_Exception( const Serial_Exception &source ) ;
            Serial_Exception &operator =(
                        const Serial_Exception & ) ;
                    // for copy and assignment: create deep copy
            // destructor
            ~Serial_Exception( ) ;

            // access functions
            inline const Text *message( void ) const ;
            inline const Text *description( void ) const ;
            inline Com_Error error_code( void ) const ;

            // processing functions
            Boolean report( ostream &output ) const ;
    } ;


    ostream & operator <<( ostream &os,
            const Serial_Exception &status) ;
            // same as Serial_Exception:: report()

    inline const Text * Serial_Exception:: description( void ) const
    {
            // use error code and do a table look-up
            return( descriptions[ static_cast<int> (id) + 1 ] ) ;
    }


    // other inline function definitions left out

#endif          // SERIAL_EXCEPTION_H Header File
```

Through *Serial Exception*, the *Serial Stream* class records detailed information about an exception. The ***error_message*** data member contains information that helps a software developer to locate and correct transient problems and recover from an exception. Except for the access, constructors, and assignment operator (=) functions, the following example implements the class member functions:

```
//              SERIAL_EXCEPTION.CPP Source File
#include <iostream.h>           // Stream I/O Class library
#include <string.h>             // String library
#include "serial_exception.h"   // Communication Status Class

// initialize error code description list
const Text * Serial_Exception:: descriptions[NUM_COM_ERRORS] =
{
      "No Communication Error" ,
      "Communication Buffer Overflow Error" ,
      "Communication Buffer Allocation Error" ,
      "Serial Stream Setup Error" ,
      "Communication Timeout Error" ,
      "Serial Port Parity Error" ,
      "Serial Port Interrupt Overrun Error" ,
      "Serial Port Frame Error" ,
} ;


Serial_Exception:: Serial_Exception( Com_Error error_code,
                    const Text *message )
```

```
                     : id ( error_code ) , error_message( static_cast<Text *> ( 0 ) )
        {
              // if a message is provided => copy message
              if( message )
              {
                     error_message = new Text[ strlen(message) + 1 ] ;
                     if( error_message ) // if allocation successful
                     {
                            // copy error message
                            strcpy( error_message, message ) ;
                     }
              }
        }


Serial_Exception:: ~Serial_Exception( )
{
        delete [] error_message ; // deallocate error message
}


Boolean Serial_Exception:: report( ostream &os ) const
{
              Boolean output_status = true ;

              os << *this ;// send "this" object to the output stream
                          // use the overloaded operator <<() function
              if( os.fail() ) // if a failure has occurred => report
              {
                            output_status = false ;
              }

              return( output_status ) ;
}

ostream & operator <<( ostream &os, const Serial_Exception &status )
{
        // if no output stream failure => output status
        if( !os.fail() )
        {
                     os << "Message: " ;

                     // if any message exists => output
                     if( status.message() )
                     {
                            os <<  status.message()  << "\n\t" ;
                     }
                     else
                     {
                            os << "None" << "\n\t" ;
                     }

                     // output error description
                     os <<  "Description: " << status.description() << "\n\t" <<
                            "Code: " << (int) status.error_code() << endl ;
        }

        return( os ) ;// return os reference for cascading
}
```

8.4 CLASS INTERFACES

For *passive* error reporting, the clients must query objects for status. However, in the case of *active* error reporting, the error-detecting functions throw unsolicited exceptions as they occur. For classes that use *active* error reporting, the client must know which functions throw exceptions. Normally a client does not have access to the implementation of a class member function since it resides in a source file. C++ has addressed this issue by incorporating the **throw** keyword in the function declaration:

```
return_type function_name( arguments, if any )
            throw ( type₁ , ..., typeₙ ) ;
```

By examining the class definition, the client can identify the functions that throw exceptions. In addition, the *exception specification* list identifies the type of exception thrown by these functions. The *Serial I/O Communication* library's design utilizes the *Serial Exception* class for reporting exceptions to the clients of this library. The *Serial Stream* class uses this class for active error reporting and throws instances of this class (Figure 8.3):

```
//              SERIAL_STREAM.H Header File
#ifndef SERIAL_STREAM_H
#define SERIAL_STREAM_H

        #include "buffer.h"               // Buffer Class
        #include "serial_exception.h"     // RS-232 Status Class
        #include "serial_port.h"          // RS-232 Serial Port Class
        #include "time.h"                 // Timer Class Library

        #define NUM_SERIAL_PORTS          2
                // # of interrupt requests for serial interface

class Serial_Stream
{
    private:
            // Serial Port
            Serial_Port *port ;
            ID id ;

            // Cache buffers
            Buffer input_buffer , output_buffer ;

            // Transmission/Receive timeout thresholds
            Time trx_timeout , rec_timeout ; // threshold time

            // Serial Stream Registry Table for Serial Interrupts
            static Serial_Stream
                        *registry_table[NUM_SERIAL_PORTS] ;

            // Utility functions: generic RS-232 interrupt handler
            inline static void serial_irq_handler(
                    Serial_Stream *stream ) ;
            // Utility: translates Port_Status to Communication Error
            Com_Error port_error( void ) const ;

            // ** Note: removed from design interface
            Serial_Stream( const Serial_Stream &source ) ;
            Serial_Stream &operator =( const Serial_Stream & ) ;
```

```
                        // two objects cannot point to the same stream
        public:
                // Constructors
                Serial_Stream( ID port_id,
                        Baud_Rate rate = B_9600,
                        Parity parity = NO_PARITY,
                        Stop_Bits stop_bits = ONE_STOP_BIT,
                        Length cache = DEFAULT_BUFFER_LENGTH,
                        Time timeout = MIN_TIMEOUT )
                          throw( Serial_Exception ) ;
                        // for hardware setup and allocation errors

                // Destructor
                ~Serial_Stream( ) ;

                // Stream I/O functions
                void put_string( const Text *str)
                        throw( Serial_Exception ) ;
                Length put_line( const Word *line, Length length )
                        throw( Serial_Exception ) ;
                void get_string( Text *str, Length length )
                        throw( Serial_Exception ) ;
                Length get_line( Word *line, Length length )
                        throw( Serial_Exception ) ;
                        // for timeout and buffer overflow errors

                // Access functions
                inline Boolean inbasket_full( void ) const ;
                inline Boolean outbasket_full( void ) const ;
                inline Boolean inbasket_empty( void ) const ;
                inline Boolean outbasket_empty( void ) const ;
                        // check input/output buffers

                inline Time RXD_timeout( void ) const ;
                inline Time TXD_timeout( void ) const ;
                Boolean change_RXD_timer( Time new_time ) ;
                Boolean change_TXD_timer( Time new_time ) ;
                        // receive (RXD) & transmit (TXD)
                        // timeout thresholds

                // Interrupt control functions
                Boolean enable_interrupt( void ) ;
                Boolean disable_interrupt( void ) ;

                friend void serial_irq1_handler( void ) ;
                friend void serial_irq2_handler( void ) ;
        } ;

        // inline function definitions left out

#endif          // SERIAL_STREAM_H Header File
```

In the preceding class definition, the *stream I/O* and *constructor* functions throw an exception of the *Serial Exception* type. The **throw** keyword in the interface serves two purposes:

1. **Client**: The interface tells the client the types of exceptions thrown and identifies the functions performing the throw operation. The client uses this information to incorporate **try-catch** clauses in the appropriate areas of its program.
2. **Interface Consistency Check**: The C++ compiler uses the declaration to verify that the function definition actually throws the defined exception types. The compiler performs basic data consistency checks on the exception types. If there is a data type mismatch between the function declaration (prototype) and definition (implementation), the compiler generates an error message at compile time. In addition, if the function calls other functions that throw exceptions other than the ones specified in the *exception specification list*, the anomaly is detected at run time and the **unexpected()** function is then called. This function is described at the end of this chapter.

In C++, any function can throw an exception, and the use of the **throw** keyword in the function interface is optional. Functions that do not specify an exception specification list are logically equivalent to the following declaration:

```
return_type function_name( argument_list ) throw( ... ) ;
                    // function can throw any type of exceptions
```

For instance, the *stream I/O* functions in the Serial Stream class can throw exceptions without specifying them in their interfaces. However, good programming practice dictates that the class design interface should identify the exceptions. Otherwise, the client cannot distinguish the exception-throwing functions and thus may not handle the exceptions properly.

C++ also allows the designer to create restrictive function declarations by explicitly specifying that a function cannot throw an exception:

```
return_type function_name( argument_list ) throw( ) ;
                    // function cannot throw an exception
```

Since there is no data type associated with the **throw** keyword, the syntax signifies that the function cannot throw an exception.

8.5 ERROR DETECTION AND REPORTING

Upon detecting an error, a function throws an exception by using the following syntax:

```
throw( error_object ) ; // throw object to the recovery point
```

This statement causes an exception to be "thrown." The exception is "caught" by the first higher level function that has a **try-catch** clause for the specified exception data type. The exception data type can be an instance of a class or a built-in data type. The use of an object (instance of a class) is more common because detailed information on the exception can be passed to the recovery point. Since the client has more information on the cause of exception, the error handler can be designed to make better error recovery decisions. In addition, the enhanced information can be used for data logging and post failure data analysis.

In the following example, one of the *Stream I/O* functions in the *Serial Stream* class has been implemented using C++ exception handling. The **put_string()** function writes the content of the supplied string to the internal *output_buffer*. While the buffer is not full the function continues writing to the buffer. If the buffer is full and the string data transaction has not completed within the specified time limit (*trx_timeout*), the function times out and aborts the write operation. The *Timer* class is internal to the design of *Serial Stream* member functions, as depicted by the *implementation* export control in Figure 8.3:

```
//          SERIAL_STREAM.CPP Source File
#include "serial_stream.h"// RS-232 Serial Communication Class Library
```

```
    void Serial_Stream:: put_string( const Text *str)
                                throw( Serial_Exception )
{
        const Text *current = str ; // point to the beginning of the string
        Timer trx_timer( trx_timeout ) ; // setup timer

        // check for overflow first
        if( output_buffer.overflow() )
        {
                // throw an exception on overflow
                throw( Serial_Exception( OVERFLOW_ERROR ,
                                    "Serial_Stream:: put_string") );
                        // create & throw a nameless Serial Exception object
        }
        else if( port->error() )
        {
                // throw an exception on Serial Port errors
                throw( Serial_Exception( port_error(),
                            "Serial_Stream:: put_string") );
                        // create & throw a nameless Serial Exception object
        }

        // while end of string not reached => write to output buffer
        while( *current )
        {
                // if output buffer is not full then
                // write a byte to the output buffer otherwise wait
                if( !output_buffer.full() )
                {
                        // write word and update string pointer
                        output_buffer.put_word( *current++ ) ;
                }
                else if( trx_timer.timeout() )
                {
                        // if time out occurs => throw exception
                        throw( Serial_Exception( TIMEOUT_ERROR ,
                                    "Serial_Stream:: put_string") );
                }
        }

        return ;
}
```

In the above example, the **put_string()** function throws a *Serial Exception* object when it detects an exception condition (Figure 8.9). At this time, the local objects created on the stack between the throwing point and their corresponding catching points are automatically destroyed. For example, the local *trx_timer* timer is automatically destroyed when the exception is thrown. The client catching the exception may be several layers above the throwing point such as in the scenario depicted in Figure 8.10. The **get_file()** function contains the recovery code for this type of error and the *Serial Exception* object is propagated to this function (Figure 8.9).

C++ exception handling is not restricted to normal member functions and can also be performed by nonmember and constructor functions. In the following example, the *Serial Stream* constructor throws exceptions of type *Serial Exception*. This constructor must interact with various classes in order to create a serial stream. Due to unavailability of resources, some of the objects and resources may fail to be allocated. For instance, all serial ports may be in use or there may be no available memory in *free store* for the internal buffers. In the event of failure, the *Serial Stream* constructor is unable to create a functional *Serial Stream* object and would need to

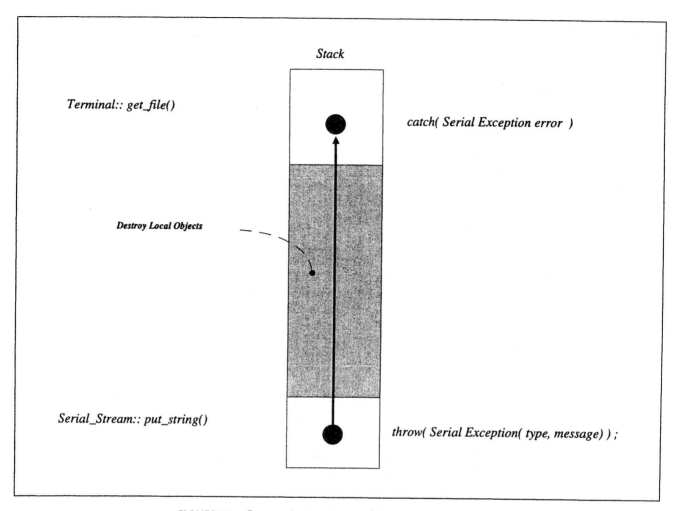

FIGURE 8.9   Communication timeout failure exception handling.

throw an exception. When an error is detected, the constructor must explicitly destroy dynamically allocated objects such as *port* since there is no automatic provisions for destroying dynamically allocated objects in C++.

```
//              SERIAL_STREAM.CPP Source File
#include "serial_stream.h" // RS-232 Serial Communication Class Library
#include "interrupt.h"      // Interrupt Vector Table Installation Library

// Serial Stream Registry Table for Serial Interrupts
Serial_Stream * Serial_Stream:: registry_table[NUM_SERIAL_PORTS] ;

Serial_Stream:: Serial_Stream( ID port_id , Baud_Rate rate , Parity parity,
        Stop_Bits stop_bits , Length cache_size, Time timeout )
                        throw( Serial_Exception )
    : port( static_cast<Serial_Port *> ( 0 ) ) , id( port_id ),
      input_buffer( cache_size ) , output_buffer( cache_size ) ,
      trx_timeout( timeout ) , rec_timeout( timeout )
{
    // if either input or output buffer has not been allocated => abort
    if( input_buffer.fail() )
    {
        throw( Serial_Exception( STREAM_SETUP_ERROR,
            "Serial_Stream::Serial_Stream() =>"
```

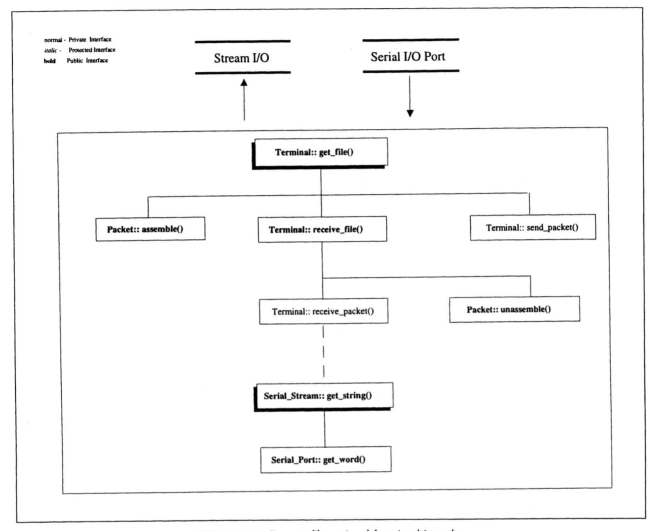

normal - Private Interface
italic - Protected Interface
bold - Public Interface

Stream I/O   Serial I/O Port

Terminal:: get_file()

Packet:: **assemble()**   Terminal:: **receive_file()**   Terminal:: **send_packet()**

Terminal:: receive_packet()   Packet:: **unassemble()**

Serial_Stream:: get_string()

Serial_Port:: get_word()

FIGURE 8.10 Remote file retrieval function hierarchy.

```
                    " Input buffer allocation error") ) ;
    }
    else if( output_buffer.fail() )
    {
        throw( Serial_Exception( STREAM_SETUP_ERROR ,
            "Serial_Stream::Serial_Stream () =>"
            "Output buffer allocation error") ) ;
    }
    else if( id >= NUM_SERIAL_PORTS )
    {
        throw( Serial_Exception( STREAM_SETUP_ERROR ,
            "Serial_Stream::Serial_Stream () =>"
            "Invalid Serial Port ID") ) ;
    }

    // create & setup serial port
    port = new Serial_Port( rate, EIGHT_BIT, parity, stop_bits ) ;
    if( port ) // if serial port created => register stream
    {
        void (*irq_handler) ( void ) ;
```

```
                    // Interrupt Request Handler function pointer

            // if serial port is in use => abort
            if( registry_table[ id ] )
            {
                    delete port ; // destroy port
                    // throw an exception on overflow
                    throw( Serial_Exception( STREAM_SETUP_ERROR ,
                        "Serial_Stream:: Serial_Stream => port in use") ) ;
            }

            // based on port id => identify Serial IRQ handler
            if( id == COM_PORT1 )
            {
                    irq_handler = serial_irq1_handler ;
            }
            else
            {
                    irq_handler = serial_irq2_handler ;
            }

            // Install the applicable IRQ handler in
            // the Interrupt Vector Table
            if( !install_interrupt( SERIAL_IRQ , irq_handler ) )
            {
                    delete port ;// destroy port

                    // throw an exception on overflow
                    throw( Serial_Exception( STREAM_SETUP_ERROR ,
                        "Serial_Stream:: Serial_Stream =>"
                        "unable to install IRQ handler") ) ;
            }

            // register "this" object in the interrupt request table
            registry_table[ id ] = this ;
            enable_interrupt() ; // enable interrupt
    }
    else
    {
            // throw an exception on Serial Port hardware setup error
            throw( Serial_Exception( STREAM_SETUP_ERROR ,
                "Serial_Stream:: Serial_Stream =>"
                "Serial Port not available"));
    }
}
```

In the above example, the constructor queries the input and output buffers and verifies that they are operational. The *Serial Stream* constructor then dynamically allocates a *Serial Port* object and reserves a serial port. Upon successful allocation, the constructor installs the applicable Serial Interrupt Request (IRQ) function in the Interrupt Vector Table and registers the *Serial Stream* object in the interrupt registry table (*registry_table*).

In real-time applications, the interrupt handler functions are normally implemented in assembly code. For presentation purposes this chapter uses C++ to implement them, but their algorithms can be translated to assembly. When a hardware interrupt is generated, an Interrupt Vector Table look-up is done and the function pointed to by the Interrupt Vector Table entry is invoked (Figure 8.11). For Serial I/O, the two interrupt handlers **serial_irq1_handler()** and **serial_irq2_handler()** are nonmember functions. These functions use the interrupt

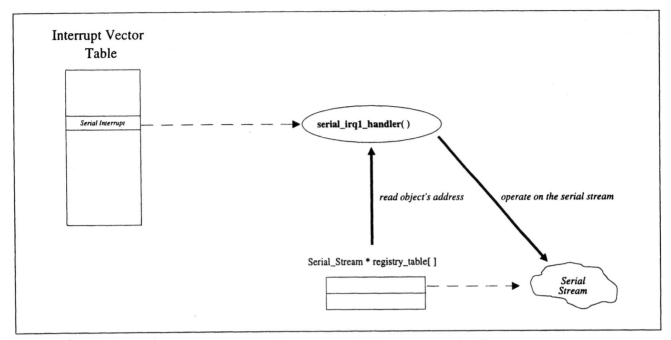

FIGURE 8.11   Serial stream access by interrupt request handler.

registry table (***registry_table***) to identify the address of the *Serial Stream* object in memory. By using the object's address, the interrupt handler can call the object back and perform the I/O operation. Since the algorithm for both functions is the same, they both use the generic **serial_irq_handler()**. This function is inlined to demonstrate there is no function call when the interrupt is being serviced. The generic function identifies the type of interrupt (transmit or receive) and transfers a data word from/to the *Buffer* object to/from the *Serial Port* object:

```
//                 SERIAL_STREAM.CPP Source File
#include "serial_stream.h"    // RS-232 Serial Communication Class Library
#include "interrupt.h"        // Interrupt Vector Table Installation Library

// Serial Stream Registry Table for Serial Interrupts
Serial_Stream * Serial_Stream:: registry_table[NUM_SERIAL_PORTS] ;

void serial_irq1_handler( void )
{
      // use generic serial IRQ handler
      Serial_Stream:: serial_irq_handler(Serial_Stream:: registry_table[0]);
}

void serial_irq2_handler( void )
{
      Serial_Stream:: serial_irq_handler(Serial_Stream:: registry_table[1]);
}

inline void Serial_Stream:: serial_irq_handler( Serial_Stream *stream )
{
      Word word ;
      // identify type of serial interrupt: transmit or receive
      if( stream->port->mode() == TRANSMIT )
      {
            // for transmit: transfer from output buffer to serial port
            word = stream->output_buffer.get_word() ;
```

```
                  stream->port->send_word( word ) ;
     }
     else
     {

              // for receive: transfer from serial port to input buffer
              // note: the following functions have been inlined
              // in order to avoid actual function calls
              word = stream->port->receive_word( ) ;
              stream->input_buffer.put_word( word ) ;
     }

     return ;
}
```

   Another reason that the *Buffer* and *Serial Port* classes use passive error detection and recovery is that the interrupt handler operates on them, and exceptions cannot be thrown within an interrupt handler. Due to improper balancing of data flow, the interrupt handler may cause a receive buffer to overflow or may cause a transmit buffer to underflow.

8.6 ERROR RECOVERY

   When the error detection and recovery points are separated by layers of functions, C++ exception handling becomes extremely useful (Figures 8.9 and 8.10). In traditional implementation, error codes are manually propagated from function to function or global error flags are set and the functions return the codes to higher levels in order to recover. C++ exception handling automates the propagation of an exception to a higher level. In addition, software reliability is improved because detected exceptions are automatically propagated. In the manual process there is the possibility that an error code may never traverse its way back to the appropriate recovery point, due to a programming error such as not checking a return value or checking a flag.
   In the *communication* module design (Figure 8.2), the error recovery functions in the *Terminal* class are separated by several layers of functions from the *Stream I/O* functions. The use of C++ exception handling in the design of the *Serial I/O Communication* class helps this library to report detected errors to the applicable *Terminal* functions (Figure 8.9).
   In C++, exceptions thrown by functions within the try block are caught and processed using the corresponding catch blocks. The type of exception in the catch statements identifies the applicable recovery code for a specified exception:

```
try
{
```

```
        // C++ code block ;
}
catch( Data_Type1 &exception_object )
{
        // error recovery code block ;
}
catch( Data_Type2 &exception_object )
{
        // error recovery code block ;
}
catch( ... )// catch any type of error
{
        // error recovery code block for any type of error ;
}
```

The **try** keyword associates a code block with one or a series of **catch** statements. When an exception is thrown from any point within the **try** block, the program execution resumes at the first **catch** statement. Based on the type of error object, the applicable **catch** block is executed. In the following example, the test driver program can catch *Serial Exception* exceptions thrown by the constructor and the stream I/O functions of the *Serial I/O Communication* class library. If any of the *Serial Stream* member functions throw an exception, the program's execution immediately resumes at the **catch** statement. If the type of raised exception does not match the ones specified in the **catch** statements, the exception propagates upward in the function call hierarchy. In the following example, exceptions other than *Serial Exception* do not propagate upward because the test driver uses a catch-all clause: **catch(...)**. Without this catch clause, exceptions other than *Serial Exception* type would have continued upward:

```
//                      Test Driver Source File
#include "serial_stream.h"

Boolean test_serial_stream( void )
{
    Boolean exception_detected = true ;

    try
    {
        char message[100] ;
        Serial_Stream stream( COM_PORT1 ) ;
            // use first Com Port

        // perform stream I/O operation
        stream.put_string( "hello world" ) ;
        stream.get_string( message, 100 ) ;
        exception_detected = false ;
    }
    catch( Serial_Exception error )
    {
        cout << error ; // report to display console
    }
    catch( ... )
    {
        cout << "Caught an error other than Communication!!" <<
                "\n\t Unexpected Error" << endl ;
    }
```

```
        return( exception_detected ) ;

}
```

In the above example, a *Serial Exception* is caught using an **error** object. It is actually better to catch an exception using a reference rather than an object. In the case of an object, the **Serial Exception( )** copy constructor is called when the thrown *Serial Exception* is caught. This introduces additional overhead because the copy constructor must be called to create a local exception object, and later the destructor must be called to destroy the object. In addition, if an exception object that is derived from the *Serial Exception* object is caught using a *Serial Exception* object, the exception handling may fail due to implicit conversions. Chapter 10 (Section 10.7) discusses this issue when it applies a design hierarchy to exception classes. ANSI C++ leaves memory allocation for an exception (temporary object) as an implementation issue for C++ compilers [ANSI 1995]. Since the implementation can vary between C++ compilers, it is best to catch an exception by using a reference. This approach avoids the construction and destruction overhead, and it also avoids implicit conversion problems associated with catching an exception using an object:

```
try
{
        // other details left out
}
catch( Serial_Exception &error )
{
        cout << error ; // report to display console
}
```

C++ allows nesting of try and catch code blocks:

```
try
{
        // C++ code block ;
}
catch( Data_Type1 &exception_object )
{
        try
        {
                // nested code block
        }
        catch( Data_Type2 &exception_object )
        {
                // error recovery code block ;
        }
}
```

8.7 PARTIAL ERROR RECOVERY

At times, a function in the path of a thrown exception may need to perform certain cleanup operations or partial error recovery. For example, functions in the path of the *Serial Exception* that have dynamically allocated objects may need to catch the exception and destroy these objects. Otherwise their addresses will become lost, resulting in memory leakage. Also, for applications that are still using the C *Standard I/O (stdio.h)* library the local streams opened in the path of an exception must be closed manually. For these types of situations, the function catches the exception, performs the necessary operations, and resumes the propagation of the exception to a higher level by rethrowing it. The following illustrates the generic syntax for a rethrowing operation:

```
try
{
```

```
          // C++ code block ;
}
catch( Data_Type1 &exception_object )
{
          // perform any local cleanup task as necessary
          if( cannot handle error at this level )
          {
                    throw ; // rethrow
          }
          // error recovery code block ;
}
```

The use of the **throw** keyword without an object causes the caught exception to be "rethrown" to a higher level. In the following example, the **receive_data_packet()** function handles the *timeout* exception only when it intercepts *Serial Exception*. When the **receive_data_packet()** function catches a serial stream *timeout*, it retries the operation several times, based on the value defined by the **NUM_RETRIES** constant. The function destroys the dynamically allocated objects and rethrows the exception for any other serial exceptions or when the number of retries is exhausted:

```
void Terminal:: receive_data_packet( char *string )
{
      Packet *data = new Packet( DATA_PACKET , string ) ;
      Packet *data_request = new Packet( DATA_REQ_PACKET ) ;

      // while # of retries has not been exhausted
      for( int i = 1 ; i <= NUM_RETRIES ; i++ )
      {
            // create data and data request packets
            try
            {
                  // transmit data request packet
                  stream.put_string( data_request.out() ) ;

                  // wait for incoming data packet
                  while( !packet_available() )
                  {
                          ;// do nothing, just wait
                  ]

                  // get packet
                  stream.get_string( data.in(), data.length() ) ;
                  delete data ; // destroy data packet
                  delete data_request ; // destroy data request packet
                  break ; // abort retry loop
            }
            catch( Serial_Exception &status )// catch Serial Exception
            {
                  // if the detected exception is other than Timeout or
                  // # of Timeout retries has been exhausted =>
                  //      destroy data packets and rethrow exception
                  if( (status.error_code() != TIMEOUT_ERROR) ||
                      (i >= NUM_RETRIES) )
                  {
                        // destroy data & request packets
                        delete data ;
```

```
                              delete data_request ;
                              throw ; // rethrow exception
                        }
                  }
            }

            return ;
      }
```

8.8 UNEXPECTED EXCEPTIONS

In C++, when exceptions are thrown and not caught, the program execution eventually works its way back to the **main()** function. At this time, the **terminate()** function is called. This is a standard library function that calls the **abort()** function to indicate an abnormal termination. The **abort()** function returns control back to the operating system or the calling process without calling the destructors of global and static objects.

If an exception is thrown by a function whose declaration does not match the exception type in the *exception specification* list, the **unexpected()** function is invoked at run time. This function then calls the **terminate()** function, which terminates the program as described above.

For applications that need to perform custom termination or unexpected recovery, the **set_terminate()** and **set_unexpected()** functions can be used to install custom functions for handling these conditions via the **except.h** header file:

```
//              EXCEPT.H Header File
typedef         void (*Error_Handler) () ;// function pointer

Error_Handler set_terminate( Error_Handler new_handler ) ;
Error_Handler set_unexpected( Error_Handler new_handler ) ;
```

For example, a patient drug delivery system may install a custom **terminate()** function that would shut down drug delivery hardware such as the system's pump and valves when it is called. This function then restarts the system at a predictable state. This approach prevents the system hardware from going into a runaway state and causing harm to a patient.

8.9 STANDARD EXCEPTION LIBRARY

Figure 8.12 depicts the C++ ANSI standard *exception* class library. The *exception* class library is based on a design hierarchy. The base *exception* class defines a standard interface for the classes derived from it. The **what()** function returns a textual description of the error condition. The *logic_error* and *runtime_error* classes are used for logical and run time exceptions, respectively.

8.9.1 Bad Exceptions

The *bad_exception* class identifies a violation of an *exception specification* specified in the function interface. The **set_unexpected()** function can be used to install a custom unexpected handler. When an *exception specification* is violated and the unexpected exception handler is invoked, this function may call **terminate()**; it may throw an exception that would satisfy the *exception specification*; or it may throw a *bad_exception*. The default **unexpected()** function calls the **terminate()** function when the *exception specification* list does not include a *bad_exception* (refer to Section 8.8).

8.9.2 Logical Exceptions

The *logic_error* class exceptions are thrown prior to the execution of a program in order to describe a logical error caused by a precondition violation:

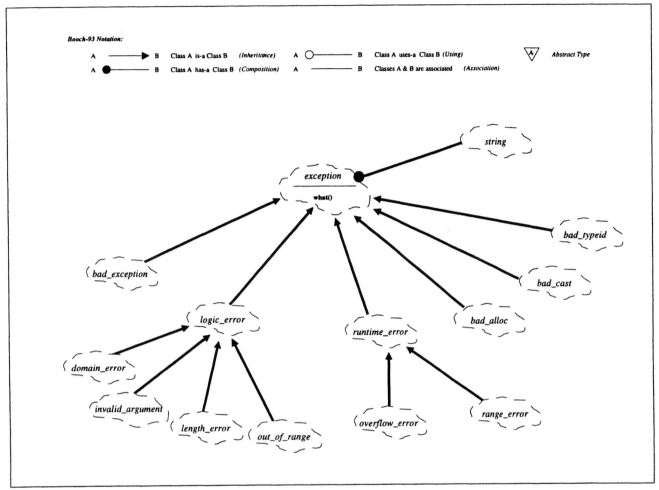

Booch-93 Notation:

A ⟶▶ B   Class A is-a Class B   *(Inheritance)*   A ◯⟶ B   Class A uses-a Class B *(Using)*   ▽A   *Abstract Type*

A ●⟶ B   Class A has-a Class B   *(Composition)*   A ⟶ B   Classes A & B are associated   *(Association)*

FIGURE 8.12   Standard exception class diagram.

1. **domain_error:** Indicates a domain violation
2. **invalid_argument:** Indicates that an invalid argument is being passed to a function
3. **length_error:** Indicates that an attempt has been made to create an object whose size is greater than the largest value specified by the *size_t* (unsigned) type
4. **out_of_range:** Indicates that the value of an argument is not in its expected range of values

8.9.3 Run Time Exceptions

The *runtime_error* class hierarchy identifies exceptions that occur when a program is being executed:

1. **range_error:** Reports a data range violation error
2. **overflow_error:** Specifies an arithmetic overflow

8.9.4 Dynamic Allocation Exceptions

The *bad_alloc* class is used by the overloaded operator **new()** function and the user-defined error handlers for reporting dynamic memory allocation failures. This class is derived from the *exception* class (Figure 8.12).

After a dynamic allocation failure, if a user-defined error handler has been defined and installed through the **set_new_handler()** function (*refer back to Section 7.4*), the **new** operator calls this function. If the user-defined error handler fails to obtain additional memory, it may exit the program or report the failure by throwing an exception of type *bad_alloc* or an exception class derived from it. In the following example, when the operator **new** fails to allocate a *Customer* object for the **UI:: create_customer**() function, it calls the **customer_alloc_recovery**() function. The recovery function deallocates the ***backup_list*** records in order to allow the allocation to succeed. In case a list does not exist, an exception of type *bad_alloc* is thrown:

```
//          UI.CPP Source File
#include <new.h>          // new support library
#include <except.h>       // C++ Exception Class library
#include <cstring.h>      // String Class library
#include "customer.h"     // Customer class library
#include "ui.h"           // User Interface class library

static Customer *backup_list ; // backup customer list (array)

void customer_alloc_recovery( ) throw( bad_alloc ) ;
              // user-defined dynamic allocation error recovery function

Customer * UI:: create_customer( void )
{
        Customer *current_customer ;
        void (*previous_handler) ( ) ;

        previous_handler = set_new_handler( customer_alloc_recovery ) ;
                // install the recovery function and save the
                // address of the previous handler.

        // obtain customer information
        Text new_name[120] ;
        cout << "Input new customer's name: \n" ;
        cin >> new_name ;

        try
        {
                current_customer = new Customer( new_name )  ;
                        // dynamically allocate a Customer object. On dynamic
                        // allocation failures, the customer_alloc_recovery()
                        // function is called.
        }
        catch( bad_alloc )
        {
                // if recovery function fails then return a null value
                current_customer = static_cast<Customer *> ( 0 ) ;
        }

        set_new_handler( previous_handler ) ;
                // restore previous error handler

        return( current_customer ) ;
}

void customer_alloc_recovery( )
                throw( bad_alloc )
{
        // if a backup list exists then destroy it and reset the pointer
        if( backup_list )
        {
```

```
          delete [ ] backup_list ;
          backup_list = static_cast<Customer *> ( 0 ) ;
  }
  else
  {
          throw( bad_alloc( string(" Recovery Failure" ) , 0 ) ) ) ;
          // throw a bad_alloc exception
  }

      return ;
}
```

8.9.5 Data Type Exceptions

The *exception* class hierarchy supports two types of exceptions for run-time data type conversions and comparisons:

1. **bad_typeid**: This exception is caused when a null pointer is passed to **typeid()**. This function is a C++ reserved keyword and returns type information for an object or class type.
2. **bad_cast**: When a dynamic cast operation fails on an object reference, this exception is thrown.

The above exceptions are described in detail in Chapter 10.

SUMMARY

An object model must address exceptions in order to prevent the objects in the model from transitioning into illegal states. The design may be based on *passive* or *active* error handling, or on a combination of the two.

In the *passive* approach, the member functions detecting an exception record the condition using a status flag in the object. The client queries the object for status in order to determine whether or not the object is in a degraded state. This approach is used for applications in which error conditions occur in the normal course of events or when the error recovery can be handled locally. The drawback of this scheme is that an exception may go undetected if the client fails to query the status of the object. This may affect the system's reliability.

In the *active* approach, the function detecting an error raises an exception and throws it automatically to a higher level function. The client functions are responsible for catching the exception and performing the applicable recovery operation. This scheme effectively automates the propagation of an exception. On the other hand, there is a degradation in program performance due to the overhead caused by automating this process. C++ exception handling should be used for errors that cannot be handled locally within a software component and should be handled by a higher level function of the function hierarchy. C++ exception handling is extremely useful where point of error detection and recovery are separated by layers of intermediate functions and where the error condition is truly an unexpected condition (exception).

C++ supports *active* error handling through the **throw, try,** and **catch** keywords. A function detecting an error uses the **throw** keyword to raise the exception. In C++, the thrown exception can be of a built-in data type or an object (*instance of a class*). The use of an object allows the detection point to provide detailed information about the error condition and the event that caused it. When an exception is raised, the exception is automatically propagated to higher level functions and is caught by the first function containing an applicable **try-catch** clause. The **try** keyword associates a block of code (group of C++ statements) with one or more **catch** clauses. Since there may be different types of thrown exceptions, the **catch** block associates the exception type with the applicable recovery procedure.

C++ automates the destruction of local objects between error detection and recovery points. However, the programmer is responsible for the destruction of dynamically allocated objects and arrays. For these objects, functions in the path of a thrown exception need to delay the throw operation by catching the exception, destroying the objects, and rethrowing the exception.

C++ provides some data consistency checking in addition to providing mechanisms to handle unexpected and unprocessed exceptions. When an exception is not caught, the exception propagates to the highest level in the program. At that time, the **terminate()** function is called, and program execution is terminated through a call to the **abort()** function. In addition, when an exception is thrown through a function whose *exception specification* list does not match the exception type, the **unexpected()** function is called. A design may override these standard library functions by installing custom unexpected and termination functions via the **set_unexpected()** and **set_terminate()** functions, respectively.

In addition, the ANSI C++ provides a standardized *exception* class library, which is depicted in Figure 8.12. This library can be used as a baseline for software development. By using C++ inheritance, this library can be customized and custom exceptions can be derived from the existing classes. This approach allows the software design to be based on a standardized exception library.

Exceptions are unexpected conditions. When they occur, the function detecting the condition is usually unable to recover, and the condition needs to be handled by functions at an object higher up in the design hierarchy. C++ exception handling can be used effectively for providing a consistent error recovery strategy.

GLOSSARY

Active error handling

The process of reporting an unsolicited exception to a client

Catch

Catching and handling an exception

Exception

An unexpected condition such as a fatal error, divide-by-zero, and so on

Passive error handling

The process of capturing and recording information in status flags and requiring the client to query for status

Specification list

An optional part of a function declaration that identifies the type of exceptions that may be thrown by the function

Throw

Raising an exception

Try

In C++, a **try** block associates a set of C++ statements with a set of **catch** blocks. The exceptions thrown within the **try** block can be handled by the corresponding catch blocks

CHAPTER 9

Inheritance

INTRODUCTION

During system analysis and design, the *object model* provides a *logical* view of the system. As discussed in Chapter 2, the *object model* undergoes reviews and refinements in order to transform the *logical* view to the *development* view. In these reviews, the *object model* is examined for classes that exhibit common characteristics and relationships. These classes are then organized into hierarchical architectures (that is, tree architectures) by identifying their common features and attributes. These common properties are then captured into a *base* (*superclass*) class. The classes in the hierarchical architecture inherit data and functions of their base class and thus build on an existing design. These *derived* (*subclass*) classes inherit from their *base* class and add features and attributes specific to their needs. The *base* and *derived* classes form a parent-child association, referred to as an *"is-a"* relationship (Figure 9.1).

In Figure 9.2 a general *Account* class, maintaining basic account information such as customer information, is used in the design of bank accounts. Through *inheritance*, the *Savings* and *Checking* classes acquire *Account* attributes and operations. For instance, both classes inherit customer's ***name, picture***, **withdraw()**, and **deposit()** from the *Account* class. These two classes then add features and operations specific to savings and checking accounts. In Figure 9.2, the *Money Market* class inherits from two classes. This class *"is-a" Savings* account with limited *Checking* privileges. By inheriting from the *Savings* and *Checking* classes, the *Money Market* class reuses the tested features of both. Since *Money Market* directly inherits from two base classes, its design is based on *multiple inheritance*.

The *design hierarchy* is one of the four major components of an object model's framework, and Chapter 9 examines the purpose and importance of inheritance. The difference between **protected** and **public** design interfaces is then discussed. The primary focus is on the implementation of inheritance in C++ by describing semantics, syntax, types of single inheritance, and multiple inheritance. The chapter concludes by illustrating the use of inheritance in the design of the *Stream I/O class* library.

9.1 PURPOSE OF INHERITANCE

Through *inheritance*, a new class obtains the data members and member functions of an existing class. The use of the existing design reduces software development and testing costs. In addition, projects evolve and grow

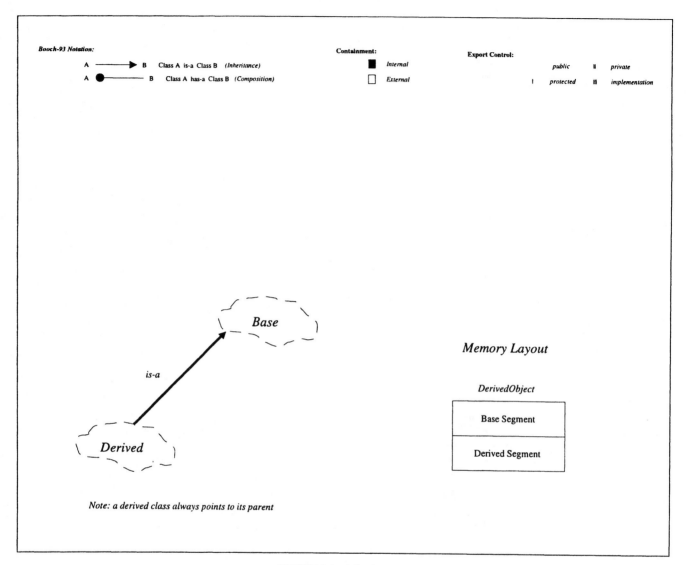

Booch-93 Notation:

A ——————▶ B   Class A is-a Class B   (Inheritance)

A ●—————— B   Class A has-a Class B   (Composition)

Containment:

■ Internal

□ External

Export Control:

public   ‖   private

| protected   ‖‖   implementation

Base

is-a

Derived

Memory Layout

DerivedObject

| Base Segment |
| Derived Segment |

Note: a derived class always points to its parent

FIGURE 9.1   Inheritance.

systematically by building on existing designs. In Figure 9.3, a word processor application operates on different types of files: *Text*, *Binary*, *Image*, *WordPerfect*, and *Microsoft Word*. A hierarchical architecture is used in the design of the *File* class library in order to meet the following objectives:

1. **Commonality:** The *base* class captures the common information (*attributes*) and features (*operations*) of the derived classes. In Figure 9.3, the *File* class maintains the file's basic attributes such as file name, path, length, and read/write permission. In addition, common features such as the **copy()** function are included in the *File* class.

2. **Customization:** An existing class is used to create a customized version of the class. The *WordPerfect* file format and architecture may vary depending on different versions of WordPerfect. The common aspects of this type of file are defined using the generic *WordPerfect* file. The differences between the versions can then be modeled and captured by customized versions of the *WordPerfect* file. For instance, the *WordPerfect 5.x* file inherits from the *WordPerfect* file and adds features and properties that are specific to the 5.x versions.

3. **Common Design Interface:** A *base* class may define the design requirements for its *derived* classes by specifying a set of member functions that are required to be provided by each of its *derived* classes. In Figure 9.3, the *File* class defines the **display()**, **search()** and **compare()** operations. The *File* class does not

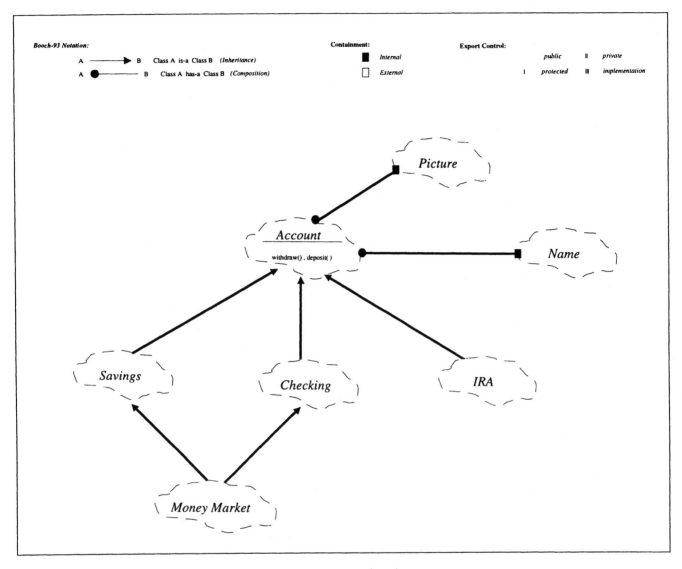

FIGURE 9.2   Account class diagram.

have an implementation for any of these functions, and in fact an implementation of these functions at the *File* class level would be meaningless. For instance, the search mechanism for a piece of information is different in a *text* file than in a *word processor* file. However, the function declarations in the *base* class create a common design interface among the *derived* classes. The *derived* classes use the specified signatures for these functions and provide the appropriate implementations.

The use of a standard interface among the derived classes allows the client to operate on any of the *derived* files in a generic way without becoming dependent on the specific file type in the hierarchy. For example, the client invokes the **search()** function on a file object whether the file is a text, binary, or word processor file. The use of inheritance to create a standard interface is explored in the next chapter, on *polymorphism* (Chapter 10).

9.2 INHERITANCE IS-A RELATIONSHIP

Inheritance adheres to an **"is-a"** relationship, which governs its use in the design of a class. For example, a *Binary File* **is-a** *File* (Figure 9.3). However, the reverse is not true, that is, not every *File* is a *Binary File*. Inheritance is used in the design of a new class when the following statement holds true:

```
"proposed_derived_class is-a base_class"
```

Applicability of the above property determines the use of inheritance. For instance, the bank *Account* in Figure 9.2 maintains a customer picture. An *Picture* class can be used for maintaining the customer's picture. Should the designer use inheritance to derive the *Account* class from the *Picture File* class? To answer this question, consider the following statement:

Account is-a *Picture*

Clearly, the above statement is false. *Account* **is-not-a** *Picture* but *Account* **has-a** *Picture*. *Inheritance* is an inappropriate approach and the design should instead use *composition* by making *Picture* a member of the *Account* class (Figure 9.2).

9.3 INHERITANCE IN C++

This section shows how inheritance is implemented in C++ by describing the following components:

1. **Base Class Design:** The *File* class (*base*) and the supporting *File Exception* class are used in the design of the *derived* classes, such as the *Text File* class.
2. **External Design Interfaces:** C++ provides two external interfaces: **public** and **protected**. This section describes the **protected** interface and its purpose.
3. **Derived Class Design:** The last part of this section presents the implementation of the *Text File* class, which is a *derived* class (Figure 9.3).

9.3.1 Base Class

The *File* class library abstracts different types of files by allowing the client to view a file stored on the disk as an object. This class hides from the client the internal details of file access, file I/O, and other related operations. For instance, the **copy()** operation hides the process of accessing the file and copying its content to another file.

The *File* class maintains common attributes and operations such as *path_name*, *file_name*, *current_type*, and the **copy()** operation (Figure 9.3). The use of inheritance avoids requiring every type of file to provide its own unique implementation. Figure 9.4 depicts the memory layout for instances of this class. Some features, such as the **size()** and **permission()** access functions do not operate on data elements and instead operate on the actual file.

```
//              FILE.H Header File
#ifndef FILE_H
#define FILE_H

    #include "file_except.h"      // File Exception class library

    typedef     bool             Boolean ;
    typedef     int              Permission ;
    typedef     unsigned long    Size ;
    typedef     char             Key ; // used for search()operation

    enum File_Type
    {
        UNKNOWN_TYPE, TEXT_FILE ,
        BINARY_FILE , IMAGE_FILE
    };

    class File
```

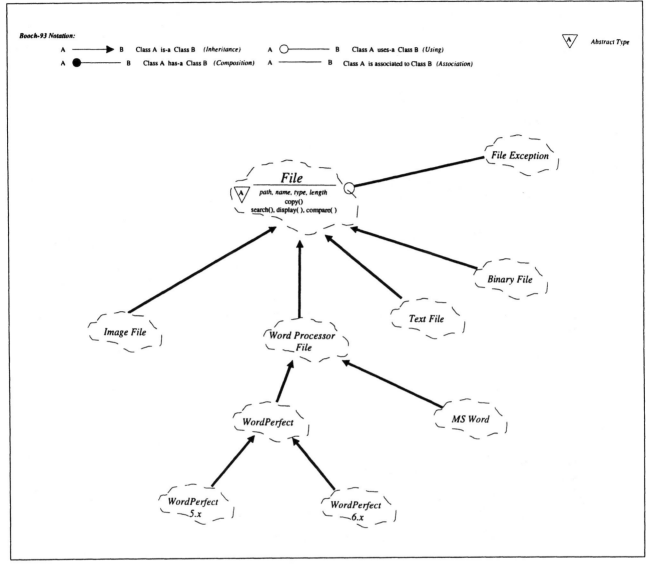

FIGURE 9.3 File class diagrams

```
        {
        private:
                Text *path_name , *file_name, *file_extension ;
                File_Type current_type ;

                // Utility functions
                Boolean find_name( void ) ;
                Boolean find_extension( void ) ;

                // NOTE: Removed from the design interface
                File( const File &source) ;
                File & operator =( const File &source ) ;

        protected:
                Boolean change_type( File_Type new_type ) ;

        public:
```

```
                            // File Constructors
                            File( ) ;
                            File( const Text *name ,
                            File_Type new_type = UNKNOWN_TYPE )
                                            throw( File_Exception ) ;

                            // File Destructor
                            ~File( ) ;

                            // File Access Functions
                            inline const Text *path( void ) const ;
                            inline const Text *name( void ) const ;
                            inline const Text *extension( void ) const ;
                            inline File_Type type( void ) const ;
                            Boolean exists( void ) const ;
                            Boolean empty( void ) const ;
                            Size size( void ) const ;

                            // File append & copy operation
                            File &operator >>( File &target )
                                            throw( File_Exception ) ;
                            void copy( File *target )
                                            throw( File_Exception ) ;
                            // Other details left out
                    } ;

              // inline function definitions

    #endif         // FILE_H Header File
```

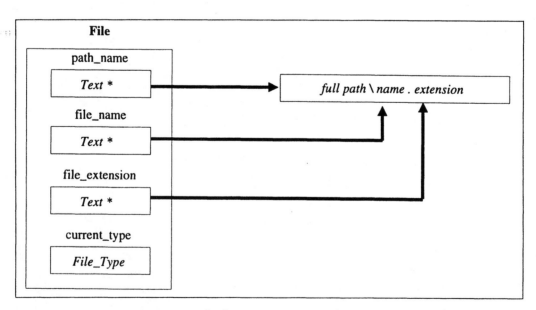

FIGURE 9.4   File class representation and architecture

The **find_name()** and **find_extension()** functions are utility functions, used by the constructors to initialize the data elements. The *copy constructor* and the *assignment* operator (=) have been declared private to prevent the client from referencing a file through duplicate file objects. Access functions such as **size()** provide basic file information to the client. The *File* class provides a **copy()** operation. The *right shift* operator (>>) has been overloaded as a file append operation. This function appends the contents of "*this*" file to the **target** file. By returning a *File* reference, this operation allows files to be cascaded.

For error detection and reporting, the *File* class uses *File Exception* to report exceptions (Figure 9.3). The *File Exception* class definition is included in the **FILE.H** header file via the **#include** directive. The design and implementation for *File Exception* are identical to that of *Serial Exception* in Chapter 8. The class captures the raw error **code** and correlates it to a description list *(descriptions)*. *File Exception* allows the classes in the *File* class library to provide meaningful error messages using the **error_message** data element. The provided information can be used by the client to identify the fatal error condition and the function that detected it:

```
//              FILE_EXCEPT.H Header File
#ifndef FILE_EXCEPTION_H
#define FILE_EXCEPTION_H

       #define NUM_FILE_ERRORS      9

       enum File_Error
       {
              FILE_ACCESS_ERROR , FILE_READ_ERROR ,
              FILE_WRITE_ERROR , FILE_CREATE_ERROR ,
              FILE_EXISTS_ERROR , FILE_FORMAT_ERROR,
              FILE_NAME_ERROR , FILE_SETUP_ERROR
       } ;
       typedef     char      Text ;

       class File_Exception
       {
       private:
              static const Text *descriptions[NUM_FILE_ERRORS];
              Text *error_message ;
              File_Error code ;
       public:
              // Constructors
              File_Exception( ) ;
              File_Exception( File_Error error_code ,
                      const Text *message ) ;
              File_Exception( const File_Exception & ) ;
              File_Exception & operator =( const File_Exception & );
                      // assignment & copy constructor:
                      //            deep copy implementation
              // Destructor
              ~File_Exception( ) ;

              // Access functions
              const Text *description( void ) const ;
              const Text *message( void ) const ;
              File_Error error_code( void ) const ;

              // Stream I/O functions
              friend ostream &operator <<( ostream &os,
                 const File_Exception &source ) ;
       } ;

#endif          // FILE_EXCEPT.H Header File
```

In the following example some of the *File* class functions are implemented:

```
//              FILE.CPP Source File
#include <stdio.h>              // Standard I/O Library
#include <string.h>             // String Library
#include <iostream.h>           // Stream I/O Class Library
#include "file.h"               // File Class Library

void File:: copy( File *target )
                throw( File_Exception )
{
        FILE *source_fp , *target_fp ;
        Boolean copy_error = false ;
        Text message[100] ;
        File_Error error_type = FILE_ACCESS_ERROR ;

        // open both files in binary mode
        if( (source_fp = fopen( path() , "rb" )) == NULL )
        {
                copy_error = true ;
                sprintf( message, "File:: copy() => unable to open %s file",
                        name() ) ;
        }
        else if( (target_fp = fopen( target->path() , "wb" )) == NULL )
        {
                fclose( source_fp ) ; // close source stream
                sprintf( message, "File:: copy() => unable to open %s file",
                        target->name() ) ;
        }
        else
        {
                int data ;
                // while no pending error on target stream
                while(!ferror( target_fp ) )
                {
                        data = fgetc(source_fp) ; // read from source stream

                        // when end of source stream reached
                        if( !ferror( source_fp ) && !feof( source_fp ) )
                        {
                                fputc( data , target_fp ) ; // write to target
                        }
                        else
                        {
                                break ;
                        }
                }

                // check for stream errors
                if( ferror( source_fp ) )
                {
                        copy_error = true ;
                        error_type = FILE_READ_ERROR ;
                        sprintf( message, "File:: copy() => unable to read"
                                " from the %s file", name() ) ;
                }
```

```
                         else if( ferror( target_fp ) )
                         {
                                 copy_error = true ;
                                 error_type = FILE_WRITE_ERROR ;
                                 sprintf( message, "File:: copy() => unable to write"
                                         " to the %s file", target->name() ) ;
                         }
                         fclose( source_fp ) ;
                         fclose( target_fp ) ;
                 }

                 // if unable to copy file => throw exception
                 if( copy_error )
                 {
                         throw( File_Exception( error_type , message ) );
                 }
         }


File:: File( const Text *name , File_Type new_type )
                                 throw( File_Exception )
             : path_name( static_cast<Text * > ( 0 ) ),
         file_name( static_cast<Text * > ( 0 ) ),
         file_extension( static_cast<Text * >( 0)),current_type(new_type)
 {
         // create a buffer for name and copy name to it
         path_name = new Text[ strlen(name) + 1 ] ;
         if( path_name != static_cast<Text *> ( 0 ) )
         {
                 strcpy( path_name, name );

                 // if file name is not found in the path then abort
                 if( !find_name( ) )
                 {
                         delete [ ] path_name ; // deallocate buffer
                         throw( File_Exception( FILE_NAME_ERROR,
                                             "Construction Error" ) ;
                 }
                  find_extension( ) ; // locate file extension if it exists
         }
         else    // allocation error => abort
         {
                 throw( File_Exception( FILE_SETUP_ERROR,
                                             "Allocation Error" ) ) ;
         }
 }


// Destructor
File:: ~File()
{
        delete [] path_name ;
}
```

9.3.2 Protected Design Interface

As discussed in Chapter 3, a class can support one internal (**private**) and two external (**public** and **protected**) design interfaces. The **private** interface is accessible only to member functions and friends (classes and functions) of the *base* class. This rule ensures that *encapsulation* is maintained for a *base* class. Even when *inheritance* is used, data coupling between *base* and *derived* classes can be minimized. All of the *File* class data members are **private** and are therefore inaccessible to the *derived* classes (refer to the example below).

At times, it may be necessary to differentiate between types of clients by providing additional features to the clients who inherit from the *base* class. As an analogy, we give our children privileges not enjoyed by other people, such as lending them the 1957 Corvette (which might be a mistake, but oh well...). C++ provides the **protected** access level for this purpose. The **protected** members of a class are accessible by the *base* class member functions, friends, and the *derived* class member functions. Note that the **protected** members of a class are not accessible to other types of clients, such as those based on a ***"has-a"*** relationship.

In the *File* class example, the class provides two external design interfaces: **public** and **protected**. In Figure 9.5, the *File* class has two types of clients: *Text File* and *Disk*. Both the *Text File* and *Disk* classes have access to

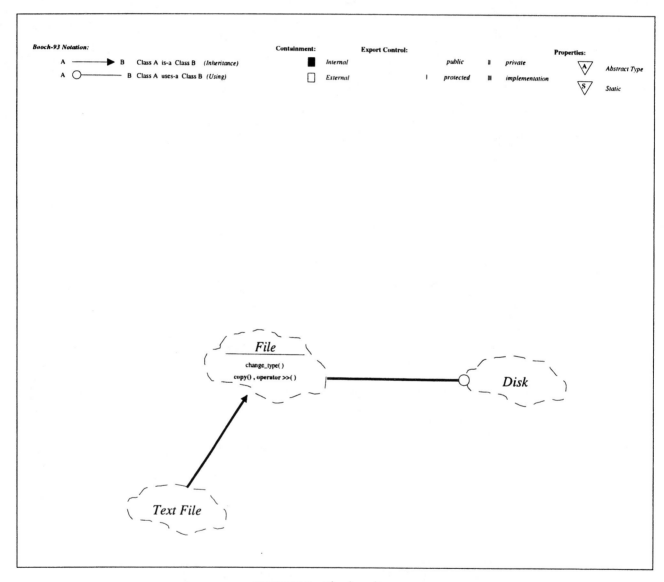

FIGURE 9.5   File class diagram

public members. However, only the *Text File* class has access to **protected** members of the *File* class. The C++ compiler does not permit classes not inheriting from the *File* class to access the **protected** members of that class:

```
//              FILE.H Header File

// For additional details, refer to Section 9.3.1
class File
{
        private:
                Text *path_name , *file_name, *file_extension ;
                File_Type current_type ;

        protected:
                Boolean change_type( File_Type new_type ) ;
                        // accessible by the derived classes
        public:
                // File append and copy operation
                File &operator >>( File &target ) throw(File_Exception);
                void copy( File *target ) throw( File_Exception ) ;
                        // accessible by all types of classes only
                // Other details left out
} ;
```

The above design allows only a *derived* class to change the type of file dynamically through **change_type()**. Another alternative is to make the *current_type* data element **protected**. To minimize data dependencies between the *base* and any *derived* classes, the design relies on member functions. In addition, the **protected** mode should not replace the **private** access level for data. The **private** access level encapsulates data and keeps the internal data representation hidden from other classes.

The use of **protected** data members makes the *derived* classes dependent on the design of their *base* class. The loss of data encapsulation in reference to the *derived* classes affects maintainability of the class hierarchy. When the *base* class architecture changes, the d*erived* class member functions are also affected by the changes. The use of **protected** data members should be carefully assessed for the implementation of the class. The primary use of the **protected** interface is to provide additional functional capabilities to *derived* classes while denying them to other clients.

9.3.3 Derived Class

In C++, a class is derived from a base class using the following notation:

```
class Derived_Name: access_level Base_Name
{
        // data member definitions & function declarations ;
} ;
```

The memory layout of a *derived* object consists of its *base* class data members followed by its *derived* class data members (Figure 9.6). In the following example, the *Text File* class inherits the properties of the *File* (*base*) class and adds new features to support a text file:

```
//          TEXT_FILE.H Header File
#ifndef TEXT_FILE_H
#define TEXT_FILE_H

        #include "file.h"              // need base class definition

        #define FIRST                 1
        #define BUFFER_LENGTH         150
        #define NULL_CHAR             '\0'
```

```
typedef        unsigned long       Counter ;

class Text_File: public File     // Text File inherits from File
{
        private:
                Counter total_lines ;
        public:
                // constructor
                Text_File( const Text *name ) ;

                // Text File operations
                Boolean search( const Key *key, ostream &os = cout)
                                    throw( File_Exception ) ;
                Boolean operator ==( const Text_File &baseline )
                                    throw( File_Exception ) ;
        } ;


#endif
```

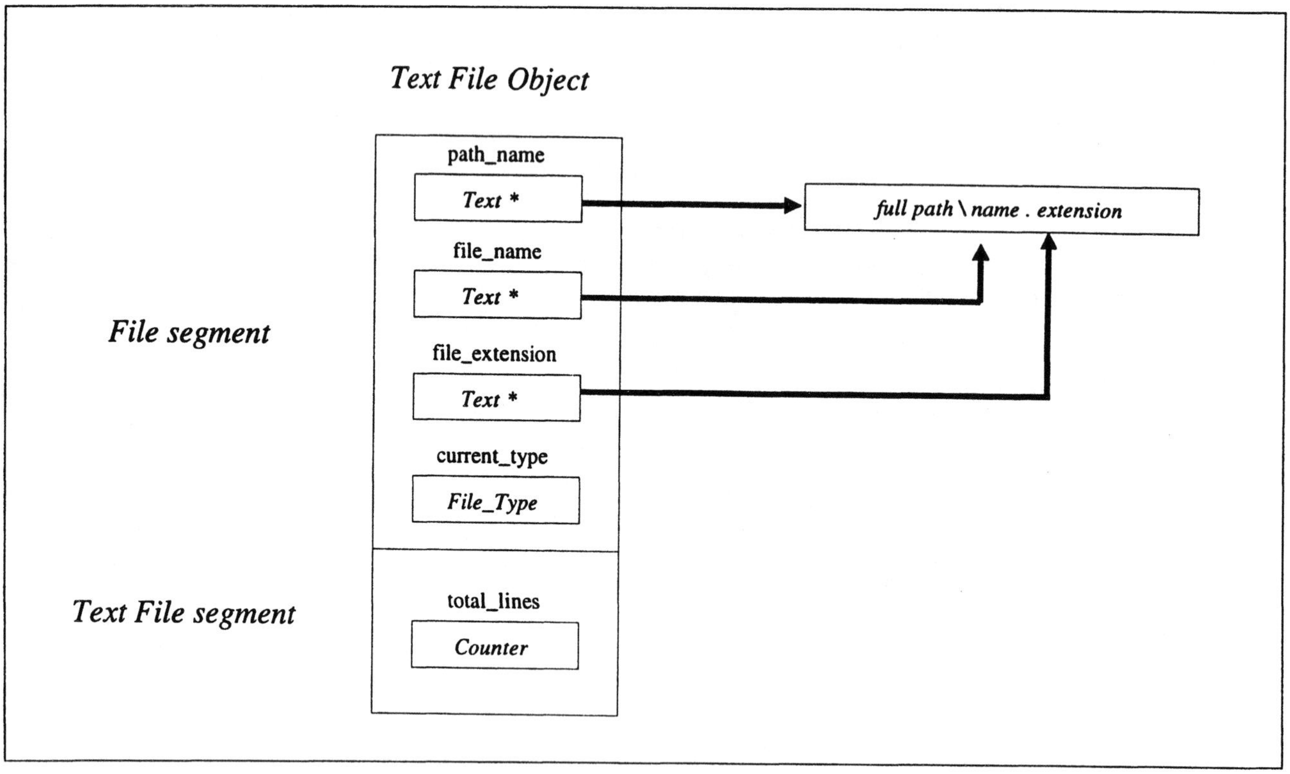

FIGURE 9.6   Text file object memory layout

The above syntax instructs the compiler to use the existing resources and attributes of the *File* class for the *Text File* class. The member functions of *Text File* have access to the **public** and **protected** members of the *File* class. A *Text File* object contains both a *File* and a *Text File* segment (Figure 9.6). The *base* class information always appears first followed by the *derived* class members. The *File* member functions encapsulate the *base* segment of the object from the *Text File* member functions.

   In the above example, *Text File* is *publicly* derived from *File*. Use of the **"public"** keyword in the declaration of *Text File* does not affect the access levels of member functions of *Text File*. Public inheritance affects the clients of *Text File* and how they perceive the use of inheritance in the design. Section 9.4 describes the types of inheritance in greater detail.

The following example implements the **Text_File:: search()** member function. This function obtains the filename by using the **File:: path()** and **File::name()** member functions. Using the *base* class features, the **search()** function opens the file and, using the designated search key, searches the file one line at a time. It writes the result of the search operation to an output stream. If the function encounters a fatal error, it throws a *File Exception*:

```
//              TEXT_FILE.CPP Source File
#include <stdio.h>            // Standard I/O Library
#include <iostream.h>         // Stream I/O class library
#include <iomanip.h>          // Stream I/O manipulator definitions
#include <string.h>           // String library
#include "text_file.h"        // Text File class library

Boolean Text_File:: search( const Key *key, ostream &os )
                                 throw( File_Exception )
{
    Text message[100] ;
    Boolean key_found = false , search_error = false ;
    File_Error error_type = FILE_ACCESS_ERROR ;
    FILE *fp ;

    fp = fopen( path() , "r" ) ; // open text file
    if( fp != NULL )
    {
        Text line_buffer[BUFFER_LENGTH] ;
        Counter line_ctr = FIRST ;
        os << "\n File: " << path() << endl ;
        while( !ferror(fp ) )
        {
            *line_buffer = NULL_CHAR ;
                    // initialize to null string

            // if line buffer is read => process line
            if( fgets( line_buffer, BUFFER_LENGTH, fp ) )
            {
                // if the search key is found in the line=>
                //      display line
                if( strstr(line_buffer,key) )
                {
                    // identify key matched
                    key_found = true ;
                    // output line to output stream
                    os << setw( 4 ) << line_ctr << ": "
                                    << line_buffer ;
                }
                ++line_ctr ;
            }
            else if( feof( fp ) ) // abort on end-of-file
            {
                break ;
            }
        }

        // if file read error => specify the condition
```

```
            if( ferror(fp) )
            {
                    search_error = true ;
                    error_type = FILE_READ_ERROR ;
                    sprintf( message, "File:: search() => read error"
                            " %s file", name() ) ;
            }
            else
            {
                    total_lines = line_ctr ; //update total # of lines
            }
            fclose( fp ) ; // close file stream
    }
    else// if file not opened
    {
        search_error = true ;
        sprintf( message, "File:: search() => unable to open %s file",
            name() ) ;
    }

    // if unable to search file => throw exception
    if( search_error )
    {
        throw( File_Exception( error_type, message ) );
    }

    return( key_found ) ;
}
```

9.4 TYPES OF INHERITANCE

In C++, a *derived* class may inherit the properties of a *base* class using different types of *inheritance*:

```
class Base_Name
{
        // base class elements and member function prototypes
} ;

class Derived_Name: access_level    Base_Name
{
        // derived class elements and member function prototypes
} ;
```

C++ supports three types of inheritance through the **access level** keywords: **public, protected,** and **private.**The **access level** is optional and may be omitted, which forces the compiler to use the default settings of *private* and *public* for the **class** and **struct** keywords, respectively. It is a good programming practice always to use explicit definitions and avoid relying on default settings.

The type of inheritance does not impact the member functions of the *derived* class. It only affects the ability of its clients to access the *base* class segment. The following sections and Figure 9.7 demonstrate the differences between the types of inheritance and their impact on the *Text File* clients: *Source File* and *Floppy Disk*.

9.4.1 Public Inheritance

Public inheritance is the most widely used type of inheritance and provides an open architecture to all types of clients. With public inheritance, all the clients are aware of the use of inheritance in the design of the *derived* class. For example, both the *Floppy Disk* and *Source File* classes know that *Text File* inherits from the *File* class.

With public inheritance, the *base* class members maintain their access levels and the *inheritance* is visible to the clients of the class. For instance, the *Source File* client derives from *Text File* and has access to the public and protected members of the *File (base)* segment of the *Text File* object such as **change_type()** and **copy()**:

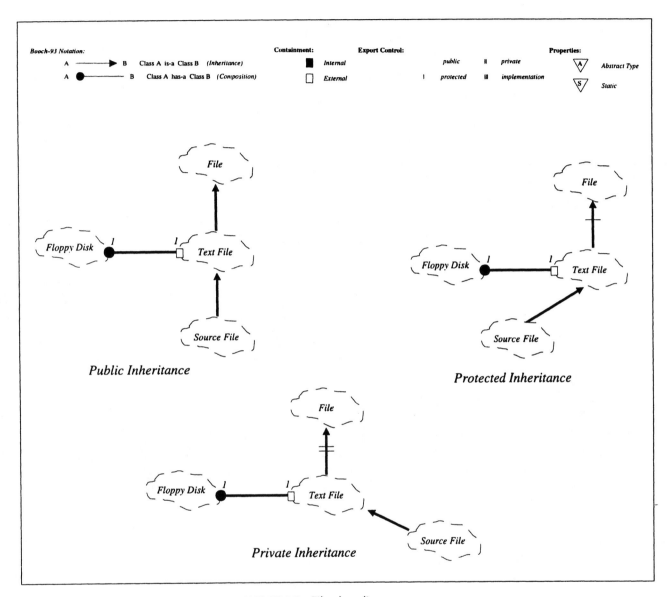

FIGURE 9.7 File class diagram

```
//              FILE.H Header File
// For additional details, refer to Section 9.3.1
class File
{
        private:
                Text *path_name , *file_name, *file_extension ;
                File_Type current_type ;
```

```
protected:
        Boolean change_type( File_Type new_type ) ;

public:
        // File Access Functions
        Permission access_mode( void ) const ;
        Boolean exists( void ) const ;
        Boolean empty( void ) const ;

        // File append & copy operation
        File &operator >>( File &target ) throw(File_Exception);
        void copy( File *target ) throw( File_Exception ) ;

        // Other details left out
} ;

//              TEXT_FILE.H Header File
#include "file.h"

// For additional details, refer to Section 9.3.3
class Text_File: public File
{
        private:
                Counter total_lines ;
        public:
                Text_File( const Text *name ) ;
                Boolean search( const Key *key , ostream &os );
        // Other details left out
} ;
```

Since *Text File* is inherited publicly from *File*, the *File* class **public** and **protected** members are part of the design interface. The derived *Source File* client has access to both public and protected members of its *File* class. In the following example, a *Source File* class inherits from the *Text File* class. The *Source File* member functions have access to both **protected** and **public** members of the *Text File* and *File* classes (Figure 9.7):

```
//              SOURCE_FILE.H Header File
#include "text_file.h"

class Source_File: public Text_File
{
        // other details left out
        public:
                void include_files( ostream &os )
                        throw( File_Exception ) ;
} ;

//              SOURCE_FILE.CPP Source File
#include "source_file.h"

void Source_File:: include_files( ostream &os )
                        throw( File_Exception )
{
        // if file exists =>
        //      search for "#include" and send result to output stream
        if( exists() )
        {
```

```
                         search( "#include" , os ) ;
        }
        return ;
}
```

In the above example, **include_files()** uses *Text File* and *File* member functions to search through a C/C++ program for **#include** directives. The output of the search is then sent to the console.

The public derivation allows the clients that *"have-a"* or *"use-a"* *Text File* to have access to the public members of the *File* class. In the following example, the *Floppy Disk* client uses the *Text File* and has access to public members of the *base* and *derived* classes in a *Text File* object. The **move_file()** operation uses the **access_mode()**, **exists()**, and **copy()** functions from the *File* class:

```
//                         FLOPPY_DISK.H Header File
#include "text_file.h"

class Floppy_Disk
{
        private:
                Text_File &active ;
        public:
                Boolean move_file( const Text *new_path ) ;
                // other details left out
 } ;

//                         FLOPPY_DISK.CPP Source File
#include <stdio.h>                // Standard I/O library
#include <string.h>               // String library
#include "floppy_disk.h"

Boolean Floppy_Disk:: move_file( const Text *new_path )
{
        Boolean file_moved = false ;

        // catch File Exceptions if any are thrown
        try
        {
                // create a target file
                Text_File target_file( new_path ) ;

                // if file exists and they are not referencing the same file
                if(  active.exists() &&
                     !strcmp( target_file.path() , active.path() ) )
                {
                        // copy from the active file to the target file
                        active.copy( target_file ) ;
                        file_moved = true ;

                        // delete active file
                        remove( active.path() ) ;
                }
        }
        catch( File_Exception &error )
        {
                cerr << error ;
        }
```

```
        return( file_moved ) ;
}
```

For all types of clients, inheritance is part of the software design interface and is therefore visible to the clients. Thus, the *derived* class cannot remove the use of inheritance from its design because that would adversely affect the client's design. *Inheritance* has become a part of the class design. For instance, changes to the *Text File* class and its use of inheritance will have a direct impact on any client programs. If the *Text File* class is changed to the following, unless the *Text File* class implements the features provided by the *File* class that are no longer inherited, the C++ compiler will generate error messages during the compilation of the *Floppy Disk* and *Source File* classes:

```
class Text_File  // removed inheritance from the design
{
        public:
                // must provide File's features to avoid compilation errors
                void copy( *target_file ) throw( File_Exception ) ;
        // other details left out
} ;
```

9.4.2 Protected Inheritance

Protected inheritance causes the *base* class public and protected members to become protected in the *derived* class.

```
//              TEXT_FILE.H Header File
#include "file.h"

class Text_File: protected File
{
        public:
                Text_File( const Text *name ) ;
                Boolean search( const Key *key , ostream &os );
        // Other details left out
} ;
```

The **public** and **protected** members of the *File* class become protected through the *Text File* class. The access levels of the *Text File* class members remain unaffected.

Protected inheritance makes the *base* segment of the *derived* class transparent to the clients who use or have that *derived* class. For instance, the *Floppy Disk* client is unable to access the **public** and **protected** members of the *base* class because these members are protected through the *derived* class. The following function will not compile because the *File* class is not visible to the client using the *Text File* class:

```
Boolean Floppy_Disk:: move_file( const Text *new_path )
{
        Boolean file_moved = false ;

        // catch File Exceptions if any are thrown
        try
        {
            // create a target file
            Text_File target_file( new_path ) ;
```

```
                 // illegal, will not compile because the
                 // clients conceptually do not know about the File portion
                 // if file exists and they are not referencing the same file
                 if( active.exists() &&
                     !strcmp( target_file.path() , active.path() ) )
                 {
                          // copy from the active file to the target file
                          active.copy( target_file ) ;
                          file_moved = true ;

                          // delete active file
                          remove( active.path() ) ;
                 }
        }
        catch( File_Exception &error )
        {
             cerr << error ;
        }

        return( file_mowed ) ;
}
```

Clients such as the *Source File* class who inherit from the *derived Text File* class are still able to operate on the public and protected members of the *File* class. For these clients, *inheritance* is part of the software design interface and the *File* (*base*) segment of the derived object is visible to them. The **Source_File:: include_files()** function has access to its *File* class public and protected members:

```
//                      SOURCE_FILE.CPP Source File
#include "source_file.h"

void Source_File:: include_files( ostream &os )
                         throw( File_Exception )
{
        // Source File knows about the base (File) segment of the
        // Text File and can access the public/protected features of File
        if( exists() )
        {
                 search( "#include" , os );
        }
        return ;
}
```

9.4.3 Private Inheritance

Private inheritance removes the use of inheritance from the software design interface, that is, inheritance is hidden from the client. Private inheritance forces the public and protected members of the *base* segment to become *private* in the *derived* class. This access level prevents all types of clients from having direct access to any of the *base* class members via the *derived* class.

```
//                      TEXT_FILE.H Header File
#include "file.h"

class Text_File: private File
{
        public:
```

```
        Text_File( const Text *name ) ;
        Boolean search( const Key *key , ostream &os );
    // Other details left out
} ;
```

Since the *Text File* class is privately derived, any derived classes of *Text File* cannot access the members of their *File* class. The *File* class segment is invisible to these classes. For example, the *Source File* member functions (Figure 9.7) cannot access *File* public or protected members.

In addition, the clients who have or use a *derived* class cannot access the *base* segment's members. The **Floppy_Disk:: move_file()** examples in Section 9.4.1 will not compile when *File* is privately inherited by *Text File*.

Private inheritance is used when the *derived* class (that is, **Text File** class) wants to remove the use of inheritance (that is, **File** class) from its design interface for all types of clients. The clients of the *derived* class can access and operate on the *base* segment of the derived object only through the *derived* class member functions. Through private inheritance, functionality of a class is reused without providing subtyping (base/derived) interface. Private inheritance allows a design to reuse functionality without conveying inheritance.

9.5 INHERITANCE ACCESS LEVEL SUMMARY

Table 9.1 summarizes the access levels for the *base* segment of a *derived* class, and how the clients perceive the *base* class members through the *derived* class.

TABLE 9.1   Base Class Members Access Level

Base Class Member Access	Public Inheritance	Protected Inheritance	Private Inheritance
public	public	protected	private
protected	protected	protected	private

To maintain encapsulation, the **private** access level for the *base* class members remains unaffected by the types of inheritance, and is not reflected in Table 9.1.

With **private** and **protected** inheritance, C++ allows the protected and public members of the *base* segment in the *derived* class to be promoted back to their original access levels through a *using declaration*:

```
class Derived_Name: protected Base_Name
{
    original_access_level:
        using Base_Name :: member_name ;
} ;
```

In the following example, *Text File* is privately inherited from *File,* which makes *File* public and protected members private through the *Text File* class. However, the *Text File* class has explicitly promoted some of the features in the *File* class. The *Text File* class has promoted **exists()** to its previous **public** level, while the **type()** function has been promoted only to the **protected** level.

```
//          FILE.H Header File
class File
{
    public:
        // File Access Functions
        inline File_Type type( void ) const ;
```

```
                    Boolean exists( void ) const ;
                    // Other details left out
} ;


//              TEXT_FILE.H Header File
#include "file.h"


class Text_File: private File
{
        protected:
               // File class member using declarations
               using File:: type ;
        public:
               using File:: exists ;
               Text_File( const Text *name ) ;
               Boolean search( const Key *key , ostream &os );
        // Other details left out
} ;
```

In the *using declaration* statements, the data types and function prototypes are left out. The *using declarations* allow certain members of a *base* class to be selectively placed back into the design interface, such the one depicted in the above example. To prevent the feature from being abused, C++ prohibits the use of a *using declaration* for promoting a member's access level to a level higher than its original level. For instance, the **path_name** data element in the *File* class cannot be promoted from **private** to **protected** through the *Text File* class. Using declarations should only be used for selected members of the class. If a derived class needs to use this feature extensively, the designer should consider a less restrictive inheritance, such as public inheritance.

9.6 OBJECT CONSTRUCTION

A *derived* object is constructed by reserving memory space to store both the *base* and *derived* data members. After that, the *base* and *derived* constructors are invoked to initialize the reserved memory space. During the construction process, the *base* portion of the object is initialized first, followed by the *derived* portion (Figure 9.8). The order of initialization ensures that the *base* portion is in a stable state if the *derived* constructor needs certain information from its *base* portion. The *base* and *derived* class constructors interface with each other through the *derived* constructor's *initialization list*. In the following example, the *Text File* constructor interfaces and passes initialization data to the *File* constructor.

```
//              FILE.CPP Source File
#include "file.h"          // File class library

File:: File( const Text *name , File_Type new_type )
                          throw( File_Exception )
        :path_name( static_cast<Text * > ( 0 ) ),
         file_name( static_cast<Text * > ( 0 ) ),
         file_extension( static_cast<Text * > ( 0 ) ),current_type(new_type)
{
     // refer to Section 9.3.1 for the implementation of this function
}


//              TEXT_FILE.CPP Source File
#include "text_file.h"        // Text File class library

Text_File:: Text_File( const Text *name )
        : File( name , TEXT_FILE ) , total_lines( 0 )
{
}
```

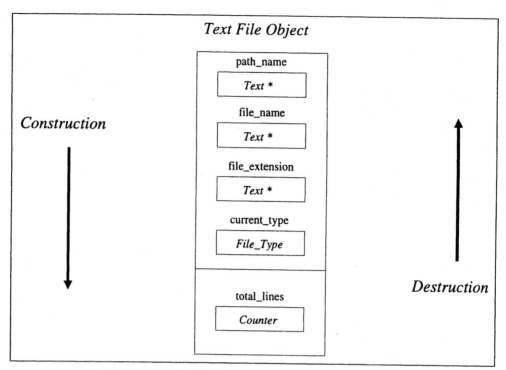

FIGURE 9.8   Text file object construction and destruction

Since the *File* portion of a *Text File* object does not have an explicit name, the *Text File* constructor uses the appropriate *File* constructor explicitly. The C++ compiler resolves the call to the *base* class constructor by using the supplied argument list in the derived constructor's *initialization list*. In the above example, the *File* constructor is called to initialize the *File* portion of the object. After the initialization statements in the *File initialization list* are performed, its body is executed. Control then goes back to *Text File* and the rest of the *Text File's initialization list* is processed. Finally, the body of *Text File* constructor is executed to complete the initialization process.

In the event the *derived* class constructor does not call a *base* class constructor explicitly in its *initialization list*, the compiler incorporates a call to the default constructor in the executable code to ensure the *base* portion is in a *predictable (stable)* state when the body of the *derived* constructor is executed. If the default constructor for the *base* class does not exists, the compiler generates a compilation error.

9.7 OBJECT DESTRUCTION

The order of destruction is inverse to that of the construction process (Figure 9.8). The *derived* portion is destroyed first, followed by the base segment. The *Text File* object is destroyed by calling the ~**Text File**() function first, followed by ~**File**(). The order of destruction ensures that the *derived* destructor can complete its cleanup operation in case it needs to obtain information from its *base* segment.

9.8 DOMINANCE

When inheritance is used, it is possible that the *derived* and *base* classes use the same names for some of their members. In this case, the name in the *derived* class dominates. Operations performed by the client of the *derived* class on these members are resolved by using the *derived* member. However, the base class element can be accessed explicitly by using the member's full signature: *Base_Name:: element*:

```
class File
{
```

```
        private:
                File_Type current_type ;
        public:
                File_Type type( void ) const ;
        // Other details left out
} ;

enum Text_Type
{
        ASCII_TYPE , SOURCE_TYPE , HEADER_TYPE
} ;

class Text_File: public File
{
        private:
                Text_Type current_type ; // name collision
        public:
                Text_Type type( void ) const ; // name collision
        // Other details left out
} ;

//              Test Driver Source File
#include <iostream.h>              // Stream I/O class library
#include "text_file.h"            // Text File class library

int main( int , char ** )
{
        Text_File sample_file( "text_file.cpp" ) ;

        cout << "\n\t name: " << sample_file.name() ;
        cout << "\n\t Type : " << static_cast<int> ( sample_file.type() ) ;
                        // call the Text File:: type() implementation

}
```

Name collisions are caused by poor naming convention, acronyms, and abbreviations. Even though C++ handles name collision through dominance, a class should use meaningful unique names for its members to avoid name collisions. Name collision difficulties are an indication of poor programming practice and a lack of programming standards.

9.9 FEATURE MAPPING

An important design issue is the applicability of a member function to its class. Prior to incorporating a feature, review and scrutinize its fit with respect to the functionality and purpose of the class and the derived classes. Improper placement of a feature leads to design flaws, which of course the compiler cannot detect. In the following example, the *File* class has incorporated the **num_lines()** function. This feature is fine for text and word processor files that have lines associated with them. However, for *Image* and *Binary* Files, this feature is meaningless.

```
class File
{
        public:
                Counter num_lines( void ) const ;
                // other details left out
} ;
```

Instead, it is better to incorporate the **num_lines()** function in each *derived* class that lines are applicable to:

```
class Text_File: public File
{
        private:
                Counter total_lines ;
        public:
                Counter num_lines( void ) ;
} ;
```

For classes to be reusable, the operations and features they provide should make sense. The *client needs* govern the design of a class because it is a client that uses the class to perform an operation or create new classes. The external features and operations provided by a class affect software maintainability since they support both the class and its clients.

When the need for or role of a function is not clear, the function should not be included in the class design. If the need does arise, the operation may be incorporated later on. It is more difficult to remove public and protected features than to add them because they are part of the external design interface, and their removal or changes to their signatures may adversely affect the client source files that have become dependent on them.

9.10 DATA CONVERSION

Since C++ creates an *"is-a"* relationship between a *base* and a *derived* class, the objects, pointers, and references of a *derived* class can be converted to the type of its *base* class either implicitly or explicitly. A **publicly** *derived* object can be implicitly converted to a *base* class object by extracting the *base* class portion from the *derived* object. The *derived*-to-*base* object conversion is a unidirectional process. The converse operation is not permitted because the *derived* members' values would be indeterminate (Figure 9.9).

```
base_object = derived_object ; // legal operation
derived_object = base_object ; // illegal operation
```

A *base* class pointer can point to a *derived* object but it can invoke only the base member functions[1] and only the *base* portion of the object is visible to it (Figures 9.9 and 9.10). In the **main()** function (*see example below*) the beginning address of the *sample_file* object is passed to the **test_file()** function as a *File* class pointer. Since the *current* pointer is of type *File*, the **test_file()** function can access only the base class members:

```
//                      Test Driver Source File
#include <iostream.h>                  // Stream I/O class library
#include "text_file.h"                 // Text File class library

int main( int , char ** )
{
        Text_File sample_file( "text_file.cpp" ) ;
        .
        test_file( &sample_file ) ;
        .
}

void test_file( File *current )
{
        cout << "\n\t name: " << current->name() ;
        cout << "\n\t path: " <<  current->path() ;
```

_____

[1]This restriction does not apply to *virtual* functions, which are discussed in Chapter 10.

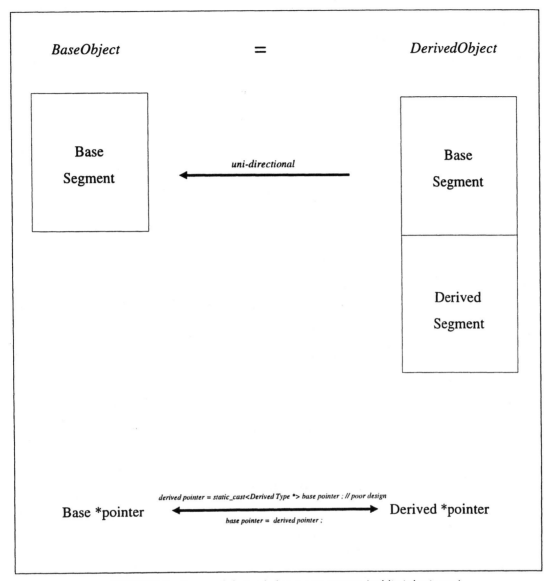

FIGURE 9.9 Base and derived object conversions (public inheritence)

```
      // call the File class implementation
current->search( "include" , cout ) ;
      // illegal operation: search() is a Text File member
}
```

In the above example, **current** points to a *derived* class object (**sample_file**). However, the **current** pointer can invoke only the *File* class member functions and is unable to invoke the *derived* class functions such as **search()**.

When a *base* and *derived* class member function names collide, the compiler resolves the function call by determining how the object is being accessed. If a *derived* object is accessed directly or by using a pointer of type *derived* class, the *derived* version has dominance and the derived implementation is called. If the *derived* object is accessed by using a *base* class pointer, the *base* class version is invoked because the *derived* segment of the object is not visible through the *base* class pointer. This is why design flaws resolved through dominance may not work (*refer to Section 9.8*):

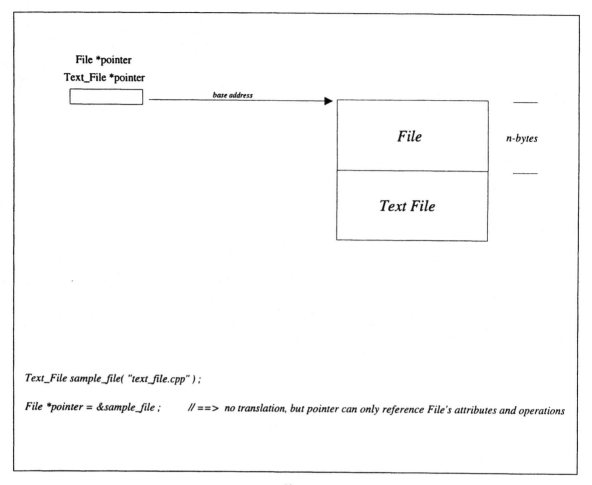

File *pointer
Text_File *pointer

base address

File

n-bytes

Text File

Text_File sample_file("text_file.cpp") ;

File *pointer = &sample_file ;   // ==> no translation, but pointer can only reference File's attributes and operations

FIGURE 9.10   Text file pointer convers

```
// Using class definitions from Section 9.8
Text_File sample_file( "sample.txt" ) ;
Text_File &tfile = sample_file ;
File *file = &sample_file ;
file->type() ;              // use File:: type()
tfile.type() ;              // use Text_File:: type()
sample_file.type() ;        // use Text_File:: type()
```

For a publicly *derived* class, a *base* class pointer can be converted to a *derived* class pointer. However, the conversion must be explicitly defined using the following notation:

derived_pointer = static_cast<derived_name *> base_pointer ;

In the following example, a *File* class pointer is converted to a *Text File* class pointer. In most cases, the **above conversion is a bad design** and this pointer conversion should not be used, because this design cannot guarantee the type of *derived* object pointed to by a *base* class pointer:

```
void test_file( File *current )
{
      cout << "\n\t name: " << current->name() ;
      cout << "\n\t path: " <<  current->path() ;
          // call the File class implementation
```

```
Text_File *sample = static_cast<Text_File *> current ;
        // poor design even though language supports it
sample->search( "include" , cout ) ;
}
```

Using the above example, an *Image File* object would be treated as a *Text File* object! This program will behave unpredictably when executed:

```
//                    Test Driver Source File
#include <iostream.h>        // Stream I/O class library
#include "image_file.h"      // Image File class library

int main( int , char ** )
{
        Image_File sample_file( "lift_off.bmp" ) ;
        .
        test_file( &sample_file ) ;
        .
}
```

The data and pointer conversions for **private** and **protected** inheritance have been restricted in C++. For **private** and **protected** inheritances, the conversion between base and derived classes is not implicitly allowed and is performed via a cast.

9.11 MULTIPLE INHERITANCE

M. Reese

A class may be derived from two or more classes (*multiple inheritance*). In *multiple inheritance*, a *derived* class uses the resources and features of several *base* classes in its design. For *multiple inheritance*, a *derived* class is defined using the same format as for single inheritance:

```
class Derived_Name : access_level Base_Name _1 , ...,
                     access_level Base_Name_n
{
} ;
```

Base classes are inherited by specifying the type of inheritance through the use of the **public, protected,** or **private** keywords. In Figure 9.2, the *Money Market* class inherits publicly from *Savings* and *Checking.*

As with single inheritance, multiple inheritance is used when the "**is-a**" relationship is satisfied for each of the base classes used:

```
proposed_derived_class "is-a" base_n_class
```

In the previous example, *Money Market* "*is-a*" *Savings* and "**is-a**" *Checking.*

Multiple Inheritance has a higher overhead than single inheritance, therefore programs using *multiple inheritance* tend to run slower. For single inheritance, the *base* data segment resides at the beginning of the *derived* object and the *base* and *derived* pointer conversion is a simple task. For multiple inheritance, the offsets for each of the *base* classes must be tracked. These requirements increase the run-time overhead:

```
class Money_Market: public Savings , public Checking
{
        // details left out
} ;
```

At the design level, *multiple inheritance* is more cumbersome to understand and maintain than single inheritance and should be used sparingly. The software developer maintaining a design based on multiple inheritance must study the design hierarchy in detail prior to making changes. A complicated inheritance lattice can make the software maintenance difficult. For instance, a change in the protected interface of one of the base classes may have an adverse effect on its derived classes. When used wisely, *multiple inheritance* can reduce the design time by reusing existing features. For example, the *Stream I/O Class* (**iostream.h**) library effectively uses *multiple inheritance* and provides a good case study.

9.12 VIRTUAL BASE CLASS

In certain applications a class may be indirectly inherited twice by a derived class (Figure 9.11):

```
class Account
{
        // details omitted
} ;

class Savings: public Account
{
        // details omitted
} ;

class Checking: public Account
{
        // details omitted
} ;

class Money_Market: public Savings, public Checking
{
} ;
```

In this design, there will be two versions of the *base* class in the *derived* class object (Figure 9.11). The *Money Market* class contains elements of both the *Savings* and *Checking* classes. Since both *Savings* and *Checking* each contain an instance of *Account*, the *Money Market* object obtains two instances of *Account*. This is an undesirable situation because the member functions of *Account* and *Savings* operating on a *Money Market*

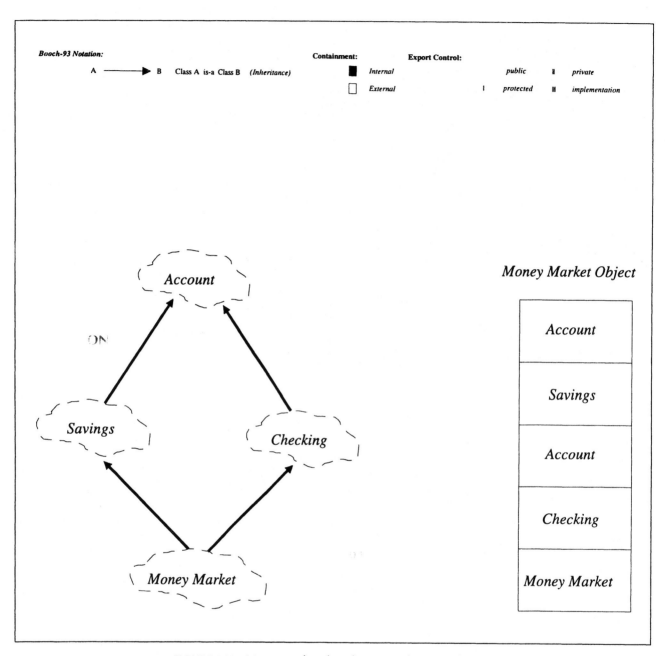

FIGURE 9.11 Money market class diagram and memory layout.

object change the *Account* information in their separate *Account* instances. Thus, the two *Account* segments in the *Money Market* object contain information inconsistent with each other.

To avoid duplication of class data members, C++ allows the data members of a *base* class to be included only once. The **virtual** keyword is used to tell the C++ compiler that the *base* class is indirectly inherited multiple times and that it should include only a single instance of the *base* class. By modifying the *Savings* and the *Checking* class definitions, the *Money Market* class will have only one instance of the *Account* class (Figure 9.12):

```
class Account
{
      // details omitted
} ;
```

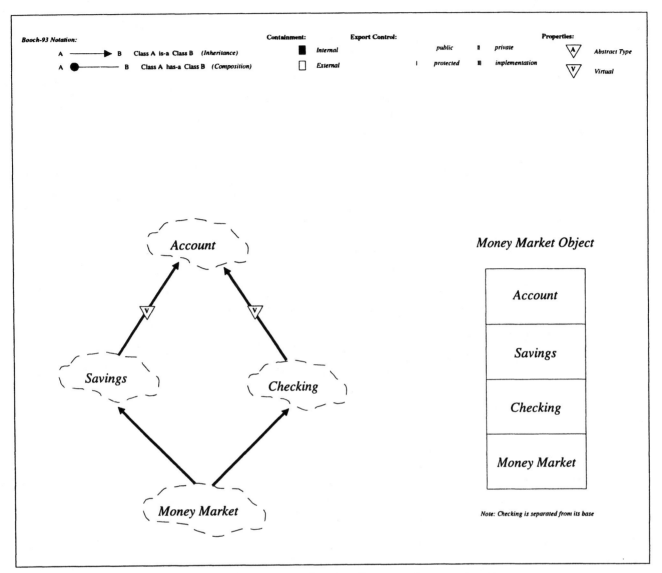

FIGURE 9.12   Money market class diagram and memory layout.

```
class Savings: virtual public Account
{
      // details omitted
} ;

class Checking: virtual public Account
{
      // details omitted
} ;

class Money_Market: public Savings, public Checking
{
} ;
```

The **virtual** keyword causes the *Money Market* object to have only one *Account* portion. The member functions of *Money Market, Savings,* and *Checking* then operate on the protected and public members of the common *Account* segment.

C++ places the following restrictions on *virtual base* classes:

1. **Initialization:** A *virtual base* class must be initialized by the most derived class. The constructor for *Money Market* must be the one to invoke and initialize the constructor function of the *Account* class.

```
Money_Market:: Money_Market( const Account &source )
     : Account( source ) , Savings( ) , Checking( )
{
     // details left out
}
```

2. **Pointer Conversion:** A pointer to a *virtual base* class cannot be converted to a *derived* pointer type.

9.13 OBJECT-ORIENTED CONSIDERATIONS

A design hierarchy is one of the major components of an object-oriented design. The use of inheritance in the design of classes requires the use of certain techniques to create maintainable and reusable software. The following guidelines summarize the high-level issues discussed earlier in this chapter:

1. **Inheritance Usage:** Inheritance should be used in the design of a class when an *"is-a"* relationship exists. If a class does not satisfy the *is-a* relationship, inheritance is not an appropriate approach.
2. **Data Members:** The *base* class should capture the information common to the *derived* classes. In the bank account example, the *Account* class maintains the customer's name, address, and picture, which are utilized by all the *derived* accounts. The *derived* classes should then focus on information and operations that are specific to them.
3. **Features:** Similar to data members, common operations should also be mapped to the *base* class. This approach allows the *derived* classes to build on a mature and tested foundation. When the requirements change and the implementations of the *base* functions need to be modified, only one set of changes needs to be made; the *derived* classes remain unaffected. If the *derived* classes had provided their own unique implementations, the change would have to be replicated within all of the *derived* classes. This significantly lengthens the software modification, retesting, and revalidation processes.

   Most importantly, care must be taken when mapping features to a class in a design hierarchy. The feature must make sense for the *base* class and its *derived* classes. Ambiguous or questionable features should be left out of the class design. If the need for a feature arises, the operation may be incorporated later on. Generally, it is easier to add features than to remove them. Existing public and protected features are part of the design interface, and changes to these features affect the client application.
4. **Type of Inheritance:** Using **protected**, **private**, or **public** access levels, the visibility of the base class(es) to the client of a *derived* class is controlled and regulated.

   For applications in which use of inheritance in the design interface is hidden, the *derived* class uses private or protected inheritance. Private and protected inheritance add unnecessary complexity to the design and are not commonly used.

   Most designs are based on public inheritance. This chapter discusses two areas where inheritance is utilized: to capture common operations and attributes, and to create customized classes. Inheritance is also used to create a common design interface among a group of *derived* classes. For example, the *File* class specifies the signature (prototype) for the **search()** operation (Figure 9.3). The function declaration establishes the interface requirements for all of the *derived* classes. Even though the function implementation varies between the *derived* classes, the interface is the same. A common design interface among the *derived* classes is established when inheritance is part of the design interface and the implementation is based on public inheritance. Since object-oriented designs usually use inheritance to capture common attributes, define common design interfaces, and create customized classes, public inheritance is the most common approach.

5. **Member Naming Convention:** Member names should be descriptive and a designer should avoid using acronyms. At times, the *base* and *derived* class member names may collide. Name collisions can indicate either a real design flaw or poor naming conventions.

6. **Member Access Levels:** The access levels should be defined cautiously in order to maintain the data encapsulation of the class hierarchy. The class design should rely on private data members with public and protected class member functions acting as the gatekeepers between the clients of the class and the class data. Furthermore, by encapsulating the *base* class architecture from the *derived* classes, the *derived* classes are decoupled from the *base* class architecture. The protected interface provides additional features that are meaningful for the *derived* classes.

9.14 STREAM I/O CLASS HIERARCHY

The standard *Stream I/O Class* library uses multiple inheritance and operator overloading and provides a versatile and consistent interface for reading and writing information to different types of streams: file, memory, and console. The library's design makes the C++ compiler responsible for selecting the appropriate stream I/O function based on the specified data type. This property creates a type-safe interface and is demonstrated in Chapter 4.

Figure 9.13 depicts the *Stream I/O* class hierarchy. The library is based on a set of key classes that create the framework for stream I/O:

1. **ios:** This class maintains the common attributes and operations for its *derived* classes, and some of them are identified below:

   a. *Stream I/O State*: Soft failure, hard failure, end-of-file
   b. *Stream Seek Direction*: Beginning, current, end
   c. *Mode*: Read, write, truncate, append
   d. *Type*: Binary, text
   e. *Data Format*: Hexadecimal, octal, decimal, justification, width, precision, scientific, fixed notation

   Through the resources provided by the *ios* class, a client changes the format of data by using one of the *stream manipulators* such as the **hex()** function. In the following example, the **hex()** manipulator is used to send the contents of the *status* flag to the console in hexadecimal format:

```
#include <iostream.h>// Stream I/O Class library
#include <iomanip.h>// I/O Manipulator

void output_status( long status )
{
        cout << "System Status : " << hex << status << endl ;
            // The contents of status are sent to console using
            // hexadecimal format. In the above example,
            // the address of hex() is passed to
            // a stream handler function which then invokes
            // the hex() function. hex() then operates on
            // the applicable data member of ios.
}
```

The *Stream I/O* class library provides a stream handler function that takes a function pointer as its argument and invokes the function:

```
ostream & ostream:: operator<<( ostream &(*f)(ostream &) )
{
        return( (*f)( *this ) ) ;
```

```
                    // return reference to ostream for cascading
}
```

The above feature operates on *manipulator* functions like **hex()**. The following is the required format for custom manipulators that do not take any arguments:

```
ostream & manipulator( ostream &os )
{
        // operate on output stream
        return( os ) ; // return reference to allow cascading
}
```

2. **streambuf:** This class maintains the stream buffer and captures common attributes and operations for file and memory (string) buffering. The *filebuf* and *strstreambuf* classes are derived from *streambuf* to provide features specific to file and string buffering, respectively.

3. **istream:** This class is responsible for reading information from an input stream. The *istream* class inherits from *ios* and overloads the *right shift* operator (>>) as a **formatted** input stream operator for all of the built-in data types. In addition, it provides several nonoperator functions:

   a. Unformatted read functions for char, string, and line: **get()** and **getline()**
   b. Undo functions: **unget()** and **putback()**
   c. Seek functions: **seekg()** and **tellg()**

   For file and string input streams, the *ifstream* and *istrstream* classes are derived from *istream* and provide the associated capability. The *istream_withassign* class handles console input (**cin**) capability.

4. **ostream:** This class is responsible for writing information to an output stream. The *ostream* class is inherited from *ios* and overloads the *left shift* operator (<<) as a **formatted** output stream operator for all of the built-in data types. In addition, it provides several nonoperator functions:

   a. Unformatted write functions for char and buffer: **put()** and **write()**
   b. Output stream flush function: **flush()**
   c. Seek functions: **seekp()** and **tellp()**

   For file and string output streams, the *ofstream* and *ostrstream* classes are derived from *ostream* and provide the associated capability. The *ostream_withassign* class handles console output (**cout**, **clog**, and **cerr**) capability.

5. **iostream:** This class combines the input stream and output stream capability of *istream* and *ostream*, and provides input/output capability on a stream. To avoid obtaining two instances of *ios* in an *iostream* object, *istream* and *ostream* **virtually** inherit from the *ios* class features.

   For file and string stream I/O, the *fstream* and *strstream* classes are derived from *iostream* and add the necessary features to handle file and memory I/O.

Figure 9.13 provides a simplified view of the *Stream I/O class* hierarchy. The ANSI C++ implementation requires the implementation of this library to support both ASCII (**char** type) and wide character literals (**wchar_t** type). A discussion of the full ANSI C++ implementation is beyond the scope of this chapter and can best be obtained in a C++ compiler reference manual.

By adding features such as custom *stream manipulators* or classes that handle new streams such as a windowing stream, the *Stream I/O class* library can be expanded by a developer. To support a window I/O stream, a user-defined *window* class inherits features from the *iostream* class (Figure 9.14). In addition, it provides several custom manipulators such as **set_cursor()**, **set_back_color()**, and **set_fore_color()**. These manipulators operate on the window stream by moving the cursor within a window and altering the background and foreground colors. Since these *manipulators* take arguments, their design and implementation are more involved than those shown earlier for manipulators like **hex()**. A sample implementation is included in the accompanying floppy disk.

```
wstream << set_cursor( x , y ) << set_fore_color( RED ) <<
"** Warning ** System Error Detected " << endl ;
```

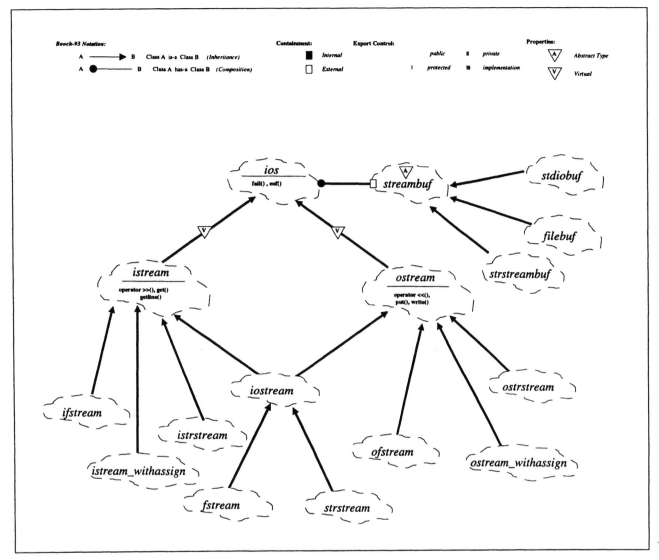

FIGURE 9.13 I/O stream library class diagram

By building on this library and designing new streams that use the same consistent interface, a client code will be able to perform stream I/O on a variety of stream types. For example, a client function could send information to a file, memory, console, or the new stream without being tied to a specific stream. By evolving this library, the software package gains a great deal of flexibility. Via this strategy, a software package can provide data logging and tracing facilities that route critical information to trace and log file streams. Most importantly, the mechanism is transparent and built into the software.

SUMMARY

Inheritance is the ability to use an existing class (*base*) and its resources to create a new class (*derived*). *Inheritance* has been built into the C++ language in order to assist the designer in reusing existing designs. Inheritance plays an important role in software development and reusability, and is used in different contexts. *Inheritance* can be used to customize an existing class and create a more specialized version. Inheritance can be used to group information common to several classes in a *base* class. Furthermore, a *base* class may define the design requirements by identifying the required member functions for each of its *derived* classes to implement. Inheritance is used in the design when a *derived* class meets the "*is-a*" relationship with the base class.

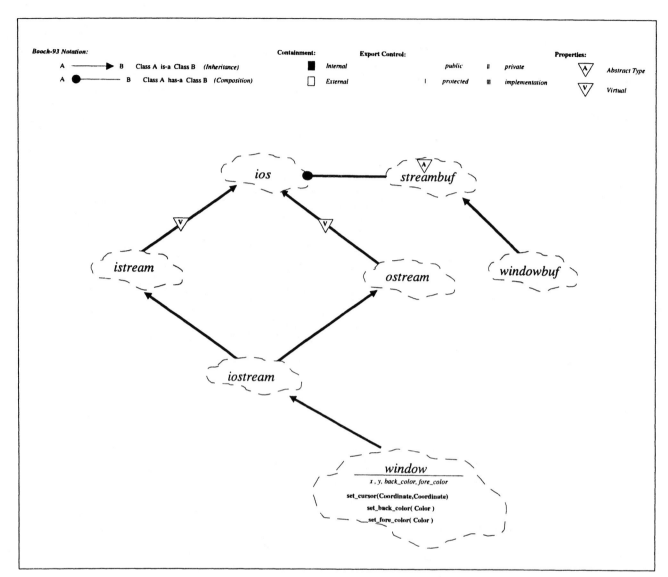

FIGURE 9.14   User defined window stream class diagram diagram

The types of inheritance control and regulate the visibility of the *base* class(es) to the client of a *derived* class. Most designs are based on public inheritance. Through protected and private inheritance, the *derived* class hides the use of inheritance in its design and removes inheritance from the design interface. The private and protected inheritance allow a *derived* class to inherit functionality without conveying use of inheritance to its clients. On the basis of the types of inheritance, Table 9.2 summarizes the visibility of the *base* class to the clients of a *derived* class.

TABLE 9.2   Visibility of a Base Class to the Clients of the Derived Class

Type of Inheritance	Visibility
Public	Inheritance is part of the design interface and the clients can access the external features of the *base* class
Protected	The classes inheriting from a *derived* class have visibility to the *base* features of a *derived* class. However, other types of clients do not have access to the *base* features of a *derived* class

TABLE 9.2   Visibility of a Base Class to the Clients of the Derived Class *(Con't)*

Type of Inheritance	Visibility
Private	Inheritance is removed from the design interface and is not visible to the clients of the *derived* class

A *derived* class may inherit from more than one *base* class in C++. This is referred to as *multiple inheritance*. Multiple inheritance allows two or more classes to be used in the design of a new class. Even though the *derived* class evolves from developed and tested software, *multiple inheritance* introduces a new level of complexity. When the design hierarchy lattice becomes complicated, it becomes difficult to maintain. The designer needs to trade off the reusability of existing classes against the maintainability of the hierarchy when contemplating multiple inheritance.

In *multiple inheritance* applications, a *derived* class may inherit a class **indirectly** multiple times. In C++, the intermediate *base* class definitions must use the **virtual** keyword. The *derived* object then inherits only one instance of that *base* class. In Figure 9.12, the *Money Market* class inherits only one instance of *Account*. This is denoted by the virtual symbol "v" on the inheritance arrow.

GLOSSARY

Using declaration
In the case of private or protected inheritance, a public or protected *base* member is promoted to a higher level (up to its original access level) by declaring the member in the *derived* class definition

Base class
In inheritance, the *base* class is used to create new classes (*derived*). The *derived* classes inherit the properties and attributes of the existing class (*base*)

Derived class
By inheriting properties and attributes of an existing class (*base*) and adding additional features, a new class (*derived*) emerges from the design

Design hierarchy
Through inheritance, a group of classes form a hierarchical architecture

Dominance
When there is a name collision between the members of *base* and *derived* classes, references to the member's name in the client code are resolved in favor of the *derived* class member, when the object is accessed directly, or by using a *derived* type pointer or reference

Inheritance
The ability to use the architecture, attributes, and properties of an existing (*base*) class in the design of a new (*derived*) class. Inheritance creates an "**is-a**" relationship between the *base* class and its *derived* class

Multiple inheritance
A derived class that inherits from two or more base classes

Subclass
Another term for a *derived* class

Superclass
Another term for a *base* class

Virtual base class
Because of multiple inheritance, a *base* class can be inherited indirectly more than once. To avoid the existence of two instances of the same *base* in the *derived* class object, the *base* class is inherited using the

virtual keyword. The **virtual** keyword causes the compiler to use only one instance of the *base* class in the memory layout of the *derived* object

CHAPTER 10

Polymorphism

INTRODUCTION

Chapter 9 introduced *inheritance* and its application to the creation of reusable designs. Inheritance was used to maintain common attributes and operations in a *base* class, and to create customized derived classes. For example, the *Shape* class in Figure 10.1 captures common shape attributes such as background and foreground colors. It also provides common operations such as the **color()** operation. The *derived* classes such as *Triangle* inherit these common features and provide unique attributes and operations such as *vertices* and **height()**. Through inheritance customized classes are provided in a design hierarchy. For instance, the *Square* class inherits from a *Rectangle* and becomes a customized *Rectangle* subtype. A *design hierarchy* also specifies a common design interface for the *derived* classes (Figure 10.1). The *base* class specifies a set of operations that are applicable to any *derived* class. The *derived* classes then provide appropriate implementations of these operations. For example, the *Shape* class requires its *derived* classes to provide the **move()**, **draw()**, **area()**, and **perimeter()** functions (Figures 10.1 and 10.2). The *Shape* class specifies only the function signatures, and the *derived* classes provide the body for these functions. Since the interface of these operations is standardized by the *base* class, the clients of the *design hierarchy* can operate on the *derived* objects in a generic way without having to worry about the specific type of object. This standardized interface creates coherency across the hierarchy and makes clients less dependent on a specific type in the hierarchy. As classes are added to the hierarchy, the client software remains unaffected. This approach makes the software more extendable and maintainable. For instance, the addition of *Trapezoid* to the *Shape* class hierarchy (Figure 10.1) will not affect existing client source code.

10.1 POLYMORPHIC BEHAVIOR

The creation of a design hierarchy allows a client program to maintain, access, and operate on different types of derived classes in a generic way. For instance, the client program does not need to provide unique functions to operate on different types of *Shapes*. The same program can draw or paint different types of derived shapes. The client program is abstracted from any specific shape. The ability to operate on and manipulate different derived objects in a uniform way is called *polymorphism*.

To implement a *design hierarchy* that supports *polymorphism*, the *base* class must specify the design interface for its *derived* classes. By declaring the required functions in the *base* class definition, the declarations

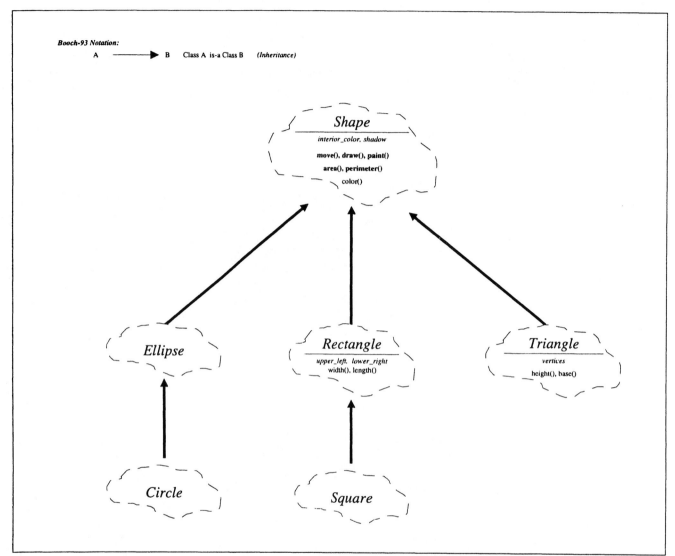

FIGURE 10.1 Shape class design hierarchy.

(*prototypes*) identify the function names, arguments, and return values. In Figure 10.2, the *Shape* class has defined a common design interface for the *Ellipse*, *Rectangle*, and *Triangle* classes: **move()**, **draw()**, **paint()**, **area()**, and **perimeter()**. The *derived* classes then define and implement the functions specified in the *base* class definition. In Figure 10.2, the *Rectangle* class provides an implementation for all of the specified functions. The *Square* class inherits the *Rectangle* **move()**, **area()**, and **perimeter()** operations. However, it provides its own unique **draw()** and **paint()** operations.

Even though each *derived* class provides a unique implementation for each function, for example, **draw()**, they are logically the same to the client. In Figure 10.3, the client is not concerned with the details of the drawing operation or with how the applicable member function is invoked to draw the object. Since the *Shape* class defines the minimum applicable operations that must be implemented by each of the *derived* shapes, the client creates lists that contain different types of shapes (*heterogeneous*) such as the one in Figure 10.3. The client operates on these shape objects by using the applicable member function of the *derived* classes. Since the *derived* classes all use the same names and interfaces for the specified functions, the client uses the same function call to operate on each different object (*polymorphism*). The client is not responsible for recognizing the type of *Shape* object and operates on different types of shapes by using a *Shape* pointer or reference. In Figure 10.3, the client traverses through a *heterogeneous* list of shapes and invokes the **draw()** and **area()** functions for any type of shape.

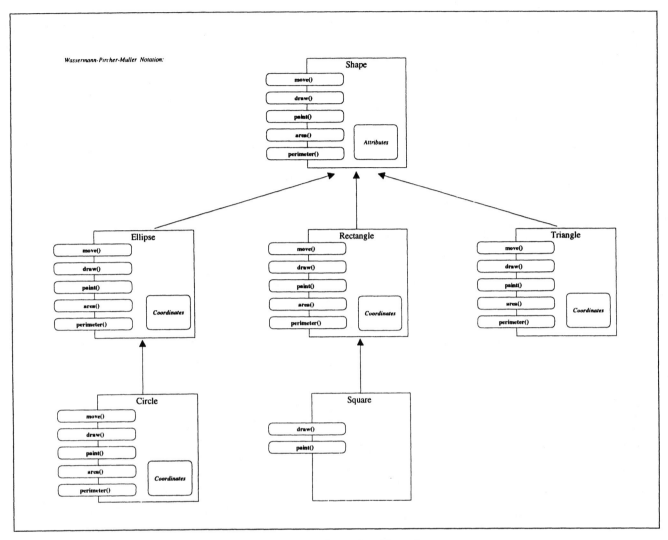

FIGURE 10.2 Shape class hierarchy.

In the following example, the client software invokes the *derived* class implementation of **area()** for all of the objects in the *Shape* list (Figure 10.3). The only important issue is to ensure that the correct **area()** function is invoked for each derived object in the list. The method of identifying the type of each object is handled by the compiler and is transparent to the designers of the *Shape* classes and their clients. The language provides the necessary tools to allow the different types of shapes to be recognized at either compile time or run time.

```
//              Test Driver Source File
#include "shape.h"
float total_area( Shape *list[], int num_shapes )
{
        float areas = 0 ;

        for( int i = 0 ; i < num_shapes ; i++ )
        {
                areas += list[i]->area() ; // compute area for each shape
        }
        return( areas ) ;
}
```

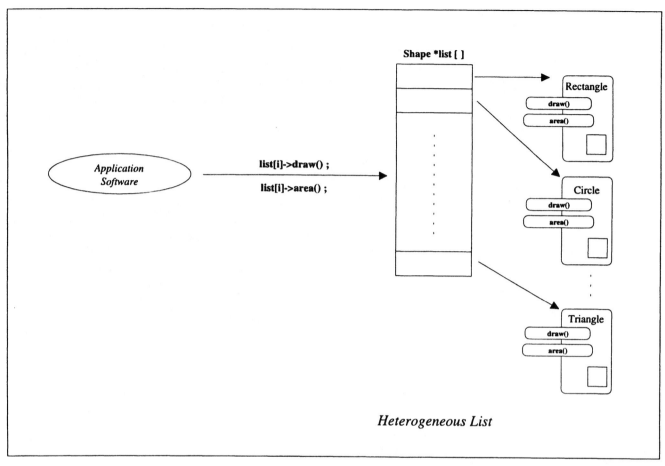

FIGURE 10.3   Application software and shape classes interaction.

In Figure 10.3 each entry in the list points to a different type of *Shape*. Since the list is based on an array of *Shape* (*base* class) pointers, the *derived* objects in the list are accessed and operated on by the client using a generic method. Thus, the design is concerned with the operations performed on the *Shape* objects, and the type of the objects is irrelevant.

Given a generic list such as the one in Figure 10.3, the compiler cannot determine the type of the objects at compile time. The type of the objects must be determined at run time in order to invoke the appropriate derived member class functions. The identification and invocation of the applicable member function are known as *dynamic binding* or *late binding*. For the above **total_area()** function, the type of each object in the *list[ ]* array is determined at run time and the correct **area()** function is invoked.

For simpler cases, the compiler is able to determine the type of a *Shape* object at compile time and use the applicable member function of the derived class. The compile time recognition of the member function is known as *static binding* or *early binding*. In the following example, if the compiler determines that the type of *Shape* being pointed to by **current** is *Circle*, the call to the **draw()** function of *Circle* would be resolved at compile time.

```
//              Test Driver Source File
#include <iostream.h>              // Stream I/O Class Library
#include "shape.h"                 // Shape Class Library

int main( int , char ** )
{
        // allocate a circle
        Shape *current = new Circle( 3 , 4 , 5, BLUE ) ;
                // center at (3,4), radius = 5, color = blue
```

```
                current->draw() ; // invoke the Circle:: draw() function
                cout << "\n\t Area: " << current->area() ;
                delete current ;

                return( 0 ) ;
}
```

10.2 VIRTUAL FUNCTIONS

Inheritance forms a design hierarchy within a group of related classes (Figure 10.1), but *inheritance* alone does not provide polymorphic behavior. As discussed in Chapter 9, the *derived* members of a class are not accessible through a *base* class pointer. Using *inheritance* alone, the client cannot access the *derived* class members using a *Shape* (base) class pointer.

```
//              Test Driver Source File
#include "shape.h"

float total_area( Shape *list[], int num_shapes )
{
        float areas = 0 ;

        for( int i = 0 ; i < num_shapes ; i++ )
        {
                areas += list[i]->area() ; // compute area for each shape
        }

        return( areas ) ;
}
```

The **total_area()** function can access only the *base* class (*Shape*) implementation of **area()**, which is only a function prototype. Even though the intention of the **total_area()** function is to access and operate on different shapes in a generic fashion, the use of inheritance alone will not enable the **total_area()** function to access the *derived* class implementations of **area()**.

C++ provides *polymorphic* behavior through the use of *inheritance* and **virtual** functions. The **virtual** keyword tells the compiler that the member function is a special type of function and is to provide *polymorphic* behavior. In the following example, the *Shape* class identifies a constructor, a **color()** access function, and five virtual functions. The virtual functions do not have a meaningful implementation at the *base* class (*Shape*) level. Obviously, it is not possible to compute the area of a generic shape. At this point, these functions have been implemented as do-nothing functions. The following sections provide a better solution via *abstract classes*:

```
//              SHAPE.H Header File
#ifndef SHAPE_H
#define SHAPE_H

        #include "point.h"      // refer to Chapter 4

        enum Color { RED, BLUE, GREEN, WHITE, BLACK, YELLOW } ;

        typedef         bool            Boolean ;

        class Shape
        {
```

```
        private:
                Color interior ;

                // ** Note:    has removed copy constructor and
                //             assignment operator (=)
                Shape( const Shape & ) ;
                Shape & operator =( const Shape & ) ;

        public:
                inline Shape( Color interior_color ) ;
                inline Color color( void ) const ;
                virtual Boolean draw( void ) const
                        { return false ; } ;// do-nothing
                virtual Boolean paint( Color new_color )
                        { return false ; } ;// do-nothing
                virtual Boolean move( Coordinate x , Coordinate y )
                        { return false ; } ;// do-nothing
                virtual float area( void ) const
                        { return 0.0 ; } ;// do-nothing
                virtual float perimeter( void ) const
                        { return 0.0 ; } ;// do-nothing
} ;

inline Shape:: Shape( Color interior_color )
        : interior ( interior_color )
{
}

inline Color Shape:: color( void ) const
{
        return( interior ) ;
}


// include the applicable subclass definitions in the hierarchy
#include "circle.h"
#include "rectangle.h"
#include "square.h"

#endif           // SHAPE_H Header File
```

Each virtual function declaration in the *Shape* class specifies the function name and interface for any of the *Shape* derived classes and, therefore, creates a uniform design interface. Since the *derived* classes use a common signature for operations such as **area()**, clients can then operate on any of the *derived shapes* using a *base* class pointer or reference. This capability allows a client to develop a function that can operate on any type of *Shape* and is not dependent on a specific type.

Typically, the *virtual* member functions in the *derived* classes have the same signature as their *base* class. ANSI C++ allows the return value of the virtual functions in the *base* and *derived* classes to differ in a limited way. A *virtual* function in the *base* class can return a pointer or reference to a *base* object, and the *derived* class version can return a pointer or a reference to a *derived* object.

The *virtual* declarations tell the compiler that the *base* class is specifying a common design interface for the *derived* classes. The compiler uses these declarations to differentiate the regular member functions that are implemented at *base* level from the virtual functions that are implemented by the *derived* classes. In the following example, the *Circle* class has been incorporated into the *Shape* class hierarchy by inheriting the properties of the *Shape* class and implementing the required virtual functions (Figure 10.4):

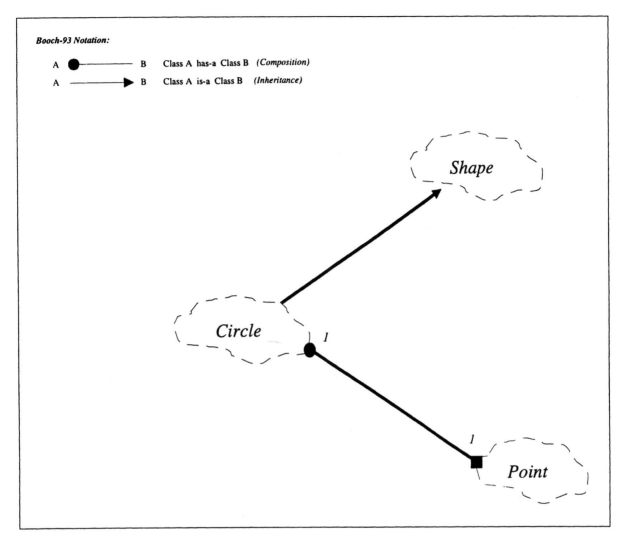

FIGURE 10.4 Circle class diagram.

```
//              CIRCLE.H Header File
#ifndef CIRCLE_H
#define CIRCLE_H

        const      double      PI = acos( -1.0 ) ;

        typedef    short       Radius ;

        class Circle: public Shape
        {
                private:
                        Point center ;       // center coordinate
                        Radius radius ;

                        // Utility function
                        Boolean erase( void ) ;

                public:
```

```
                    // Constructor
                    Circle( Coordinate x, Coordinate y, Radius new_radius,
                            Color interior_color) ;

                    // Graphical processing functions
                    virtual Boolean draw( void ) const ;
                    virtual Boolean paint( Color new_color ) ;
                    virtual Boolean move( Coordinate x , Coordinate y ) ;

                    // Arithmetic processing functions
                    virtual float area( void ) const ;
                    virtual float perimeter( void ) const ;
            } ;

#endif                 // CIRCLE_H Header File
```

The *Circle* class implements the virtual functions by using the prototypes defined in the *Shape* class. The use of the **virtual** keyword for *Circle* member functions is optional. However, as a good programming practice, the **virtual** keyword is used to differentiate the *Circle* virtual and nonvirtual functions.

```
//              CIRCLE.CPP Source File
#include "shape.h"

Circle:: Circle( Coordinate x, Coordinate y,
      Radius new_radius,  Color interior_color)
      : Shape( interior_color ) , // initialize base class elements
      center( x , y ) , radius( new_radius )
{
}

Boolean Circle:: move( Coordinate x , Coordinate y )
{
      Boolean status_flag = true ;

      // move circle to the new coordinate
      center = Point( x , y ) ;

      // invoke graphic primitives to erase the current circle

      // redraw circle by invoking graphic primitives
      status_flag = draw() ;
      return( status_flag ) ;
}

Boolean Circle:: draw( void ) const
{
      // invoke graphic primitives
}

Boolean Circle:: paint( Color new_color )
{
      // invoke graphic primitives
}

float Circle:: area( void ) const
{
```

```
        float current_area = radius * radius * PI ;
        return( current_area ) ;
}

float Circle:: perimeter( void ) const
{
        float current_perimeter = 2 * PI * radius ;
        return( current_perimeter ) ;
}
```

The **Circle()** constructor uses the **Shape()** and **Point()** constructors to initialize a *Circle* object. First the **Shape()** constructor initializes the base segment (color), then the **Point()** function initializes the *center* coordinates (Figure 10.5). The interaction diagram illustrates the order of object construction for the composed elements and the base segments.

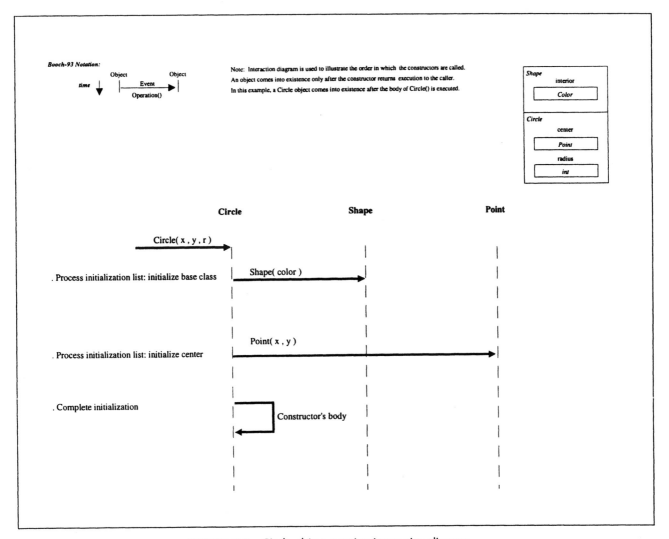

FIGURE 10.5   Circle object creation interaction diagram.

Using the above virtual definitions for *Circle*, **test_shape()** is implemented to access the *Circle* (derived) class member functions:

```
//                Test Driver Source File
#include <iostream.h>        // Stream I/O Class Library
#include "shape.h"           // Shape Class Library
int main( int , char ** )
{
        Circle round_shape( 1 , 3 , 4, RED) ;
                        // center: (1,3) , radius = 4, Color = Red

        test_shape( cout, round_shape ) ;
                        // reference the round_shape object using a
                        // Shape reference (Upcasting)
        return( 0 ) ;
}

void test_shape( ostream &output_stream, Shape &current )
{
        output_stream << "\n\t Area of Shape:"  <<
                        current.area() ;
        output_stream << "\n\t Perimeter of Shape:" <<
                        current.perimeter() ;
        return ;
}
```

The **test_shape()** function obtains the address of a *Circle* object (**round_shape**). Through a base class *Shape* reference (*upcasting* or *widening*), the **test_shape()** function invokes the applicable *Circle* class member functions. After the type of shape referenced by the **current** pointer is recognized, the relevant member functions are invoked. The generic implementation of the **test_shape()** function also allows the function to operate on other types of shapes.

In the following example, the *Shape* class is used to create a new *Rectangle* shape (Figure 10.6):

```
//            RECTANGLE.H Header File
#ifndef RECTANGLE_H
#define RECTANGLE_H

        class Rectangle: public Shape
        {
                private:
                        Point upper_left , lower_right ;
                                // upper left and lower right coordinates
                public:
                        Rectangle( Coordinate x1, Coordinate y1,
                                Coordinate x2, Coordinate y2,
                                Color interior_color ) ;
                        virtual Boolean draw( void ) const ;
                        virtual Boolean paint( Color new_color ) ;
                        virtual Boolean move( Coordinate x , Coordinate y ) ;
                        virtual float area( void ) const ;
                        virtual float perimeter( void ) const ;
        } ;

#endif// RECTANGLE_H Header File
```

As is evident, the *Rectangle* class provides the same design interface as *Circle* but the virtual functions' implementations are different. The use of inheritance incorporates the *Rectangle* class into the *Shapes* library. By compiling and linking the new *Shape* library with the client software, functions such as **test_shape()** will be able to handle *Rectangle* shapes. Because C++ supports *polymorphism*, the client source files remain unaffected by changes to the *Shapes* library. The resulting flexibility plays an important role in software evolution, maintainability, and reusability.

```
//                    RECTANGLE.CPP Source File
#include <stdlib.h>            // Standard Library
#include "shape.h"             // Shape Class Library

Rectangle:: Rectangle( Coordinate x1, Coordinate y1,
                       Coordinate x2, Coordinate y2,  Color interior_color )
     : Shape( interior_color ), upper_left( x1 , y1 ) , lower_right( x2 , y2 )
{
}

Boolean Rectangle:: move( Coordinate x , Coordinate y )
{
      // invoke graphic primitives
}

Boolean Rectangle:: draw( void ) const
{
      // invoke graphic primitives
}

Boolean Rectangle:: paint( Color new_color )
{
      // invoke graphic primitives
}

float Rectangle:: area( void ) const
{
      float current_area, width , length ;

      // use coordinates to compute length and width
      length = abs( upper_left.x_coordinate() -
                         lower_right.x_coordinate() ) ;
      width = abs( upper_left.y_coordinate() -
                         lower_right.y_coordinate() ) ;
      // use length and width to compute area
      current_area = length * width ;
      return( current_area ) ;
}

float Rectangle:: perimeter( void ) const
{
      float current_perimeter , width , length ;

      // use coordinates to compute length and width
      length = abs( upper_left.x_coordinate() -
                         lower_right.x_coordinate() ) ;
      width = abs( upper_left.y_coordinate() -
                         lower_right.y_coordinate() ) ;
      // use length and width to compute area
      current_perimeter = 2 * (length + width) ;
      return( current_perimeter ) ;
}
```

Polymorphism also applies to indirectly inherited classes. For example, the *Square* class is derived from the *Rectangle* class to create a more customized version of *Rectangle* (Figure 10.6):

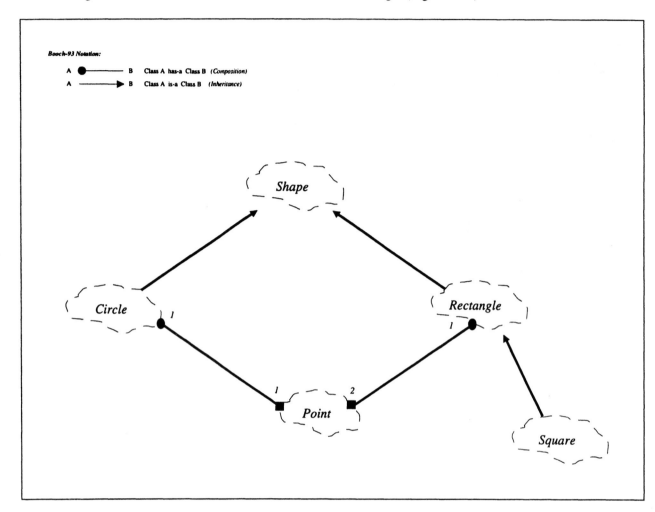

FIGURE 10.6   Rectangle and square class diagram.

```
//           SQUARE.H Header File
#ifndef SQUARE_H
#define SQUARE_H

    typedef     unsigned short      Length ;

    class Square: public Rectangle
    {
        public:
            Square(Coordinate x1, Coordinate y1, Length side,
                Color interior_color ) ;
            virtual Boolean draw( void ) const ;
            virtual Boolean paint( Color new_color ) ;
    } ;

#endif         // SQUARE_H Header File
```

The *Square* class uses the symmetry of a square shape to provide faster implementations for the **draw()** and **paint()** functions. For this purpose, the *Square* class uses most of the existing resources of *Rectangle* and reimplements only a few of the features provided by the *Rectangle* class. For example, the *Square* class uses the existing data elements in *Rectangle* to identify the coordinates of a square object, and it also reuses the *Rectangle* implementation of the **move()**, **area()**, and **perimeter()** functions:

```
//              SQUARE.CPP Source File
#include "shape.h"

Square:: Square(Coordinate x1, Coordinate y1, Length side,
                                Color interior_color )
        : Rectangle( x1, y1, x1 + side , y1 - side , interior_color)
               // initialize base elements
{
}

Boolean Square:: draw( void ) const
{
        // invoke optimized graphic primitives for square
}

Boolean Square:: paint( Color new_color )
{
        // invoke optimized graphic primitives for square
}
```

In the above example, the *Square* class does not specify any data members of its own. Therefore, the **Square()** constructor needs only to use the **Rectangle()** constructor to complete the initialization process. Figure 10.7 illustrates the construction process for a *Square* object.

In the absence of an implementation for a virtual function at the *derived* class level, the compiler uses the *base* class implementation. In the following **test_shape()** function, the *Square* class implementation of the **draw()** function is used to operate on a *Square* class object. For the **perimeter()** and **area()** functions the *Rectangle* class implementations are invoked:

```
Boolean test_shape( ostream &output_stream, Shape &current )
{
        Boolean status ;

        output_stream << "\n\t Area of Shape:"  <<
                        current.area() ;// same as rectangle
        output_stream << "\n\t Perimeter of Shape:" <<
                        current.perimeter() ;// same as rectangle
        status = current.draw() ;// unique to square

        return( status ) ;
}
```

10.3 DYNAMIC BINDING

In the previous examples, the calls to the shape library functions are somehow resolved by first recognizing the type of the object, and then calling the appropriate derived class member functions. C++ provides the ability for determining the applicable derived class member function at run time (*dynamic binding*) or compile time (*static binding*), but how does this process work?

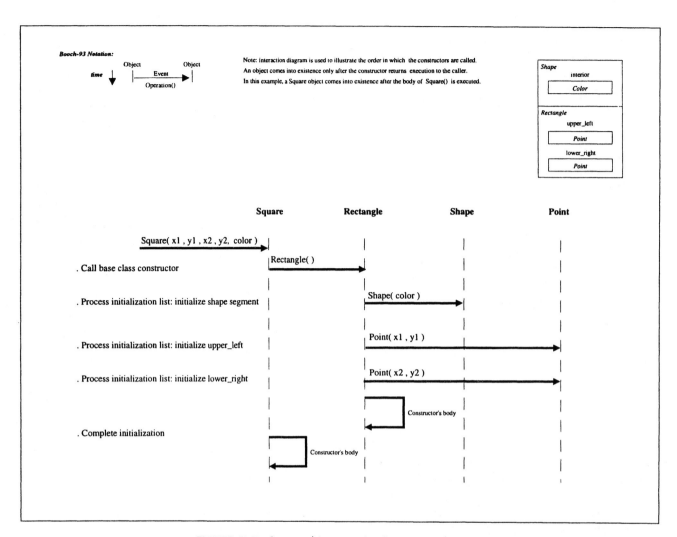

FIGURE 10.7   Square object creation interaction diagram.

The actual process of object recognition varies among C++ compilers but the concept is similar. Most C++ compilers use function pointer tables for implementing *dynamic binding*. This mechanism keeps the data recognition and implementation hidden from the software developer, and at the same time provides an efficient solution for object recognition. For each class containing virtual functions the compiler creates a *virtual-table*, also known as a *v-table*. The *v-table* is a function pointer table that contains the address of every virtual function in a class. The *Circle*, *Rectangle*, and *Square* classes each have a distinct *v-table* in memory that will contain the starting addresses of their virtual member functions (Figure 10.8). Each instance of the *Circle*, *Rectangle*, and *Square* classes will have a hidden pointer to its applicable *v-table*. Using this hidden pointer in the object (Figure 10.8), the **test_shape()** function locates the *v-table* in memory, performs a table lookup to obtain the address of the virtual function, and invokes the virtual function. Since the compiler requires the same design interface for all derived classes, and the same function names and prototypes are used in each class, the applicable functions are easily invoked via the *v-table* function pointers. Most importantly, the process is transparent to software developers.

For *derived* classes (such as the *Square* class) that do not support their own implementation of a virtual function, the *v-table* entry for the virtual function points to the *base* class implementation. Since the *Square* class has not provided an implementation for the **move()**, **area()**, and **perimeter()** functions, the *Square* class *v-table* entries will point to the *Rectangle* class implementations, but the **draw()** and **paint()** functions point to the *Square* class implementations (Figure 10.9).

Through *polymorphism*, a client program can create a *heterogeneous* list (Figure 10.3). A *heterogeneous* list is used to maintain different but related data objects. In the following example, the **main()** function creates a *heterogeneous Shape* list by using the **make_shape()** function. The **test_shape()** function is then used to operate

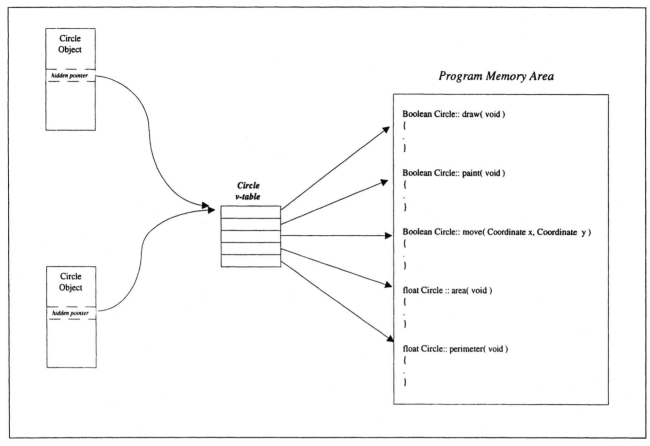

FIGURE 10.8 Circle class virtual table overview.

on the members of the *heterogeneous* list by displaying the area and computing the perimeter of each. Finally, the *heterogeneous* list is destroyed by using the **delete_shape()** function to perform the cleanup operation.

```
//              Test Driver Source File
#include <iostream.h>              // Stream I/O Class Library
#include "shape.h"                 // Shape Class Library

#define MAX_NUM_SHAPES            3

Shape * make_shape( int i ) ;
void delete_shape ( Shape *current ) ;
Boolean test_shape( ostream &output_stream, Shape *current ) ;

int main( int , char ** )
{
    Shape *list[MAX_NUM_SHAPES] ;
    int i ;

    // create a heterogeneous list and fill the Shape list array
    // using different shapes
    for( i = 0 ; i < MAX_NUM_SHAPES ; i++ )
    {
        list[i] = make_shape( i ) ;
    }
```

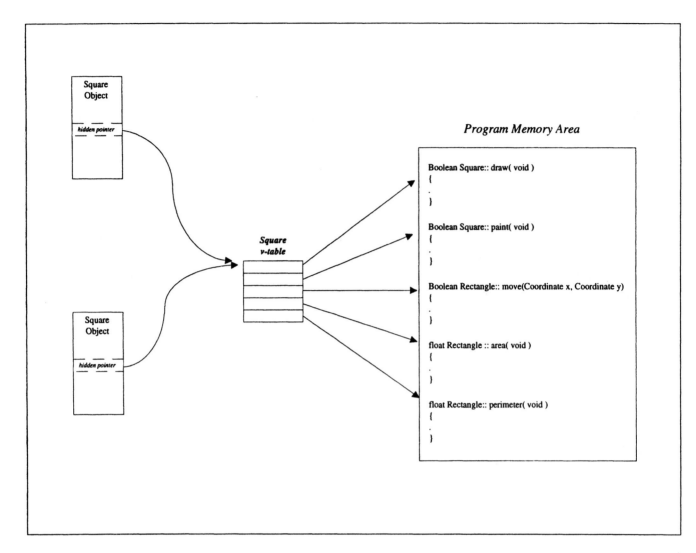

FIGURE 10.9 Square class virtual-table overview.

```
        // process each shape in the list
        for( i = 0 ; i < MAX_NUM_SHAPES ; i++ )
        {
            test_shape( cout, list[i] ) ;
        }

        // clean up the shape
        for( i = 0 ; i < MAX_NUM_SHAPES ; i++ )
        {
            delete_shape( list[i]  ) ;
        }
}

Boolean test_shape( ostream &output_stream, Shape *current )
{
        Boolean status ;

        output_stream << "\n\t Area of Shape:"  <<
            current->area()  ;
```

```
        output_stream << "\n\t Perimeter of Shape:" <<
            current->perimeter() ;
        status = current->draw() ;
        return( status ) ;
}


Shape * make_shape( int i )
{
        Shape *current ;
        if( i == 0 )
            current = new Circle( 1 , 3 , 4 , RED ) ;
        else if( i == 1 )
            current = new Rectangle( 8, 5, 12, -2, GREEN ) ;
        else
            current = new Square( -6 , 3 , 3 , BLUE ) ;
        return( current ) ;
}


void delete_shape ( Shape *current )
{
        delete current ;
}
```

Owing to the nature of *polymorphism* and *dynamic binding*, virtual functions cannot be inlined. The rationale behind this restriction is as follows:

```
class Rectangle: public Shape
{
        public:
            inline virtual Boolean draw( void ) ;  // meaningless
        // other details left out
} ;


//          Test Driver Source File
Boolean test_shape( ostream &output_stream, Shape &current )
{
        // other details left out
        status = current.draw() ; // cannot expand body here
}
```

The compiler cannot expand the body of the virtual **draw**() function in the calling function, because at compile time, the call to the applicable **draw**() function cannot be resolved. Since **test_shape**() can operate on any derivation of the *Shape* class, requiring the body of the virtual function (inline) to be expanded is a meaningless operation. The compiler will ignore inline requests for virtual functions and use the functions as

10.4 ABSTRACT CLASS

Abstract Cookies

Concrete Cookies

When *inheritance* is used to provide polymorphic behavior, at times there are no suitable implementations for the virtual functions in the base class. For instance, there are no real implementations for the **perimeter()**, **area()**, and **draw()** functions for the *Shape* class. In Section 10.2, for the sake of completeness the virtual functions in the *Shape* class were implemented with *do-nothing* functions. In the client software, the *Shape* class alone does not serve any purpose and the do-nothing function implementations introduce an incipient danger by allowing the client program to define instances of the *Shape* class. The following code could be written:

```
int main( int , char ** )
{
      Shape generic_shape ; // meaningless operation

      cout << "Area: " << generic_shape.area() ;
      test_shape( &generic_shape ) ;

}
```

A function such as **test_shape()** invokes the do-nothing functions but these virtual functions do not perform any real task. The do-nothing functions are logically inappropriate and this kind of a design is not good programming practice. Most importantly, **do-nothing virtual functions in the base class do not enforce the implementation of a common design interface for a design hierarchy, because they do not require the derived classes to provide an implementation for the virtual functions**. In the above example, the purpose of *Shape* is to allow a client to treat different types of shapes such as *Circle* and *Rectangle* homogeneously.

If the designer of the *Circle* class does not implement a corresponding virtual function, the programs operating on the *Circle* shapes would then use the *base* class (*Shape*) implementation. Since the *Shape* class functions are do-nothing functions, the client programs get meaningless results. The do-nothing implementations at the *base* level make the implementations of the virtual functions at the *derived* level optional, and the compiler cannot enforce their implementation.

When a *base* class does not have a meaningful implementation for a virtual function, the designer should define the function as a *pure virtual* function. A *pure virtual* function is a null set and explicitly tells the compiler that the *base* class does not have a suitable implementation for the function and that the virtual function prototype specifies only the design interface.

```
class Name
{
      access_level:
```

```
        virtual function_prototype( ) = 0 ; // pure virtual function
} ;
```

A *pure virtual* function is defined by terminating the virtual function prototype with an *assignment* operator (=) and zero. The following example uses the *pure virtual* functions for the *Shape* class. This class definition reflects the fact that there are no suitable implementations at this level and that the function declarations are only identifying a common design interface:

```
//              SHAPE.H Header File
#ifndef SHAPE_H
#define SHAPE_H

    enum Color { RED, BLUE, GREEN, WHITE, BLACK, YELLOW } ;

    typedef      bool    Boolean ;

    class Shape
    {
        private:
                Color interior ;

        public:
                inline Shape( Color interior_color ) ;
                inline Color color( void ) const ;

                virtual Boolean draw( void ) const = 0 ;
                virtual Boolean paint( Color new_color ) = 0 ;
                virtual Boolean move( Coordinate x , Coordinate y ) = 0 ;
                virtual float area( void ) const = 0 ;
                virtual float perimeter( void ) const = 0 ;
                        // better implementation than the one in Section 10.2
    } ;

    inline Shape:: Shape( Color interior_color )
            : interior ( interior_color )
    {
    }

    inline Color Shape:: color( void ) const
    {
            return( interior ) ;
    }

    // include the applicable subclass definitions in the hierarchy
    #include "circle.h"
    #include "rectangle.h"
    #include "square.h"

#endif              // SHAPE_H Header File
```

A class containing at least one *pure virtual* function is called an *abstract class*. For example, the above *Shape* class contains five *pure virtual* functions, which makes it an *abstract class* (Figure 10.10).

C++ prevents a program from defining an instance of an *abstract class* (object). For example, the client program cannot define instances of the *shape* class.

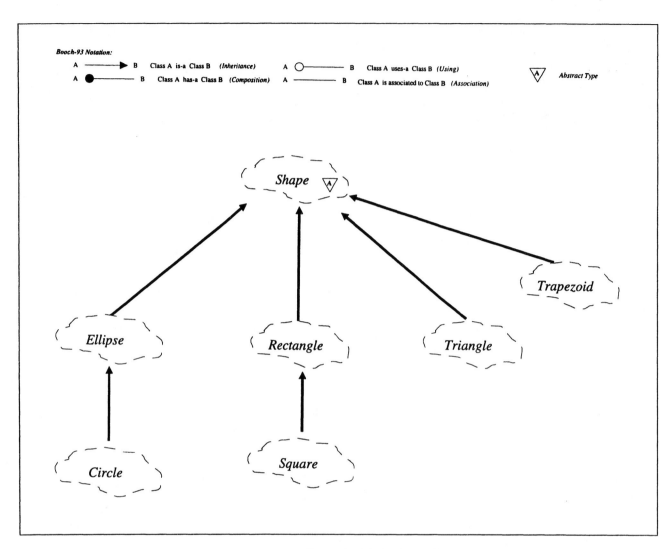

FIGURE 10.10 Shape class design hierarchy.

```
//              Test Driver Source File
#include "shape.h"
int main( int , char ** )
{
      Shape generic_shape ; // illegal definition, compiler error

      generic_shape.draw() ;
      // other details left out
}
```

The above ***generic_shape*** definition results in a compiler error because *Shape* is an *abstract class*. If the above ***generic_shape*** definition were allowed, the client would be able to invoke any of the *pure virtual* functions. However, since there are no implementations for these functions, the program would crash. The restriction prevents a client from invoking the *pure virtual* functions inadvertently. In contrast to the *Shape* class, the *Rectangle, Circle*, and *Square* classes provide implementations for their virtual functions and a client can freely define instances of these classes. These classes are referred to as *concrete* classes. A *concrete class* does not contain any *pure virtual* functions, and thus a client can define instances of the class.

Through the *pure virtual* functions, an *abstract* class also enforces the implementation of *pure virtual* functions in the derived classes. If a derived class does not have an implementation for a *pure virtual* function of the base class, then the derived class also becomes an *abstract class* and instances of the derived class cannot be defined. Since the compiler applies the same restriction to the derived class, the derived class is forced to provide implementations for the virtual functions. For example, the *Shape* class requires its derived classes such as *Circle* to provide implementations for the *pure virtual* functions. If the *Circle* class does not provide an implementation for the **draw()** function, the *Circle* class also becomes an *abstract class*, and a designer will be unable to define instances of *Circle*. If the *Shape* class uses the do-nothing functions defined in Section 10.2 instead of *pure virtual*, the *Circle* class will not be forced to implement the virtual functions.

In a design hierarchy, an *abstract class* creates and enforces a standard design interface for its current and future *derived* classes. *Pure virtual* function declarations explicitly specify the minimum design requirements for the implementation of a *derived* class.

10.5 POLYMORPHISM AND CLASS MANAGEMENT

A constructor function cannot be a **virtual** function, because in the absence of an implementation for the derived class, the **virtual** keyword tells the compiler to use the *base* class implementation. To construct a *derived* object, both *base* and *derived* constructors must be called to initialize the applicable memory spaces of the object. Thus, a virtual constructor becomes meaningless. In addition, the type of the object is known at the point of construction, and creation of polymorphic behavior is unnecessary. In the following example, the definition specifies that a *Circle* object is being dynamically allocated. After the allocation of the memory space, both **Shape()** and **Circle()** constructors must be called. Even though the object is being referenced using a *base* class pointer, the exact type of the object is known at the point of creation:

```
Shape *current = new Circle( 1 , 3 , 4 ) ; // create a circle object
```

However, a destructor function can be defined as **virtual**. Actually, if a *base* class contains virtual functions, the *base* class destructor must also be a virtual function. A virtual destructor guarantees proper object cleanup. The following example demonstrates the need for a virtual destructor. The following *Shape* class uses a regular destructor function:

```
//          SHAPE.H Header File
#ifndef SHAPE_H
#define SHAPE_H

    enum Color { RED, BLUE, GREEN, WHITE, BLACK, YELLOW } ;
    typedef      bool      Boolean ;

    class Shape
    {
        private:
            Color interior ;
        public:
            inline Shape( Color interior_color ) ;
            ~Shape() ;
            inline Color color( void ) const ;
            virtual Boolean draw( void ) const = 0 ;
            virtual Boolean paint( Color new_color ) = 0 ;
            virtual Boolean move(Coordinate x, Coordinate y) = 0;
            virtual float area( void ) const = 0 ;
            virtual float perimeter( void ) const = 0 ;
    } ;
    // other details left out

#endif            // SHAPE_H Header File
```

Any client program using the above *Shape* class definition will not behave properly when a derived shape is destroyed by using the *Shape* class pointer or reference. A derived *Shape* object must be destroyed by calling the applicable destructor function, and then the memory space is deallocated. The **delete_shape()** function (in Section 10.3) operates on a derived *Shape* object (for example, circle) using a *base* class pointer. However, the actual type of *Shape* is not known. During object destructions, only the destructor for the *Shape* class is invoked. The *derived* portion of the object is not cleaned up because the *derived* class destructor is never called:

```
void delete_shape( Shape *current )
{
        delete current ;
                // only invokes the destructor for the Shape class.
                // The derived class destructor is never called.
}
```

The **delete_shape()** function does not provide enough information to identify the type of shape at compile time. The type of shape must then be recognized at run time. Therefore, the compiler must be instructed to put provisions for dynamic binding of object destruction into **delete_shape()**. The current implementation of the *Shape* class does not provide enough information to incorporate dynamic binding in the **delete_shape()** function. By making the *Shape* destructor **virtual**, the compiler can solve the problem of object destruction in the **delete_shape()** function. The virtual destructor causes the compiler to capture the addresses of destructors into *v-tables*. Programs such as the **delete_shape()** function can then recognize the type of object and invoke the applicable destructors.

```
//              SHAPE.H Header File
#ifndef SHAPE_H
#define SHAPE_H

    class Shape
    {
            private:
                Color interior ;

            public:
                inline Shape( Color interior_color ) ;
                virtual ~Shape() ; // fixes the problem with destruction
                inline Color color( void ) const ;
                virtual Boolean draw( void ) const = 0 ;
                virtual Boolean paint( Color new_color ) = 0 ;
                virtual Boolean move(Coordinate x , Coordinate y) = 0;
                virtual float area( void ) const = 0 ;
                virtual float perimeter( void ) const = 0 ;
    } ;

    // other details left out

#endif       // SHAPE_H Header File
```

Using the above definition, the virtual destructor allows a C++ program to properly destroy an object by invoking the *derived* class destructor followed by the base class destructor. **As a design rule, any class containing a virtual function must also use a virtual destructor.**

C++ restricts a destructor from being defined as *purely virtual*. Since a destructor is always called, a *pure virtual* destructor would cause the program to crash.

```
class Shape
{
    public:
            virtual ~Shape() = 0 ; // illegal, compiler error
} ;
```

C++ has placed several additional restrictions on the interaction of constructor and destructor functions with the virtual functions of the class. If a *base* class constructor invokes one of the virtual functions, the *base* class version is invoked instead of its *derived* implementation.

```
class Shape
{
    private:
            Color interior ;
    public:
            inline Shape( Color interior_color ) ;
            virtual Boolean draw( void ) const ;
                // other details left out
} ;

Shape:: Shape( Color interior_color )
    : interior( interior_color )
{
    draw() ;// invoke base class: Shape:: draw() implementation
}
```

At the time of *base* class construction, the *derived* elements have not been initialized. To invoke the *derived* class version is meaningless, because the *derived* class implementation may use the uninitialized values of the *derived* data members. Therefore, calls to the virtual functions in the *base* class constructor function cause the *base* class implementation to be invoked. However, if the *base* class functions are *purely virtual*, then the program's behavior would become unpredictable.

```
class Shape
{
    private:
            Color interior ;
    public:
            inline Shape( Color interior_color ) ;
            virtual Boolean draw( void ) const = 0 ; // pure virtual function
                // other details left out
} ;
```

The **Shape()** class constructor (above) calls the base class implementation of **draw()**. However, **draw()** is a *pure virtual* function and does not have an implementation for *Shape*. In this case, the program will produce unpredictable results and may crash.

The above limitation does not apply to a *derived* class constructor. The following *Rectangle* class constructor will invoke the *Rectangle* **draw()** function for both *Square* and *Rectangle* objects.

```
class Rectangle: public Shape
{
    private:
            Point upper_left , lower_right ;
                // upper left and lower right coordinates
    public:
```

```
        Rectangle( Coordinate x1, Coordinate y1,
              Coordinate x2, Coordinate y2,
              Color interior_color ) ;
        virtual Boolean draw( void ) const ;
              // other details left out
} ;
Rectangle:: Rectangle( Coordinate x1, Coordinate y1,
              Coordinate x2, Coordinate y2,  Color interior_color )
      : Shape( interior_color ), upper_left( x1 , y1 ) , lower_right( x2 , y2 )
{
      draw() ; // invokes the derived class: Rectangle:: draw() implementation
}
```

In the case of a *Square* object, If *Rectangle* did not have an implementation for its virtual **draw**() function, the *Shape purely virtual* **draw**() function would be used and again the program's behavior would become unpredictable.

C++ applies the same restrictions to destructor functions. A call to a virtual function in the *base* class destructor causes the *base* class implementation to be invoked. During destruction of the *base* segment, the *derived* portion of the object has already been destroyed and its content is no longer predictable. If the *base* class implementation is purely virtual, the program's behavior would be unpredictable.

10.6 DYNAMIC CASTING

The clients of a design hierarchy (with polymorphic behavior) can use a pointer or reference to the *base* class type to operate on instances of *derived* classes. By effectively utilizing the polymorphic behavior, the client minimizes its dependencies on specific types of *derived* classes in the hierarchy. As new classes are added to the hierarchy, the client's code remains unaffected.

At times, however, a client may need access to features and operations unique to a *derived* class. For example, a client referencing a *Circle* object through a *Shape* pointer may need to use the **radius**() function, which is unique to *Circle*. In such a situation, the client must convert the *base* class pointer or reference to a *derived* class pointer or reference. The conversion allows the client to operate on the *derived* object and access features unique to it. The conversion of the *base* class pointer or reference to a *derived* pointer or reference is known as *downcasting* or *narrowing*. C++ supports *narrowing* through *dynamic casting*:

```
Derived_Type *derived_ptr =dynamic_cast<Derived_Type *> ( base_ptr ) ;
if( derived_ptr ) // if object is the expected type (narrowing is successful)
{
      // operate on the object
}
```

The C++ *dynamic cast* is a type-safe downcast. At run time, the casting operation is performed by comparing the data type information for the *derived* object to the specified data type in the cast. If the specified data type in the cast matches the one for the object, the *narrowing* is performed. Since the *derived* object may be a different type than the one specified by the cast, a *dynamic cast* may fail. For example, if a *Shape* pointer references a *Circle* object, an attempt to dynamically cast a *Shape* pointer to a *Rectangle* pointer will fail. Thus, this restriction prevents a *Circle* object from being treated as a *Rectangle*. When the *dynamic cast* fails, a null pointer is returned. In the following example, the **highlight**() function narrows the *Shape* object pointer to *Circle* and operates on it only if it is an instance of *Circle*:

```
//            CAD.CPP Source File
#include "shape.h"        // Shape Class Library

void CAD:: highlight( Shape *current )
```

```
{
        Circle *round = dynamic_cast<Circle *>( current ) ;
        if( round ) // if shape is actually a circle
        {
                // do operations specific to Circle such as round->radius()
        }
}
```

Since a *derived* object can also be accessed through a *base class reference*, *dynamic casting* also applies to references. A *dynamic cast* for a reference is slightly different than the one for a pointer. Since a null address cannot be returned for a reference when the *dynamic cast* fails, the C++ standard **bad_cast** exception is raised (*refer to Chapter 8*):

```
try
{
        Type & derived_reference =
                        dynamic_cast<Type &>( base_reference ) ;
}
catch( bad_cast ) // when specified cast fails
{
        // recover from invalid cast
}
```

In the following example, the **highlight()** function is reimplemented using the reference implementation:

```
//                      Test Driver Source File
#include "shape.h"// Shape Class Library

void CAD:: highlight( Shape &current )
{
        try
        {
                Circle &round = dynamic_cast<Circle &>( current ) ;
                // do operations specific to Circle such as round.radius()
        }
        catch( bad_cast ) // if shape is not a circle do not do anything
        {
                ;       // do-nothing
        }
}
```

The use of exception handling for *reference downcasting* increases the software execution overhead. Since the pointer implementation does not include the overhead of C++ exception handling, it may be a better alternative when failures are common.

Since the data type information is stored in the *derived* class's *v-table*, a dynamic cast only applies to design hierarchies with polymorphic behavior. When a dynamic cast is applied to the objects of a class which does not support **virtual** functions, the program's behavior becomes unpredictable.

The compiler incorporates provisions in the executable code for allowing a *base* class reference to be narrowed to an intermediate data type at run time. For instance, a *Shape* reference to a *Square* object can be narrowed to a *Rectangle* reference (Figure 10.1). Thus, the narrowing operation can performed to the level appropriate for accessing the unique features of a class. In addition, the C++ *dynamic casting* feature handles type conversions for complex design hierarchies such as those using multiple inheritance and multiple layers of single inheritance (Figure 10.11). For example, a *Base 1* pointer referencing a *Derived 4* object can be narrowed to a *Base 2, Derived 1*, or a *Derived 3* pointer.

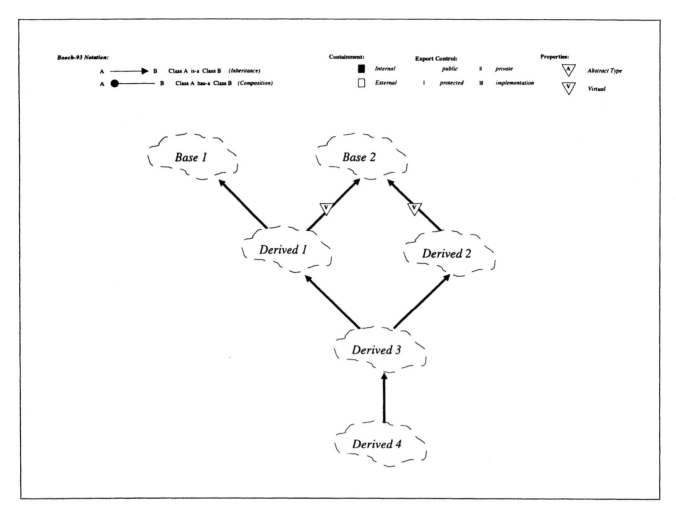

FIGURE 10.11   An example of a complex class design hierarchy.

Dynamic casting allows the clients of a design hierarchy to invoke operations unique to the *derived* classes. In the previous example, the **CAD:: highlight**() function keeps its parameter list independent of the derived *Shape* objects by using the *Shape* class pointer. Within the body of the function, the *Circle* objects are treated uniquely. This approach allows the client's interface to remain independent of a specific derived type in the hierarchy while still accessing unique features of a *derived* type.

10.7 RUN-TIME TYPE IDENTIFICATION

C++ provides another mechanism for identifying the type of an object through *Run-Time Type Identification (RTTI)*. Although the actual implementations vary among compiler vendors, a *type_info* class is used to maintain information for a data type. For instance, a *concrete* derived class contains a *type_info* class (Figure 10.12). The *type_info* class maintains the *derived* class data type information. A C++ programs access the *type_info* class through the *type_info* library and the **typeid**() keyword. For example, the type of a *derived* object accessed through a *base* class pointer or reference is determined by using the **typeid**() keyword. This function returns a constant reference to the *type_info* object. The member functions of the *type_info* class are used to recognize the type of object.

The *type_info* class provides the following member functions: **operator==( )**, **operator !=( )**, **name**(), and **before**(). In the following example, **typeid**() is used to access *type_info* for a *Circle* object:

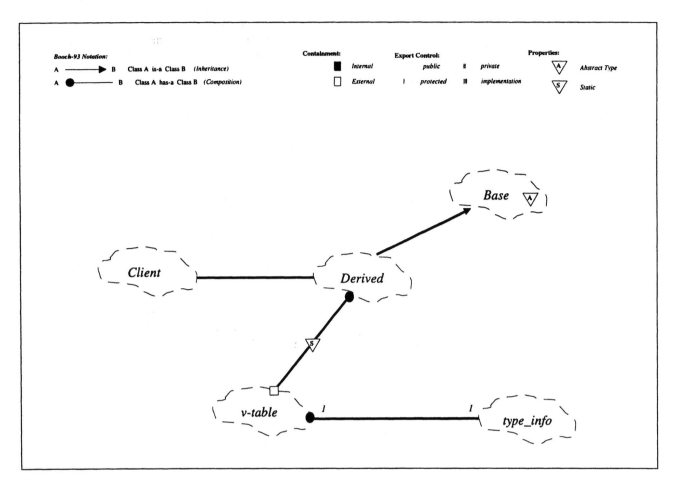

FIGURE 10.12 RTTI class diagram.

```
//              Test Driver Source File
#include <typeinfo.h>        // type_info class definition
#include "shape.h"           // Shape Class Library

void shapes_type( Shape *current )
{
        // display the data type information for the shape
        cout << "Shape's Type:" << typeid( *current ).name() << endl;

        // if shape is a circle => display radius
        // is treated as:
        // typeid( *current ).operator ==( typeid( Circle ) )
        if( typeid( *current ) == typeid( Circle ) )
        {
                Circle *round = dynamic_cast<Circle *>( current ) ;
                cout << "Radius: " << round->radius() << endl ;
        }
}
```

The **typeid()** function takes a pointer or a reference to an object and returns a constant reference to *type_info*, which contains the data type information. The **typeid()** keyword provides an interface to RTTI while

encapsulating the implementation and internal details of RTTI across compilers. The following list identifies the
typeid() prototypes based on usage:

```
const type_info & typeid( Type *object_pointer )
                            throw( bad_typeid ) ;
const type_info & typeid( Type &object_reference ) ;
const type_info & typeid( Type ) ;
```

The **typeid(Type *)** function throws a **bad_typeid** exception whenever a null pointer is passed to it. This
exception is part of the ANSI *exception* class library (*refer to Chapter 8*).

The *type_info* object accessed through the **typeid()** function supports the following operations:

1. **Data Type Comparison**: The *equality (==)* and *nonequality (!=)* operators have been overloaded for the
   type_info class and are used to compare the data types of the objects to one another. In the previous
   example, the **typeid()** function returns references to *Circle type_info* and the object referenced by **current**.
   The **type_info:: operator ==()** is then called to compare the data types:

   ```
   if( typeid( *current ) == typeid( Circle ) )
           // typeid( current ).operator ==( typeid(Circle) )
   ```

   The data type comparison compares the specified type and not the actual data type. For example, the
   current pointer is a *Shape* pointer and must be dereferenced in order to determine whether the object
   pointed to by **current** is a *Circle* or not.

2. **Name**: The **name()** function returns a constant text string identifying the type of data referenced by the
   pointer or reference. In the previous example, the **type_info:: name()** function displays the text description
   for the shape's type:

   ```
   cout << "Shape's Type:" << typeid( current ).name() << endl;
   ```

3. **Data Type Ordering**: The **type_info:: before()** function specifies whether the type of an object appears
   before another object's type in the hierarchy:

   ```
   Boolean type_info:: before( type_info &reference_object ) ;
   ```

4. In the following example, the ordering of data types for *Rectangle* and *Square* objects is verified:

   ```
   if( typeid( rectangle_object ).before( typeid( square_object ) ) )
   {
           // do something based on the order of data
   }
   ```

The **typeid()** function has lower overhead than the C++ *dynamic cast* because it does not do all of the tasks
performed by the dynamic cast, such as downcasting to an intermediate level. When a client needs only to
recognize an object type and perform a task, the **typeid()** function is more suitable than *dynamic casting*. In the
following example, *derived* exception objects are caught using a *base System Exception* reference (Figure 10.13).
For exceptions that are an instance of the *Patient Exception* class, an alarm is sounded.

```
//       MONITOR.CPP Source File
Boolean Monitor:: log( ostream & os )
{
        Boolean data_logged = false ;
        try
        {
```

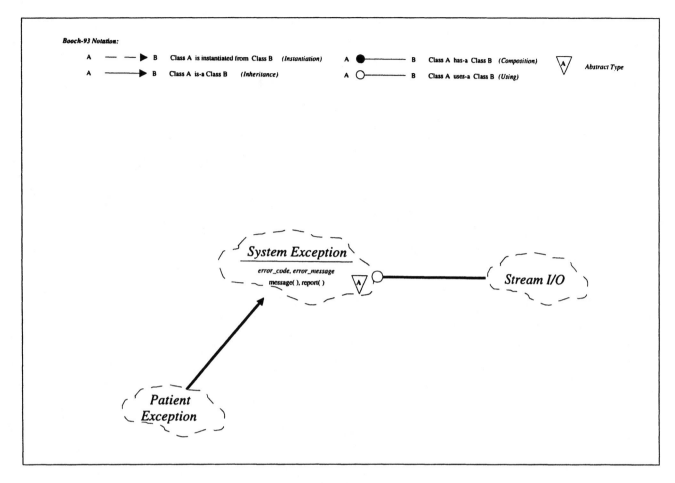

FIGURE 10.13 Circle object creation interaction diagram.

```
        // log patient's heart beat and temperature to the output stream
        os << "Heart Beat (PPM) : " << patient.heart_beat( ) <<
              "Temperature (C):    " << patient.temperature( ) ;
        data_logged = true ;
    }
    catch( System_Exception &error )
    {
        // log exception
        os << error.report() ;

        // sound an audio alarm for any type of error associated
        // with a patient
        if( typeid( error ) == typeid( Patient_Exception ) )
        {
            // sound alarm
            alarm.on() ;
        }
    }

    return( data_logged ) ;
}
```

When a hierarchy supports **virtual** functions, and a client requires access to the unique features of a *derived* class, *dynamic casting* is used. Section 10.6 provides several examples of *dynamic casting*.

10.8 APPLICATION OF DESIGN HIERARCHY TO ERROR HANDLING

As discussed in Chapter 2, error detection and handling is a *strategic* (global) issue and must be handled at the system architecture level. Since error detection and recovery span across the system architecture, a cohesive strategy will allow a standardized mechanism to detect and report exceptions across *module* and *subsystem* boundaries. By addressing error detection and recovery at the system architecture level, the class libraries provide a uniform and cohesive error-handling strategy. This approach prevents different development teams from creating their own unique interfaces and reporting mechanisms. In addition, the coupling between the client program and specific exception types is minimized.

In an object-oriented design, objects interact with each other. When an exception is detected by a member function of an object, it reports the condition to the applicable object(s), which then perform the necessary recovery procedure. The exception data types are incorporated in the design interface of the class libraries. On the basis of the design interfaces, the clients incorporate try-catch clauses in the appropriate places in order to catch and handle a thrown exception. In the following example, **method**() provides unique catch clauses for *File* and *Printer Exceptions*. In this implementation, there is a close coupling between the exception types and **method**(), because of how exceptions are defined:

```
#include "class.h"          // Class library

Client_Class:: method( )
{
      try
      {
            // code block
      }
      catch( Printer_Exception &perror )
      {
            // catch and handle printer errors
      }
      catch( File_Exception &ferror )
      {
            // catch and handle file errors
      }
}
```

With implementations such as the one illustrated in the above example, when a new type of exception is added to the software, each client method that needs to handle the exception must be updated. Since there is no relationship among the exceptions, the client code becomes affected and requires updating. The incorporating and handling for the new exception may require substantial software retesting and revalidation effort.

The use of a design hierarchy provides the means to standardize the error detection/recovery across the system architecture, such as the one depicted in Figure 10.14. The base *System Exception* class specifies standard interfaces for all types of exceptions that can occur during the execution of a program. Furthermore, the design hierarchy allows the functions in the software to catch any of the *derived* exceptions using a *System Exception* (*base*) reference or pointer:

```
#include "exception.h"//          Program's Exception library

Client_Class: method()
{
      try
```

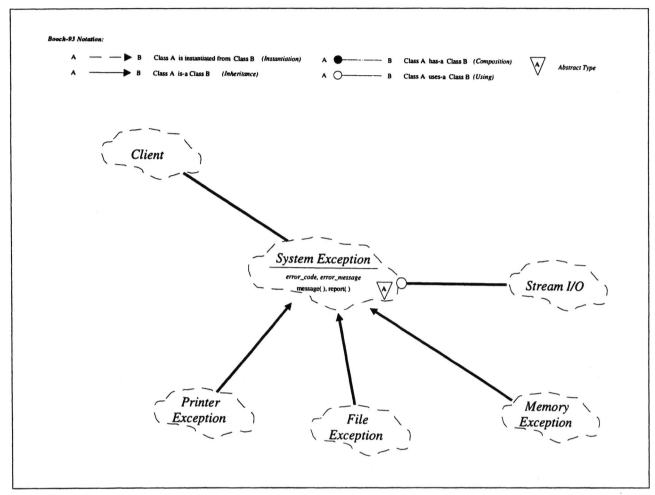

FIGURE 10.14 Circle object creation interaction diagram.

```
{
        // code block
}
catch( System_Exception &error ) // catch any type of exception
{
        // Handle all types of exceptions. For unique
        // exceptions use RTTI to recognize the specific type
        if( typeid( error ) == typeid( Derived_Name ) )
        {
                // handle the unique exception
        }
}
}
```

The above interface allows the client to catch any exception type defined in the design hierarchy. As new exceptions are added to the hierarchy, the client code remains unchanged. These programs need only to be recompiled and linked to the new version of the exception library. The above approach increases code extendibility and maintainability. For situations that require unique handling of a specific exception, *dynamic casting* and **typeid**() can be used in the **catch** block for identifying the exception type and then taking the appropriate steps.

A C++ based object-oriented design can be further evolved by combining the developed software error detection and reporting with the standardized C++ exception library. In Figure 10.15, the *System Exception* class inherits from the ANSI C++ *exception* class library and adds features unique to the software requirements. This approach allows the software design to build on a standardized library already equipped with resources. In addition, the software does not need to provide separate **catch** blocks for the C++ standardized *exception* and the custom exception design hierarchy. By extending the exception class library, the client's program catches both custom and ANSI C++ exceptions (Figure 10.15):

```
try
{
      // code block
}

      catch( exception &error )  // catch any type of exception
{
      // Handle any type of exception
}
```

10.9 OBJECT-ORIENTED PROGRAMMING CONSIDERATIONS

The classes in a design hierarchy exhibit the common characteristics of having the *base* class capture the common operations and attributes of the *derived* classes. In addition, the hierarchy specifies a common design interface for the *derived* classes through the use of **virtual** functions. The *derived* classes provide customized features through the regular member functions that address their unique needs. The following paragraphs define some guidelines for designing classes that provide *polymorphic* behavior:

1. **Virtual Functions**: Functions defined as **virtual** in the *base* class must be applicable to all of the *derived* classes. For instance, the **area()** and **draw()** functions specified in the *Shape* class make sense for any two-dimensional shape, whereas **width()** is applicable only to a *Rectangle* or *Square*. The **width()** function should be defined as a nonvirtual function at the *Rectangle* level (Figure 10.16):

    ```
    class Shape
    {
          public:
                // the following functions apply to any
                // two-dimensional shape:
                virtual Boolean draw( void ) const = 0 ;
                virtual Boolean area( void ) const = 0 ;

                // poor design: not applicable to shapes such as Circle
                virtual float width( void ) const ;
    } ;
    ```

2. **Implementation Enforcement**: **Virtual** functions that do not have a meaningful implementation at the *base* class level must be defined as *purely virtual*. The **draw()** function in the above example can be defined only for the *derived* classes. This practice will make implementations of these functions a requirement for the *derived* classes.

3. **Nonvirtual Functions**: The *base* class captures attributes and functions that are common to all derived classes. For example, the **color()** and **has_shadow()** functions are applicable to any type of shape and are mapped to the *Shape* class. Since the implementation for these functions does not vary between the *derived* classes, they are defined as nonvirtual:

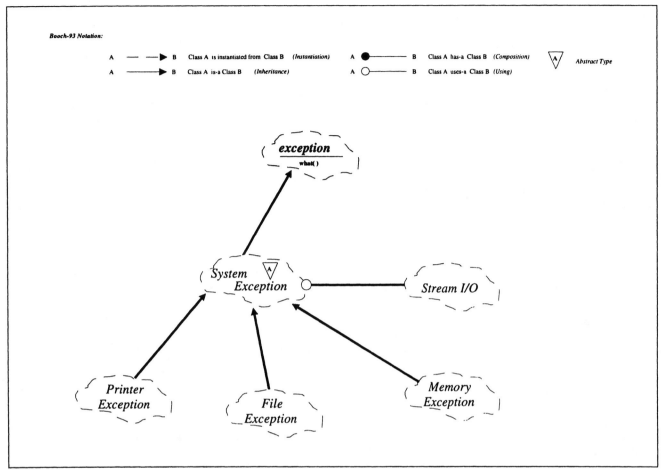

FIGURE 10.15 Custom exception class diagram.

```
class Shape
{
    private:
            // common attributes
            Color interior ;
            Boolean shadow ;
    public:
            // Access Functions
            Color color( void ) const ;
            Boolean has_shadow( void ) const ;
} ;
```

The *derived* classes provide the customized features unique to them. When these features do not need to be overridden by classes inheriting from the *derived* classes, they are declared and implemented as nonvirtual. For example, the **width()** and **radius()** functions are implemented as nonvirtual by the *Rectangle* and *Circle* classes, respectively.

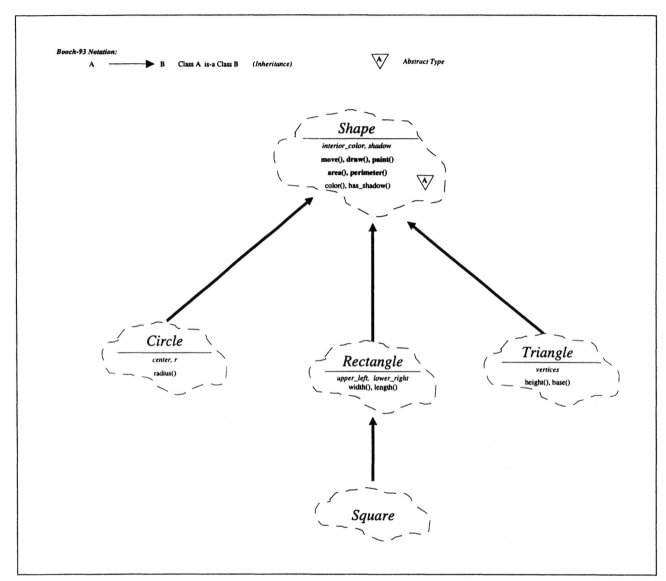

FIGURE 10.16 Shape class design hierarchy.

SUMMARY

Inheritance can be used to create a design umbrella for a group of derived classes. The *base* class defines the operations and features needed for the *derived* classes by specifying the function prototypes. The identified function declarations in the *base* class are then implemented by the *derived* classes. This approach permits the client to design programs that operate on different *derived* objects in a generic way. The ability to define similar operations and tasks for a group of *derived* classes is called *polymorphism.*

Polymorphic behavior is implemented in C++ using inheritance and **virtual** functions. **Virtual** functions are declared in the *base* class. These declarations instruct the compiler that the base class is requiring its *derived* classes to use the same interface and to provide an implementation for these functions. In addition, the **virtual** definition causes the *derived* class implementation to be invoked when a client accesses a *derived* object using a *base* class pointer or reference. For the *derived* classes that do not provide an implementation for a **virtual** function, the first immediate *base* class implementation is invoked instead.

Objects accessed using *base* class pointers permit designers to create programs that operate on different *derived* classes. This flexibility creates the *polymorphic* behavior but, naturally, increases complexity. The compiler must be able to recognize the type of objects at compile time (*static binding*) or create the object recognition provisions for the program's use at run time. The capability to identify objects at run time is known as *dynamic binding*. *Dynamic binding* is transparent to software developers and is implemented by the compiler using function pointer tables. The compiler creates a function pointer table (*v-table*) for each class containing virtual functions. At run time, the program accesses the *v-table* and invokes the applicable virtual function. With function pointers, *dynamic binding* has been efficiently implemented in the language.

For implementing and enforcing the design hierarchy, the base class may use *pure virtual* functions. A *purely virtual* function tells the compiler that there is no suitable implementation at the *base* class level, and that the function declaration is only identifying the design interface for all *derived* classes. Since no definition exists for the *purely virtual* function at the *base* class level, the compiler prevents a client from defining instances of the class. Thus, the *base* class becomes an *abstract class*. The *abstract class* permits the compiler to enforce the implementation of the *purely virtual* functions at the *derived* levels. If a *derived* class does not provide an implementation for a *purely virtual* function, the *derived* class also becomes an *abstract class*. This property allows the *base* class to enforce compliance with its design hierarchy.

Through *Run-Time Type Identification (RTTI)* and *dynamic casting*, C++ allows the client to identify the type of a *derived* object through its *base* class pointer or reference at run time, and then perform an operation specific to the *derived* type. With a *dynamic cast*, a *base* reference/pointer to a *derived* object is converted to a *derived* reference/pointer. If the type of object matches the one specified by the cast, the pointer or reference will be converted at run time. By using a *derived* pointer or reference, the client then accesses features unique to the *derived* class.

RTTI is provided through the **typeid()** keyword, which returns a constant reference to a *type_info* object at run time. This object contains data type information on a class in a design hierarchy. Using the *type_info* object, the client recognizes the type of an object and performs the applicable tasks. For data type comparison and recognition, *RTTI* provides the overloaded relational operators: **operator ==()** and **operator !=()**. It also provides a textual representation of a class name through its **name()** operation.

When a client needs to perform a task based on a unique type of an object, the use of *RTTI* is preferred over a *dynamic cast* for a design hierarchy with polymorphic behavior. This is because *RTTI* has a lower overhead than *dynamic casting*. However, when a client needs to access a method that is unique to a *derived* type, a *dynamic cast* is used instead.

Polymorphism is a powerful concept that plays a major role in the evolutionary development of software by allowing projects to build on and benefit from existing designs. C++ incorporates polymorphic behavior into the language and provides it as a tool to software developers. Through *dynamic casting* and *polymorphism*, client programs maintain their independence from specific types in the hierarchy, yet are still able to access unique features of a derived class.

GLOSSARY

Abstract class
A class whose purpose is to identify the design interface for its derived classes. In C++, a class containing at least one *purely virtual* function is an abstract class. C++ prevents a program from defining instances of an abstract class

Concrete class
A concrete class is the opposite of an *abstract* class. Since its design and implementation are complete, a *concrete* class can have instances

Downcasting
See *Narrowing*

Dynamic binding
The process of identifying the actual type of an object at run time, and invoking the applicable member function. This is also referred to as *late binding*

Dynamic casting
Converting a *base* type reference or pointer to a *derived* pointer or reference at run time

Narrowing

Converting a *base* class reference or a pointer to a *derived* reference or pointer

Polymorphism

The ability to operate on **different** but **related** data types in a generic way

RTTI

Run-Time Type Identification

Static binding

Recognizing the type of an object at compile time. It is also known as *early binding*

Virtual function

A function whose implementation is redefined by the *derived* classes. To create polymorphism, the *base* class declares a virtual function, specifying the function name and the interface for all *derived* classes

Pure virtual function

This is an *abstract* operation and specifies that there is no suitable implementation at the *base* class level. The *pure virtual* function only specifies the requirements for the implementation that must appear in any *derived* classes

V-Table

A function pointer table that contains the addresses of the applicable *virtual* functions of a class. The language implements *dynamic binding* (run time recognition) via the *v-table* (*virtual-table*)

Upcasting

Pointing to or referencing a *derived* object using a *base* reference or pointer

Widening

Another term for *upcasting*

CHAPTER 11

Templates

INTRODUCTION

In a software application, some of the modules may need to maintain a list of objects. For instance, a *Computer-Aided Design (CAD)* class needs to maintain a list of *Shapes* that its user creates. Instead of implementing and maintaining the list of *Shapes*, the *CAD* class may use a *container* class for this purpose. The *container* class hides the data maintenance and record keeping from the client, and allows the client to operate on the objects without having to be concerned with the actual physical architecture (Figure 11.1). In Figure 11.2, the *Shape* class hierarchy along with its supporting *container* class makes the *user interface* of a Computer-Aided Design (CAD) software client independent of any specific type of shape and of the topology used to maintain the shape objects in memory (Figure 11.3). The *CAD user interface* software uses the public interface defined by the abstract *Shape* class to perform graphical operations such as **draw()** on any type of shape. At the same time, the *CAD user interface* software uses the *Shape List* container class for maintaining the *Shapes* its user creates (Figure 11.2). The *Shape List* class takes care of how the shapes are maintained and accessed in memory. The container class insulates the clients from the architecture used to maintain the list of objects, and if the topology changes later on, the client remains unaffected. For instance, when the internal design is changed from the circular linked list to an array architecture the *CAD* class remains unaffected (Figure 11.1).

In Figure 11.3, the *Shape List* container class is specific to the *Shape* class library even though the concept is applicable to other data types. Traditionally, *container* classes are implemented for unique data types. Although the actual data types maintained and operated on are different, it results in the creation of programs that have the same algorithms and data architectures. This approach introduces maintainability and reusability problems. A change to an algorithm impacts each of unique implementations. In addition, for a new data type, a new implementation must be created manually.

A more versatile alternative is to create a generic design for the *container* class that is not dependent on a specific data type. The client applies the generic definition to a specific data type, and the compiler instantiates a unique implementation for the specified data type. For instance, a generic container class can be instantiated to maintain *shapes (heterogeneous list)*. This approach localizes changes to algorithms and architecture to the generic class definition. Furthermore, implementations for new data types are automatically generated.

C++ supports generic definitions through the use of *templates*. This chapter provides a detailed discussion of *templates*. Since Chapter 3 introduced template functions, this chapter's main focus will be on template classes known as *parameterized* types. This discussion of *parameterized* types begins by defining a generic *Array* class

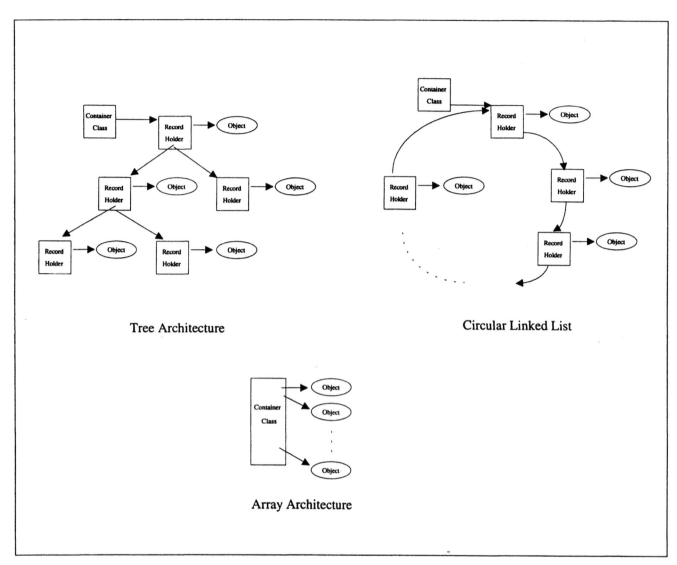

FIGURE 11.1 Container classes.

that monitors array accesses for boundary errors. *Design hierarchies* and exception handling are combined with the template applications to present sophisticated yet versatile designs for a *linked list* class library, a common application for templates. Chapter 11 concludes with an overview of the *Standard Template Library (STL)*.

11.1 TEMPLATE FUNCTIONS

Mathematical operations, data sorting, searching, or swapping algorithms can be applied to different data types. The following example defines a *template* for a **min()** function, which is a generic implementation for obtaining the minimum value of two data points. The "template" keyword specifies that the function is a *generic* definition and can be applied to any data type. The "class" keyword denotes that the *generic* definition can be used for both classes and built-in data types. The word *"Type"* is a symbolic name for a data type and is used by the compiler during instantiation of the function. When a unique data type is applied to the template definition, the compiler substitutes the actual data type for this word:

```
//           GENERAL_DEF.H Header File
#ifndef GENERAL_DEF_H
```

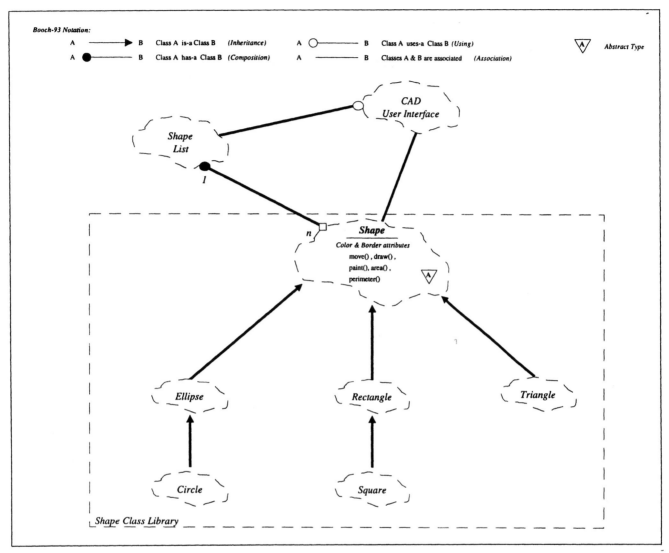

FIGURE 11.2   CAD user interface class diagram.

```
#define GENERAL_DEF_H

       template <class Type>
       Type &min( Type &data1 , Type &data2 )
       {
               Type *min_value ;

               // compare and return the min value
               if( data1 < data2 )
               {
                       min_value = &data1 ;
               }
               else
               {
                       min_value = &data2 ;
               }
               return( *min_value ) ;
       }


#endif
```

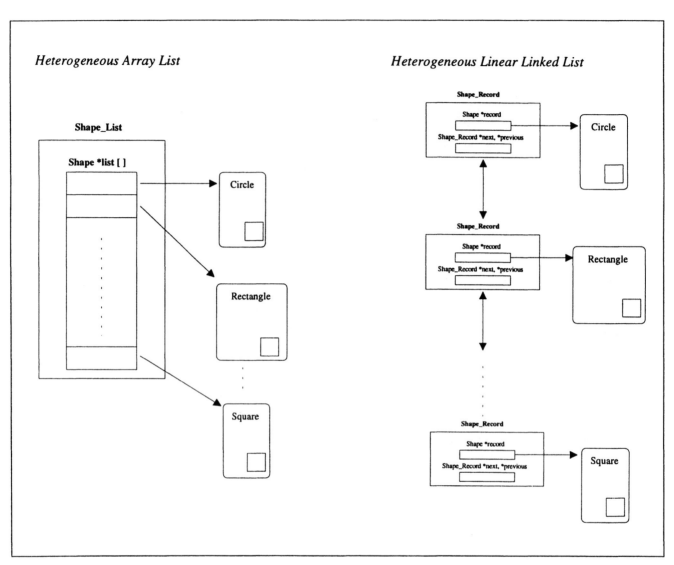

Heterogeneous Array List

Heterogeneous Linear Linked List

FIGURE 11.3   Container class architecture.

The **min()** template function can be used for classes that have overloaded the relational *Less Than* (<) operator.

The above template function arguments and return value use references instead of a copy, which avoids the overhead of copy constructor. In the following example, the test driver program applies the above **min()** definition to both float and integer data types:

```
//            Test Driver Source File
#include <iostream.h>
#include "general_def.h"

int main( int , char ** )
{
        int     i1 = 3 , i2 = 4 ;
        float   f1 = 9.8 , f2 = 10.0 ;

        // display Min(x,y) of two integer numbers
        cout << "Min( " << i1 << " , " << i2 << " ) : = " <<
                  min( i1 , i2 )   << endl ;
```

```
            // compiler generates a min() implementation
            // for integer data type

    cout << "Min( " << f1 << " , " << f2 << " ) : = " <<
                min( f1 , f2 ) << endl ;
            // compiler generates a min() implementation
            // for float data type

    return( 0 ) ;
}
```

The compiler uses the type of data passed to the generic **min()** function and automatically creates the actual implementation for the **min()** function. In the previous example, the *template* for the **min()** function is called using floating point and integer data types. The executable file will contain both an integer and a floating point implementation for the **min()** function.

With *templates*, a designer provides a *generic* definition. The client specifies the data types for the *generic* definition and the compiler creates the appropriate implementation(s) at compile time. C++ does not provide any built-in capability for code generation at run time.

Since the *template* definitions are resolved at compile time, they are typically defined in a header file. Some compilers allow template declaration and definitions to be separated into header and source files, while others require both declarations and definitions to be included in the header file.

A *template* does not reduce the number of functions in the executable code. However, the number of functions a designer must implement for a general- purpose algorithm is reduced to only one. Any changes to the function in the future will be mapped to all implementations created at compile time, making the design easier to maintain. In the above example, the executable program contains two implementations of the **min()** function but the designer had to provide only one generic implementation in the header file.

11.2 TEMPLATE CLASSES

Templates of our heroes.

In both C and C++, memory overrun is a common problem. Neither language provides any tools to detect array boundary problems. This section examines the use of *templates* in the design of a class that monitors an array for illegal accesses. By catching memory overruns, this class improves software reliability. Since the array monitoring operation applies to a variety of data types, *templates* are ideal for this application.

To address memory overrun problems, the *Array* class overloads the *array index* operator ([ ]). The Array:: operator [ ] function monitors the array indices and ensures that they are always within the array's boundaries. The design provides a nonintrusive method for monitoring array accesses, and the monitoring process is transparent to the client:

```
array_name[ array_index ] = expression ;
        // the compiler treats the overloaded statement as:
        //      array_name. operator [ ] ( int array_index ) = expression ;
```

When the *Array* class detects an error, it will need to report it to its client. For this purpose, the *Array* class uses the *Array Exception* class (Figure 11.4). The *Array* class reports errors to its clients by throwing instances of

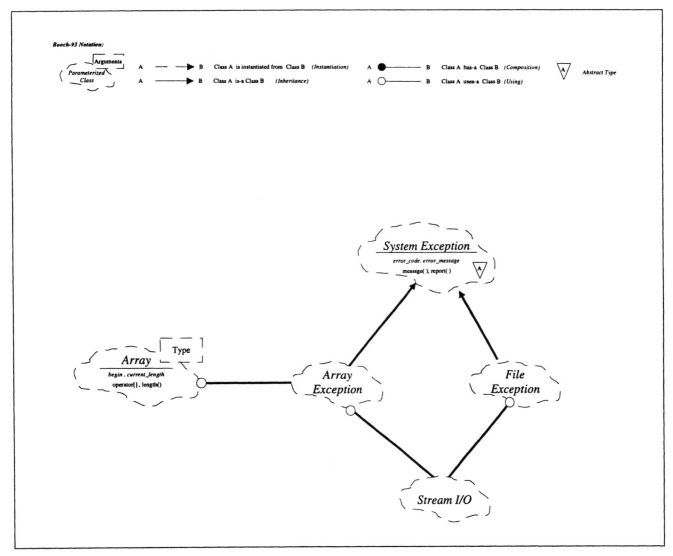

FIGURE 11.4   Array class diagram.

the *Array Exception* class. The *Array Exception* class is similar in design to the *File Exception* and *Serial Exception* classes in Chapters 8 and 9. This class needs to maintain the raw error code, a message, and an error description table. Since these classes are similar and have common attributes and operations, they can be made part of a *design hierarchy* as depicted in Figure 11.4.

The base *System Exception* class not only maintains common attributes and operations such as the **error_message** data element, but it also identifies the design interface for its *derived* classes. Using the **virtual** keyword, this class specifies the required derived functions and their signatures. The functions that cannot be implemented at the *System Exception* level are defined as *purely virtual*. Since the *System Exception* class contains purely virtual functions such as the **report()** function, it is an *abstract* class. The *Array Exception* class inherits from the *System Exception* class and provides implementations for the *purely virtual* functions. The *System Exception* class does provide an implementation for the **message()** function because the **error_message** data element is maintained at this level. However, the derived classes can override the **message()** implementation since it is declared as **virtual**. Figure 11.5 depicts the memory layout for an *Array Exception* object:

```
//          STATUS.H Header File
#ifndef STATUS_H
#define STATUS_H
```

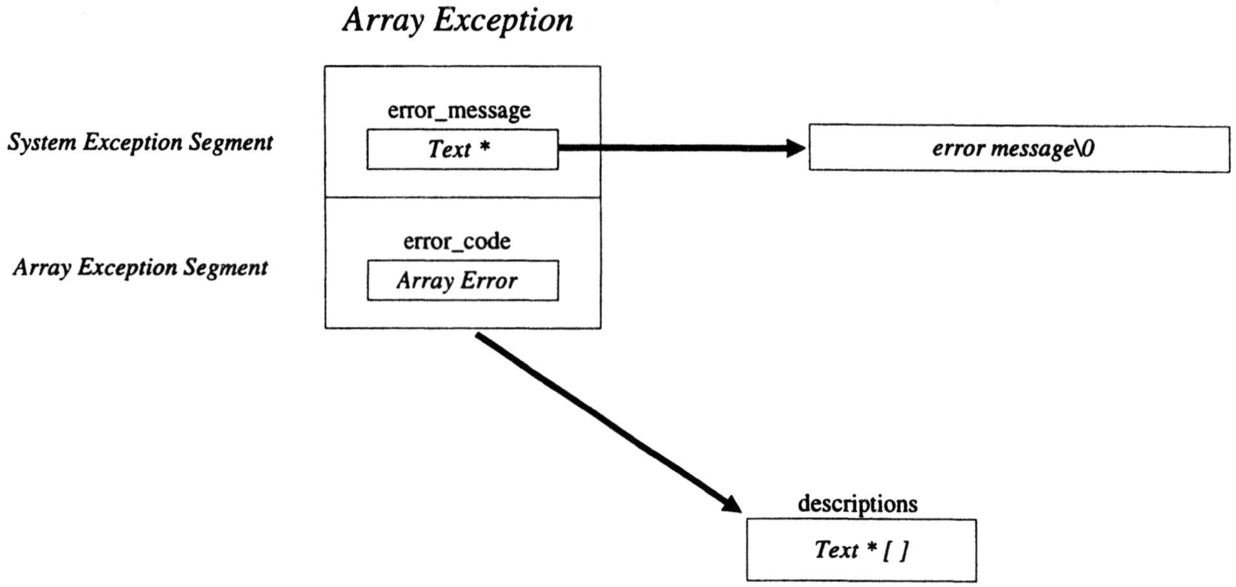

Array Exception

FIGURE 11.5 Array exception object memory layout.

```
typedef      bool              Boolean ;
typedef      char              Text ;
typedef      unsigned short    Array_Length ;
typedef      Array_Length      Array_Index ;

enum Array_Error
{
      ARRAY_SETUP_ERROR, ARRAY_ALLOCATION_ERROR,
      ARRAY_ACCESS_ERROR
} ;
#define NUM_ARRAY_ERRORS4

class System_Exception
{
      private:
            Text *error_message ;
      public:
```

```
                    // Constructors
                    System_Exception( const Text *message =
                            static_cast<Text *> ( 0 ) ) ;
                    System_Exception( const System_Exception & ) ;
                    System_Exception & operator =(
                    const System_Exception & );
                            // assignment & copy constructor:
                            //          deep copy implementation

                    // Destructor
                    virtual ~System_Exception( ) ;

                    // Access functions
                    virtual const Text *description( void ) const = 0 ;
                    virtual int code( void ) const = 0 ;
                    virtual const Text *message( void ) const ;
                    // Stream I/O functions
                    virtual Boolean report( ostream &os ) const = 0 ;
        } ;

        class Array_Exception: public System_Exception
        {
                private:
                        // Error description and raw error code
                        static const Text  *descriptions[NUM_ARRAY_ERRORS];
                        Array_Error error_code ;

                public:
                        // Constructors
                        Array_Exception( Array_Error error_code =
                                    ARRAY_SETUP_ERROR,
                        const Text *message =
                        static_cast<Text *> (0) ) ;
                        Array_Exception( const Array_Exception & ) ;
                        Array_Exception & operator =( const
                        Array_Exception & );
                                // assignment & copy constructor:
                                //          deep copy implementation
                        // Destructor
                        ~Array_Exception( ) { } ;

                        // Access functions
                        const Text *description( void ) const ;
                        int code( void ) const ;
                        inline Array_Error type( void ) const ;

                        // Stream I/O functions
                        Boolean report( ostream &os ) const ;
                        friend ostream &operator <<( ostream &os,
                                    const Array_Exception &source );
        } ;

        // the File Exception class definition left out.
        // It is similar to the Array Exception class.
#endif        // STATUS.H Header File
```

Since the *design hierarchy* provides polymorphic behavior, the client can invoke the **description()**, **message()**, **code()**, and **report()** functions to operate on any type of exception in the hierarchy. In the following example, the client program catches any type of exception in the *System Exception* class hierarchy and generates a problem report by invoking the applicable **report()** function. The derived **report()** function sends a formatted report to the error stream (*cerr*):

```
//                    Application Source File
#include <iostream.h>      // Stream I/O Class Library
#include "status.h"        // Exception Class Library


client_function( )
{
      try
      {
            // C++ code block(s)
      }
      catch( System_Exception &error )// catch all types of System Exception
      {
            // Note: Error is a reference type to a derived object. The
            // above statement catches derived objects. By using
            // polymorphism, the client's code has become
            // independent of types of derived exceptions and can operate
            // on any exception in the hierarchy.
            // An instance of the base class can never
            // be caught because System Exception is an abstract class
            // and cannot be instantiated.
            error.report( cerr ) ;  // send a report to standard error
      }
}
```

11.2.1 Template Class Definition

The following example specifies the design interface for the *Array* class. The "template" keyword specifies that the class definition can be applied to different types of data. The "class" keyword specifies that the class can be used for both classes and built-in data types. The *Array* class uses the symbolic "Type" name. During instantiation of this class, the compiler uses the client-specified data type and substitutes the actual data type for each occurrence of the "Type" name:

```
//                    ARRAY.H Header File
#ifndef ARRAY_H
#define ARRAY_H

      #include "status.h"        // Array Exception class

      template <class Type>
      class Array
      {
            private:
                  Type *begin ; // identify beginning of the array
                  Array_Length  current_length ; // length of the array

                  // Note: Removed from the design interface
                  Array( const Array & ) ;
                  Array & operator =( const Array & ) ;
```

```
        public:
                // Constructor
                Array( Array_Length length )
                            throw( Array_Exception ) ;

                // Destructor
                ~Array( ) ;

                // Array monitoring function
                Type &operator[ ]( Array_Index index )
                            throw( Array_Exception ) ;

                // Access Functions
                inline Array_Length length( void ) const ;
    } ;


    template <class Type>
    inline Array_Length Array <Type>:: length( void ) const
    {
    return( current_length ) ; // current length
    }

#endif              // ARRAY_H Header File
```

The *Array* template class definition provides the following features and attributes:

1. **Array Data Support**: Using a pointer (***begin***), the class identifies the beginning of an array. The ***current_length*** data member identifies the array's size and is used by the *array index* operator ([ ]) to verify the array indices (Figure 11.6).

2. **Array Construction**: The class maintains the ownership of the array. The *user-defined value* constructor uses the supplied length of the array and creates the array dynamically. The destructor deallocates the array.

   Since the class does not provide any array-resizing operation, the *default* constructor is meaningless. An *Array* object created with this constructor cannot support an array and therefore the *Array* object would be useless. This constructor has been removed from the design by being omitted in the class definition.

   The *copy* constructor and the *assignment* operator (=) have also been removed from the design interface because a shallow copy would cause problems for instances of this class. A deep copy degrades software performance when used to copy large arrays. Furthermore, it is a poor utilization of free store. The purpose of the class is to monitor accesses to arrays, not to create duplicate arrays. By declaring these functions as **private**, a client will be unable to make a copy of an *Array* object.

3. **Array Exception Handling**: Member functions use the *Array Exception* class to report problems. Instances of this class are thrown by the constructor and the *array index* operator functions. These functions specify error reporting in their interface definition by the use of the **throw** keyword.

4. **Class Access Functions**: After construction, the client does not need to keep track of an array's length. This is provided via the **length()** function.

5. **Array Access**: A client accesses an array by using the array index operator:

```
array_name[i]   = expression ;
```

Since the array index operator ([ ]) is overloaded for the Array class, this function is called whenever the client accesses an element in the Array object. This function checks the index value and returns a reference to the proper element in the array. If the array index does not fall within the range of the array, then the operator function performs its error recovery by throwing an exception.

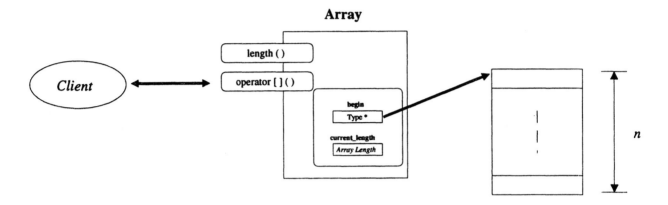

Wassermann-Pircher-Muller Notation:

FIGURE 11.6 Array block diagram.

11.2.2 Template Class Implementation

The implementation of the member functions in a parameterized class is slightly different in syntax than for typical class member functions. The following identifies the general notation used to define a template member function:

```
template <class Type>
return_type class_name<Type>:: function_name ( arguments, if any)
{
        // function body
}
```

The template class member functions use the **template** keyword. The "*<Type>*" identifier is part of the class member function signature. The notation also tells the compiler that the function is a generic definition and needs to be instantiated for a specific data type.

Some compilers require *parameterized* member function definitions to be included in the header file. The following implementation assumes a compiler that allows the template class definition and its member functions to be separated in a header and source file:

```
//              ARRAY.CPP Source File
#include <iostream.h>    // Stream I/O Class Library
#include "array.h"       // Array Class Library

template <class Type>
Array<Type>:: Array( Array_Length length )
                                throw( Array_Exception )
        : begin( static_cast<Type *> ( 0 ) ) , current_length( length )
{
      Text message[100] ;

      // if array's length is valid => set up array
      if( current_length > 1 )
      {
            // allocate array dynamically
            begin = new Type[ current_length ] ;
            if( !begin ) // on dynamic allocation failures => abort
            {
                  // create an error message
                  sprintf( message,"Array(): Allocation error on "
                        "(length =%u)", current_length);

                  // throw an array allocation exception
                  throw( Array_Exception(
                        ARRAY_ALLOCATION_ERROR, message) ) ;
            }
      }
      else
      {
            // create an error message
            sprintf( message,"Array(): invalid length (%u): ",
                  current_length);

            // throw an array setup error
            throw( Array_Exception(
                  ARRAY_SETUP_ERROR, message ) );
      }
}

template <class Type>
Array<Type>:: ~Array( )
{
      delete [ ] begin ;  // destroy dynamic array
      begin = static_cast<Type *> ( 0 ) ; // clear out the memory
      current_length = 0 ;
}

template <class Type>
Type & Array<Type>:: operator[ ]( Array_Index index )
                                throw( Array_Exception )
{
      // throw an exception on an invalid index
      if( index >= current_length )
```

```
        {
                Text message[100] ;

                // create an error message
                sprintf( message,"operator[ ]: Array Access error on %u "
                                 "(length =%u)", index, current_length);
                // throw an array access exception
                throw( Array_Exception(
                         ARRAY_ACCESS_ERROR, message) ) ;
        }

        return( begin[index] ) ; // return a reference to the data member
}
```

The *array index* operator ([ ]) verifies that the location accessed in the array is valid and will not cause a memory overrun.

11.2.3 Template Class Usage

The client uses the above generic definition and specifies the data type to be maintained by the *Array* class. The compiler uses the client-defined data type and generates an implementation for the class and its member functions. In the following example, the test driver uses the *Array* class for *Circle* and floating point data types. The compiler generates a unique instantiation for each data type (Figure 11.7). The instantiation of the *Array* class is shown using a dashed line, and the data type used to instantiate the unique implementation is defined in the solid rectangular box:

```
//              Test Driver Source File
#include <iostream.h>          // Stream I/O Class Library
#include "shape.h"             // Shape Class Library
#include "array.h"             // Array Class Library

void test_array( Array_Length n )
{
        try
        {
                // create a list of Shape class pointers
                Array<Circle> circles( n ) ;
                Array<float> areas( n ) ; // set up a floating point list
                      // note for n = 0 or 1: Array constructor throws an exception
                create_shapes( circles ) ;
                      // load coordinates & radius from a file

                for( Array_Index i = 0 ; i < circles.length() ; i++ )
                {
                        // compute areas
                        areas[ i ] = circles[ i ].area() ;
                                // treats as:
                                //    areas.operator[ ]( i ) =
                                //          circles.operator[ ] ( i ) .area( ) ;
                                // if i were invalid => the [ ] function
                                //    would have thrown an exception
                }

                for( i = 0 ; i < circles.length() ; i++ )
                {
```

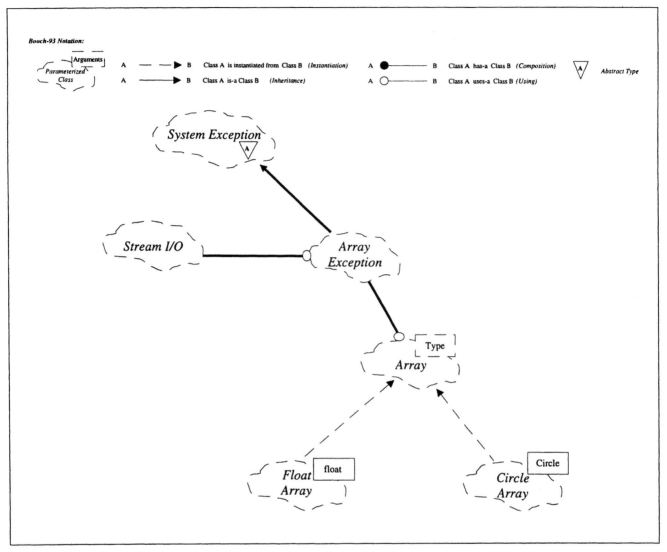

FIGURE 11.7 Array class diagram.

```
                // display computed areas
                cout << "Areas: " << areas[ i ] << endl ;
            }
        }
        catch( System_Exception &error )
        {
                error.report( cerr ) ; // report error to the standard error stream
        }
    }

    void create_shapes( Array<Circle> &list )
    {
        for( Array_Index i = 0 ; i < list.length() ; i++ )
        {
                // load list from a file: details left out
        }
    }
```

During software testing, the *Array* class monitors the functions that could cause memory overrun. Since the *array index* operator ([ ]) is called for each element of the *Array* object, the monitoring operation has a high overhead. After the software has completed its qualification tests, the *array index* operator ([ ]) function can be replaced by a more efficient implementation. This implementation provides the same behavior as the built-in array index operator. The deliverable software is recompiled using the nontest environment template definition:

```
//          ARRAY.H Header File
template <class Type>
class Array
{
        public:
                inline Type & operator [ ] ( Array_Index index ) ;
        // Other details left out
}

template <class Type>
inline Type & Array<Type>:: operator [ ] ( Array_Index index )
{
        return begin[index] ;
}
```

The above inline function always returns a reference to an element of the array. Since there is no function call overhead, the above function is equivalent to the built-in array index operator. Naturally, there is no more boundary error checking. By providing two different *Array* implementations for the test and development environments, the software can be checked for boundary problems during software testing with a nonintrusive class library. The deliverable code still remains nearly as efficient as an implementation using the built-in operator.

11.3 TEMPLATES AND DESIGN HIERARCHY

In C++, templates can inherit from each other. This section designs a *Linked List container* class hierarchy. A *container* class maintains a *heterogeneous* list of objects, which includes instances of different data types in a design hierarchy, or a *homogeneous* list, which includes instances of the same data type. Figure 11.1 depicts the different types of architectures used in the design of *container* classes. The purpose of the *container* class is to hide the data architecture and mechanisms used in maintaining a list of objects. Thus, changes to the architecture become localized to the *container* class and its member functions. In Figure 11.8, the client uses the overloaded *array index* operator ([ ]) to access an object in the list. The *container* object searches through the list for the specified object and returns a reference to it.

Figure 11.9 depicts the class diagram for the *Linked List* template class library. The *Linked List* class uses the *List Exception* class in the *System Exception* class hierarchy for reporting errors associated with the linked list. The *Record* class is an auxiliary class and is used by the *Linked List* class to maintain the addresses of the specified objects. In addition, it maintains the address of *previous* and *next Records* in memory, and is thus said to have the *reflexive* property (Figure 11.9):

```
//          LIST.H Header File
#ifndef LIST_H
#define LIST_H

        #include "status.h"      // Array Exception class
        typedef      unsigned short      Index ;
        typedef      index               Size ;

        template<class Type>
```

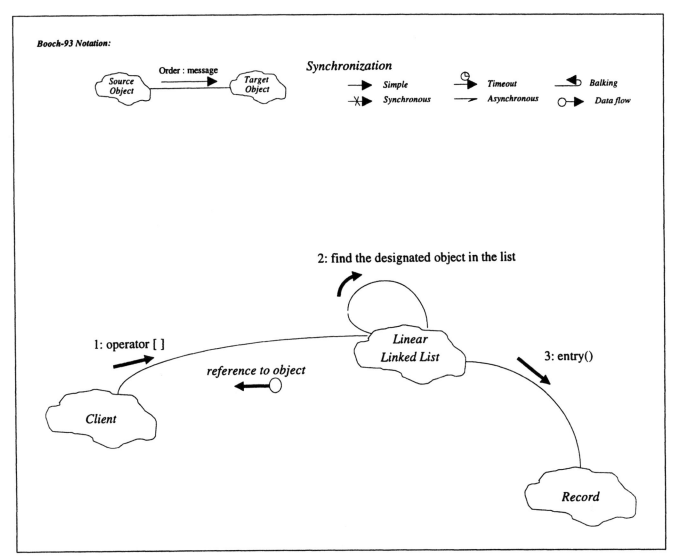

FIGURE 11.8 Linked list object diagram.

```
class Record
{
        private:
                Type *object ;
                Record *next_record , *previous_record ;

                // Note: remove from the design interface
                Record( const Record &source) ;
                Record & operator = ( const Record &source) ;
        public:
                // Constructor
                Record( ) ;
                Record( Record *previous, Record *next,
                 Type *new_object );

                // Destructor
                ~Record( ) ;
```

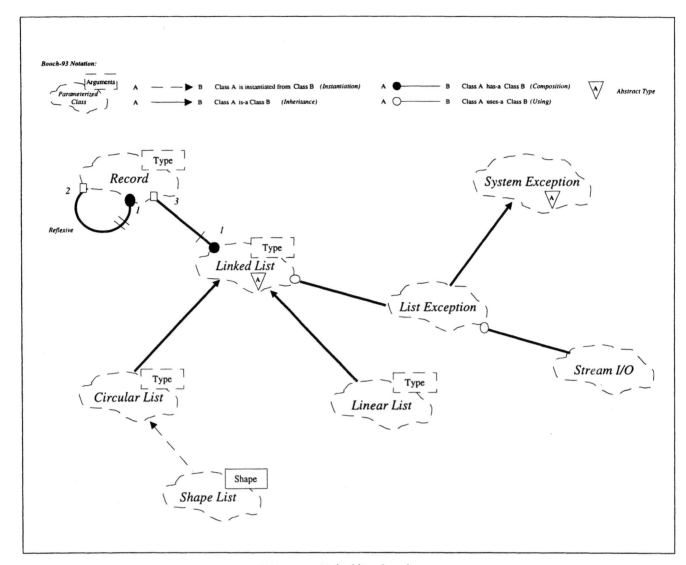

FIGURE 11.9 Linked list class diagram.

```
// Access Functions
inline Record<Type> *next( void ) const ;
inline Record<Type> *previous( void ) const ;
inline Type *entry( void ) const ;
} ;


template <class Type>
inline Record<Type> * Record<Type>:: next( void ) const
{
      return( next_record ) ;
}


template <class Type>
inline Record<Type> * Record<Type>:: previous( void ) const
{
      return( previous_record ) ;
}
```

```
template <class Type>
inline Type * Record<Type>:: entry( void ) const
{
        return( object ) ;
}


template <class Type>
class Linked_List
{
        private:
                // Note: removed from the design interface
                Linked_List( const Linked_List & ) ;
                Linked_List & operator = ( const Linked_List & ) ;

        protected:
                Record<Type> *begin ; // pointer to the first record
                Record<Type> *end ;// pointer to the last record
                Record<Type> *current ;// current entry
                Index current_index ;// current entry's id
                Size total_record , max_records ;
                // # of records in the list
        public:
                // Constructor
                Linked_List( ) ;
                Linked_List( Size n ) ;

                // Destructor
                virtual ~Linked_List( ) ;

                // Access Functions
                Size num_entries( void ) const ;
                Size max_entries( void ) const ;
                Type *current_entry( void ) const ;
                Type *first_entry( void ) const ;
                Type *last_entry( void ) const ;

                // Processing Functions
                virtual Type &operator[ ]( Index i )
                        throw( List_Exception ) = 0 ;
                virtual void insert( Index i , Type *object )
                        throw( List_Exception ) = 0 ;
                virtual void remove( Index i )
                        throw( List_Exception ) = 0 ;
} ;

#endif              // LIST_H header file
```

The *Linked List* class provides the following features:

1. **Data Members**: The common data and operations among the derived classes are captured by the *Linked List* class. The *Linked List* data elements are defined using the **protected** access level. Even though this approach tightly couples the derived classes to the *Linked List* class, the linked list access and processing time is minimized. The design hierarchy still encapsulates data representation and architecture from other clients.
2. **Design Interfaces**: The member functions of the linked list allow the clients to insert, remove, and access objects in the list. The client operates on the objects maintained in the list using the *array index* operator ([

]) function. Through this operator, the client perceives the list as an array. The derived classes in the hierarchy need the same information for maintaining their linked lists. The search algorithms for *Linear* and *Circular Linked lists* vary slightly. Thus, the *Linked List* class defines the search functions as **virtual**, which creates a common interface for these classes. The member functions abstract and encapsulate the search process from their clients.

The *Circular* and *Linear Linked lists* are derived from the *Linked List* base class, and they provide implementations for the *purely virtual* functions:

```
//                    LIST.H Header File
#ifndef LIST_H
#define LIST_H

    #include "status.h"// Array Exception class

    typedef     unsigned short     Index ;
    typedef     Index              Size ;

    template<class Type>
    class Record
    {
        // details left out
    } ;

    template <class Type>
    class Linked_List
    {
        // details left out
    } ;

    template <class Type>
    class Circular_List: public Linked_List<Type>
    {
        private:
            // Note: removed from the design interface
            Circular_List( const Circular_List & ) ;
            Circular_List & operator = ( const Circular_List & ) ;

        public:
            // Constructor
            Circular_List( ) ;
            Circular_List( Size n ) ;

            // Destructor
            ~Circular_List( ) ;

            // Processing Functions
            virtual Type &operator[ ]( Index i )
                    throw( List_Exception )  ;
            virtual void insert( Index i , Type *object )
                    throw( List_Exception )  ;
            virtual void remove( Index i )
                    throw( List_Exception )  ;
    } ;
```

```
        template <class Type>
        class Linear_List: public Linked_List<Type>
        {
                // similar to Circular list
        } ;
```

```
#endif                   // LIST_H header file
```

In the following example, the *linked list* class definition is used by the test driver program to create a specific container class for a geometrical *shape* library:

```
//              Test Driver Source File
#include "shape.h"// from Chapter 10
#include "list.h"// List Class Template Definition

int main( int , char ** )
{
        try
        {
                Circular_List<Shape> list( 2 )  ;
                        // shape_list supports different shapes
                Shape *current ;

                // create a shape list
                current = new Rectangle( 1, 3, 2, 5, RED ) ;
                list.insert(  0 , current ) ;
                current =new Circle( 4, 3 , 2, BLUE ) ;
                list.insert( 1 , current ) ;

                // compute area & perimeter of each shape in the list
                for( Index i = 0 ; i < list.num_entries() ; i++ )
                {
                        cout << "Area: " << list[ i ].area() << endl ;
                        cout << "Perimeter: " << list[ i ].perimeter() << endl ;
                }
        }
        catch( System_Exception &error )
        {
                error.report( cout ) ; // catch and report problems to cout
        }
        catch( ... )
        {
                cout << "\n\t Unknown Error ... " << endl ;
        }

        return( 0 ) ;
}
```

The above application uses the generic definition of the *Circular List* container class to create a container class for *Shapes.* The client uses the container class member functions to create the list, retrieve records from the list, and operate on the records maintained in the list, for example, the **area()** operation.

The use of a generic container class allows different libraries to reuse the code and algorithms of the container class. This approach increases productivity by reducing the software development time needed to create a specific container class for every library.

11.4 STANDARD TEMPLATE LIBRARY

The *Standard Template Library (STL)* is an ANSI standard C++ library developed by Hewlett-Packard and adopted by the ANSI/ISO C++ standard committee. This library provides a set of container classes and generic algorithms (template functions) that can be combined to perform operations on both classes and built-in data types. In addition, the STL is designed to be extensible with custom algorithms and libraries. For example, a designer may define a specialized container class and use the STL sort function to sort it. While the STL interfaces are an ANSI standard, the implementation of the functions in the library is not.

STL is a complicated and, correspondingly, a powerful library. It differs from most C++ libraries because it was purposely designed with an architecture that is not completely object-oriented. For example, the *Stream I/O* class library makes maximum use of encapsulation and inheritance. In contrast, the STL separates the tasks (algorithms) to be performed from the representation of the structures (container classes). STL is therefore viewed as a collection of algorithms and also as a collection of data structures that can be manipulated using the algorithms. If the normal object-oriented approach were taken, each of the algorithms would have to be developed for each of the data structures. This requires many more member functions than are actually implemented using the separated approach.

STL is a complex library, consisting of many components. Detailed coverage of this library is beyond the scope of this book. This section provides a high-level overview of STL, its components, and its capability. For a detailed description, a C++ compiler manual should be consulted.

11.4.1 Structure of the Library

The library contains five main kinds of components as well as numerous predefined types and primitive classes [HP 1995]:

1. **Container**: This component maintains a set of classes that contain data items, such as vector, list, double-ended queue, and set classes.
2. **Iterator**: This component provides the capability for an algorithm to traverse through the list of data elements maintained by a container class. The simplest example of an iterator is a pointer used to index an array.
3. **Algorithm**: The generic algorithms define computational procedures or steps, such as a Quicksort algorithm.
4. **Function**: This component is used in conjunction with generic algorithms. It has a set of classes that operate on other classes that have overloaded the *parenthesis* operator.
5. **Adaptor**: These template classes provide interfaces for container, iterator, and function components.

The *Standard Template Library* consists largely of template declarations. The actual classes and functions are instantiated in the client software just like the user-defined templates discussed in earlier sections of this chapter. STL is divided into several header files to reduce code complexity. Table 11.1 identifies some of the STL header files.

TABLE 11.1   Standard Template Library Header File

STL Library	Header File(s)	Description
Containers	bvector.h	bit_vector class
	deque.h	deque class
	list.h	list class template
	map.h	map class
	multimap.h	multimap class
	multiset.h	multiset class
	set.h	set class
	vector.h	vector class template
Iterators	iterator.h	Iterator definitions, stream iterators, and iterator adaptors

TABLE 11.1   Standard Template Library Header File *(Con't)*

Algorithms	algo.h	Algorithm templates
	bool.h	simulate bool type
Functions	function.h	Operators, function objects, and adaptors
Adaptors	stack.h	stack class

11.4.1.1 Container

The supported container classes consist of the following categories:

1. **Sequence containers**: Consists of the *vector*, *bit-vector*, *list*, and *deque* classes

   A *vector*, similar to an array, is an indexed data structure: $<v_0, v_1, ..., v_{n-1}>$. The elements within the *vector* class are accessed similarly to an array with the *array index operator* ([ ]). The size of a *vector* can dynamically grow:

```
//              VECTOR.H Header File
template <class T, template<class U> class Allocator = allocator>
class vector
{
        public:
                // Constructors
                vector();
                vector(size_type n, const T & value = T());

                // Destructor
                ~vector();

                // Access functions
                size_type size() const ; // current size
                size_type max_size() const ; // upper limit on vector
                size_type capacity() const ; // max storage space
                bool empty() const;
                reference operator [ ] (size_type n) ;
                const_reference operator [ ] (size_type n) const;


        // Other details left out
} ;



//              TEST.CPP Source File
#include <iostream.h>        // Stream I/O class library
#include <vector.h>          // STL: Vector class

using namespace std ;        // namespace used by STL components

void test_vector( int n )
{
        vector<float> image( n ) ; // the image object holds n-elements
        float ctr = 0.0 ;
        int i ;

        // initialize elements to a counter pattern
        for( i =  0 ; i < image.size() ; i++ )
        {
                image[i] = ctr++ ;
```

```
        }

        // display contents of the vector: <v₀, .. , vₙ₋₁>
        cout << "\n\t Vector = < " ;
        for( i =  0 ; i < image.size() ; i++ )
        {
                cout <<  image[i] ;
                if( i + 1 != image.size() )
                {
                        cout <<  " , " ;
                }
        }
        cout << " >" ;

        return ;
}
```

A *deque* container is a "double-ended queue." It is similar to a *vector*, but it provides efficient insertion at both the beginning and end of the list (a *vector* provides an efficient insertion only at the end). The elements within the *deque* class can also be accessed by using the *array index operator* ([]).

A *list* container provides efficient storage of data by allowing a client to add or remove data from the beginning, middle, or end of a list. The time required for removing and adding data anywhere within the list is constant and is also independent of the size of the list.

2. **Associative containers**: Consists of the *set*, *multiset*, *map*, and *multimap* classes

The *set* container class is an ordered collection of items. It is optimized for insertion and removal of elements. Similar to *list*, a *set* can expand and contract dynamically. Unlike a *list* class, the *set* **insert()** method ignores insertion requests for values that are already in the list. A *multiset* class is basically a *set* that allows multiple occurrences of the same value in the set.

A *map* is an ordered and indexed data structure. Similar to a *vector*, its elements can be accessed by using the *array index operator* ([]). A *map* can be indexed by an integer value, a float, or a string (which is referred to as a *key*). A *map* does not allow insertion of values that use an existing *key*. However, a *multimap* class allows multiple values to use the same *key*.

```
//                    TEST.CPP Source File
#include <iostream.h>        // Stream I/O class library
#include <map.h>             // STL: Map class
#include <string.h>          // String class library

using namespace std ;        // namespace used by STL components

string months[12] =
{
        "January" , "February", "March", "April",
        "May", "June", "July", "August",
        "September", "October", "November", "December"
} ;


map<string, int, less<string> > calendar_table ;
        // table holds integer values and is indexed using a string

void setup( void )
{
        int i :
```

```
        // for each month: initialize calendar to corresponding
        // numerical value, January - 1, Feb - 2, ...
        for( i =  0 ; i < 12 ; i++ )
        {
                calendar_table[ months[i] ] = i + 1 ;
                        // table is being indexed using a string object
        }
        // display contents of the table
        cout << "\n\t Calendar " ;
        for( i =  0 ; i < 12 ; i++ )
        {
                cout << '\n' << calendar_table[ months[i] ] <<
                << ". " <<  months[i];
        }

    return ;
    }
```

11.4.1.2 Iterator

Iterators are a key factor in the design of the STL. They are used to traverse through data maintained by the *container* classes. An *iterator* is a generalized pointer, and acts as an intermediary between the containers and clients of the STL library. Since there are different ways of traversing through a list of data in a container object, there are five categories of iterators: *input, output, forward, bidirectional*, and *random access*. Each category has a set of requirements that standardizes the interface, semantics, and complexity assumptions. Table 11.2 identifies the general properties of the supported iterators.

TABLE 11.2 Iterator Classes

Iterator	Property
Input	Forward moving, read-only
Output	Forward moving, write-only
Forward	Forward moving, read and write
Bidirectional	Forward and backward moving, read and write
Random access	Random access, read and write

In addition to the above iterators, STL provides *stream iterators*. This allows algorithms to work directly with the *Stream I/O* class library.

11.4.1.3 Algorithm

STL specifies generic algorithms for a broad range of data manipulations, such as searching, sorting, merging, copying, and transforming. For example, the binary_search() algorithm searches through a list for a specified value.

11.4.1.4 Function

Function objects are objects with an operator() defined. This component is used by an algorithm component, and provides arithmetic, comparison, and logical operations using the overloaded *parenthesis* operator. This allows the algorithms to work with arbitrary function objects, instead of just function pointers.

11.4.1.5 Adaptor

Adaptors are template classes that provide interface mappings [SUN 1995]. They are typically implemented by using the other components of the library, and they provide a specific functions. STL provides the following adaptors:

1. **Container Adaptors**: This component consists of the *stack, queue,* and *priority queue* classes. A *stack* is a *last in, first out* (LIFO) data structure, and a *queue* is a *first in, first out* (FIFO) data structure.
2. **Iterator Adaptors**: There are two types of iterator adaptors: insert and reverse. The insert adaptor is used for data insertion. For bidirectional and random access iterators, a reverse iterator adaptor provides the capability to traverse in the opposite direction.
3. **Function Adaptors**: This adaptor works only with the function object classes that have argument types and return value types. There are several types of function adaptors: negators, binders, and pointers to functions.

11.4.2 Design Concepts

When using the STL architecture, the following issues should be taken into consideration:

1. **Flexibility**: Algorithms and classes can be used for both conventional pointers/arrays as well as for objects.
2. **Efficiency**: The library is modular and provides an efficient method for dealing with specific data structures and algorithms.
3. **Iterator Mismatches**: Iterators add generality to the STL, but given the separation of algorithms and data structures it is not possible to verify that iterators are matched. Using a beginning iterator from one container and an ending iterator from another class, for example, will produce unpredictable results.
4. **Debugging**: Errors generated when using generic algorithms and classes can be obscure since they are often defined multiple levels deep in template expansions.
5. **Overhead**: Due to STL's heavy reliance on templates, programs can grow to be larger than expected. The cost, in terms of memory and performance, of multiple instantiations of multiple templates must be considered when using STL.
6. **Usage**: STL supports many different types of container classes. The designer should select the appropriate container class by comparing characteristics of the candidate container class to the software requirements. For example, if the design requirements call for insertion of data anywhere within a list, the *list* class becomes more appropriate than the *vector* or *deque* classes.
7. **Multithreading**: The STL must be used with care in a multithreaded environment. Iterators, because of their separation from the containers that they operate on, cannot be passed safely between threads.

SUMMARY

In C++, a template provides the capability to define generic definitions for algorithms and data classes. These generic definitions are used by the client with specific data types. On the basis of the type of data specified by the client, the compiler creates an instantiation of the class.

Template functions are useful for general sort, search, and mathematical operations. Templates are widely used for list and queue classes. In the case of container classes, a template class can maintain a list of objects using a tree, array, or linked list architecture. The container class encapsulates the data architecture and representation from its clients. Since the class definition is not unique to a data type, the client can apply the generic definition to a specific data type (homogeneous list) or different data types in a hierarchy (heterogeneous list).

The use of templates reduces the software design, implementation, and test effort by eliminating source code duplication. Instead of defining several implementations of a bubble sort function, for example, a designer specifies only one generic bubble sort function and utilizes the compiler to create the actual code for the required data type.

Templates also enhance software reusability and maintainability by eliminating the need to modify the library when an implementation for a new data type is required. The compiler automatically creates a new implementation for the new data type, using the generic definitions. A template is a basic code generation tool in C++ and applies to both functions and classes.

In C++, inheritance can be used in the design of templates. This capability allows a template to use a base class to maintain common attributes and features, to have customized derived versions of itself, and to use a base class to define the design interface for the derived template classes. In addition, the resulting coherency permits the clients to switch between the template classes in the hierarchy.

The Standard Template Library (STL) was developed by Hewlett-Packard and has been adopted by the ANSI C++ committee. It provides a common set of algorithms and container classes (data structures). Interfaces to the library components are well specified, ensuring the widespread utility of the STL. The design of the library is somewhat different than that of the other C++ libraries in that it is not completely object-oriented. There is a separation between the implementation of the algorithms and the design of the container classes. This orthogonal design allows programmers to use library data structures with their own algorithms, and their own data structures with library algorithms. This design also has the advantages of flexibility and efficiency; it also comes with some side effects such as larger code size and obscure error messages.

GLOSSARY

Container class
A container class is a list and maintains a group of related (heterogeneous) or identical (homogeneous) objects. A container class is a supporting class whose purpose is to hide the topology used for maintaining the list of objects in memory

Heterogeneous list
A list containing objects of different but related types. The objects are related through a base class, such as a list of different types of bank accounts

Homogeneous list
A list containing objects of identical data types, such as a list of savings accounts

Iterator class
A class that is used to traverse through the objects maintained by a container class

Parameterized class
A generic class definition; it is not instantiated until the client provides the needed information. A parameterized class is also referred to as a template class

Reflexive association
When an instance of a class is associated with other instances of the same class, the resulting association is referred to as reflexive

STL
Standard Template Library

Template
A generic algorithm or class definition, which is independent of any particular data type

CHAPTER 12

Distributed Objects

INTRODUCTION

In client/server applications, an *object model* spans across hardware and process boundaries, and objects are distributed across platforms. For example, the *object model* for a banking system will be distributed across a network of embedded computer systems such as *automated teller machines (ATMs)*, mainframes, and workstations. The objects in such a network reside on different systems, and they interact with each other through well-defined interfaces. This architecture forms a *heterogeneous* computing system. An *ATM* object residing on an embedded system interacts and operates on the *Savings* objects on a mainframe (Figure 12.1). The objects no longer are within a single process or platform, and are *distributed*.

In single-process applications, C++ features provide built-in support for object construction, interaction, and destruction. An object-oriented language such as C++ addresses the basic needs of an object model that resides within a single process and address space. However, C++ does not have built-in support for a *distributed object model*, which introduces additional complexities in design and implementation. For example, an object on one platform cannot directly call the constructor or methods of an object on a different platform. Some of the increased complexity associated with distributed objects is in the following areas:

1. Object Construction and Destruction
2. Object Interaction
3. Persistence
4. Concurrency

In recent years, there have been several efforts to provide standards and software tools that will facilitate the design of *distributed objects*. Most notable are the *Common Object Model (COM)* by Microsoft, and the *Common Object Request Broker Architecture (CORBA)* standard proposed by a consortium of companies called the *Object Management Group (OMG)*.[1] Standards such as *CORBA* provide mechanisms by which *distributed objects* can interact with each other independent of programming language, operating system, hardware platform, and

---

[1]The primary contributors to the OMG are Digital Equipment Corporation, Hewlett-Packard, HyperDesk Corporation, NCR, Object Design, and Sun Microsystems.

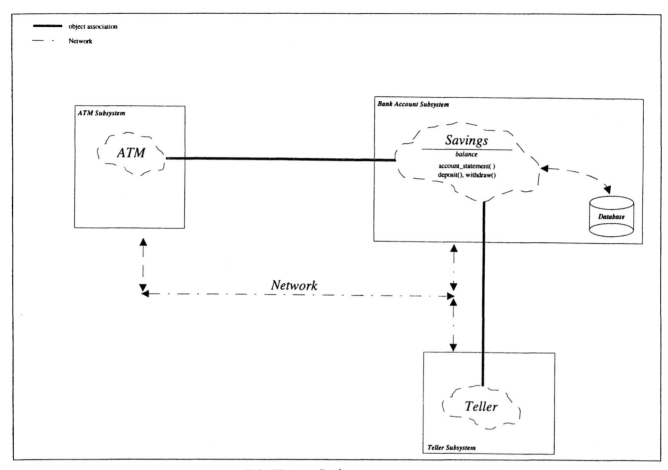

FIGURE 12.1 Bank account system.

network connectivity dependencies. CORBA identifies an underlying framework that will allow *distributed objects* to create, interact with, and destroy each other.

Concurrency support is essential for distributed objects and multitasking applications. C++ does not provide built-in concurrency support. However, C+- (C-plus-minus), which is a C++ extension, has incorporated concurrency support [Seizovic 1994].

This chapter discusses emerging object-oriented technologies for distributed applications. The discussion also includes the complexities associated with *distributed objects*, and how off-the-shelf software development tools based on CORBA can mitigate these complexities. The following describes the organization of the chapter:

1. **CORBA**: This section provides a high-level overview of CORBA.
2. **Distributed Objects**: This section then describes the design complexities and issues specific to distributed objects, and how CORBA and its supporting software development platforms address them.

   The discussion refers to different design patterns used in distributed objects such as a *factory*, *proxy*, and *adaptor*. These patterns are based on the definitions in *Design Patterns: Elements of Reusable Object-Oriented Software* [Gamma et al., 1994] They are briefly described in order to discuss the role they play in a *distributed object* design. The reader should refer to this book for a description of many design patterns.

12.1 COMMON OBJECT REQUEST BROKER ARCHITECTURE (CORBA)

The *Common Object Request Broker Architecture (CORBA)* standard has been developed by the *Object Management Group (OMG)*, a consortium of more than 500 companies. Some of the primary contributors are identified earlier in footnote 1 of this chapter. This standard is designed to allow object-oriented applications designed on different platforms and languages to interact with each other through "middleware" software. The CORBA-based middleware software makes communication protocols and hardware dependencies transparent to the objects within the applications. Through the middleware software, applications developed on different hardware platforms and languages can interact with each other. For example, in Figure 12.1, an *ATM* object, which may have been developed using C++ on a Motorola-based system, interacts with a *Savings* object developed, perhaps, in Ada 95 on a mainframe.

Two of the commercially available software development environments that are based on CORBA are Orbix, by IONA Technologies, and NEO, by Sun Microsystems. CORBA provides interoperability capability for software applications through the following framework (Figure 12.2):

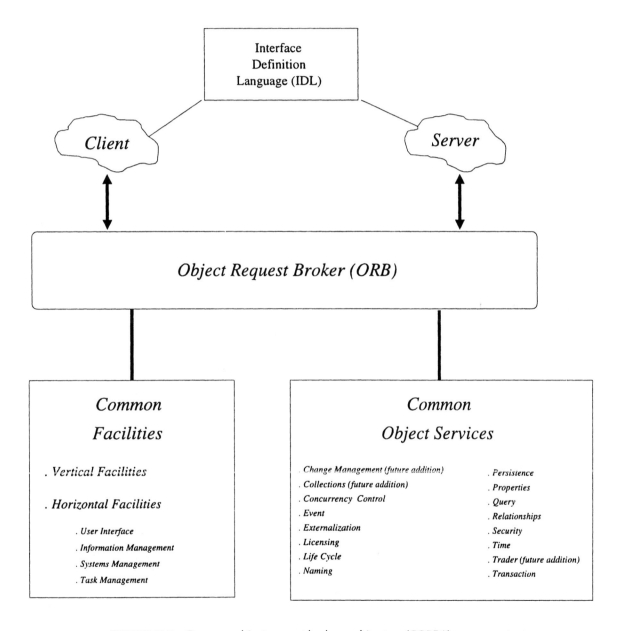

FIGURE 12.2 Common object request broker architecture (CORBA) components.

1. Interface Definition Language (IDL)
2. Object Request Broker (ORB)

3. Common Object Services
4. Common Facilities

The following sections describe these components.

12.1.1 Interface Definition Language (IDL)

To avoid system dependencies, CORBA focuses on the interfaces between the distributed objects instead of on their implementation. CORBA uses an *Interface Definition Language (IDL)* to describe the external interface of distributed objects. A *distributed object* specifies the data and functions accessible to its clients through an IDL specification. The object-oriented applications developed in different languages and platforms use IDL declarations to obtain information on features and operations available to them. The use of IDL establishes a well-defined interface between an object and its clients. Additionally, it separates the design interface from the implementation. While the interface for a distributed object is defined using IDL, its implementation may be in Ada, C++, Java, or any other language. Thus, objects implemented using different object-oriented languages can interact with each other through the interfaces defined by IDL. The following example identifies the design interface for a distributed *Account* class library:

```
//              ACCOUNT.IDL File
#ifndef ACCOUNT_IDL
#define ACCOUNT_IDL
module Bank_Account_Library
{
      // Interface definition for a bank account object
      interface Account
      {
              // typedef declarations
              typedef        float           Currency ;

              // exception type declarations
              exception insufficient_funds{ } ;

              // data attributes visible in the interface
              readonly attribute Currency balance ;
                      // The attribute keyword causes IDL compiler to
                      // generate the set_balance() and get_balance() access
                      // functions. However, the readonly keyword makes the
                      // "balance" data attribute read-only, thus preventing
                      // set_balance() from being created.

              // operations
              void deposit( in float amount ) ;
              void withdraw( in float amount )
                      raises( insufficient_funds ) ;
                      // if a withdraw operation causes the balance to
                      // become negative, the withdraw() function throws an
                      // insufficient funds exception.
              boolean account_statement( ) ;
      } ;
} ;
#endif                  // ACCOUNT_IDL File
```

In the preceding example, the **module** keyword specifies the scope of the *Account* IDL identifiers. The **interface** keyword specifies the external design interface for *Account*, which is used by clients to operate on an *Account* object. Using the above interface, an *ATM* object can prepare account statements, make a deposit, or withdraw money from an *Account* object. For the operations, the **in**, **out**, and **inout** keywords specify the direction in which parameters are passed. For example, the ***amount*** for deposit and withdraw requests are passed into these functions. The **raises** keyword is used for operations that raise an exception, such as the **withdraw()** operation. Using the above interface, clients can interact with *Account* objects.

An IDL interface does not provide or specify an implementation for its functions. For example, an *ATM* object implemented in Ada 95[2] interacts with the *Account* object implemented in C++ through the IDL interface. By separating interfaces and implementations, CORBA becomes a programming language-neutral standard.

IDL data types, syntax, and grammar are similar to C++. The language supports the following data types:

1. **Basic Types**: IDL supports the following types:

   a. *Char*: 8-bit character
   b. *Octet*: An 8-bit character that cannot undergo conversion by the communication protocol when it is transmitted to another system
   c. *Boolean*: Takes FALSE or TRUE values only
   d. *Short* and *unsigned short*: 16-bit integer
   e. *Long* and *unsigned long*: 32-bit integer
   f. *Float* and *double*: IEEE-32 single precision and IEEE-64 double precision
   g. *String*: An unbounded character string
   h. *Any*: Any of the above IDL types

2. **Enumerated Type**: IDL uses the same notation as C/C++ for declaring an enumerated type:

```
enum Color
{
     BLUE , RED , GREEN
} ;
```

3. **Data Structure**: IDL uses the same notation as C/C++ for declaring a data structure:

```
struct Point
{
     short x , y ;
} ;
```

4. **Union**: A union declaration is slightly different than in C/C++. An IDL union is used for operations that return different but predefined data types. The following is the generic syntax for declaring an IDL union:

```
union name
switch( expression )
{
        case Constant1:
             type declaration ;
        case Constant2:
             type declaration ;
        default:
             type declaration ;
} ;
```

5. **Sequence**: A sequence type is a one-dimensional array whose maximum size is statically (compile time) determined and whose actual length is dynamically (run time) determined. The dynamic length is less than or equal to the static size. In the following example, the maximum length of the string sequence is 32 bytes:

---

[2]As of March 1996, the CORBA standards have specified only C and C++ mappings. IDL mapping for Ada 95 and Java are being added to the standards.

```
string<32> name ;
```

After an IDL interface is defined, it is compiled using an IDL compiler. This compiler generates language specific output files for a *server* and a *client*. These files contain the class definitions and function skeletons. For a C++ mapping, the IDL compiler generates the following C++ header and source files:

1. **Server**: On the server (implementation) side, the header file contains the generated class definition based on the IDL interface. The source files contain the skeleton of the class member functions. A designer then modifies these files and adds functionality to the body of these functions. For example, the designer of the *Account* object modifies the bodies of the **deposit()** and **withdraw()** functions, and provides an implementation for them.

2. **Client**: On the client side, the declarations in the header file are used by a client that interacts with the *Account* object. For example, the *ATM* object uses the C++ declarations for **deposit()** and **withdraw()** to operate remotely on an *Account* object. The *Account* source file on the client side is a stubbed implementation that interacts with the CORBA-based middleware. The stubbed *Account* is referred to as a *proxy*. An *Account proxy* provides the identical interface to the *Account* class on the *server* side. However, a *proxy* does not provide any functionality, and handles routing of data to the middleware, which routes the information to the *Account* server. The *proxy* object also routes data returned by the *Account server* object to the client (Figure 12.3).

Similar to C++ classes, an IDL's **interface** can inherit from another **interface**. In the following example, the *Savings* IDL interface inherits from the *Account* interface and adds income capability:

```
//              SAVINGS.IDL File
#ifndef SAVINGS_IDL
#define SAVINGS_IDL
#include "account.idl"            // Account interface definition

module Savings_Account_Library
{
     // Savings inherits from Account
     interface Savings: Bank_Account_Library:: Account
     {
            // typedef declarations
            struct Interest_Table
            {
                   float rate ;
                   string<9> begin_date ;
                   unsigned short num_days ;
            } ;

            // data attributes visible in the interface
            readonly attribute Interest_Table interest ;

            // operations
            Bank_Account_Library:: Currency income( ) ;
     } ;
} ;


#endif             // SAVINGS_IDL File
```

Unlike classes in C++, *Savings* inherits only the interface of *Account* and does not inherit its implementation. When the above IDL is compiled using a C++ mapping, the *Savings* class on the server side must provide an implementation for its *Account* operations such as **deposit()**, **withdraw()**, and

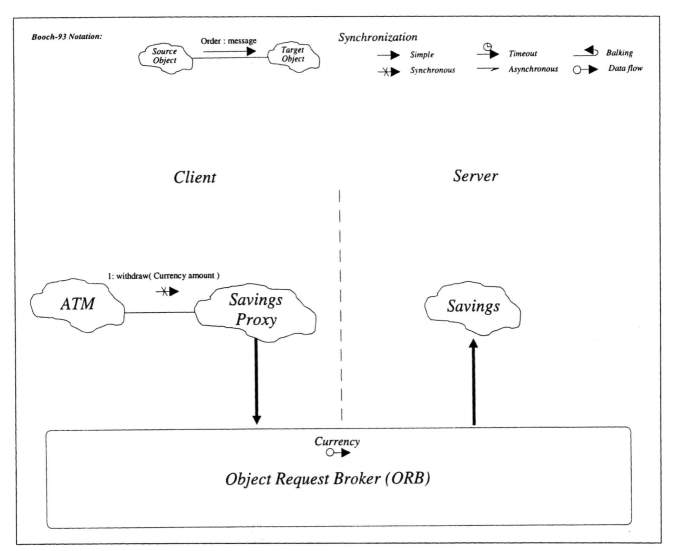

FIGURE 12.3 ATM and savings interaction.

account_statement(). Since IDL does not specify the implementation of an interface, the implementations for the IDL's operations cannot be inherited.

12.1.2 Object Request Broker (ORB)

In a distributed object model, objects are distributed across several systems. These systems may be connected with each other via a network, Internet, or other physical connections. A client interacts with a *distributed object* through a middleware software component referred to as an *Object Request Broker (ORB)*. The ORB hides communication protocols, connectivity, and other physical dependencies from the distributed objects. It is conceptually a data bus that coordinates routing and transfer of information between objects (Figure 12.4).

When a client invokes an operation on a distributed object, the ORB intercepts the call, locates the object, passes the parameters over the physical boundaries, invokes the corresponding function implementation on the *server* side, and then passes the return value back to the client. In Figure 12.4, the ORB transparently allows *ATM* to locate the *Savings* object, and invoke the deposit( ) or withdraw( ) operations on it.

An ORB provides the following capabilities:

1. **Method Invocations:** Through an ORB, the calls to the functions of an object are either determined statically at compile time or are resolved dynamically at run time.

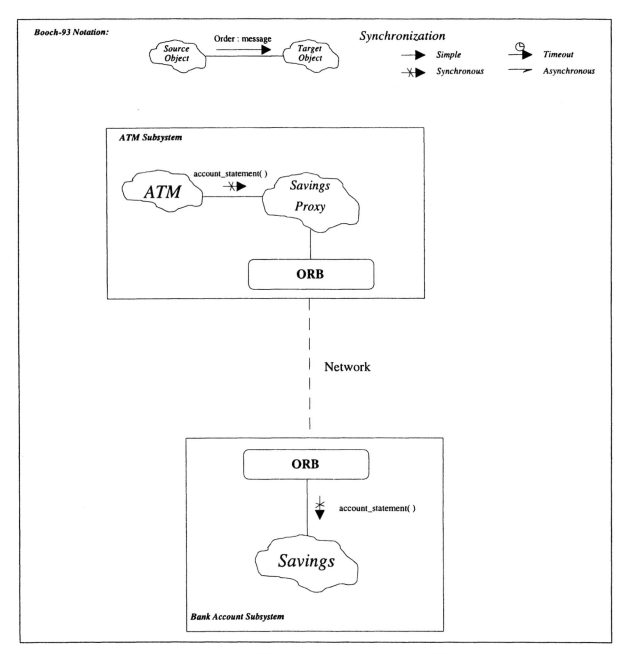

FIGURE 12.4 ATM and savings interaction via an ORB.

2. **Language Independence:** A client developed in C++ can invoke the method of an object developed in Ada 95. By separating implementation from interfaces through IDLs, an ORB makes the language used to implement the server object irrelevant to the client.

3. **Data Transactions:** When a client invokes an operation and passes information via the function's parameters, an ORB handles the data transfer and any transformations needed between the client and server objects. For instance, it handles byte reordering for representation of multibyte data types on different hardware platforms. One system may order storage of a floating point value from the most to least significant bytes, and another system may do the opposite.

4. **System Transparency:** By being a broker between the objects, an ORB hides physical dependencies as well as operating system dependencies from the distributed objects. All of the objects may reside within multiple processes on one system, or they may be scattered across several systems connected via a Local Area Network (LAN) or a Wide Area Network (WAN).

12.1.3 Common Object Services

CORBA specifies the following collection of services to assist the design and implementation of *distributed object models* (Figure 12.2):

1. **Naming Services:** For a client to operate on a specific object, the object must first be located. This service provides name look-up capability for locating an object on the applicable platform. By identifying where the object resides, the data parameters can be routed to the appropriate platform and the requested operation can then be invoked on it.

2. **Life Cycle Services:** These services govern how distributed objects are created, moved, copied, and destroyed.

3. **Persistence Services:** Some objects cannot be destroyed without storing their current state for future requests. For example, after an *ATM* invokes the withdraw() operation on a *Savings* object, the *Savings* account information must be permanently updated to reflect the withdrawal operation. For this purpose a database is used to store the state of *Savings*. Through the persistence service, CORBA provides a uniform interface for storing an object's information to a variety of persistent storage facilities such as a database or a file.

4. **Event Services:** In a distributed model, objects not only interact with each other through the functions specified in their IDLs, but they can also interact through *events*. Event services allow objects to associate themselves with an event, and become a *supplier* or a *consumer* of an event. When a *supplier* initiates an *event*, the information is passed to the *consumer* objects via an *event channel*. The concept is similar to a bulletin board, where one person posts a message and people with access to the bulletin board look for the message.

   This service provides several types of *event channel* models, the description of which are beyond the scope of this book.

5. **Concurrency Control Services:** This service prevents deadlocks from occurring when two clients try to access the same object at the same time. Through a concurrency control mechanism, usually a *semaphore*, the clients access an object in an orderly and systematic manner.

6. **Transaction Services:** In distributed applications, some requests must be managed from the point of initiation until they are actually completed. These requests are denoted as *transactions*. For instance, a withdraw( ) request by an *ATM* object should be handled as a *transaction* because the *Savings* object should not *commit* to the withdraw request until the *ATM* object dispenses the money to its customer and notifies *Savings*.

   A *transaction* allows the system to recover from a failure by rolling back to a previous predictable state. For instance, if the *ATM* object is unable to open its money dispenser tray due to a mechanical failure, the withdraw() transaction can be canceled.

7. **Externalization Services:** Similar to C++ Stream I/O, this service uses a stream-based design for obtaining and passing data between objects through a *stream* object.

8. **Relationships Services:** This service provides the capability for assigning roles and relationships to distributed objects without changing their implementations. This service addresses the *containment* and *cardinality* aspects of the design.

9. **Properties Services:** This service allows a set of attributes to be dynamically associated with an off-the-shelf software component without the use of an IDL.

10. **Licensing Services:** This service provides metering capability and allows software applications to collect fees from clients of an object. Through this service, a client may be charged when an object is created or used, or when an object is being used based on a session, site, or node.

11. **Query Services:** For database applications, CORBA provides object query operations using an Object Query Language (OQL).

12. **Security Services:** This service provides security features in order to restrict access to sensitive information. For example, an *ATM* object can operate only on a *Savings* object after the *ATM* object has been authenticated. This is performed by a third-party *principal* object that provides the *Savings* and *ATM* objects with an *authenticated ID*. The *ATM* object uses this ID to interact with the *Savings* object when it is accessing the account information. Through security services, the client's access rights are specified. After *ATM* has been authenticated, the *Savings* object then uses an *Access Control List (ACL)* to control *ATM* access.

The security services provide *audit* capability, and make clients accountable. These services monitor objects and keep a log of the interactions on a secured object. The security services also provide *encryption* capability which avoids unauthorized reading of data by an outside party during data transmission. For example, transmission of a *Credit Card* object over a medium such as the Internet must be kept confidential. Through data encryption, the account number, person's name, and other transaction information are protected while data are being transported.

   13. **Time Services:** For event tracking, this service allows the clock on the distributed systems to be periodically synchronized.

OMG is adding other additional services to other versions of CORBA, such as trader, collections, and change management [Orfali 1996].

12.1.4 Common Facilities

To facilitate management of a distributed object model and build on standardized IDL interfaces, CORBA specifies a collection of common facilities known as *horizontal* and *vertical* common object facilities. The following is a list of *horizontal* facilities (Figure 12.2):

   1. **User Interface (UI):** Provides UI editing services
   2. **Systems Management:** Defines the interfaces for managing, installing, and configuring distributed objects
   3. **Information Management:** Provides data exchange facilities
   4. **Task Management:** Provides e-mail service, long transactions, and scripting

The *vertical* facilities provide standardized IDL interfaces for retail, finance, medical, and other applications.

12.2 DISTRIBUTED OBJECT

Similar to a C++ object, a *distributed object* must be created before it is operated on. When a client finishes using the object, the object may be destroyed. This section describes design considerations in reference to the following issues:

   1. Construction
   2. Interaction
   3. Destruction
   4. Persistence
   5. Concurrency

12.2.1 Object Construction

Through constructors, the C++ language provides the capability to create objects automatically. A client statically declares an object or uses the new operator in order to create an object dynamically. At run time, the memory space allocation for an object is reserved and the applicable constructor is called.

C++ cannot handle automatic creation of objects when they reside in a different process or another address space. The language and physical hardware limitations require the object model to include provisions for creating a *distributed object* prior to operating on it. For example, the *ATM* object depicted in Figure 12.3 operates on a *Savings* object. Since the two objects reside in different address spaces, the *ATM* object somehow must create a *Savings* object remotely prior to making the deposit( ) and withdraw( ) requests.

The creation of a *distributed object* introduces the notion of a *factory*, which is an object that creates instances of other objects [Gamma et al., 1994]. In the banking system example, an *ATM* object does not have access to the *bank account* subsystem and its local resources. This prevents the *ATM* object from creating a *Savings* object directly. However, *ATM* can remotely create a *Savings* object by using an intermediary *Bank* object (Figure 12.5). The *ATM* object supplies the *Bank* with the account ID recorded on the *ATM* card. *Bank* uses this information to locate the customer's profile and balance information in the local database. On locating the information, the factory then creates an instance of *Savings* on the target system via a *Savings* constructor. The *Bank* factory then supplies the *ATM* object with a *remote object reference* to the *Savings* object. This reference is analogous to a C++ pointer or reference, and it allows *ATM* to operate on the *Savings* object remotely.

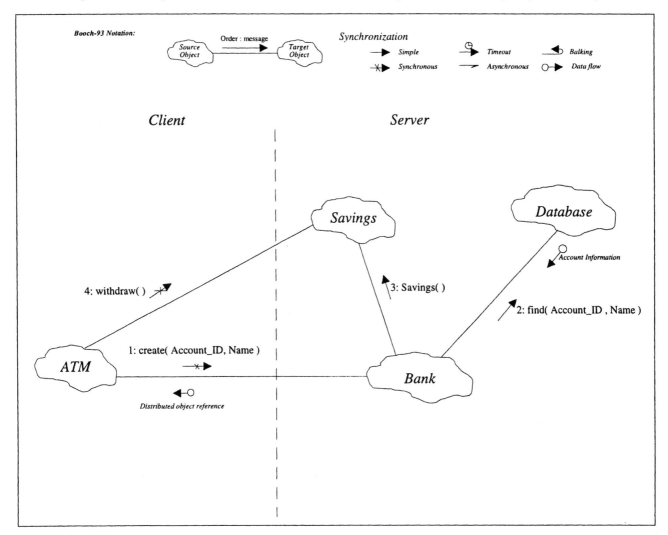

FIGURE 12.5 Savings object creation and interaction.

Since an *ATM* object operates on different types of bank accounts, the *Bank* factory should be able to handle different types of accounts. If the creation of bank account objects varies on the basis of their types, then unique factories are needed for each specific type of bank account. In this case, a *factory* design hierarchy is used to address differences and commonality while providing a common design interface (Figure 12.6). By making *Bank* an *abstract factory*, the common operations are then handled by an abstract *Bank* class, and the derived *factories* define the unique implementations for each type of bank account. Since the *factory* design hierarchy provides a uniform design interface, this hierarchy makes *ATM* independent of specific types of bank factories.

In the CORBA standard, objects are created as an outcome of a client request and there should be no special mechanism for creating an object. For a CORBA-compliant object model, the notion of *factories* can be encapsulated from a client in the object model.

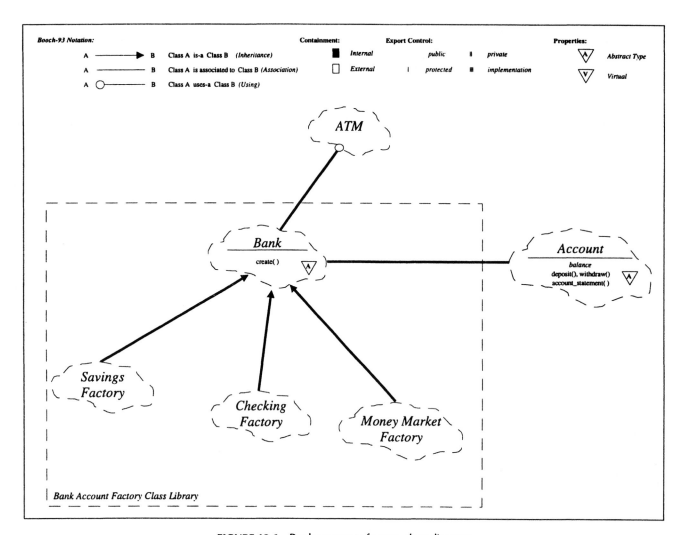

Booch-93 Notation:

A ──────▶ B   Class A is-a Class B   *(Inheritance)*

A ────── B   Class A is associated to Class B *(Association)*

A ○────── B   Class A uses-a Class B *(Using)*

Containment: ■ *Internal*   □ *External*

Export Control: *public*   I *protected*   II *private*   III *implementation*

Properties: ▽A *Abstract Type*   ▽V *Virtual*

FIGURE 12.6   Bank accounts factory class diagram.

12.2.2 Object Interaction

The interaction between two C++ objects is performed simply by invoking a member function and passing the "**this**" pointer to it. For instance, an *ATM* object operates on a *Savings* object by using the following notation:

```
savings_object.deposit( amount ) ;
```

When the **deposit()** function is invoked, the "**this**" pointer and the ***amount*** parameter are passed to **deposit()** on the *stack*. Since both data and program reside in the same memory, the member function in the *program segment* accesses the *Savings* data members stored in the *data segment*. After the member function finishes executing, the return value is passed back to the caller on the *stack*.

In a distributed object architecture, a client object resides in its own memory area and its functions do not have access to an external data segment containing another *distributed object*. For instance, *ATM* member functions do not have direct access to *Savings* data and functions (Figure 12.7). The distributed architecture introduces several logistical and complexity issues with respect to object interaction:

1. **Arguments and Return Value**: Parameters and return values must be passed across physical and/or process boundaries. In the case of a physical boundary, the information must be transmitted over network, Internet, or wireless mediums. In the bank example, when the *ATM* object operates on *Savings* and invokes **Savings:: deposit()**, the deposit ***amount*** must be passed over some type of network boundary. The data transfer will require the information to be packaged according to a specified network communication protocol, such as TCP/IP, and sent over to the bank account subsystem (Figure 12.7). The bank account subsystem, which maintains the applicable *Savings* object, then unpacks the information. This process is referred to as *data marshalling*. The *Savings* member function is then invoked and the parameters are passed to it. The **deposit()** function's return value is then returned to *ATM* via the same *data marshalling* process as the arguments.

   In a CORBA-compliant system, the data-marshalling operation is performed by the *Object Request Broker (ORB)*. The ORB's components are responsible for finding the distributed object, marshalling the request to the server object, invoking the method, and passing parameters to it. The ORB then marshals the return value to the client.

2. **Interface**: The client of a distributed object operates on the object even though the object does not reside in the same address space. The client must somehow have information on the class and its external interfaces. For instance, the *ATM* object needs the *Savings* interface in order to operate on a *Savings* object.

   In C++ applications, the client of a class uses the class definition stored in a header file for obtaining information on the class external interface. For a distributed application, a client must have access to the

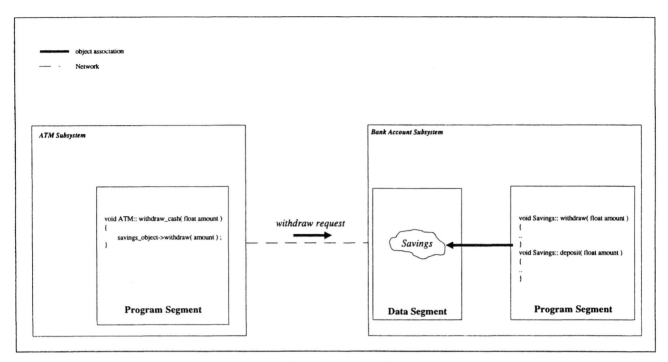

FIGURE 12.7 Distributed object block diagram.

distributed object's interface. For CORBA-based applications, an IDL specification provides this capability. During the compilation of an IDL interface, the IDL compiler creates a stubbed version (*proxy* object) of the interface. A *proxy* object is a stubbed version of the *server* object, and provides the same interface. The client issues requests to the *server* object via the *proxy* object. In Figure 12.3, the *ATM* object operates on the *Saving* object through a *Savings proxy* object. The *proxy object* handles the interaction with the distributed object development platform, and hides the *distributed aspects* of *Savings* from *ATM*. From *ATM's* perspective it is operating on the actual *Savings* object:

```
account->deposit( amount ) ;
```

A distributed function call takes substantially more time than simple C++ function calls because the object must be located, the parameters must be transmitted over a network medium, the object must be activated if it is inactive, the method must be invoked, and the return value must be sent back over the same medium. To minimize this overhead, a proxy object at times maintains its own copy of the commonly needed information of a server object. The local copy may be either a subset or a complete copy of server's data. If a proxy maintains its own local copy of data, distributed calls are reduced. Thus, the network traffic is reduced and software response time would be faster. For example, the Savings proxy object may store balance and interest information locally. For operations that do not affect the state of the object, such as balance queries, the Savings proxy uses the local information. However, when an operation is invoked that changes the state of the object, the Savings proxy would then make a distributed call to the real Savings object. A proxy object that maintains its own local copy of data is referred to as a smart proxy. Since a smart proxy maintains its own local copy of data, it gains functionality and is no longer a stubbed version of the server object. The use of smart proxies may improve performance but at the same time it introduces additional complexities. An implementation would need to keep a smart proxy's information in sync with the server object. When there are two or more smart proxies for an object, not only the original server object must be updated when one proxy changes state, but also all other proxies must be notified. This design must then formulate policies that would prevent a smart proxy from operating on old and invalid data. For instance, the actual server object may keep track of its proxies and notify them automatically when its state changes.

Another application of a smart proxy is to hide the notion of factories from the client. For example, the constructor of a Savings proxy may be used to interact with the Bank factory object that creates the server Savings object in the bank account subsystem. The ATM would then be unaware of the Bank factory object.

3. **Reference**: In C++, a client operates on an object by using a reference or a pointer. In distributed objects, a client will need a similar tool to gain access to the object. These references are generated by the CORBA-based development environment and contain the applicable information that would allow an ORB to locate and operate on the object. In the following example, the ATM object uses a Savings object reference:

```
Boolean ATM:: dispense_cash( ODF_ObjRef<Savings> &current,
                    Currency amount )
{
    Boolean dispensed = true ;
    try
    {
        // make withdraw request
        current->withdraw( amount ) ;

        // if no exceptions, open cash tray
        tray.open( ) ;

        // dispense n $20.00 bills
        tray.dispense( amount % 20 ) ;
        // wait until money has been taken out of tray
        while( !tray.empty() ) ;
        tray.close() ;
    }
    catch( CORBA:: Exception &error )
    {
        dispensed = false ;
        // recovery code
    }

    return( dispensed ) ;
}
```

12.2.3 Object Destruction

When a C++ object goes out of scope or a dynamically allocated object is deleted, the destructor for the object is called and its memory space is deallocated. In the case of a distributed model, the object's lifetime may or may not be associated with the process that created it. For example, if an *ATM* object creates and operates on a specific *Savings* object, the *ATM* object cannot destroy the *Savings* object when *Savings* is also being operated on by a *Teller* object (Figure 12.1). The lifetime of the *Savings* object is not coupled to the process that created it.

The implementation of the model must ensure that objects are destroyed only after all the clients finish using them. An approach commonly used is that an object keeps a reference count of the number of clients with which it is interacting. When a client finishes using the object it notifies the object, which decrements its reference count. The object is destroyed when the last client finishes using the object and the reference count reaches zero. This approach prevents an object from being destroyed prematurely while it is being accessed by a group of objects. However, this approach requires the clients' cooperation. If a client does not notify the object or the notification is lost due to an error, then the object is never destroyed because it assumes there are still valid clients. These side effects would require the need for some type of garbage collection system, or use of time-out features in order to allow proper cleanup.

12.2.4 Object Persistence

Some of the objects in a distributed model may require their state to be stored for future requests. The *Bank Account* classes are examples of these classes, which require persistence. When a *Bank Account* object is destroyed, the deposit() and withdraw() transactions performed must be permanently reflected. The member functions of these objects need to interface to a database and record the transactions. By using a database, *the state of the object can then transcend through time and space* [Booch 1994].

Through *Persistence Object Services (POS)*, CORBA supports persistence for a distributed object model. POS provides the capability for the objects to store their contents to a file that has a low performance overhead (*lightweight*) or to a database that has a higher overhead (*heavyweight*).

CORBA's *Persistent Object Services* provide several benefits:

1. **Uniform Interface:** POS uses a uniform interface that allows objects in memory to interface with any of the following types of persistent storage: relational database manager (RDBM), object-oriented database manager (ODBM), file, and other special persistent storage mediums (Figure 12.8).

   In Figure 12.8, an object inherits from the *Persistent Object* (PO) IDL, which specifies the underlying interface for persistent storage. Through the *Persistent Object Manager (POM)*, POS encapsulates an object from the underlying persistent storage facility, such as use of a file or an ODBM. The *Persistent Object Manager* routes information from an object to the applicable persistent data storage facility. The actual data storage is performed by the *Persistent Data Services (PDS)* component, which interfaces with the applicable *Datastores* such as an ODBM or a file.

2. **Persistence Abstraction:** POS encapsulates and abstracts the use of persistent storage from a client. An object can reside in memory or be maintained in external storage such as an ODBM. From the client's perspective the object is available at all times. For example, a *Savings* object may be inactive and its state stored in an ODBM. When an *ATM* invokes a withdraw() operation, the *Savings* object is activated, the request processed, and the result is stored back into the database. The use of persistent storage is completely hidden from the client. This approach is referred to as a *single-level store*.

   In some other applications, memory and persistent storage are separated from each other, and clients become aware of the use of persistent storage in the design. This approach allows a client to become involved in the actual storage of data, and is referred to as a *two-level store* [Orfali 1996].

12.2.5 Object Concurrency

Objects in a distributed model need to address concurrent access by multiple clients. To prevent an object from going into an unpredictable state, some of the member functions must incorporate locking mechanisms that will protect the data members from simultaneous access. For example, when the *ATM* object invokes the withdraw() operation, this function needs to lock the *Account balance* while it is processing the withdrawal request. If a *Teller* client invokes the print_statement() function at the same time, this function must wait until the lock for the *Account balance* information is released. By controlling simultaneous access to the *balance* information, the *Teller* client does not obtain invalid and stale data.

Critical code or data are protected by the *semaphore* locking mechanism. A *mutex* is the simplest form of a *semaphore*. It is a Boolean flag, and indicates whether the protected information is currently locked or not. The locking mechanisms can become complicated by providing different levels of protection. For example, a *semaphore* may provide a partial lock for simultaneous read operations, and a full lock when the state of the object is being changed (write). CORBA's *concurrency services* provide semaphores that allow a distributed object to protect its critical information from concurrent operations.

12.3 DESIGN ISSUES

The design of a distributed system introduces many levels of complexity. Two main issues that must be addressed in the design of such a system are performance and error detection/recovery. As discussed in Chapter 2, these are *strategic* issues that the system architecture must address:

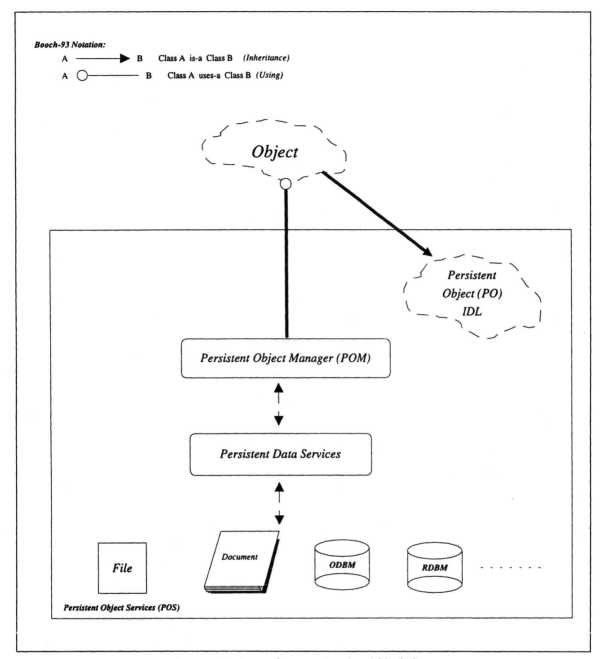

FIGURE 12.8 Persistent object services (POS) block diagram.

1. **Performance:** The interactions between the distributed objects increase software overhead. For methods that have numerous parameters or complex objects in their argument lists, the distributed calls may adversely affect the system performance.

   There are design techniques and strategies that address the performance issues. For example, the information on the client side is typically cached in order to reduce the amount of network traffic and distributed calls (*refer to smart proxies in Section 12.2.2*).

2. **Error Detection/Recovery:** The design of distributed objects not only has to deal with exceptions that occur with the software operation, it must also encompass exceptions that occur with distributed platforms. For example, a message sent to an object may be lost due to loss of a communication link, a system crash, or other factors. The application software cannot leave these types of exceptions as an implementation

issue. Instead, the system design needs to specify a system wide cohesive error detection/recovery strategy. This approach can allow the system to continue operating in a degraded mode, and may prevent complete system failure.

For an indepth discussion on distributed object design, the reader may refer to *Distributed Objects: Methodologies for Customizing Systems Software* [Islam 1996].

SUMMARY

In distributed applications, objects become scattered across hardware and process boundaries. Proper distribution of objects enhances system throughput, because objects interacting with each other can perform tasks in parallel. The resulting parallelism helps in better utilizing the computing resources, but it also introduces additional design complexities. With distributed objects, the design and implementation must explicitly address issues that are automatically handled by an object-oriented language in a single-process application. Some of these issues are as follows:

1. **Object Construction:** Since a distributed object does not have access to the resources and facilities of another system, it needs to interact with an intermediate factory object in order to create an instance of another object. For example, an ATM object interacts with a Savings Factory object, which searches its local database for specific savings account information, and then creates an instance of Savings.
2. **Object Interaction:** When a distributed object invokes a method on a distributed server object, the parameters must be sent over a network using a communication protocol, to the system containing the server object. The applicable method of the object is then invoked. The return value is also routed back over the same medium to the caller. To encapsulate this process, proxy objects are used. A proxy object resides on the same platform as the client and provides the same interface as the server object but with no real functionality, other than routing requests. It simply locates the real server object, sends the applicable parameters to it, and routes the return value back to the client.

   At times proxy objects cache some of the server object's data in order to reduce distributed calls. By reducing distributed calls, system performance is improved and network traffic is reduced. These proxy objects must then provide some limited functionality, and are referred to as smart proxies. However, when an object has several smart proxies, the design must address how its data are kept in sync with its proxies.
   A critical issue in the design of distributed objects is concurrency. Since the objects in the model are distributed, they could attempt to interact with each other at the same time. There is a need to synchronize and control access to an object in order to prevent simultaneous requests from corrupting information maintained by the distributed object. Semaphores, which are locking mechanisms, are used to synchronize and control interactions.
3. **Object Destruction:** Unlike a single process application, the lifetime of an object cannot be tied to the process that created it. A distributed object can be created by one object but may be destroyed only when its last client issues a destroy request. For this purpose, a distributed object may need to keep a log of its clients, and only respond to a destroy request from its last client. While this approach solves the destruction issue, it also introduces a reliability issue. If a client's process dies or a destroy request is lost, then the object is never destroyed. This requires use of garbage collection.

To facilitate design and implementation of distributed objects, the Common Object Request Broker Architecture (CORBA) standard was created by a consortium of companies. This standard allows distributed objects to interoperate with each other independent of platform, underlying implementation, communication protocol, and types of network. CORBA specifies the following features and resources that address complexities associated with distributed objects:

1. **Interface Definition Language (IDL):** This language is similar in syntax to C++ and is used to specify the interface for a distributed object. It is on the basis of their IDL interfaces that distributed objects interact with each other. The use of an IDL hides the underlying implementation of distributed objects, and they can even be implemented in different languages.

2. **Object Request Broker (ORB):** An ORB is like a data bus that intercepts a distributed call; locates the target object using an object naming service; routes the passed parameters over the network; invokes the applicable method on the server object; and routes the data back to the client object.
3. **Common Object Services:** CORBA specifies a collection of services that facilitate the design and implementation of a distributed model. Some of these services are naming, concurrency control, persistence, and timing.
4. **Common Facilities:** These facilities provide standardized IDL interfaces for development of vertical applications such as a biomedical application. The horizontal facilities provide support for system configuration, information, and task management, such as e-mail capability and software installation.

GLOSSARY

CASE tool
Computer-Aided Software Engineering tool

COM
Common Object Model

CORBA
Common Object Request Broker Architecture

Data marshalling
The process of packing data being supplied by a client and transmitting it over a network to the server object

Factory
An object that creates an instance of another object

Flat file
A file that does not contain any relational information or references within it, such as a file containing text or a picture

IDL
Interface Definition Language

LAN
Local Area Network

Mutex
A binary semaphore

Multiprocess
When several processes execute concurrently

Multithreaded
Threads refer to the segments of a program that execute concurrently

OMG
Object Management Group

ORB
Object Request Broker

Process
A process consists of one or more threads

Proxy
An object that provides the same interface as its server object but does not have any functionality. During a method invocation, it routes data to the true server object and sends back the return value to the client

Semaphore

A locking mechanism used to lock critical code or data. Through a semaphore only one client can access the locked information at a time

Server

An object that is accessed by a client object

Smart proxy

A smart proxy is a proxy that caches some of the information of its server object and provides some limited capability. It is used to reduce distributed calls

Thread

Sequence of instructions executed within a program

Transaction

A transaction is a request that is managed from the point of initiation until it has been completed

WAN

Wide Area Network

CHAPTER 13

Introduction to Java

INTRODUCTION

Java is an object-oriented language developed by Sun Microsystems. Java uses features and syntax from C++ and adds support for concurrency. Since Java is similar in syntax to C++, its rising popularity warrants an overview of this language. Java is developed based on the following objectives [Sun 1995]:

1. **Platform Independence**: Java is a platform-neutral language. Unlike a C++ compiler, the Java compiler does not generate processor-specific executable code (*binary code*). Instead it generates *byte code*, which is an intermediate representation not specific to a particular processor. Java's run-time environment *interprets* and executes the generated *byte code*.

   By using an intermediate-level representation instead of a machine's native binary code, a compiled Java program may be easily ported to any platform having a Java run time environment. A *heterogeneous* architecture can dynamically share Java applications.

2. **Security**: Java's run time environment has the following built-in security features:

   a. Imported Java applications are checked for viruses.
   b. Imported applications are given limited access to critical resources such as the file system.
   c. Java's *byte code verifier* checks the integrity of the imported *byte code*. For example, it checks for stack overflow and underflow, illegal data conversions, illegal instructions, and illegal access levels.
      For distributed designs, security is an important design issue. Since objects interact across hardware and geographical boundaries, information as well as the computing system must be guarded against unauthorized accesses, viruses, trojan horses, and so on. Even though Java provides several security features, there are security deficiencies and problems that need to be resolved [Dean et al., 1996].

3. **Concurrency**: Java provides *multithreading* capability through language features and library support. This capability allows an application to perform concurrent operations such as displaying a picture, loading images from disk, and playing music, all at the same time.

4. **Performance**: Since Java is interpreted, special care has been taken to reduce overhead and provide an optimized environment.

5. **Robustness**: The Java development environment has been designed to reduce programming errors, such as memory leakage. For example, Java does not support *pointers* and pointer arithmetic. By eliminating a

program's access to physical address locations, Java's memory management has more control over the data memory space. Java also provides automatic *garbage collection* to reclaim objects that are no longer in use by a program.

Java is not only used for standalone applications such as C++ applications, but is also used to develop World Wide Web service applications known as *applets*. Additionally, Sun Microsystems has provided CORBA support for Java through a CORBA-IDL to Java mapping. Java's syntax and features are quite similar to C++, which makes transitioning from C++ to Java relatively easy [Sun 1995]. This chapter compares Java to C++ and provides an overview of the language in terms of the *object model* framework in the following areas:

1. Encapsulation
2. Abstraction
3. Modularity
4. Design Hierarchy
5. Concurrency
6. Typing

The discussion also includes basic features of the language such as exception handling and interface definition, and an overview of development environment.

13.1 BUILT-IN DATA TYPES

Java built-in data types are similar to C++ and are outlined in Table 13.1.

TABLE 13.1   Java Built-in Data Types

Type	Range
Boolean	false, true
byte	8-bits: -2^7 to 2^7-1
short	16-bits: -2^{15} to 2^{15}-1
int	32-bits: -2^{31} to 2^{31}-1
long	64-bits: -2^{63} to 2^{63}-1
char	16-bit unsigned unicode character set
float	IEEE-32
double	IEEE-64

In terms of *typing*, Java is most similar to Ada and does not permit mixing data types in an expression without explicit casts. For example, an expression that contains both float and integer variables requires an explicit cast. As discussed in Chapter 1, a *strongly typed* language reduces logical errors caused by implicit conversions:

```
float circum , r ;
.
circum = (float) 2 * PI * r ;     // circumference of a Circle
```

Java supports only **signed integers** based on a 2's complement representation. To accommodate unsigned integer operations, Java provides an *unsigned binary right shift* operator (>>>). In the following example, this operator uses a leading zero for the most significant bit of ***temp_radius*** during the *binary right shift* operation:

```
//      CIRCLE.JAVA File
class Circle
{
        // internal data representation
        private int radius ;
        private Point center ;

        // graphics member functions
        public boolean reduce( int n )
        {
                boolean reduced = false ;
                int temp_radius = radius ;

                // if n is within the valid range then reduce radius
                if( n > 1 && n < 15 )
                {
                        // divide by 2 n
                        temp_radius = temp_radius >>> n ;
                }
                else
                {
                        temp_radius = 0 ;
                }

                // if reduction has not caused radius to become zero
                //reduce radius and redraw circle
                if( temp_radius != 0 )
                {
                        radius = temp_radius ;
                        reduced = true ; // reduce request granted
                        redraw( ) ; // redraw circle
                }

                return( reduced ) ;
        }

        public void redraw( void )
        {
                // body of redraw() method
        }

        // Other details omitted
}
```

In Java, integer expressions are evaluated as an **int** or **long** type. If an operand is a **long** integer, the result of the evaluation is **long**, otherwise the expression type is **int**. Similar to C++, Java uses leading **0** and **0x** for *octal* and *hexadecimal* representations, respectively:

```
long low_mask = 0xffff ; // hexadecimal
short permission = 0753 ; // octal
```

Java's **char** type is similar to C++'s **wchar_t** (*wide character type*). The use of an unsigned integer to represent a character gives a Java application the ability to represent international characters and a character set larger than the traditional ASCII 8-bit character set:

```
char control_char = '\f' ;
        // Java uses the C++ symbols for representing non-printable
        // characters, such as \r - carriage return, \b - backspace,
        // \\ - backslash, and \' - single quote
```

Java does not support preprocessor directives such as **#define** and **#include**. Constants can be defined only as constant variables by using the **final** keyword. For example, PI is defined as:

```
final double PI = java.lang.Math.acos( -1.0 ) ;
        // the above declaration denotes PI cannot be changed after
        // it is defined. Incidentally, Java's math library provides a
        // definition for PI.
```

In Java, arrays are created in two stages: the memory space is allocated and then it is initialized. In the following example, the memory space for an array of *Circle* objects is allocated, and is then initialized by using the *default* constructor:

```
Circle list[ ] = new Circle[ n ] ;         // allocate an array of Circle objects
for( int i = 0 ; i < n ; i++ )
{
        list[i] = new Circle( ) ;
                                // invoke constructor to initialize memory space
}
```

Java treats arrays as objects. This is similar to the *Array* template class defined in Chapter 11, which provided the array boundary check and the **length()** functions. Java provides a *length* variable that identifies the length of an array, and its run time environment checks for array boundary exceptions:

```
// display area of circles in the list
for( i = 0 ; i < list.length ; i++ )
{
        System.out.println( "Area of Circle: " + list[i].area( ) ) ;
}
```

As method arguments, built-in data types are passed by value. However, objects and arrays in Java are passed by reference.

To avoid the errors that normally result with the use of pointers, Java does not support pointers and pointer arithmetic. By removing a program's ability to access a memory location using its physical address, Java can then control the program's access to its data memory space. As discussed earlier, Java's run time environment checks for array boundary violations. In addition, it provides an automatic *garbage collection* mechanism. When an object is no longer being used, it is reclaimed by the run time *garbage collector* and its memory space is returned to the available memory pool. In the following example, *c1* is used to reference two different objects. When the first object referenced by *c1* is replaced by a new one, the first one is freed and its memory space can be reused by the memory manager for other allocation requests:

```
//      TEST.JAVA File
import java.lang.System       ; // Use Java's System console I/O library
import Shapes.*               ; // Use Shape Library
public class Test_Driver
{
        // Similar to the main() function in C++, a standalone Java application
        // requires an entry point which is denoted by the main() method.
        // This method must be a static member of a class. In this case, it is
        // a static member of the Test_Driver class.
```

```
        public static void main( String args[ ] )
        {
                Circle c1  ;// declare a reference for a Circle object

                // instantiate and reference a Circle object
                c1 = new Circle( 1 , 2 , 4 ) ;

                // Display areas on the console
                System.out.print( "Area of Circle: " + c1.area( ) ) ;

                // instantiate and reference a new Circle object
                // the previous object is automatically returned to the
                // available memory space pool.
                c1 = new Circle( 3 , 5 , 6 ) ;
                System.out.print( "Area of Circle: " + c1.area( ) ) ;
        }
}
```

Unlike C++, the preceding *"Circle c1"* statement is a *declaration* and not an *instantiation*. An object is created only when its memory space is allocated and its constructor executed. With a declaration, an object is not created. The above declaration specifies that *c1* is a reference to a *Circle* object. Until it references a valid object, it is initialized to null. A *Circle* object is created when the **new** command is used to allocate memory and the applicable *Circle* constructor is called. After a *Circle* object is instantiated by using **new**, *c1* will reference the *Circle* object.

13.2 PACKAGE

In C++, a group of related classes is organized and packaged using a namespace. Java provides the same capability through a **package**. For example, the classes within the *Shape* class hierarchy in Chapter 10 can be organized into the *Shapes* library package (Figure 13.1):

```
//      SHAPE.JAVA File
package Shapes  ;// Specifying Shape Library package

class Shape
{
        // body
}

// Circle inherits from Shape
class Circle extends Shape
{
        // body
}

// Rectangle inherits from Shape
class Rectangle extends Shape
{
        // body
}

// Square inherits from Rectangle
class Square extends Rectangle
{
```

```
            //  body
        }
```

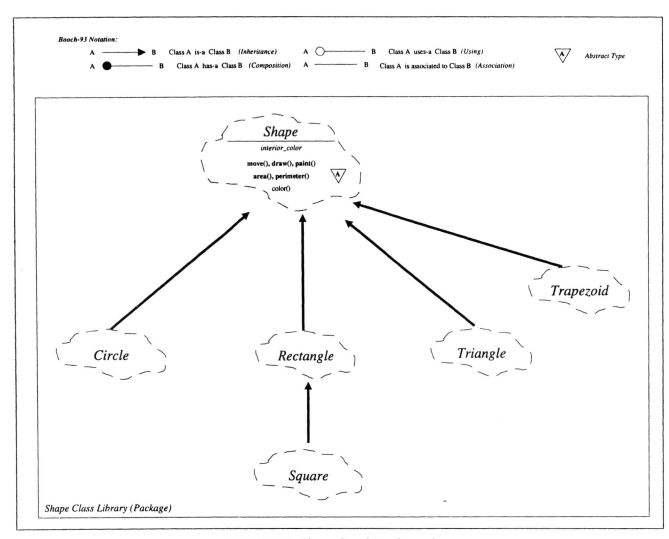

FIGURE 13.1   Shape class design hierarchy.

The client accesses features from a package by using the **import** keyword:

```
//        CAD.JAVA File
import Shapes.*;
            // Use all of the classes within the Shapes Library
```

This example is similar to a C++ *using directive*. In this case, the client can access all classes defined in the package. Java also provides more inclusive importing capability by allowing a client to import a specific class within a package, similar to the C++ *using declaration*:

```
//        CAD.JAVA File
import Shapes.Circle ; // Use Circle from the Shapes Library
```

To standardize package names, Sun Microsystems recommends that package names be preceded by reversing the Internet domain name [Tyma 1996]. On the basis of this convention, the preceding package is renamed using the "**com.parta.Shapes**" label.

Java's package feature provides a built-in mechanism for logically organizing classes into a set of loosely coupled and cohesive libraries. By creating *modular* designs, core libraries can be shared among different software applications.

13.3 CLASS DEFINITION

Since Java is an object-oriented language, classes provide the fundamental underlying components of the language. The syntax for a Java class is similar to a C++ class:

```
class Name
{
        [access_level] type data_members ;

        [modifier] [access_level] return_type method_name( parameters )
                                          [throws exception_list]
        {
                // method's body
        }
}
```

In Java, the member functions of a class are referred to as *methods*. Java does not support nonmember and standalone functions. In the following example, a *Circle* class has been defined using the above syntax:

```
//      CIRCLE.JAVA File
package Shapes  ;// Specifying Shape Library package

class Circle
{
        // internal data representation
        private int radius ;
        private Point center ;

        // default constructor
        public Circle( )
        {
                // constructor's body
        }

        // user-defined value constructor
        public Circle( int x , int y , int r )
        {
                // constructor's body
        }

        // graphics member functions
        public boolean reduce( int n )
        {
                // body of reduce( )
        }

        boolean enlarge( int n )      // default access level
        {
                // body of enlarge( )
```

```
        }

        public void redraw( )
        {
                // body of redraw( )
        }
        public float area( )
        {
                // body of area( )
        }
        public float perimeter( )
        {
                // body of perimeter( )
        }
}
```

In the preceding example, *center* and ***radius*** are data elements with the **private** access level. The *Circle* class provides a variety of member functions such as **area()**.

When a class is declared **public**, it is visible to classes outside its package. A class declaration that omits an access level is visible only within its own package:

```
//      CIRCLE.JAVA File
package Shapes  ;// Specifying Shape Library package

// visible outside the Shapes Library
public class Circle
{
                private int radius ;
                private Point center ;
                // other details left out
}


// only visible within the Shapes Library
class Point
{
                private int x , y ;
                // other details left out

}
```

Java supports **static** data members and methods. Java's static members are subject to the same restrictions as those in C++. A static method cannot access nonstatic methods or data in a class. The static data members are initialized at class load time, and a class may provide an *initialization block* that is executed only once. In the following example, the *Savings* class may provide different interest rates based on the account's balance. By using an ***interest_rates*** table, a *Savings* object can dynamically change its interest rate information using its balance and this table. Since the interest rates are common for all of the objects, the ***interest_rates*** table is declared as **static** and it is initialized to values retrieved from a file when the *Savings* class is loaded into memory:

```
class Savings
{
        // static data member declaration
        static private float interest_rates[5] ;

        // static data initialization block
        static
        {
```

```
                    for( int i = 0 ; i < 5 ; i++ )
                    {
                            // load interest rates from a file
                    }
          }
          // other details left out
}
```

13.4 ENCAPSULATION

Through access levels, Java implements and enforces encapsulation. A Java class regulates access to its members via five different access levels. These access levels are an expanded version of the C++ access levels. Table 13.2 describes the access levels and their similarities to their C++ counterparts.

TABLE 13.2   Java's Access Levels

Access Level	Description
private	The same as C++, a **private** member is internal to the design of the class
private protected	It is the same as the protected access level in C++. A **private protected** member is accessible only by the derived classes
default	A **default** member can be accessed by any class within the same **package**. There is no C++ equivalent
protected	A **protected** member is accessible by the derived classes and also any nonderiving classes that have been defined within the same **package**. There is no C++ equivalent
public	The same as C++, a public member is accessible to any type of client

In the previous Circle example, the client operates on the **private** data members by using the **public** member functions. The access level specification is optional, and the compiler uses the **default** access level for members that do not declare an access level. In the previous example, the Circle's **enlarge()** method has been defined without an access level (**default**). This method is accessible only to any type of class ("**use-a**," "**has-a**," or "**is-a**") within the **Shape Library** package.

13.5 ABSTRACTION

The member functions of the class not only protect data members but also abstract the internal operations and algorithms from a client. This section provides an overview of the different types of methods and their syntax. The methods are partitioned into several categories:

1. Constructor
2. Regular Methods
3. Static Methods
4. Destructor

13.5.1 Constructor

For construction of an object, classes in Java may provide two different types of constructors: default and user-defined values constructors. In the following example, the Circle class provides three constructors:

```
//     CIRCLE.JAVA File
package Shapes  ; // Specifying Shape Library package

import java.lang.Math ;      // use Java's Math Library

class Circle
{
        // internal data representation
        private int radius ;
        private Point center ;

        // default constructor
        public Circle( )
        {
                // use user defined constructor: Circle( int, int, int )
                this( 0 , 0 , 0 ) ;
        }

        // user-defined value constructor
        public Circle( int x , int y , int r )
        {
                if( r < 0 )
                {
                        r = Math.abs( r ) ; // Math Library's absolute value
                }
                radius = r ;
                center = new Point( x , y ) ;
                        // use the Point class constructor and create a
                        // Point object
        }

        public Circle( int r )
        {
                this( 0 , 0 , r ) ; // use the above constructor
        }
}
```

In the preceding example, the *Circle* class specifies a *default* and two *user-defined* values constructors. Unlike C++, a *Circle* constructor can call another Circle constructor without any ill effects. This approach allows class constructors with complex algorithms to share implementations, and is demonstrated in the above example.

Java requires that the first statement in the body of a constructor be a call to another constructor. Except for one of the user-defined values constructors, the first statement in the constructors is a call to the **Circle()** constructor.

Java uses the same guidelines as C++ for method overloading. A method can be overloaded on the basis of the number and types of arguments, but cannot be overloaded on the basis of the return value. In the preceding example, *Circle* uses method overloading for its constructors.

13.5.2 Regular Methods

A method takes the following generic format:

```
[modifier] [access_level] return_type name( parameters, if any )
                                        throws exception_list
{
```

```
                // method's body
}
```

In the following example, the Circle class specifies two arithmetic methods for calculating the area and circumference of a Circle object:

```
//      CIRCLE.JAVA File
package Shapes  ;  // Specifying Shape Library package
import java.lang.Math ;      // use Java's Math Library
class Circle
{
        // internal data representation
        private int radius ;
        private Point center ;

        // default constructor
        public Circle( )
        {
                // body
        }

        // user-defined value constructor
        public Circle( int x , int y , int r )
        {
                // body
        }

        public Circle( int r )
        {
                // body
        }

        // arithmetic member functions
        public double area( )
        {
                return( (double) (radius * radius) * Math.PI ) ;
                                        // use math library's PI
        }

        public double perimeter( )
        {
                return( 2.0d * Math.PI * (double) radius ) ;
                        // trailing d for 2.0 denotes a double precision
        }
}
```

A client operates on instances of *Circle* by using the above operations. In the following example, the test driver creates and operates on two instances of *Circle*:

```
//      TEST.JAVA File
import java.lang.System          ; // Use Java's System console I/O library
import Shapes.*                  ; // Use Shape Library

public class Test_Driver
{
        public static void main( String args[ ] )
        {
```

```
Circle c1 , c2 ;          // declare references to Circle object

// instantiate and reference Circle objects
c1 = new Circle( 1 , 2 , 4 ) ;
c2 = new Circle( ) ;

// Display areas on the console
System.out.print( "Area of C1: " + c1.area( ) ) ;
System.out.print( "Area of C2: " + c2.area( ) ) ;
    }
}
```

An optional modifier at the beginning of a method specifies special characteristics of the method. The following identifies the supported modifiers:

1. **Abstract:** An **abstract** method is equivalent to a C++ *purely virtual* function. It is used by an abstract base class in order to specify a common design interface for the *derived classes*. In the following example, the *Account* class specifies the signature for the **print_statement()** method, and *derived* classes such as *Savings* will provide an implementation for it:

```
public abstract class Account
{
        // specify a common design interface for derived classes
        abstract public boolean print_statement( ) ;
}

public class Savings extends Account
{
        // Savings provides a body for this method
        public boolean print_statement( )
        {
                // body
        }
}
```

2. **Final**: In addition to being used for constants, this keyword is also used as a method modifier. When so used, it denotes that the implementation for the method is final and a derived class cannot override it by providing a new implementation.

```
class Rectangle extends Shape
{
        final public boolean draw( ) ;
}
```

3. **Synchronized:** These methods are used for concurrent applications and regulate access to critical information in a multithreaded program in a structured way. These methods are discussed in Section 13.7 on concurrency.

4. **Native:** This keyword is used to allow a Java application to interact with a non-Java method such as a C or C++ function. Since this feature provides an interface to an application compiled for a specific platform, the Java application having one or more native methods loses its architecture-neutrality, and cannot be ported dynamically to a different platform. This modifier should be used sparingly, and only when portability is not an issue and desired performance can be achieved only by using the native system's hardware and processing capability.

13.5.3 Static Methods

Similar to a C++ application, a static method operates on static data members. In the previous sections, several examples of **static** methods, such as the **main**() method, have been presented.

13.5.4 Destructor

Since Java's garbage collector takes care of reclaiming the memory space of a discarded object, the need for a destructor is diminished. For classes that reference external entities such as a hardware device, a destructor may become necessary. For example, Java's *Stream I/O* library uses a destructor to close file handles. A destructor in Java has the following signature:

```
class Name
{
        // destructor
        void finalized( ) ;
}
```

Before the object is reclaimed by the garbage collector, this method is automatically invoked.

13.6 DESIGN HIERARCHY

In Java all classes inherit from **java.lang.Object**. When a class does not inherit explicitly from any other class, **Object** automatically becomes its base class. This default inheritance is equivalent to the following statement:

```
class Name extends java.lang.Object
{
        // body
}
```

Classes in Java inherit from each other by using the **extends** keyword. In the following example, the Shape class hierarchy in Chapter 10 has been reimplemented in Java:

```
//              SHAPE.JAVA File
package Shapes ;         // Specifying Shape Library package

public abstract class Shape        // Abstract Class
{
        private byte interior_color ;

        // specify a constant color list for shapes
        static final public byte RED    = 0 ;
        static final public byte BLUE   = 1 ;
        static final public byte GREEN  = 2 ;
        static final public byte WHITE  = 3 ;
        static final public byte BLACK  = 4 ;
        static final public byte YELLOW = 5 ;

        // user-defined value constructor
        public Shape( byte color )
        {
                // implicit call to the constructor of the Object class
                interior_color = color ;
```

```
        }

        // default constructor
        public Shape( )
        {
                // use RED as the default value and use the Shape class
                // user-defined constructor
                this( RED ) ;
        }

        // access
        public byte color( )
        {
                return( interior_color ) ;
        }

        abstract public boolean draw( ) ;
        abstract public boolean paint( byte new_color ) ;
        abstract public boolean move( int x , int y ) ;
        abstract public double area( ) ;
        abstract public double perimeter( ) ;
}
```

In the preceding example, the Shape class maintains the common information for its derived classes. For instance, **interior_color** is a common attribute. In addition, Shape specifies the common design interface for its derived classes. The **abstract** keyword is used to denote the methods that are only declarations and therefore must be implemented by the derived classes. The derived classes inherit from the **Shape** class via the **extends** keyword, and provide unique implementations for all of the Shape **abstract** functions:

```
// Circle inherits from Shape
public class Circle extends Shape
{
        // internal data representation
        private int radius ;
        private Point center ;

        // default constructor
        public Circle( )
        {
                // Invoke base class constructor
                super( ) ;

                // use default values
                radius = 0 ;
                center = new Point( ) ;
        }

        // user-defined value constructor
        public Circle( int x , int y , int r, byte color )
        {
                // Invoke base class constructor
                super( color ) ;

                if( r < 0 )
                {
```

```
                    r = Math.abs( r ) ; // Math Library's absolute value
                }
            radius = r ;
            center = new Point( x , y ) ;
                        // use the Point class constructor and create a
                        // Point object
        }

    public Circle( int x , int y , int r )
    {
            // Invoke other Circle constructor
            this( x , y , r , Shape.RED ) ;
    }

    // arithmetic member functions
    public double area( )
    {
            return( (double) (radius * radius) * Math.PI ) ;
                            // use math library's PI
    }

    public double perimeter( )
    {
            return( 2.0d * Math.PI * (double) radius ) ;
                    // trailing d for 2.0 denotes a double precision
    }

    public boolean draw( )
    {
            // method's body
    }

    public boolean paint( byte new_color )
    {
            // method's body
    }

    public boolean move( int x , int y )
    {
            // method's body
    }
}
```

In the preceding example, the **super** keyword is used by the **Circle( )** constructor to call the base class constructor. **super** is a reference to the base segment of a derived class. In Java, the first statement in a constructor must be a call to another constructor, and the above **Circle( )** constructors satisfy this requirement.

Similar to C++, if a derived class in Java does not provide an implementation for an **abstract** method, it is also considered an abstract class, and cannot have an instance. In the preceding example, Circle is a concrete class because it provides an implementation for the required **abstract** methods.

Unlike C++, classes in Java can inherit only from one class and *multiple inheritance is not permitted*.

The clients of a design hierarchy can use a base class reference to access and operate on derived classes in a generic way (polymorphic behavior):

```
//      TEST.JAVA File
import java.lang.System        ; // Use Java's System console I/O library
import Shapes.*                ; // Use Shape Library
```

```
public class Test_Driver
{
      public static void main( String args[ ] )
      {
            Circle c1 ; // declare a reference for a Circle object
            Rectangle r1 ; // declare a reference for a Rectangle object

            // instantiate and reference a Circle object
            c1 = new Circle( 1 , 2 , 4 ) ;

            // instantiate and reference a Rectangle object
            r1 = new Rectangle( 1 , 2 , 3 , 4 ) ;

            // Display information on a Circle
            test_shape( (Shape) c1 ) ;
                            // upcast a Circle reference to Shape
            // Display information on a Rectangle
            test_shape( (Shape) r1 ) ;
                            // upcast a Rectangle reference to Shape
      }

      // general purpose shape tester
      static void test_shape( Shape current )
      {
            System.out.print( "Information on Shape: " );
            System.out.print( "Area: " + current.area( ) ) ;
            System.out.print( "Perimeter: "+ current.perimeter() );
      }
}
```

In the preceding example, the **main**() function creates Circle and Rectangle objects and uses the **test_shape**() method to display their area and perimeter. Since the references to derived objects are upcast to a base class reference, the **test_shape**() method operates on any type of Shape.

In Java, all regular methods are analogous to C++ virtual functions, and a derived class can override its base class method. As long as the base method is not **private**, a derived class overrides its base implementation by using the same signature:

```
public class File
{
      public boolean copy( String target_name )
       {
            // body
       }
}

public class Text_File extends File
{
      public boolean copy( String target_name )
      {
            // body
      }
}
```

In the preceding example, the Text File class overrides the **copy**() method and provides its own implementation. The clients operating on a Text File object implicitly use the derived class implementation for **copy**():

```
Text_File source_file = new Text_File( "sample.txt" ) ;
source_file.copy( "sample.bak" ) ; // use Text_File.copy()
```

A design hierarchy can place a limitation on the depth of a hierarchy by declaring its last derived class as **final**:

```
final class Name extends Base_Name
{
        // body
}
```

The **final** keyword prevents any further inheritance from the above derived class, and the class becomes a leaf of the class hierarchy.

13.7 CONCURRENCY

In multithreaded applications, different segments of a program execute concurrently. The objects within different threads interact with each other through shared memory, or through synchronous or asynchronous method invocations. For example, a multimedia application may be reading data sequentially from CD-ROM, displaying images on a display, and sending recorded voice data to the speakers. Since these devices are slow, the processor may frequently be idle. The sequential execution provides a poor utilization of system resource. In addition, it also makes synchronization of voice and images more cumbersome. A better alternative is to allow parts of the multimedia application to execute concurrently. This approach improves performance and resource utilization. The *CD-ROM* object within an information retrieval thread can be reading video and sound stored on a CD-ROM and storing them to shared sound and video buffers. Concurrently, the *Display and Speaker objects* within other threads retrieve the *Video* and *Voice* data in the shared memory and display and play them, respectively.

Java supports concurrency through **synchronized** methods and the **java.lang.Thread** library. The thread library provides a Java application with the capability to control the execution of threads by assigning different levels of priorities for threads: *low*, *normal*, and *high*. This library also provides methods for operating on a thread, such as suspending and resuming execution. To use this library, the preceding CD-ROM object inherits from the *Thread* class (Figure 13.2), and overrides the **run()** method from the Thread class. This method is executed when a thread is started (Figure 13.2):

```
public class CD_ROM extends Thread
{
        // data representation for a CD-ROM
        // override base class implementation
        public void run( )
        {
                // forever read from CD-ROM (until thread is destroyed)
                while( true )
                {
                        // read data from CD-ROM
                        // if data is voice send to the Voice object
                        // if data is an image send to the Image object
                }
        }

        // constructor: references to the shared Voice and Image objects
        CD_ROM( Voice voice , Image image )
        {
                // initialize CD-ROM object
        }
```

```
        // other details left out
}
```

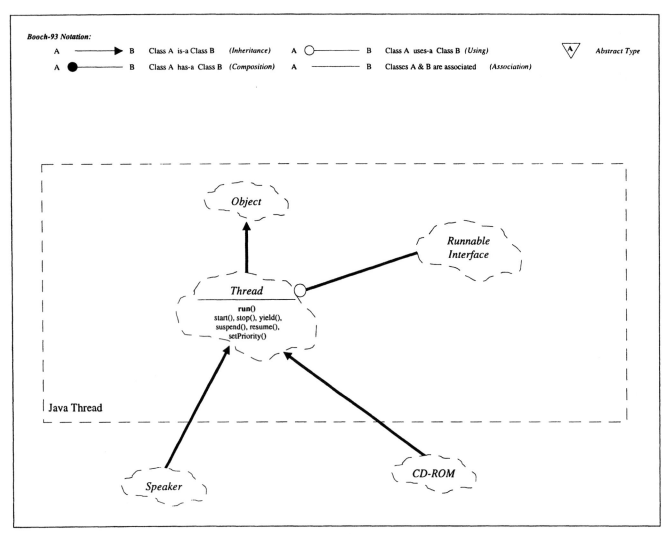

FIGURE 13.2   Thread class diagram.

By inheriting from the Thread class, a CD-ROM object's thread can be controlled by the base class methods such as **start()**, **stop()**, **yield()**, **suspend()**, **resume()**, and other thread control operations (Figure 13.2).

The **synchronized** methods allow objects from different threads to interact with each other in a systematic and controlled manner. For instance, a *CD-ROM* object and a *Speaker* object from different threads operate on a *Voice* object. Only one of these objects can operate on the *Voice* object at one time, otherwise the voice information may become corrupted. By declaring the applicable *Voice* object's methods as **synchronized**, only one client operates within any of *Voice's* **synchronized** methods. Other threads must wait until the active thread finishes executing within the **synchronized** method. The synchronization is implemented by associating a *semaphore* with an object. When the active thread is executing within the **synchronized** method, the object's semaphore is used to lock critical code and/or data. The lock is automatically released when the thread finishes executing the **synchronized** method:

```
public class Voice
{
        synchronized public fill( long data[ ] )
        {
```

```
                   // Other details left out
        }

        synchronized public read( long data[ ] )
        {
                   // Other details left out
        }

        public boolean filled( void )
        {
                   // Other details left out
        }
}
```

A detailed discussion of Java's concurrency is beyond the scope of this section. The reader is referred to a Java programming language book, such as *Java Primer Plus* [Tyma et al. 1996].

By using the concurrency capability of Java and the network (**java.net**) library, Java applications can interact with each other across a network, thus creating a distributed architecture.

13.8 EXCEPTIONS

Java's exception handling is based on C++ exception handling. An exception is raised by using the **throw** keyword. The *recovery point* uses the try-catch block to catch and handle an exception.

Exceptions in Java are derived from the *Exception* or *Throwable* class (Figure 13.3). For an object to be throwable, it must be directly or indirectly derived from the *Throwable* class. As in C++, a client catches and handles exceptions using a try-catch block. In the following example, the *Teller* client catches *List Exception* as well as other types of exceptions in the hierarchy, and handles them uniquely:

```
//             TELLER.JAVA File
import Account_List_Library.*   ; // use Bank Account List library

public class Teller
{
        boolean process_transactions( Account_List list )
        {
                boolean processed = false ;

                try
                {
                        for( long i = 0 ; i < list.num_entries( ) ; i++ )
                        {
                                // access list and process transactions
                        }

                        // other details left out
                        processed = true ; // no exceptions
                }
                catch( List_Exception list_error )
                {
                        list_error.report( ) ; // display pending errors

                        // recovery code
                }
```

```
         catch( Exception error ) // catch other types of exceptions
            {
                  // recovery code
            }
         catch( Throwable error ) // catch any throwable object
            {
                  // recovery code
            }

         return( processed ) ;
      }
   }
```

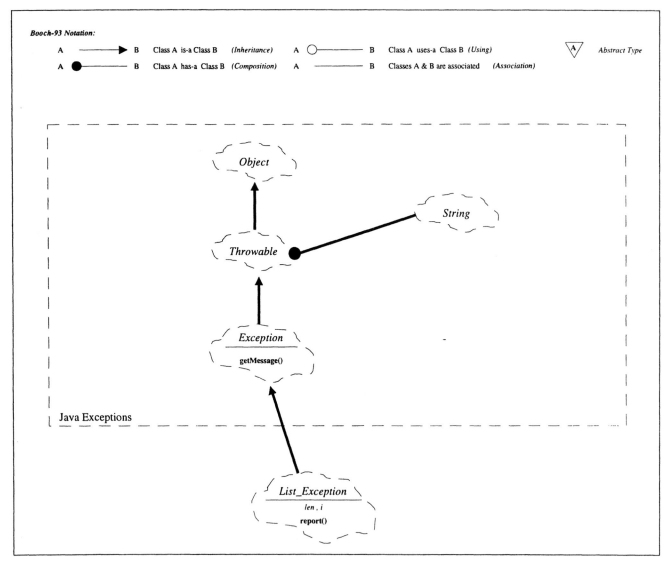

FIGURE 13.3   List exception class diagram.

13.9 INTERFACES

In Java, an application may specify a design interface. An interface provides declarations for a method or collection of methods, but does not specify an implementation for them. An interface may contain data elements but must be declared **static** and **final**:

```
interface Name
{
        return_value method_declaration( parameters, if any ) ;
}
```

In the following example, the *Persistent Object* interface provides a standard interface to load and download data to a persistent storage area. Hypothetically, the **flatten( )** method requires conversion of the object's data to raw data bytes, which are then stored to a file by a persistent object manager. Afterward, the persistent object manager returns a unique ID for future loading operations. The clients use this interface and provide unique implementations for these methods in order to interact with the persistent object manager:

```
interface Persistent_Object
{
        public long flatten( byte record[ ] ) ;
        public void unflatten( long persistent_id, byte record[ ] ) ;
}
```

A persistent object manager does not know the type of data members in a class, and this interface allows the persistent object manager to provide a consistent and standard mechanism for objects to interact with it.

A client class implements an interface by using the **implements** keyword:

```
class Name implements Interface₁ , Interface₂ , ... , Interfaceₙ
{
}
```

For example, the *Savings* class inherits from an Account class, and provides an implementation for the methods specified by the *Persistent Object* interface (Figure 13.4):

```
public class Savings extends Account implements Persistent_Object
{
        public long flatten( byte record[ ] )
        {
                // body
        }

        public void unflatten( long persistent_id, byte record[ ] )
        {
                // body
        }
        // other details left out
}
```

The preceding *Persistent Object* interface allows different types of Account classes that require persistence to build on a standardized interface rather than create their own.

C++ does not support an interface mechanism. However, an interface can be emulated by inheriting from an *abstract class* with no data members.

13.10 JAVA ENVIRONMENT

Java applications can be either standalone or interfaced with a Web browser that supports Java, such as HotJava by Sun Microsystems or Netscape Navigator by Netscape. Java applications for Web pages are referred to as *applets,* and use the Internet as their communication medium. Using this medium, objects are distributed across hardware boundaries, and they interact with each other and share resources. For example, a Web application

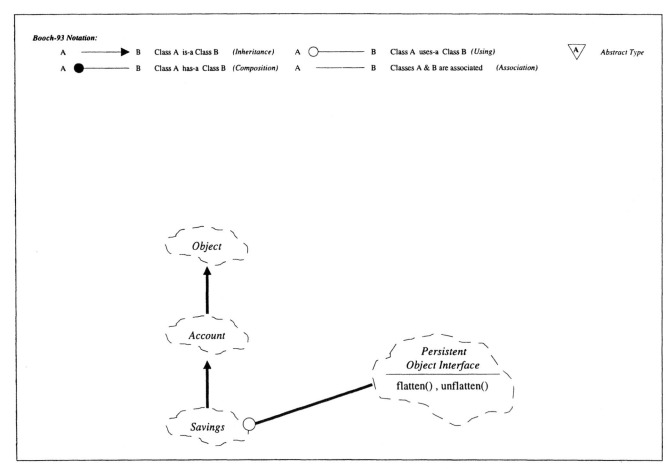

FIGURE 13.4 Thread class diagram.

dynamically downloads the *byte code* for a Java *WordPerfect* applet that displays a WordPerfect document. By reconfiguring itself dynamically the first time it encounters a WordPerfect document, the Web application can then automatically handle future WordPerfect documents when it downloads them from an external host. This capability could be used by a software vendor for making software updates available electronically.

For distributed objects and computing, Java has incorporated a Remote Method Invocation (RMI) capability, and it supports COM/OLE through its Java Bean component technology. This new component allows OLE to be combined with Java. As mentioned earlier, Java applications can also be used in CORBA based applications through an IDL-to-Java mapping.

As previously described, the Java environment includes a garbage collector for memory management. The garbage collector is a low-priority process that runs asynchronously in the background. It checks every valid memory reference. It verifies memory areas that are still in use. The locations that still have valid references are marked in a master list. After the marking phase has been completed, the garbage collector traverses back through its master list, removes the unmarked pieces, and makes memory space available for future allocations [Tyma 1996].

13.11 JAVA LIBRARY

Like any other language, Java's development environment supports different types of libraries. These are as follows [Sun 1995]:

1. **Language Foundation Classes:** The **java.lang** library package consists of math, threads, exception, string, and other basic support methods.

2. **I/O Class Library:** The **java.io** library package provides stream I/O support similar to the C++ stream I/O capability.
3. **Abstract Window Toolkit Class Library**: The **java.awt** library package provides support for a graphical user interface (GUI), such as button and scroll bar support.
4. **Utility Class Library:** The **java.util** library package provides vector, stack, hash table, date, and time support.
5. **Network Interface Class Library:** The **java.net** library package provides telnet and socket interfaces for distributed applications. Using this library, the objects can be distributed across a network.

SUMMARY

Sun Microsystems introduced the Java programming language in 1995. Java is an object-oriented language whose syntax is heavily influenced by C++. An advantage of Java over C++ is that it is an architecture-neutral language and has built-in concurrency support. The Java compiler translates a Java program to an intermediate byte code representation. The run time environment then interprets and executes the byte code. By not translating a Java program to the executable level, compiled Java applications can be dynamically shared by various computers in a heterogeneous system. As long as there is a Java run time environment on each system, any system can download the *byte code* from a different platform and execute it. Java's run time environment provides garbage collection to reclaim memory space from discarded objects. It also provides security features to prevent unauthorized access and damage by an imported Java application. For example, all Java applications imported from an external system are checked for viruses.

Papers by Sun Microsystems and books on Java claim that Java is an object-oriented language and that C++ is a hybrid language [Sun 1995; Tyma 1996]. A language is a vehicle for implementing a design, and its use does not imply that a piece of software is or is not object oriented (OO). Adherence of the design to the object model's framework discussed in Chapter 1 determines whether the design is object-oriented. Merely using OO methodologies, OO computer-aided software engineering (CASE) tools, and OO languages does not guarantee an object oriented system. Both C++ and Java can be used to create classes that fail to satisfy the basic definition of an object.[1] These languages only provide the features necessary to implement an object-oriented design. The design and implementation of an object-oriented system require human intelligence, which cannot be replaced by any method or language.

GLOSSARY

Byte code
A Java compiler generates an intermediate-level representation from the Java source code that is interpreted by Java's run time environment

CASE tool
Computer-Aided Software Engineering tool

LAN
Local Area Network

Multiprocess
When several processes execute concurrently

Multithreaded
Threads refer to the segments of a program that execute concurrently

Process
A process consists of one or more threads

---

[1]An object is an entity that has a state, behavior, and identity.

Semaphore

A locking mechanism used to lock critical code or data. Through a semaphore only one client can access the locked information at a time

Thread

Sequence of instructions executed within a program

WAN

Wide Area Network

CHAPTER **14**

Unified Modeling Language

INTRODUCTION

This book has presented examples of object-oriented programming (OOP) using Booch-93 notation. The Booch method represents the architecture, organization, logic, and design of a software system using a graphical notation. To express different aspects of the design, the notation uses different types of diagrams as discussed in Chapter 1. They capture the static and dynamic aspects of a system.

In addition to Booch, there are other methods used by software engineers, such as the Object-Modeling Technique (OMT) developed by James Rumbaugh, Real-Time Object-Oriented Modeling (ROOM), the Shlaer-Mellor method, and the Coad-Yourdon method. In the past several years, James Rumbaugh and Ivar Jacobson have joined Grady Booch at the Rational Software Corporation. They have been collaborating to combine their notations into what is currently known as the *"Unified Modeling Language for Object-Oriented Development."* By combining these leading OO methods, the basis for a *de facto* standard OOA and OOD methodology is being established [Rational 1996].

The Unified Modeling Language (UML) encompasses both the static and dynamic portions of the object model, as do the other individual methods. The following sections briefly describe the application of this new notation to some of the previously developed concepts and examples. The major diagram types are presented but are not described exhaustively. The reader should contact the Rational Software Corporation (// www.rational.com) for documentation that provides a more complete description of the method. This chapter describes the notation in terms of static and dynamic behavioral issues.

14.1 STATIC MODEL

In Booch notation the static model is depicted by the following diagrams (see Chapter 1):

1. Process diagram
2. Component diagram
3. Category diagram
4. Class diagram
5. Class specification

The Unified Modeling Language depicts the static model via similar diagrams:

1. Deployment diagram
2. Component diagram
3. Class diagram
4. Operation specification

There is a strong correlation between the diagram types regardless of how the diagrams are drawn, especially with respect to the *component* and *class* diagrams. The following sections describe the characteristics and notation of the above cited Unified Modeling Language diagrams.

14.1.1 Deployment Diagram

The *deployment* diagram captures the physical components of a system, such as processors, workstations, and network. Processors and peripheral devices are denoted using 3-D boxes, and are referred to as *nodes*.

In the *deployment* diagram, the purpose and the physical number of each *node* are documented by using *role* and *multiplicity* features. Figure 14.1 illustrates the *deployment* diagram for a credit union banking system. The bank system is a distributed system consisting of several servers, personal computers (PCs), automated teller machines (ATMs), and a printing system. To denote there are many ATMs and PCs, the *multiplicity* symbol is used to indicate that there are n-servers, 20 PCs, and n-ATMs. The *role* of the PCs is defined as *Teller*.

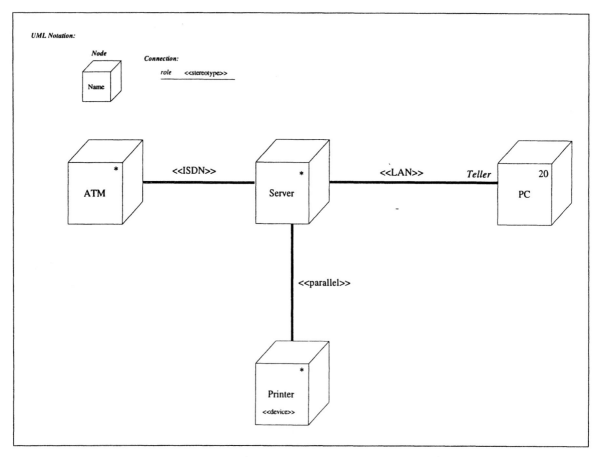

FIGURE 14.1   Bank account system platform diagram.

A stereotype is used to specify the type of a *node*. For example, a peripheral device is not computationally interesting, and to differentiate it from a processor the <<device>> stereotype is used to specify the type of *node*.

In Figure 14.1, the printers are labeled as a device. In addition, the type of connections between the nodes are specified using the stereotype symbol. For example, the server and the printer are connected via a parallel interface (Figure 14.1). UML specifies the following stereotypes for a *node* [Rational 1996]:

1. Device
2. Processor
3. Memory

Processes, threads, and active objects can be associated with a given processor in the *deployment* diagram.

14.1.2 Component Diagram

Similar to the *module* diagram in Booch-93, the *component* diagram provides a high-level overview of the system physical software architecture. This diagram is used in a high-level design document. By providing a *strategic* view of a system, it helps multiple teams in a development environment to coordinate their activities (*refer to Chapter 2*).

A *component* diagram presents the development view of a system. The *component* diagram consists of *modules*, which are grouped in *packages*. Each *package* contains the definition and implementation of a class or a group of logically organized classes. The dependencies between *packages* are denoted by dashed arrows. Figure 14.2 depicts a high-level overview of the banking system architecture, using the Unified Modeling Language. The *ATM* and *Teller packages* are dependent on the *Bank package*. Even though the internal details of the *packages* are not shown, each *package* can consist of other *packages* and classes.

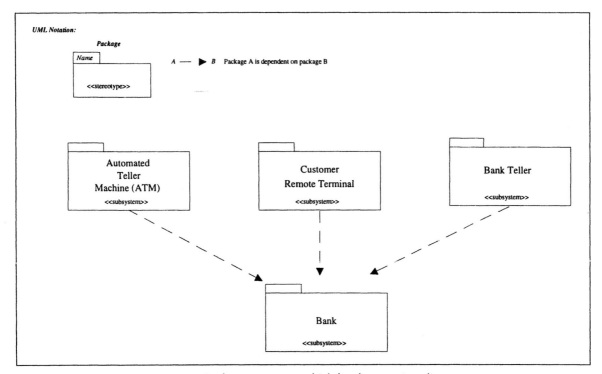

FIGURE 14.2   Bank account system high-level component diagram.

The design of a large system requires a dedicated organizational work for presentation of the system's object model. The *component* diagram is purely organizational and is used for configuration control and partitioning of components for parallel development. *Packages* help organize the design of a *module* or a *subsystem* into a collection of logically related class definitions. For a complicated system, a *component* diagram conveys the relationships between a group of *packages* without having to expose the underlying internal class architectures, relationships, export controls, and other details. In addition, *packages* provide the reference point for other model elements, such as use-cases, which specify the behavior of the system as a whole [Rational 1996].

A *package* is represented by a folder icon. *Packages* can share the following relationships:

1. Dependency: Dependencies among the *packages* are shown by dashed arrows.
2. Composition: For nested *packages*, a package icon appears inside another package.
3. Versioning: To denote different versions of a *package*, an inheritance symbol (a filled arrow) is used.

Figure 14.3 depicts the *component* diagram for the automated teller machine (ATM) subsystem. The highest level package, *Controller*, is dependent on the *Peripherals* and *Graphical User Interface (GUI)* packages. The *Peripherals* package contains several other packages, such as *Printer*. Owing to variations in graphical user interfaces (GUIs), different windowing systems are presented using the Unified Modeling Language versioning feature. This notation indicates that only one of the GUIs will be linked in at a time.

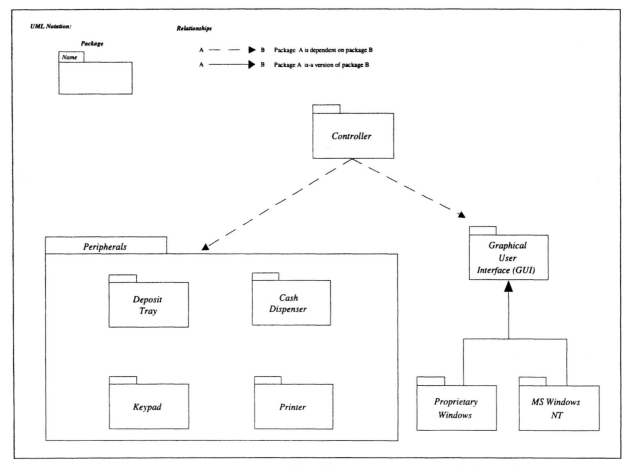

FIGURE 14.3 Automated teller machine (ATM) component diagram (preliminary).

A class definition is "owned" by only one package, but can be imported into other packages. The class name of an imported class contains the package name, similar to a namespace in C++, as shown here:

```
Package_Name:: Class_Name
```

The UML specifies the following **stereotypes** for a *package* [Rational 1996]:

1. Subsystem

2. Module group
3. Category
4. Processor group
5. Service package
6. Use-case group

Figure 14.2 illustrates the use of a **stereotype** in a *component* diagram.

14.1.3 Class Diagram

The *class* diagram shows the internal structure of a system, its components, and their interfaces and relationships to each other in terms of classes. This section describes the semantics of a class diagram. In the Unified Modeling Language, a class is represented by a solid outline box with three compartments (Figure 14.4):

1. Name: The class name resides in the top compartment.
2. Attributes: The class data members are located in the middle compartment.
3. Methods: The bottom compartment contains the list of member functions.

To reduce complexity, the designer may choose not to show the compartments explicitly. However, an empty attribute and/or method compartment denotes that there are no elements in that part of the class definition.

14.1.3.1 Class Name Compartment

The name compartment identifies the class and other pertinent information such as the class properties. In Figure 14.4, the *Account* class consists of three compartments, the first of which contains the following information:

1. Class: A class name appears in boldface characters, and an abstract class appears in *italic-bold face* characters. In Figure 14.4, the *Account* class is designated as an *abstract* class, which specifies the design interface for its derived classes and the common operations and attributes.

   As mentioned earlier in the discussion of a *component* diagram, the class name can be scoped by using the scope resolution (::) operator. In Figure 14.4, the *Account* class has been associated with the *Bank Accounts* package.
2. Properties: Similar to Booch-93 notation, the class diagram in the Unified Modeling Language specifies class properties: *virtual, abstract, readonly, designer,* and so on. Unlike Booch-93 notation, the Unified Modeling Language allows user-defined properties. The properties are documented using *italic* letters and appear underneath the class name.
3. Stereotype: This feature specifies the type of class, such as a *proxy, actor, server, agent, factory, interface, exception,* and so on. The type of a class is not restricted to any specified list and is in fact user defined. A stereotype appears above the class name and is enclosed in two sets of angle brackets (*<<stereotype>>*). In Figure 14.7, this feature is used for the *List Exception* class.

UML has defined the following stereotypes for a class [Rational 1996]:

1. Event: An event that triggers a transaction
2. Exception: An event that is thrown
3. Interface: Designates the interface of a package or a class, such as a Java interface
4. Metaclass: A class of classes
5. Utility: A collection of standalone functions and data logically organized

Since the *properties* and *stereotype* features can be user defined, the names should be standardized across a development organization for maintaining architectural and documentation coherency.

14.1.3.2 Attributes Compartment

The attributes compartment contains a full or partial list of data members. The following identifies the format used to specify a data member:

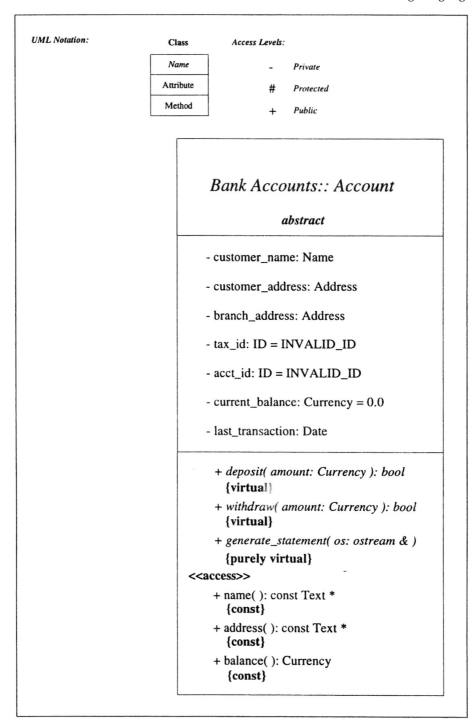

FIGURE 14.4 Account class diagram.

```
[visibility] data_member_name: Type = initial_value
```

The *visibility (export control)* is denoted by the following symbols:

1. Private: minus (-)
2. Protected: pound (#)
3. Public: plus (+)

When *visibility* is left out, it indicates that it is being omitted for presentation purposes. In Figure 14.4, *visibility* is defined for all of the data members as **private**.

The *initial value* setting is optional and its specification is language dependent. Some of the data members in Figure 14.4 such as ***tax_id*** are initialized to a specific value by the default constructor.

The **static** data members are preceded by a dollar symbol ($). In the following example, the ***interest_rate*** data member is a private static member and is of the *Interest_Table* type:

```
-$ interest_rate: Interest_Table
```

14.1.3.3 Class Methods Compartment

The methods compartment specifies the member functions and their interfaces. The following specifies the syntax for a class method:

```
<<stereotype>>
[visibility] name( parameter_name: Type = default_value, ...): return type
{ constraints }
```

The following briefly describes the preceding notation:

1. **Stereotype**: A **stereotype** is not only used for nodes, packages, and association, but it is also used for class elements. For member functions, it is used to classify the functions such as access, helper, and arithmetic operations. In Figure 14.4, the **balance( )**, **name( )**, and **address( )** functions are classified as **access** functions. The other member functions do not have a stereotype.
2. **Visibility**: The static symbol ($) and the visibility symbols described in the previous section also apply to the function declarations, and follow the same guideline as the data members.
3. **Function Declaration**: Regular member functions appear in normal text, and abstract (purely virtual) functions appear in italic characters. In Figure 14.4, the **generate_statement( )** function is an abstract function and the **balance( )** function is a regular member function.

   For functions that do not return a value (**void**), the colon and return type are left out, such as in **generate_statement( )** (Figure 14.4). For functions that return multiple values, the return type becomes a list. If the function does not take any arguments, an empty set of parentheses is used. For instance, the **balance( )** function in Figure 14.4 does not take any arguments.
4. **Constraints**: Constraints are language dependent, such as constant, virtual, and abstract. The constraints allow a design to specify additional criteria for a member function. In Figure 14.4, the Account class specifies several common methods and attributes such as **balance( )** and **customer_name**. The Account class also specifies the design interface for its derived classes by specifying the signature for the **generate_statement( )** and **deposit( )** methods, which are **purely virtual** and **virtual**, respectively. For read-only operations such as **name( )**, the **const** constraint specifies that the member function does not change the state of the object.

   The actual method declaration is flexible and all data except the name may be omitted to reduce diagram complexity. The extra detail becomes useful when class diagrams are used to support detailed design and coding. As a guideline, when detailed information such as argument lists, types, and constraints is available it should be made part of the class diagram.

14.1.3.4 Relationships among Classes

The classes in a design form associations that are structural relationships between the objects. Most associations are binary and are represented by solid lines between pairs of classes as depicted in Figure 14.5. In Figure 14.5, different types of bank accounts are associated with each other. At the end of each association a "rolename" is assigned, which shows how a class is viewed by the opposite class.

Similar to Booch notation, UML shows multiplicity, that is, how many instances of a class can be associated with an instance of the opposite class. Multiplicity is represented using the following syntax:

```
Exactly one relationship:          1
Unlimited number (0 or more):      *
Zero or more:                      0 ... *
One or more:                       1 ... *
Range:                             10 ... 30
Range and number:                  2 ... 4 , 8
```

The asterisk (*) symbol is used to indicate the "many" relationship.

Each association is independent of other associations between the same two classes. Associations may have attributes, may themselves be defined as a class, and may have qualifying conditions specified.

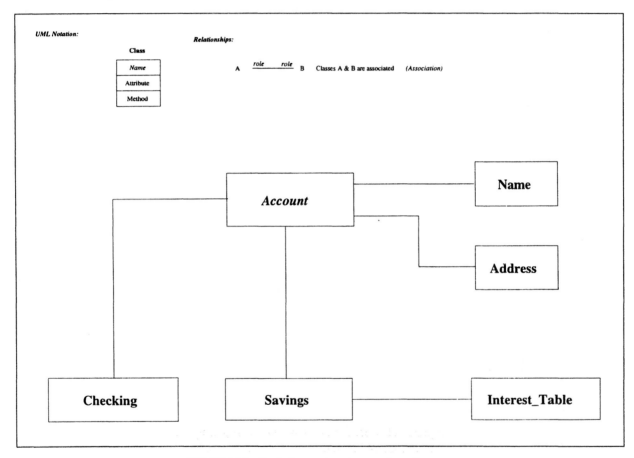

FIGURE 14.5 Bank Accounts category class diagram.

During software design and modeling, the roles among the classes are quantified and loosely associated relationships are replaced by concrete relationships. This is done iteratively. Some of the associations lead to common relationships, which are identified as follows:

1. **Aggregation**: This relationship denotes a "whole-part" relationship and is a type of composition. It is represented by a diamond on the role attached to the "system" class. The type of containment is denoted by filling the diamond or leaving it blank. A darkened diamond denotes internal containment, and a white diamond denotes external containment.

   In Figure 14.6, the *Savings* class "**has-an**" *Interest Table*, and external containment is used. This approach allows the *Savings* class to switch dynamically between different interest rate tables. The *Account* class uses composition to maintain name and address information. Since an *Account* can be a joint or a single account, external containment is used to dynamically associate multiple *Names* with an *Account*.

2. Generalization: The relationship between a base class (superclass) and its derived classes (subclasses) is represented as a solid line with a filled triangular arrowhead on the superclass end.

Inheritance as well as other associations are shown in Figure 14.6. In Figure 14.6, the *Account* class is an **abstract** class and cannot have direct instances. The *derived Savings* class inherits from this class and implements the specified purely virtual functions. The *Savings* class is a *concrete* class.

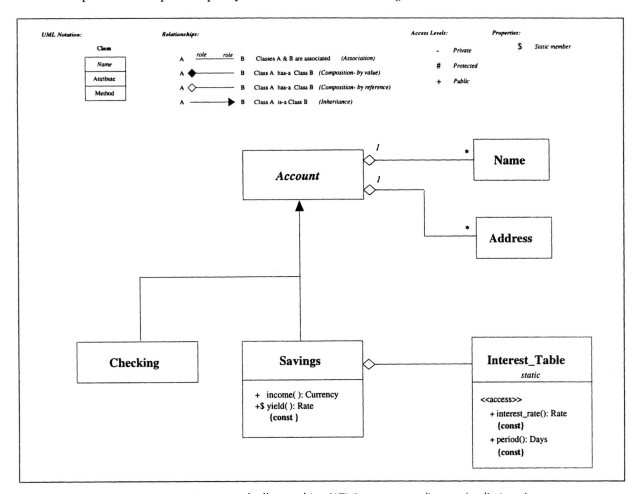

FIGURE 14.6 Automated teller machine (ATM) component diagram (preliminary).

For **parameterized** (template) classes, the class symbol is superimposed with a small dashed box in the upper right-hand corner. In Figure 14.7, the *Linked List* template class from Chapter 11 is represented using the Unified Modeling Language. The base *Linked List* class is an **abstract** class and specifies three *purely virtual* operations that must be implemented by the derived classes, such as *Circular List*. The *Linked List* class uses the *List Exception* class to report problems with accessing, creating, and manipulating records within the list. The *Record* class is a helper class that maintains references to a designated object. In addition, a *Record* object maintains references to the next and previous *Records* (Figure 14.7). This is referred to as the *reflexive* property. Since the types of objects maintained by the *Linked List* and *Record* classes are not known until instantiation, both have been defined as template classes. A client must specify the type of object, as denoted by the *Type* parameter in the dashed box in the class diagram.

A **utility** class logically groups a set of global attributes and standalone functions, i.e., nonmember functions. For instance, the functions and global variables in the math libraries of C and Java may be organized into a utility class. In Figure 14.8, some of the features provided by Java's *math* library are depicted. Utilities may also be templates. A utility class is shown as a class box and is stereotyped as a **utility**.

An *interface* specifies the external interface of a class or package, which includes a list of member functions and constraints. The constraints specify the order in which the functions can be called. This feature is useful for specifying a Java language interface or a Common Object Request Broker Architecture (CORBA) based Interface Definition Language (IDL). In Figure 14.8, the *Account* **deposit( )** member function uses the *math* **abs( )** function. The **save( )** and **retrieve( )** member functions use the *persistent storage* interface.

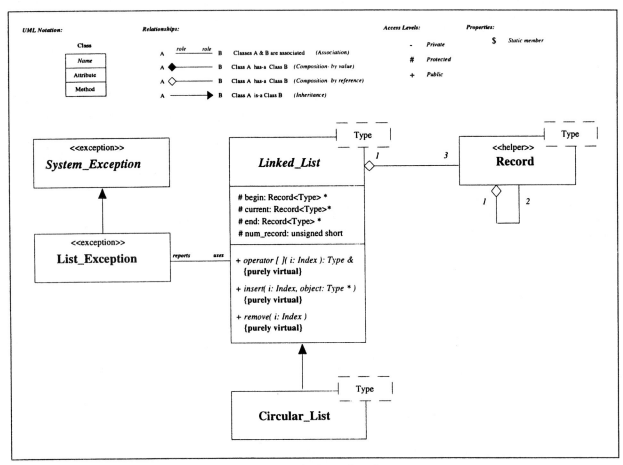

FIGURE 14.7   Linked List class diagram.

14.1.4 Operation Specification

The *operation specification* denotes all of the semantics of each method in the functional model. For example, the *operation specification* captures what happens before and after a method is performed. The before condition describes the state of the system prior to executing the operation, and the after condition describes the state of the system after the execution of the operation. An operation specification is textual and essentially presents data flow information. In the following example, the **Savings:: withdraw( )** function is documented using the *Operation Specification* notation:

Operation:	Savings:: withdraw( )
Responsibilities:	Withdraws a specified amount of money from an active or inactive *Savings* account
Inputs:	Amount - a nonzero floating value
Returns:	Boolean flag - denotes if withdrawal was accepted or denied
Modified objects:	Modifies "this" object

Preconditions:	The *Savings* object may be in one of the following states:

Preconditions: The *Savings* object may be in one of the following states:
1. **Active (good standing)**: Current *balance* is greater than $0.00
2. **Inactive**: Account has not been accessed for more than 60 days

Postconditions: Depending on the following states of the *Savings* object, the method will perform one of the following:
1. **Active**: If the amount of the withdrawal request would not cause the *Savings* account to become overdrawn, the method accepts the request and posts it, and returns a "true" flag. Otherwise, it returns a "false" flag to denote that the request has been rejected
2. **Inactive**: The method performs the same operation as described above, and if successful will also change the state of the *Account* to active

For any other state, the withdrawal request will be denied.

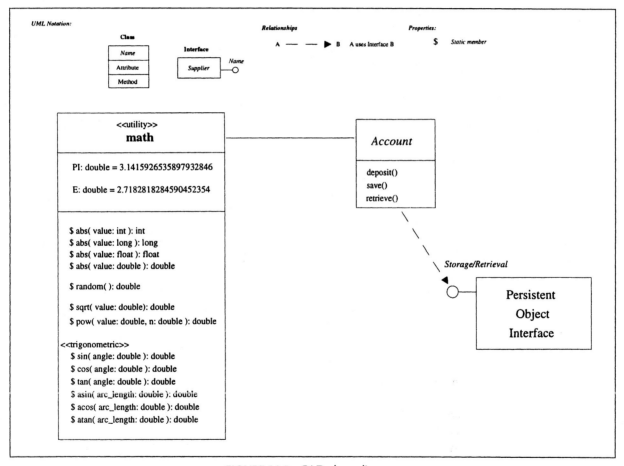

FIGURE 14.8 CAD class diagram.

14.2 DYNAMIC MODEL

In Booch-93 notation, the following diagrams represent the dynamic characteristics of a design:

1. State transition diagram
2. Interaction diagram
3. Object diagram

Similarly, the Unified Modeling Language utilizes the following diagrams for the dynamic model:

1. State diagram
2. Sequence diagram
3. Collaboration diagram
4. Use-case diagram

Except for the use-case diagram, there are strong similarities between Booch and Unified Modeling Language diagrams. The sequence and collaboration diagrams are called interaction diagrams. The use-case diagram is new and does not exist in Booch-93. The following sections describe the characteristics and notation of the above cited Unified Modeling Language diagrams.

14.2.1 State Diagram

A *state* diagram specifies the behavior of an object. This diagram identifies all of the permissible states for an object. It also describes the transitions between the states in response to either the invocation of member functions or external events, such as an interrupt. The *state* diagram is useful for describing objects that have many states and transitions (*complex behavior*). Each state diagram is associated with either a class or with a higher level state diagram.

Similar to Booch-93 notation, a *state* diagram is a collection of states denoted by rounded rectangles. Each rectangle contains the following information (Figure 14.9):

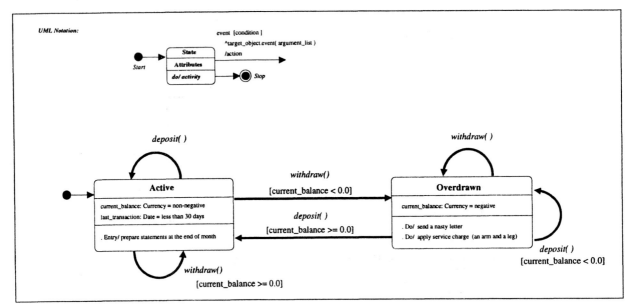

FIGURE 14.9   Account class state diagram.

1. **State:** It contains the name of the specified state. Figure 14.9 illustrates a simple *state* diagram for the *Account* class. The state of the object (either *Active* or *Overdrawn*) is determined on the basis of the *current_balance* of the *Account* and on how recent the last transaction was.
2. **Selected Attributes:** For a state, the values of a selected group of attributes may be explicitly specified. The value of a state variable is shown using the following syntax:
   attribute_name: Type = value
   In Figure 14.9, the value of current_balance in the Overdrawn state is negative:

   current_balance: Currency = negative

3. **Activity**: A state may specify a set of *activities* that require time to complete. When an event occurs that causes a transition, the *activity* is then interrupted, even if has not been completed. Similar to Booch, the

Unified Modeling Language supports the following types of activities:
Entry / operation
Do / operation
Exit / operation

In Figure 14.9, each state calls for a specific set of *activities*.

The state transitions are connected by directed lines. Transitions are caused by a method or an external event. Similar to Booch-93, when an event that causes a state transition occurs, the following takes place:

1. **Guard Condition**: The guard condition is evaluated and the transition takes place only when the condition is "**true**." The guard condition is enclosed in brackets. Figure 14.10 illustrates a more elaborate state diagram for the *Account* class. Most of the state transitions are based on some condition. For example, the *Account* object transitions from an *Overdrawn* state to the *Active* state on a **deposit( )**, only when the *current_balance* becomes nonnegative (Figure 14.10).

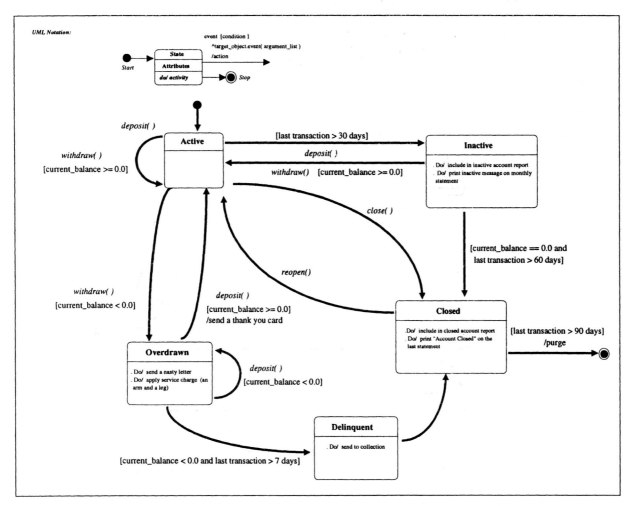

FIGURE 14.10   Account class state diagram.

A guard condition is optional. If it is left out, the transition becomes automatic with the occurrence of the event. In Figure 14.10, the *Account* object transitions from the *Inactive* state to the *Active* state on any type of **deposit( )**.

When a transition does not specify an event and contains only a guard condition, the transition occurs any time the condition becomes "**true**." In Figure 14.10, if the *Account* object has been *Active* and has not been accessed for more than 30 days, it automatically transitions to the *Inactive* state without any event occurring.

A state may also have a **single** transition without any labels. In this case, when all *activities* within the state are complete, the transition occurs automatically. In the *Delinquent* state, when the collection department has been notified, *Account* is automatically *Closed*.

2. **Events**: Before the state of an object changes, the object may send an event to another object or broadcast it to a collection of objects. The following syntax denotes transmission of an event:

^ target_object_name(s). event_name(argument list)

3. **Action**: This feature has the same notation and behavior as in Booch-93 notation. An action is not interruptable and conceptually takes zero processing time. In Figure 14.10, a thank-you card is sent (action) when the object transitions from Overdrawn to Active.

Similar to Booch-93 notation, the state diagram also supports substates, where a group of states are logically associated with a superstate. This book has used this feature in the state transition diagrams in Chapters 2 and 8. At times, when a state diagram uses substates, some of the transitions from an external state to the substates are identical. Instead of drawing unique transition lines to each of the applicable substates, the use of a state with history prevents the diagram from becoming cluttered. The Unified Modeling Language supports the history feature by using an "**H**" enclosed in a circle. The transition line from the external state becomes directed to the history symbol.

The Unified Modeling Language also provides the following additional features, which are not discussed in detail here:

a. **Concurrency Support**: Multithreaded applications whose number of threads may vary within the state of an object introduce the need for representing concurrent substates. For example, this feature is useful for representing the state of objects within a distributed object model, such as a Common Object Request Broker Architecture (CORBA)-compliant system.

b. **Composite States**: A composite state is a high-level state, which contains a collection of lower level states. The lower level states respond to lower level events, which are not visible at the higher level. At the lower level, there is an entry state and an exit state.

Timing Mark: A timing mark designates the time at which a transition occurs.

c. The reader may refer to the "Unified Modeling Language for Object-Oriented Development" for a more detailed description of these features [Rational 1996].

14.2.2 Sequence Diagram

A sequence diagram is almost identical to the object interaction diagram (Booch-93). This diagram shows the full details of a scenario and the messages that flow between the objects over time. The lifetime of an object is drawn as a solid vertical line. The interactions between the objects can be shown with respect to time and the lines are vertically downward. Events or messages are represented by horizontal arrows from the sending to the receiving object's line.

Figure 14.11 depicts the sequence diagram for a savings withdrawal scenario for an Automated Teller Machine (ATM). The ATM and Savings objects reside on different systems (distributed objects). The withdrawal request requires some time to complete, due to network traffic, communication protocol, and other processing overhead. To depict this event, the event line is slanted downward, and a timing mark is used to represent specific message delivery times.

The creation of an object is denoted by leveling the object icon with the operation that creates it. The destruction of an object is denoted by a large "X." In Figure 14.11, the Account constructor is leveled with the Account object icon, and the Account object is destroyed by a call to the Account destructor.

The Unified Modeling Language also provides the following additional features, which are not discussed in detail here:

1. **Guard Condition**: Similar to a state diagram, a guard condition enclosed in brackets is used for conditional branching. The guard condition appears before the message above the arrow.

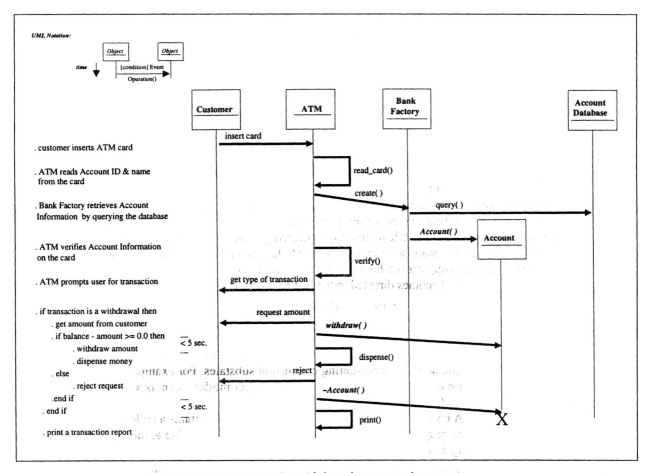

FIGURE 14.11 ATM withdrawal sequence diagram.

For complicated and nested branching, it is better to use multiple diagrams.

2. **Recursive Call**: A recursive call is denoted by stacking multiple activities on the object lifeline.

The reader may refer to the "Unified Modeling Language for Object-Oriented Development" for a more detailed description of these features [Rational 1996].

14.2.3 Collaboration Diagram

A collaboration diagram conveys the same information as the object diagram in Booch-93 notation. A collaboration diagram is a scenario that shows the flow of messages within an object diagram as nodes in a graph. It emphasizes the relationships between objects, rather than the sequencing. A message can be either a procedure call or an asynchronous link (an operation or an event) between objects.

An object in the collaboration diagram is represented using a rectangle and the class name is underlined (Figure 14.12). It contains two compartments for the object name and a list of attribute values, respectively. Typically, the list of attributes compartment is suppressed, unless it is important to depict them for informational purposes.

The collaboration diagram supports the following Booch-93 features for messages (Figure 14.12):

1. **Simple**: The standard arrow depicts a single thread of control from a source to a target object.
2. **Synchronous**: A synchronous message is shown by an arrow with an "X."
3. **Timeout**: Timeout synchronization is shown by the clock above an arrow to indicate that the event or operation must be completed within a specified amount of time.
4. **Asynchronous**: An asynchronous message is shown by a modified arrow (ó).

5. **Balking**: Balking synchronization is shown by an arrow that points back to the source object. The message is passed to the target object only if the target object is ready to receive it. The operation is abandoned if the target is not ready.

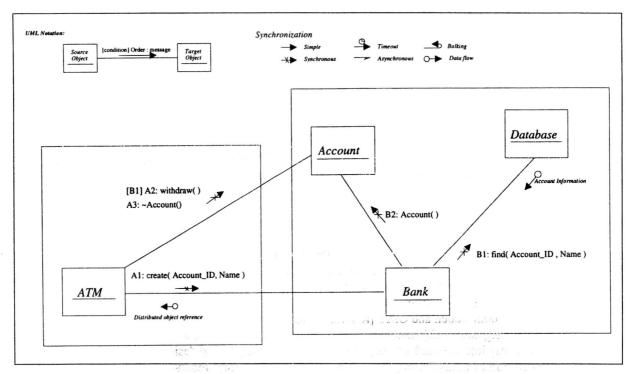

FIGURE 14.12   Account collaboration diagram.

In Figure 14.12, the messages between the objects are synchronous. In addition, the data flow feature of the object diagram is also utilized by the collaboration diagram.

For concurrent applications, the collaboration diagram has enhanced message ordering. The normal sequential numbering system (1, 2, 3, ...) for concurrent messages is inadequate. Therefore, the Unified Modeling Language proposes a different labeling for multithreaded applications. Each thread is assigned a single letter (A, B, and so on), and the messages within the thread are then sequentially numbered. For example, a thread is assigned letter "A" and the concurrent messages within this thread are then numbered A1, A2, and so on. Simple messages to passive objects within the thread are denoted using the simple call symbol (full arrowhead) and are labeled using a nested numbering system: A1.1, A1.2, and so on. Figure 14.12 provides a simple example using this notation.

There are usually dependencies between threads. Therefore, when a specific message must wait until a message from another thread completes, the dependency is shown using the following syntax:

[dependent message(s)] message id

For example, [A4] B5 specifies that B5 occurs after A4 and B4. In Figure 14.12, the A2 message occurs after A1 and B1.

For object interactions that are dependent on a condition, a guard condition is used. The guard condition is enclosed in brackets, and uses the same notation as for synchronizing threads (refer to the preceding example). By using a guard condition, branches can be shown in a collaboration diagram.

Similar to Booch-93, the collaboration diagram can specify that the link between the objects is permanent or temporary, such as a link to a local object. These associations are denoted by one of the following symbols enclosed in a small square at the target object:

1. Association (A)
2. Field (F)

3. Global (G)
4. Local (L)
5. Procedure (P)
6. Self reference (S)

14.2.4 Use-Case Diagram

A *use-case* diagram describes a subset of the behavior of the system, organized into a set of transactions/ interactions in response to an initial event. As shown in Chapter 2, *use-cases* are usually written as an informal text description of the sequences of interactions between two objects and/or external entities. By using *use-case* analysis, the behavior of the system can be described for every scenario. The *use-case* descriptions are then used to design an object model for a system.

The *Unified Modeling Language* incorporates the use-case model developed by Jacobson. The description of the use-case model is beyond the scope of this chapter. The reader may refer to *Object-Oriented Software Engineering* by Ivar Jacobson [Jacobson 1992].

SUMMARY

The *Unified Modeling Language (UML)* is a third-generation method for visualizing, specifying, and documenting the artifacts of an object-oriented system under development. The Unified Modeling Language represents the unification of the Booch, OMT, and Object-Oriented Software Engineering (OOSE) methods, and in addition incorporates ideas from a number of other methodologies. The Unified Modeling Language is the direct successor to both Booch and OMT [Rational 1996].

Since the emergence of object-oriented analysis and design techniques in the late 1980s, many permutations have made their way into the marketplace. As object-oriented analysis and design continued to mature and grow, a second generation of methods/notations gained popularity, notably Booch-93 and Rumbaugh's OMT. Both enjoy considerable automated support from Computer Aided Software Engineering (CASE) tools that provide diagram drawing support as well as code generation. Both methods were growing together, albeit independently, so it made sense to combine them in an attempt to prevent proliferation of mutually OOA/OOD notations.

This book has presented a snapshot of the *Unified Modeling Language (UML)* based on the 0.9 documentation set provided by Rational Software Corporation. UML has been evolving and is undergoing further changes in different areas such as design patterns and traceability. The reader should refer to Rational Software Corporation for future updates.

GLOSSARY

Aggregation
Composition

Association
A relationship between two or more classes

Attribute
A data member

Behavior
The sequence of operations performed by the system with respect to its objects

Class
A type definition that has instances with identity, state, and behavior

Composition
A class that contains other objects

Event
> A signal between two objects that conveys control and information, such as an interrupt

Member
> Either an attribute or an operation

Message
> A communication from one object to another. It may be either a procedure call or an event

Object
> An instance of a class

OOSE
> Object-Oriented Software Engineering

Package
> An organizational unit for class models

Role
> Each association identifies the role that the applicable classes perform with respect to each other

Transition
> A change in state in response to a received event

Use-case
> Describes how a system is used. Specifies threads through the state model of the entire system

References

TEXTBOOKS

1) [Booch 1994] Booch, G. *Object-Oriented Analysis and Design with Applications.* Redwood City, California: Addison-Wesley, 1994.

2) [Rational 1995] Booch, G. and Rumbaugh, J. *Unified Method for Object-Oriented Development Documentation Set*, version 0.8. Santa Clara, California: Rational Software Corporation, 1995.

3) [Rational 1996] Booch, G., Rumbaugh, J., and Jacobson, I. *The Unified Modeling Language for Object-Oriented Development Documentation Set*, version 0.9. Santa Clara, California: Rational Software Corporation, 1996.

4) [Brooks 1995] Brooks, F. *The Mythical Man-Month.* Reading, Massachusetts: Addison-Wesley, 1995.

5) [Davis 1993] Davis, S. *C++ Programmer's Companion.* Reading, Massachusetts: Addison-Wesley, 1993.

6) [Ellis et al., 1990] Ellis, M. and Stroustrup, B. *The Annotated C++ Reference Manual.* Reading, Massachusetts: Addison-Wesley, 1990.

7) [Islam 1996] Islam, N. *Distributed Objects: Methodologies for Customizing Systems Software.* Los Alamitos, California: IEEE, 1996.

8) [Gamma et al., 1994] Gamma, E., Helm, R., Johnson, R., and Vlissides J. *Design Patterns: Elements of Object-Oriented Software.* Reading, Massachusetts: Addison-Wesley, 1994.

9) [Jacobson 1992] Jacobson, I., et al., *Object-Oriented Software Engineering.* Reading, Massachusetts: Addison-Wesley, 1992.

10) [Kernighan and Ritchie 1988] Kernighan, B. and Ritchie, D. *The C Programming Language.* Englewood Cliffs, New Jersey: Prentice-Hall, 1988.

11) [Kreyszig 1983] Kreyszig, E. *Advanced Engineering Mathematics.* New York: John Wiley & Sons, 1983.

12) [Murray 1993] Murray, R. *C++ Strategies and Tactics.* Reading, Massachusetts: Addison-Wesley, 1993.

13) [Selic et al., 1994] Selic, B., Gullekson, G., and Ward, P. *Real-Time Object-Oriented Modeling.* New York: John Wiley & Sons, 1994.

14) [Stroustrup 1991] Stroustrup, B. *The C++ Programming Language.* Reading, Massachusetts: Addison-Wesley, 1991.

15) [Tyma et al., 1996] Tyma, P., Torok, G., Downing, T. *Java Primer Plus.* Corte Madera, California: Waite Group Press, 1996.

PUBLICATIONS

1)   [Adler 1995] Adler, R. "Emerging Standards for Component Software." *Computer* March 1995, pp. 68–77.

2)   [Boehm 1988] Boehm, B. "A Spiral Model of Software Development and Enhancement."*Computer* May 1988, pp. 61–72.

3)   [Dean et al., 1996] Dean, D., Felten, C.D., and Wallack, D. "Java Security: From HotJava to Netscape and Beyond." *Proc. 1996 IEEE Symposium on Security and Privacy* 1996, pp. 26–37.

4)   [Jones 1995] Jones, C. "Patterns of Large Software Systems: Failures and Success." *Computer* March 1995, pp. 86–87.

5)   [Moyers 1995] Moyers, W. "Taligent's Common Point: The Promise of Objects." *Computer* March 1995, pp. 78–82.

6)   [Paulk 1995] Paulk, M. "How ISO 9001 compares with the CMM." *IEEE Software* January 1995, pp. 74–82.

7)   [Saiedian 1995] Saiedian, H. "SEI Capability Maturity Model's Impact on Contractors." *Computer* January 1995, pp. 16–26.

8)   [Stroot 1987] Stroot, Jacquelyn R. "Software Quality Assurance." *Quality* February 1987, pp. 38–40.

STANDARDS

1)   ANSI Committee. *The ANSI-C++ Programming Language.* New Jersey: 1995.

2)   CCITT. *Terminal Equipment and Protocols for Telematic Services, Recommendations T.0-T.63*, Volume VII. 1991.

3)   DOD-STD-2167A. *Military Standard: Defense System Software Development.* US Department of Defense, Washington D.C.: February 1988.

4)   IEEE. *IEEE Software Standards.* Piscataway, New Jersey: 1994.

5)   ISO-9000. *International Standard: Quality Management and Quality Assurance Standards*, ISO, Geneva, 1987.

6)   Object Management Group (OMG). *Common Object Request Broker Architecture (CORBA): Architecture and Specification*, version 2.0. August 1995.

MISCELLANEOUS

1)   [Sun 1995] Gosling, J., and McGilton, J. *The Java Language Environment* Sun Microsystems, May 1995.

2)   [PARTA 1991] PARTA Corp. *Software Coding Standards.* Agoura Hills, California: PARTA Corp., 1991.

3)   [PARTA 1993] PARTA Corp. *Graphical On-Line Documentation (GOLD) System Phase- I SBIR Research Proposal.* Agoura Hills, California: PARTA Corp, 1993.

4)   [Paulk 1993] Paulk, M. and Weber, C. *Key Practices of the Capability Maturity Mode.* Pittsburgh: Software Engineering Institute (SEI), 1993.

5)   [RPI 1994] RPI. *Standard Template Library Reference.* Renesselaer Polytechnic Institute (RPI), 1994.

6)   [Seizovic 1994] Seizovic, J. *The Architecture and Programming of a Fine Grain Multicomputer.* CalTech-CS-TR-93-18. Pasadena, California: California Institute of Technology Press, 1994.

7)   [HP 1995] Stepanov, A. and Meng, L. *The Standard Template Library.* Palo Alto, California: Hewlett-Packard, July 7, 1995.

About the Author

Babak Sadr was president and founder of PARTA Corporation, a software development consulting and research company. He also taught Object Oriented Design and Programming courses at UCLA for 8 years. He received a BS and an MS in Electrical Engineering from the University of Southern California. The courses he taught at UCLA and his overall experience with software development, particularly in OO methodology, are the basis of this book.

Unfortunately, in May of 1996 Babak was diagnosed with cancer and on 23 Jan. 1997 he died of that disease. He was very young when he died, only 33 years old, but he has left a rich legacy. His influence and knowledge live on, both in this book and via the students that he taught and inspired. He will be greatly missed by the software engineering community.